Gorbachev
and
Glasnost
Viewpoints from the Soviet Press

D0815580

Edited by
Isaac J. Tarasulo

A Scholarly Resources Imprint
WILMINGTON, DELAWARE

©1989 by Scholarly Resources Inc.
All rights reserved
First published 1989
Printed and bound in the United States of America
Second printing 1990

Scholarly Resources Inc.
104 Greenhill Avenue
Wilmington, DE 19805-1897

Library of Congress Cataloging-in-Publication Data

Gorbachev and glasnost : viewpoints from the Soviet press /
  edited by Isaac J. Tarasulo.
    p. cm.
    Thirty-three articles translated from Russian newspapers and magazines published in 1987 and 1988; twenty articles translated by the editor.
    Includes bibliographies and index.
    ISBN 0-8420-2336-4 (alk. paper). — ISBN 0-8420-2337-2 (pbk. : alk. paper)
    1. Soviet Union—Politics and government—1985– 2. Glasnost.
I. Tarasulo, Isaac J., 1939– .
DK286.5.G64 1989
947.085 4—dc20   89-10510
                                                                CIP

B. Yakovlev, "New in Town: A Jewish Café, At Joseph's," *Vechernyaya Moskva*, May 24, 1988.

Nina Andreyeva, "Polemics: I Cannot Waive Principles," *Sovetskaya Rossiya*, March 13, 1988.

Mikhail Antonov, "At the Turning Point," *Moskva*, no. 3, 1988.

Nina Fokina, "Who Will Pick the Red Flower?" *Dalnii Vostok*, no. 1, 1988.

Andrei Sakharov, "The Inevitability of *Perestroika*," *Knizhnoe Obozrenie*, no. 25, June 17, 1988.

V. Sanatin, "Smog over the City," *Komsomolskaya Pravda*, April 6, 1988.

Nikolai Shmelyov, "Advances and Debts," *Novy Mir*, no. 6, 1987.

———, "New Worries, " *Novy Mir*, no. 4, April 1988.

Vasily Selyunin, "Sources," *Novy Mir*, no. 5, 1988.

"Principles of *Perestroika*: The Revolutionary Nature of Thinking and Acting," *Pravda*, April 5, 1988.

Vladimir Petrov, "Pamyat and Others," *Pravda*, February 1, 1988.

Georgy Ovcharenko, "Cobras over Gold," *Pravda*, January 23, 1988.

The Naval Combat Training Department of the Editor's Office, "Pooling Resources to Get a Computer," *Krasnaya Zvezda*, May 3, 1988.

Sh. Salimgareev, "No, I Do Not Want to Be a 'Granddad,' " *Krasnaya Zvezda*, May 3, 1988.

D. Klimov, "Five Years of SDI: What Next?" *Krasnaya Zvezda*, March 23, 1988.

V. Letov, "The Family Farm of the Shaposhnikovs," *Izvestiya*, March 30, 1988.

Lev Semeyko, "Instead of Mountains of Weapons: On the Principle of Reasonable Sufficiency," *Izvestiya*, August 13, 1987.

Georgy Melikyants et al., "There Were No Previous Models for the Development of National Relations," *Izvestiya*, March 22, 1988.

Tatyana Zaslavskaya and Yelena Manucharova, "19th Party Conference: Considering the CPSU Central Committee Theses and Fundamental Questions of *Perestroika,*" *Izvestiya,* June 4, 1988.

Dmitry Volkogonov, "The Stalin Phenomenon," *Literaturnaya Gazeta,* December 9, 1987.

Fyodor Burlatsky, "Khrushchev: Sketches for a Political Portrait," *Literaturnaya Gazeta,* February 24, 1988.

———, "Brezhnev and the End of the Thaw: Reflections on the Nature of Political Leadership," *Literaturnaya Gazeta,* September 14, 1988.

Viacheslav Dashichev, "East-West Quest for New Relations: The Priorities of Soviet Foreign Policy," *Literaturnaya Gazeta,* May 18, 1988.

"Letter about Brezhnev's Portrait in Art Rock Parade," *Sovetskaya Kultura,* April 30, 1988.

Alexander Gelman, "Time to Assemble Forces," *Sovetskaya Kultura,* April 9, 1988.

Lev Ovrutsky, "Impasses of Sobering Up," *Sovetskaya Kultura,* July 16, 1988.

Abel Aganbegyan, "People and Economics," *Ogonyok,* nos. 29 and 30, July and August 1987.

Galina Belikova and Alexander Shokhin, "Black Market: People, Goods, Facts," *Ogonyok,* no. 36, September 1987.

Kim Tsagolov and Artyom Borovik, "Afghanistan: Preliminary Results," *Ogonyok,* no. 30, July 1988.

Alexander Nezhny and Konstantin Kharchev, "Conscience Is Free," *Ogonyok,* no. 21, 1988.

Ilya Smirnov, "Lucky Ticket: A Few Meetings with Yuri Shevchuk," *Selskaya Molodyozh,* no. 6, 1988.

"Rock: Music? Subculture? Life-style?" *Sotsiologicheskie Issledovaniya,* June 1987.

"Mikhail Gorbachev Addresses the United Nations," *Soviet Life,* special supplement, no. 2, February 1989.

Contents

Chapter Five   Foreign and Military Issues, 217

Chapter Six   Party Struggle and Political Reform, 267

About the Editor

A native of the Soviet Union, Isaac J. Tarasulo was educated at the University of Leningrad and at Yale University, from which he received a Ph.D. in Russian history. He also has been a research fellow at the Kennan Institute for Advanced Russian Studies. Since 1986, Dr. Tarasulo has been director of the Bethesda Institute for Soviet Studies, a nonpartisan research organization.

Editorial Note

I have selected these thirty-three articles published in Soviet newspapers and magazines in 1987 and 1988 to best reflect the most important developments taking place in the Soviet Union today. These are not necessarily the most provocative items that have appeared in the Soviet press, but they discuss the most significant issues. With *glasnost* escalating daily it was difficult to choose which articles to include, because it seems certain that even more interesting articles have yet to be published.

Twenty of the articles were translated either by myself or under my guidance. I had assistance from several graduate students in the Washington, DC, area, including Helen Shapiro and Darcy Weber. Translations of the remaining thirteen articles were done by FBIS (Foreign Broadcasting Information Service, a U.S. government service), with the exception of Mikhail Gorbachev's UN speech, for which the translation published by *Soviet Life* was used.

Most of the articles have been carefully abridged to fit space requirements. All editorial interpolations within the documents are confined to footnotes or brackets. Transliteration was based on the Library of Congress system, with a few modifications to conform with generally accepted usage.

Acknowledgments

I would like to express my gratitude to Professor Richard Stites of Georgetown University for his support of this project and willingness to give advice when needed.

Stuart Anderson provided invaluable research and editorial assistance in preparing the introductory essays for the chapters and articles. Susan Brent was extremely helpful in correcting the translations and copyediting.

I also would like to thank the book's editor at Scholarly Resources Inc., Tricia Andryszewski, for her attentive reading, patience, and valuable advice.

Introduction

This book is designed to provide Western audiences with a representative sample of articles from the Soviet press on the most important problems currently facing the Soviet Union. Under Mikhail Gorbachev's policies of *glasnost* and *perestroika*, the Soviet press has emerged as a serious forum for political debate. For Western scholars, the Soviet press has become an indispensable source of information on Soviet history, politics, and economics.

The word *glasnost* means "openness" or "publicity" in English, but most important is how its definition has evolved in the Soviet Union. Although *glasnost* originally referred to the publicizing of economic shortcomings, it has developed into greater openness in the arts, history, politics, and even in foreign and military affairs. Throughout the process of *glasnost*, political leaders have criticized press articles, but liberalization has gathered a momentum far beyond what anyone expected. Rather than being a gradual process, *glasnost* has burst forth in an unpredictable torrent whose final destination is yet unknown.

Gorbachev's policy of *glasnost* has challenged many conventional Western stereotypes of the Soviet Union. Only four years ago the Soviet mass media did not address such taboo subjects as homosexuality, drug abuse, train wrecks, and crime. Soviet scholars and writers did not openly discuss Soviet history. Even dissidents did not dare to call for the rehabilitation of Bolshevik leaders, such as Nikolai

Bukharin, Lev Kamenev, and Grigory Zinoviev, who were killed during Stalin's purges. No one anticipated the publication of such long-banned novels as Boris Pasternak's *Dr. Zhivago* or Yevgeny Zamyatin's *We*, much less George Orwell's *1984* or the Bible.

All attempts to define the limits of *glasnost* have failed. It has taken on a momentum of its own, becoming a powerful modernizing force in an outmoded and oppressive political system. Judging by the breadth of the discussion, by the number of political, social, and moral issues addressed, and by the sheer number of the participants, one may say that this is an absolutely new phenomenon for the Soviet Union and for the whole socialist camp. Such a pronounced period of openness cannot be compared to anything in Russia's historical experience. Regardless of the wishes of its creator, *glasnost* has turned into a revolutionary process and has revealed much of the vitality and intellectual energy of various nationalities in the Soviet Union.

Neither Russian nor Soviet citizens have ever experienced true freedom of the press. In eighteenth- and nineteenth-century Russia, czars tightened or loosened press censorship at their discretion. After the Bolshevik Revolution in 1917, the first measures taken by the new government were to close "bourgeois" newspapers and to establish new censorship laws. Although greater liberalization developed under the New Economic Policy (1921–1928), Joseph Stalin's reign turned the press into a mere mouthpiece of the Communist party. Under Nikita Khrushchev and Leonid Brezhnev the press developed greater freedom on only a limited number of subjects, such as the performance of industry and agriculture. The hopes inspired by the 20th Party Congress in 1956 followed by the strict censorship enforced under Brezhnev led to the development of the *samizdat* into an important vehicle of expression for the Soviet people. The government imprisoned many dissident writers during the 1960s and 1970s.

The unexpected atmosphere of *glasnost* has fostered ever-rising expectations, and Mikhail Gorbachev himself proudly proclaimed on April 7, 1989, in London that the Soviet Union "is guided by the internationally recognized highest criteria of *glasnost* and the right to be informed which also conform to our ideals and cultural and historical traditions." Whether Gorbachev, pushed by liberal reformers and former dissidents, is actually willing to live up to such an international standard is doubtful, but the statement itself reflects a current of change in the thinking of the Soviet leader. To anyone who has closely studied Russian history, it is clear that the cardinal revision of political, social, and moral stereotypes undertaken under *glasnost* is a phenomenon without precedent in Russian history.

The fierce political battle over Mikhail Gorbachev's reforms and the nation's future is played out daily in Soviet periodicals. The divisions of opinion are clearly established: Publications that consistently represent the views of ardent reformers include the newspapers *Izvestiya*, *Sovetskaya Kultura*, and *Moscow News*, the monthly journals *Novy Mir*, *Znamya*, *Neva*, and *Druzhba Narodov*, and the weekly magazine *Ogonyok*. Strongly conservative views are expressed in the military newspaper *Krasnaya Zvezda*, the newspaper of the Russian republic *Sovetskaya Rossiya*, and the monthly journals *Moskva*, *Molodaya Gvardiya*, and *Nash Sovremennik*. The press in provincial towns and in the various republics is controlled by local party leaders and generally espouses conservative views. (The local press of the Baltic republics is an exception.) Among the more centrist periodicals are the weekly *Literaturnaya Gazeta* and *Pravda*, the official newspaper of the Communist party.

Rival periodicals have attacked one another for their political views. On January 18, 1989, *Pravda* printed a letter signed by seven leading conservative writers which criticized the liberal magazine *Ogonyok*, charging that the magazine had at times misrepresented the country's culture and values. The conservative journal *Molodaya Gvardiya* has attacked the ethics of *Ogonyok*'s outspoken editor, Vitaly Korotych.

Articles in newspapers and magazines have inflamed passions across the political spectrum in the Soviet Union. For the first time in Soviet history the press is playing an important role in the daily lives of the country's citizens. People now line up to buy newspapers and magazines, just as they do for other valuable items in the Soviet Union. Subscriptions to "reform" publications have increased dramatically, while the circulation of conservative journals has lagged behind.[1] The reason is clear: Some periodicals are increasing their popularity by addressing the most compelling issues facing Soviet society. In the summer of 1988 emotions erupted in major cities when the bureaucracy sharply reduced the number of available subscriptions, particularly for proreform periodicals. Although this was ostensibly done to conserve paper, reformers correctly interpreted the action as an effort to restrict democratization. Thousands of letters to the press protested the restrictions and finally forced the authorities to rescind the order—a rare victory for public opinion in the Soviet Union.

Under *glasnost* Soviet newspapers and magazines have developed into semi-autonomous bodies. Princeton University's Professor Robert Tucker notes that "editors are being given rights to make decisions about what can or cannot appear in their journals or in their newspapers, whereas until recently this has not been the case. The person who was saying, 'No, you can't print that' was likely to be some party person in the apparatus of that newspaper."[2]

The political ideology of the editor plays an important role in shaping the viewpoint of a Soviet periodical. Under the editorship of Alexander Tvardovsky, who was removed by Brezhnev, *Novy Mir* became a journal of bold political and literary discourse. Today, *Pravda*'s editor Viktor Afanasiev is a conservative, Brezhnev-era holdover. Consequently, Afanasiev resists *glasnost* and reportedly has published liberal articles only at the behest of such figures as Gorbachev ally Alexander Yakovlev. In contrast, *Moscow News* has become a leading voice for reform during the tenure of its current editor, Yegor Yakovlev, Alexander Yakovlev's brother.

The debate in the press clearly reflects a struggle within the party and among the top leadership. Under

---

[1] Subscriptions to *Ogonyok* doubled in 1987, from 561,415 to 1,313,349. Total periodical subscriptions increased by 18 million in 1987. Wishnevsky, "A Guide to Some Major Soviet Journals," *Moscow News*, no. 8, 1988.

[2] U.S. Congress, House, Testimony of Robert Tucker, Hearings before the Subcommittee on Europe and the Middle East of the Committee on Foreign Affairs, *U.S.-Soviet Relations*, 100th Cong., 2d sess., 1988, 1:66.

Brezhnev Soviet citizens first experienced a period of improvement in living standards followed by severe shortages of food, consumer goods, and services during the late 1970s and early 1980s, while political and military leaders grew more concerned about the increasing technology gap between the West and the Soviet Union. Therefore, when he became general secretary in March 1985, Mikhail Gorbachev had a mandate to improve the overall state of the Soviet economy. This was his only mandate; the party leadership did not grant him leave to change the nation's ideology and its fundamental institutions. Gorbachev believes that his assignment is to achieve results and that the economy dictates a need for change, so he is willing to compromise ideological principles for economic progress. Herein lies the essence of the confrontation between reformers and conservatives: The struggle is between different interpretations of Marxist ideology. According to the reformers, the Lenin-Bukharinist interpretation of Marxist ideology, in contrast to the Stalinist version, is better suited to the realities of Soviet life at the end of the twentieth century.

Reforms in Russia and the Soviet Union have always been initiated from above. In the absence of a democratic multiparty system the personality of the reformer and his political acumen are pivotal. To be successful, a ruler-reformer must exhibit certain outstanding characteristics, including courage, fervor, and an unbridled hope for the future of Russia. As a leader Mikhail Gorbachev exhibits strong persistence and a desire to win by all reasonable means. Former *Washington Post* Moscow correspondent Robert Kaiser writes that "one of the miraculous aspects of the present situation is the fact that this scared, bureaucratized political organization produced the likes of Gorbachev, his principal associate Alexander Yakovlev, and the other leading figures of reform."[3]

Gorbachev was born in 1931 in the Privolnoe settlement in the Stavropol territory. This territory in Northern Caucasia emerged as one of the outposts of the cossacks in the Russian colonial drive to the south at the end of the

---

[3] Robert Kaiser, "The USSR in Decline," *Foreign Affairs*, Winter 1988/1989, p. 107.

eighteenth century. These frontier settlers displayed a pioneer spirit and earned a reputation for fierce independence from the central authorities. Gorbachev's early years reveal nothing that would indicate he was destined to become a leader of the Soviet Union. He followed the normal path of thousands of Soviet party officials by becoming a Komsomol worker during his studies at the law department of Moscow State University.

A turning point in Gorbachev's life came well after his graduation in 1955 and his return to Stavropol as a party worker. Over the next two decades Gorbachev moved up the party hierarchy in his native city. Two other Stavropol men—notorious party leaders Yuri Andropov and Mikhail Suslov, both pillars of the Brezhnev regime—were instrumental in advancing Gorbachev's career at that time.[4] Then in 1978 the sudden death of the Politburo's youngest member, Fyodor Kulakov, led to Gorbachev's appointment as a secretary of the CPSU. With unusual speed, in October 1980, Gorbachev became the youngest full member of the Politburo at the age of forty-nine.

It is ironic that Gorbachev, destined to rise to the top, was given responsibility for agricultural affairs, a position with a high potential for failure. The performance of Soviet agriculture did not improve in any discernible way during his two-year tenure, yet fate continued to propel Gorbachev toward the top. The death of Leonid Brezhnev in 1982 and the short tenures of Yuri Andropov and Konstantin Chernenko suddenly brought the top party leadership position within his grasp. On March 11, 1985, Mikhail Gorbachev became the general secretary of the Communist party of the Soviet Union.

Gorbachev is the first Soviet leader to seek the limelight relentlessly in both the Soviet and Western mass media. He travels widely inside and outside the Soviet Union and makes the most of his on-screen charisma during television appearances. Public appearances with his wife, Raisa Gorbachev, have provided the Soviet population with an unprecedented view of their "First Couple" and have influenced his image positively abroad. Gorbachev is the

---

[4] Yuri Andropov was in charge of the KGB for sixteen years, from 1966 to 1982. Mikhail Suslov was the chief Soviet ideologist during the Brezhnev years.

first Soviet leader to use television to enhance his political power by appealing directly to the masses to generate a popular mandate for his policies. He does not resort to empty Marxist rhetoric, and his speeches appear to be self-styled.

In Gorbachev's first speech as general secretary, he employed the term *glasnost* and asserted that "the more informed people are, the more consciously they will act, the more actively they will support the party, its plans, and its fundamental goals." As Toronto University's Professor Timothy Colton writes, "Gorbachev's emphasis was less on the right to know than on the utility of an informed citizenry to the regime."[5] This utilitarian approach differs from the Western concept of the right to know as a fundamental, inviolable principle rather than as a fluctuating policy adopted (or abandoned) in the interests of the state. Because of this, no one initially believed that *glasnost* and greater freedom were ends in themselves. Gorbachev appeared simply to be using liberalization to inspire workers and intellectuals to fight against the party and state bureaucrats who opposed his economic reforms. In fact, Gorbachev himself defined *glasnost* as primarily a tool to assist in *perestroika*, his plans to restructure the economy. He believed that *glasnost* should be utilized to fight corruption, inefficient management, bureaucracy, and such social ills as alcoholism.

The nuclear power plant explosion at Chernobyl in April 1986 dramatically changed both Gorbachev and the nation's perception of *glasnost*. *Glasnost* proved to be necessary for informing the population about the nuclear catastrophe and avoiding exaggerated rumors. By Soviet standards, in contrast with American perceptions, the coverage of the Chernobyl disaster was a media breakthrough, utilizing high-tech television equipment and soberly assessing the dangers of nuclear power. It was also a good lesson in humility for Soviet reporters accustomed to recording only success stories. After a disaster of that magnitude, it became easier to televise and write about industrial and transportation accidents, earthquakes, and floods in the USSR. The initial delay in the coverage of

---

[5] Timothy Colton, *The Dilemma of Reform in the Soviet Union* (New York: Council on Foreign Relations, 1986), p. 161.

Chernobyl has not recurred in the reporting of subsequent disasters. Coverage of the Armenian earthquake in December of 1988 illustrated the gains made by *glasnost*. Not only did the mass media immediately report the earthquake, but also the Soviet press sharply criticized both the low quality of construction and the Soviet bureaucratic obstacles that impeded the relief effort.

Glasnost in the press, rather than shortcomings in the economy, is at present the focus of conservative political attacks. Conservatives feel helpless in the face of *glasnost*'s flourishing, since they no longer control the press as they did in the past. Conservatives seek to preserve all the essential elements of the old system, including ministries, collective farms, centralized control, and tight control over the mass media. They persist in believing that economic performance can be improved without cardinal changes in the economy.

The conservative opposition to far-reaching reforms includes members of the military establishment, elements of the KGB, and leading party and state officials, as well as bureaucrats. A great many Communist party members are hostile toward dramatic changes in the country. Products of the Stalinist and Brezhnev systems, these party members refuse to relinquish their power, privileges, and sacred beliefs. As Columbia University's Professor Seweryn Bialer writes:

> The heart of the active opposition comes from the party's ideological, educational, and propaganda arms; a powerful minority of writers and journalists, particularly outside Moscow in the Russian Republic; some academics in the social sciences, and a large group of "semi-intelligentsia," the thousands of teachers of Marxism-Leninism in universities and high schools. . . . The writers and journalists among them are mostly masters of "socialist realism" from the provinces, risen to significant salaries and status despite simple-mindedness and a lack of talent. Their views and deepest beliefs are a mixture of Slavophile anti-Western orientation, simplified Marxist-Leninist

dogmas and commitment to the glory of past Soviet and Russian achievements.[6]

The present political conflict in the Soviet Union clearly parallels the 1840s struggle between Slavophiles and Westerners. Nationalistic slogans form a basis for popular support for the conservative platform. The most extreme conservative organization, Pamyat, is ideologically similar to the pre-Soviet Black Hundreds.

Supporters of radical political and economic reform are a distinct minority in the Soviet Union. Reform advocates come primarily from the ranks of the liberal intelligentsia and journalists. Since reformers are few in number, they have been easily alarmed by fluctuations in the political climate. For example, many people mistakenly interpreted the conservative attack on *glasnost* in the newspaper *Sovetskaya Rossiya* on March 13, 1988, as the end of the reforms (see Chapter 6). The aim of the reformers is to change this unfavorable ratio of forces by prolonging the process of change and achieving visible economic success. Until then, the future of Gorbachev's reforms will be in constant jeopardy. The memory of Nikita Khrushchev's ouster by conservatives in 1964 can never be far from Gorbachev's thoughts.

Although Mikhail Gorbachev promotes economic and political reforms, he often occupies an uneasy middle ground between archconservatives and radical reformers. His speeches consistently criticize conservative opponents of *perestroika* while also chastising the authors of extremely bold reformist articles. Although his sympathies lie more with the radical reformers, Gorbachev plays off both sides in order to protect himself politically. So far Gorbachev has successfully avoided resolutely identifying himself with one camp, but it is uncertain how long this can continue. His ambiguity has proven to be particularly costly in the area of relations among various Soviet nationalities. The ongoing expansion of democratization indicates that Gorbachev currently has no intention of stifling dramatic press revelations. Because liberal writers

---

[6] Seweryn Bialer, "The Hostile Forces He Faces at Home," *U.S. News and World Report*, December 19, 1988, p. 22.

and journalists constitute his most loyal followers, the removal of leading reform editors could be a signal that *glasnost* and *perestroika* are over.

The articles selected for *Gorbachev and Glasnost* will allow students and other interested readers to gain a deeper understanding of the current reforms in the Soviet Union. The views of both reformers and conservatives are represented to illustrate the unprecedented level of the debate. Special attention is given to articles by the country's leading figures, the "stars" in the Soviet Union, including historians Fyodor Burlatsky and General Dmitry Volkogonov, economists Abel Aganbegyan and Nikolai Shmelyov, and controversial reform advocates Alexander Gelman and Andrei Sakharov. Introductory essays in each chapter and a brief analysis of each article provide readers with the appropriate historical and political context.

The book's first chapter deals with the country's most controversial and hotly debated issue, the reinterpretation of Soviet history. For the first time in seven decades, the entire history of Soviet communism is being publicly scrutinized. In some cases, Soviet writers have more harshly criticized the country's past than have Western scholars. Because of the USSR's undeveloped and fragile democratic processes, conservatives and reformers alike seek justification for their positions in historical examples. This tendency is imbedded in Russian and Soviet political traditions. The most important historical issues currently debated in the Soviet press are the postrevolutionary period, Joseph Stalin's role in history, World War II, Nikita Khrushchev's rule, and the "period of stagnation" under Leonid Brezhnev.

Chapter 2 contains a selection of articles on the present state of the Soviet economy and the prospects for its radical reform. Leading reform economists and a conservative critic discuss economic problems and solutions. Articles also are included on agriculture, cooperatives, and the black market economy.

The third chapter deals with a new phenomenon in the Soviet Union, the development of "informal" groups. These organizations are outside of the formal framework of the socialist state and do not fall under the supervision of the Communist party. The protection of the environment is a key focus of many informal groups, but the organization that has attracted the most public attention is the Russian nationalist group Pamyat. Rock music and its relationship to Soviet youth is also addressed in this chapter. Under *glasnost*, rock music and other informal groups serve as instruments for educating the masses in social tolerance and political pluralism.

Chapter 4 deals with nationalities in the Soviet Union, the more lenient attitude toward religion, and social ills such as alcoholism and drug abuse. Before *glasnost* the press ignored controversial subjects, but the endemic nature of these problems has compelled the Soviet press to inform the population as the country gropes for solutions.

The fifth chapter focuses on changes in Soviet foreign and military policies. Mikhail Gorbachev's rule has witnessed the development of "new thinking," which reflects a diminished role for traditional Marxist ideology in Soviet foreign policy. In military policy, the theory of "reasonable sufficiency" has become the guiding principle. This section includes articles on Afghanistan, "Star Wars," and military personnel issues.

Chapter 6 addresses the struggle within the Communist party in the Soviet Union over Gorbachev's reforms. For the first time, internal party disputes have spilled over into the Soviet press. This chapter includes Nina Andreyeva's conservative attack on *perestroika*, published on March 13, 1988, in *Sovetskaya Rossiya*, as well as *Pravda*'s stinging rebuke published three weeks later. The chapter ends with a discussion of whether the Soviet economic reforms can succeed without the democratizing process of *glasnost*, political pluralism, and a freer flow of information. Gorbachev and his supporters are attempting to construct a model of socialist pluralism that will satisfy both reformers and conservatives without creating a multiparty system. It is hard to imagine how a one-party yet democratic system would function in the Soviet Union, and it is equally difficult to predict whether or not this process of *glasnost* will permanently establish new modes of political expression.

Might *glasnost* be eliminated once economic performance improves or even sooner, as a result of a clear conservative victory or other strong pressure on Gorbachev? *Glasnost* will not be irreversible until the Soviet political system undergoes a fundamental change, which will require several decades at least. It cannot survive permanently based solely on the goodwill of the Communist party leadership. Although it might be eliminated, it will not be forgotten. Even a clear-cut conservative victory would not bring about a complete return to the status quo of the Brezhnev period.

How does *glasnost* compare to Western freedoms, rights, and liberties? What are its prospects for the future? We must realize that "democratization" in the Soviet Union is not identical to Western democratic norms and civil liberties. Nonetheless, the push for *glasnost* is definitely not a sham. It is a small step in the right direction for a more efficient and productive society, a step that should neither be overplayed nor underestimated. *Glasnost* signifies the rising of the curtain for a new leadership and the dawn of a new era for the Soviet Union.

> There is no country in the world in which history has been so falsified as ours.
>
> Yuri Afanasiev

Chapter One

Reinterpretation of History

The future of the Soviet Union is being determined by the fierce debate over its past. The battle lines have been drawn, as reformers and conservatives wage a relentless ideological war for the soul of the nation. The centralized nature of power in the Soviet Union means that leaders in all facets of life, political, social, and moral, have played an overwhelmingly decisive role. Therefore, in determining what went awry during seven decades of socialist rule, the role played by individual leaders—Lenin, Nikolai Bukharin, Leon Trotsky, Stalin, Khrushchev, and Brezhnev—has become the focal point of the discussion. Articles selected for this chapter express current interpretations of these leaders and how these interpretations affect Soviet domestic and foreign policy.

The debate over Soviet history is pivotal to the aspirations of reformers. Fundamental reform requires a transformation of political, economic, and social institutions, and in the Soviet Union this requires a revision of history. The country's institutions are essentially Stalinist in origin, and to initiate change reformers must expunge Stalin's legacy. Professor Stephen F. Cohen of Princeton University, in his book *Rethinking the Soviet Experience*, identifies the unbreakable link between Stalin and the politics of reform in the Soviet Union. He writes that after Stalin's death "the conflict between reformers and conservatives was inseparable from the Stalin question because the status quo and its history were Stalinist. In advocating change, Soviet reformers had to criticize the legacy of Stalinism in virtually every area of policy. . . . And in order to defend those institutions, practices, and orthodoxies, Soviet conservatives had to defend the Stalinist past."[1]

Mikhail Gorbachev's rule has witnessed the most fascinating phase in the revision of Soviet history. Upon assuming power in March

---

[1] Stephen F. Cohen, *Rethinking the Soviet Experience* (New York: Oxford University Press, 1985), p. 100.

1985, Gorbachev concentrated his energies on economic reforms and consciously avoided such divisive issues as Stalinism and the development of socialism. Gorbachev, however, did express support for "filling in the blank spots" in Soviet history, which Soviet intellectuals interpreted as a green light to attack the Stalinist heritage.

In this new atmosphere, cultural figures were better prepared than historians to address the burning issues of the past. Startling artistic endeavors, such as Tenghiz Abuladze's film *Repentance* and Anatoly Rybakov's novel *Children of the Arbat*, had been created during Brezhnev's rule but were not permitted to reach the public until *glasnost. Repentance* was filmed in Stalin's native republic of Georgia, and the project required that Georgian party leader Eduard Shevardnadze (now foreign minister) intervene on Abuladze's behalf. The film dramatizes a dictator in the mold of Stalin, Lavrenty Beria (Stalin's chief executioner), or Adolf Hitler and deals extensively with the psychological consequences for survivors of the Stalin period. Anatoly Rybakov's novel *Children of the Arbat*, first published in the journal *Druzhba Narodov*, paints a revealing portrait of Stalin and the devastating impact of his rule on the entire society. From this remarkable example of *glasnost*, many young people learned for the first time about such prominent historical figures as Lev Kamenev, Grigory Zinoviev, and Nikolai Bukharin.

The plays of Mikhail Shatrov, the movie *Repentance*, and *Children of the Arbat* became lightning rods for conservative criticism. Shatrov's play *The Brest Peace* shows Trotsky on stage hotly debating with Lenin the Treaty of Brest-Litovsk, which ended Russia's involvement in World War I in 1918. Shatrov's production *Dictatorship of Conscience* puts Stalin's legacy on trial while engaging audience members in debates about history and politics.

The rehabilitation of and subsequent posthumous publication of the works of such Soviet writers as Boris Pasternak, Anna Akhmatova, Vasily Grossman, Yevgeny Zamyatin, and others is yet another crucial element of the historical debate. The works of these authors reveal previously repressed facts about history and send a clear message to Soviet citizens about abusive political power inhibiting creative expression. Journalists have carried the debate further by examining the issues raised by literary figures and by publishing revealing exposés about innocent people executed under Stalin.[2]

---

[2] An *Izvestiya* article describing documents from the show trials of the 1930s reveals Stalin's role: "There are three signatures underneath [the summary of the case]: Andrei Vyshinsky, Vasily Ulrikh, and Alexander Yezhov. All that was left for Stalin to do was to point his finger on the page at "1" (execution by firing squad) or "2" (10 years in camp)." Pavel Gutiontov, "Case No. 17 in Defense of Comrade Stalin Dismissed by the District Court," *Izvestiya*, September 23, 1988. Documents uncovering the existence of mass graves from Stalin's time also have astounded the public.

The historical role of Joseph Stalin is clearly at the center of the political debate in the Soviet Union. In the eyes of faithful believers, Stalin is the founder and defender of the Soviet system and the symbol of socialism. Defending Stalin and the traditional interpretations of the country's history is indispensable to conservatives like Politburo member Yegor Ligachev, many of whom favor moderate economic reform but are disturbed by ideological changes. What Ligachev and like-minded individuals fear is that a thorough revision of history may lead to the weakening of the Communist party's domination in all spheres of Soviet society. In contrast, reformers emphasize that Stalin bequeathed a rigid, centralized economy and an almost medieval intolerance toward political and social dissent.

Since Soviet leaders traditionally have played the decisive role in determining historical truth, both reformers and conservatives have looked to Mikhail Gorbachev to deliver an official policy line on Soviet history. Public pressure compelled Gorbachev to address the controversial Stalin question during his long-awaited November 2, 1987, speech on the 70th Anniversary of the October Revolution. His speech, however, disappointed supporters and, by largely sidestepping the Stalin issue, illustrated the power of his conservative opposition. On the pivotal question of Stalin's role in history Gorbachev declared:

> To remain faithful to historical truth we have to see both Stalin's indisputable contribution to the struggle for socialism, to the defense of its gains, as well as the gross political mistakes and the abuses committed by him and his circle, for which our people paid a heavy price and which had grave consequences for society. Sometimes it is said that Stalin did not know about many incidents of lawlessness. The documents at our disposal show that this is not so. The guilt of Stalin and his immediate entourage before the party and the people for wholesale repressive measures and acts of lawlessness is enormous and unforgivable. This is a lesson for all generations.[3]

Gorbachev's speech represented the type of political compromise that consistently has disappointed his ardent supporters. For, in addition to criticizing Stalin strongly, the speech elsewhere justified the policies of collectivization and industrialization and applauded Stalin for "safeguarding Leninism" in the ideological struggle against Leon Trotsky and the Trotskyites. Gorbachev hoped that his speech would be accepted as the final word on Soviet history, but by praising and condemning Stalin in the same breath he only exacerbated the debate. To this day, both sides cite passages of his speech to buttress their historical analysis.

---

[3] Mikhail Gorbachev, *October and* Perestroika: *The Revolution Continues, 1917–1987*, Moscow, 1987, p. 21.

Although Gorbachev has continued to play a neutral role in the Stalin debate, it is clear that genuine economic reform cannot take place until Stalin's heritage is destroyed. Reformers, therefore, have picked up the political gauntlet and have continued to hammer away at the long-established "truths" of Soviet history. For the first time, long-hidden facts about the history of Communist party rule are being revealed to the Soviet people. Conservatives are outraged that, with the exception of Leon Trotsky, all of the major Communist party members persecuted by Stalin have been fully rehabilitated. The Commission on Rehabilitations established by Gorbachev, in contrast to a similar committee under Khrushchev, remains very active and regularly issues detailed communiqués absolving all party "factions" accused of treason under Stalin. In this new spirit of civic activism a group dedicated to commemorating Stalin's victims, Memorial, has been established and has won the support of such leading publications as *Moscow News* and *Ogonyok*. Soviet historical revision has far exceeded the de-Stalinization policies of Khrushchev and has spread further than Western observers expected.

The reputation of Lenin, unlike that of Stalin, has not been substantially revised in the era of *glasnost* and *perestroika*. As leader of the Bolshevik Revolution and founder of the Soviet state, Lenin continues to be revered for establishing the principles of socialism in the USSR. Compelling reasons argue against a broad and substantive attack on Vladimir Illyich Lenin. First, Gorbachev and other reformers do not wish to undermine the legitimacy of the entire system that Lenin helped to establish. Second, Lenin is an appropriate figure to juxtapose against Stalin. Third, the depth and variety of Lenin's writings, which total fifty-five volumes, make his quotations suitable for justifying practically any political or economic course. Nonetheless, as early as 1975, Soviet historian Roy Medvedev, formerly a dissident and now a leading reformer, wrote of the need to "go beyond Leninism" in evaluating Soviet history and political institutions.[4] The implication is that Soviet policymakers should realize that Lenin's writings cannot provide complete solutions to the current crisis in the Soviet Union.

Although Soviet historians in general have sought to provide a more realistic portrait of Lenin's life and policies, Vasily Selyunin's article "Sources" (Document #1) is atypical in assigning Lenin blame for the destruction of the peasantry. Selyunin argues that wealthy peasants (*kulaks*) were eliminated as a class under Lenin during the period of War Communism (1918–1921). In addition to charging Lenin with setting a dangerous precedent, Selyunin asserts that this made Stalin's premise for collectivization (1928–1932) false, since only

---

[4] Roy Medvedev, *On Socialist Democracy* (New York: Oxford University Press, 1975), p. 324.

middle and poor peasants remained in the countryside after the civil war.

On Soviet television and in the press, Nikolai Bukharin, who developed Lenin's New Economic Policy (NEP), has emerged as the patron saint of *perestroika*. In 1921 economic disarray and the Kronstadt revolt of sailors compelled the Bolsheviks under Lenin to abandon War Communism and adopt NEP. After Lenin's death, Nikolai Bukharin strongly supported the continuation and expansion of this policy. NEP (1921–1928) produced significant successes in agriculture and industry, and it is seen as a useful model by proponents of *perestroika*. NEP encouraged economic freedom for the small producers who provided services and manufactured most consumer items. It also granted peasants the freedom to sell their agricultural products on the open market and permitted a liberal approach to culture and the press.

By 1928, Stalin had begun to challenge the essentials of NEP. Stalin wanted an economic policy that would correspond to his grand vision of Russia. Idolizing Peter the Great and decrying Russia's historical backwardness, he declared that "to slow down the tempo [of industrialization] means to lag behind. And those who lag behind are beaten. We are behind the leading countries by fifty to one hundred years. We must make up this distance in ten years. Either we do it or we go under."[5]

History has vindicated Bukharin's predictions about the political and economic costs of Stalin's drive for rapid industrialization and mass collectivization. In a November 1928 speech to worker and peasant correspondents, Bukharin attacked Stalin's plans. He argued that "if some kind of madmen proposed to build immediately twice as much as we are now doing, this truly should be the policies of madmen because then our industrial goods famine would intensify several times over . . . and mean a grain famine."[6] The rehabilitation of Bolshevik leaders killed under Stalin is tightly linked to Gorbachev's reform program. On the 100th anniversary of Bukharin's birth, *Pravda* published a laudatory article declaring that "Bukharin has been posthumously rehabilitated in the party and everything of value in his creative legacy . . . is being taken into the Communist party's arsenal."[7] Although conservatives still criticize Bukharin, reform historians and writers promote him as a credible historical alternative

[5] Adam Ulam, *Stalin* (New York: Viking Press, 1973), p. 340.

[6] Stephen F. Cohen, *Bukharin and the Bolshevik Revolution* (New York: Oxford University Press, 1985), p. 302. Another attack on Stalin's policies appeared in Nikolai Bukharin's "Notes of an Economist," *Pravda*, September 30, 1928.

[7] V. Naumov and V. Zhuravlev, "Back to the Truth. History through People's Fate: On the 100th Anniversary of the Birth of Nikolai Ivanovich Bukharin," *Pravda*, October 9, 1988.

that could have saved the country from Stalin. *Pravda* writes that "it must be noted that the 'Bukharin alternative' was not a matter of tactical differences of opinion with Stalin; rather, it was a matter of defending Lenin's concept of socialism against Stalinist distortions."[8] This *Pravda* article, published less than one year after Gorbachev's 70th Anniversary speech on November 2, 1987, flatly contradicts the general secretary's ambivalent remark in that speech that "no other course could have been taken" besides Stalin's in the 1930s.[9]

In contrast to Selyunin's praise of Bukharin, General Dmitry Volkogonov in "The Stalin Phenomenon" (Document #2) dismisses the idea of Nikolai Bukharin as a historical alternative to Stalin. As evidence, Volkogonov argues that Bukharin "admitted" his mistakes in not encouraging a faster pace of industrial growth. But, as Bukharin biographer Stephen Cohen points out, Bukharin was coerced into recanting his views, both in newspaper articles and later at his trial in 1938. In an example of the respect now awarded to Western scholarship, the Soviet Union is publishing Stephen Cohen's book *Bukharin and the Bolshevik Revolution.*

Leon Trotsky, in contrast to Bukharin, continues to be vilified in the conservative Soviet press. Trotsky held leadership roles in foreign affairs and defense and was considered to be the mastermind of the Bolshevik victory in the civil war. After Lenin's death, Stalin saw Trotsky as his most important rival for power and expelled him from the country in 1929. In the period that followed, many important party leaders were executed for their involvement in so-called Trotskyite activities. Then, in 1940, Trotsky was assassinated in Mexico, reportedly on Stalin's orders.[10] The next stage in *glasnost* could be a full rehabilitation of Trotsky for his alleged crimes against the country. This would be logical since his associates, the Trotskyites, have been exonerated.

Today, many articles like "The Stalin Phenomenon" still present Trotsky as a traitor yet show him as a talented speaker and writer. Reform historian Yuri Afanasiev writes that while "this may seem to present a more truthful picture, the essence of these publications is not the desire to reach the truth but the aspiration to preserve in the minds of the Soviet people the image of the 'enemy of the people' with the help of a kind of 'refined' image of Trotsky. In fact, this is a

---

[8] Ibid.

[9] Gorbachev's 70th Anniversary speech was cautious; he tried not to irritate conservatives at that point.

[10] For the first time, a Soviet press article has reported what was widely acknowledged in the West: that the Soviet government ordered Trotsky's assassination. Historian N. Vasetsky writes that "Stalin could not forget old insults. . . . Either he took the decision himself or he let his entourage know that it was time to put an end to Trotsky." N. Vasetsky, "Liquidation," *Literaturnaya Gazeta*, January 4, 1989.

reproduction of the same old Stalinist system of evaluating [Trotsky]."[11]

Volkogonov's article suggests that Stalin adopted Leon Trotsky's views on industrialization and that, therefore, he would have been even more dangerous to the country than Stalin. Although this argument appeals to conservatives, no historical evidence supports such a theory. Since the 1930s the Soviet population has not had access to Trotsky's writings and therefore cannot evaluate the arguments of this debate. On many issues conservatives complain that reform writers do not utilize archival materials to document their arguments. It is conservatives, however, who vehemently oppose opening state and party archives to researchers.

Volkogonov calls Stalin the "intellectual and emotional epicenter of the public's interest in the past." He paints a portrait of Stalin as a man who saw no grays, only blacks and whites, someone who equated disagreement with treason and who eliminated loyal followers as well as perceived enemies, leading to the conclusion that perhaps "alongside the cruelty [was] a mental illness." Volkogonov's emphasis on Stalin's personality draws criticism from reform historians who believe that concentrating on Stalin's personal characteristics obscures the need for fundamental change in the system. Yuri Afanasiev specifically cites Volkogonov's article as an attempt to "make Stalin appear as a crafty and mentally sick individual." He writes that "many would like to sacrifice Stalin for the sake of saving Stalinism. This also means circumventing the very essence of the problem, bypassing the question of the extent to which Stalin was both the creator and the product of a system which became consolidated under his rule."[12]

Another controversial issue, World War II and Stalin's role during the war, touches a nerve by focusing attention on Russian nationalism and the nation's pride in military achievements. Until recently, even ardent reformers rarely questioned Stalin's leadership role during the war. The publication, however, of previously unpublished excerpts from Marshal Georgy Zhukov's memoirs (*Pravda*, January 20, 1989) contradicts the perception of Stalin as a great military leader. During Zhukov's lifetime he was unable to publish his memoirs in full. The newly published portions reveal that Stalin sought to exaggerate his role during major operations by calling field commanders with detailed information received from Marshals Zhukov and Alexander Vasilevsky. Zhukov writes, "I have to emphasize here that when major successful

---

[11]Yuri Afanasiev, *"Perestroika* and Historical Knowledge," *Literaturnaya Rossiya*, no. 24, June 17, 1988.

[12] Ibid.

operations were conducted, Stalin tried to cast a shadow on the organizers and put himself forward."[13]

Another subject about which the Soviet press remained silent until *glasnost* is the rule of Nikita Khrushchev. Under Mikhail Gorbachev, Khrushchev has been rehabilitated as a generally positive figure. In drawing lessons for the Gorbachev era, Fyodor Burlatsky (Document #3) cites the primary reasons for the conservative victory over Khrushchev's moderate reform attempts. He argues that the party *apparat* was not prepared for the reforms. Burlatsky, however, does not add that, since bureaucracies always resist change, reforms can only be implemented against the wishes of the party *apparat*. Burlatsky also writes that during Khrushchev's time the population as a whole was not ready for radical changes; the people were neither properly informed about nor involved in the reform struggle. The absence of a tradition of participatory democracy in both prerevolutionary Russia and the Soviet Union makes reforms difficult to implement.

As for the Brezhnev era, two recent events resoundingly proclaimed the official Soviet view of Leonid Brezhnev's rule. First, late in 1988, in what many saw as a symbolic indictment of the entire Brezhnev era, the former Soviet leader's son-in-law, Yuri Churbanov, was sentenced to twelve years' imprisonment for corruption. Second, the Soviet government posthumously stripped Leonid Brezhnev of all his honors and removed his name from all public places.

Despite the official condemnation of the Brezhnev era, few analytical articles have been written on this recent historical period. Fyodor Burlatsky's article "Brezhnev and the End of the Thaw: Reflections on the Nature of Political Leadership" (Document #4) is therefore an important contribution to the nascent field of political science in the Soviet Union. Burlatsky identifies the main lessons of the Brezhnev era. He argues that the Stalinist bureaucratic system perpetuated by Brezhnev has proved incapable of serving the needs of a modern society. Burlatsky advocates establishing a more rationalized system of leadership succession to ensure that no one rises to a high leadership position by "backstage deals . . . conspiracies and bloody purges." This article reflects the general consensus in Soviet society that the Brezhnev years impeded technological development and produced a malaise, a "period of stagnation."

The fate of the Soviet Union and its institutions is at the center of the debate over the reinterpretation of Soviet history. The articles of Selyunin, Volkogonov, and Burlatsky represent only a small part of this debate. While conservatives fight against ideological change, reformers know that unless Stalinism is fully exposed the effort to

---

[13] Georgy Zhukov, "Briefly about Stalin," *Pravda*, January 20, 1989.

transform the economic and political system is doomed to failure. The final outcome of this intense struggle will determine the destiny of the nation.

Sources
Vasily Selyunin

Novy Mir, no. 5, 1988

This highly controversial article challenges two cardinal beliefs of Soviet ideology: the unquestioned wisdom of Vladimir Lenin and the unmitigated evil of capitalism. Since most Bolsheviks believed that allowing any free market would lead to capitalism, Lenin sought to liquidate the village market economy. Selyunin argues that a policy of mass repression began under Lenin that led to mass requisitions and a famine. He asserts that Lenin's strategy during the civil war set a dangerous precedent for the economic policies of Joseph Stalin.

Selyunin's article seeks to establish the essential link between New Economic Policy (NEP) and Gorbachev's reforms. The author views Nikolai Bukharin's theories from the 1920s as a useful guide for planning the current economic reforms. Selyunin states that the break with NEP in 1929 resulted in the suppression of all forms of private enterprise and the resurrection of the tactics employed during War Communism (1918–1921).

A central question throughout Soviet history is how can people be inspired to work productively? Selyunin candidly states that capitalism has historically created positive incentives to inspire people to work. In this revision of Soviet economic history, he argues that the builders of socialism in the USSR chose a path defined by coercion.

As early as November 10, 1917, speculators had been declared enemies of the people, and three months later a decree signed by Lenin included a clearly unambiguous instruction: "Speculators are to be shot at the scene of the crime." It is quite clear that, given the disorganized state of commerce at that time, any sale of food was considered to be speculation. "Not one *pood* [16 kg] of grain," the authorities decreed, "should remain in the hands of its holders, with the exception of the amount needed for planting and for feeding their families until the next harvest. Anyone possessing surplus grain and not delivering it to grain collection stations should be declared an enemy of the people and should be turned over to a revolutionary court so that the guilty party may be sentenced to confinement in prison for a term of no less than ten years, permanently expelled from the commune, and have all his property confiscated" (*History of the All-Russian Extraordinary Commission, 1917–1921*, Moscow, 1958, p. 95).

The common assumption is that this severity was due to hunger and collapse [due to World War I and the February Revolution]. But, as we have seen, it was connected to a fundamental principle, namely that if commercial production and its accompanying market were not destroyed, the October Revolution would be reduced, so to speak, to a bourgeois level. All it takes is common sense to understand that the food produced in the country would be eaten by its population. It was not famine that led to mass requisitions but rather the other way around: One consequence of mass requisitions was famine. The peasants were supposed to feed the country free of charge, without any benefits for themselves. The peasant responded to these measures at best by reducing the amount of cultivated land and at worst by brandishing a sawed-off shotgun.

Most historians, both Soviet and foreign, reduce the civil war to a conflict between Whites and Reds, with the difference lying only in the ratings they get. The facts, however, show that a third force received the major blow, the peasant rebel movement. It aligned itself with the Whites and with the Reds at different times with various levels of activity, all the while remaining a relatively independent force. Long before the revolution, in preparation for these events, Lenin wrote: "We will initially support the peasantry against the gentry wholeheartedly, by all means, including confiscation, and then (not even afterwards, but at the very same time) we will support the proletariat against the peasantry" (*Lenin, Collected Works* 11:222). In the struggle against the gentry the interests of the peasantry completely coincided with the interests of the Soviet authorities. Even the White generals understood this. For example, we have a letter from [Alexander] Kolchak to [Anton] Denikin[1] in which the luckless admiral condemns an agrarian policy "which in the peasantry

---

[1] Admiral Kolchak and General Denikin led White armies against the Bolsheviks during the civil war.

creates the idea of a restoration of gentry landownership."
As soon as this danger had disappeared, the gray warriors
[peasants] switched sides. As the civil war heated up,
Lenin noted with alarm that "the peasantry of the Urals,
Siberia, and the Ukraine are turning to Kolchak and
Denikin," and as the White movement was destroyed the
peasants' resistance got fiercer. For example, the
headquarters of the eastern front reported from the Volga
region in 1919 that "the peasants have gone mad; they are
attacking machine guns with pitchforks, stakes, and
hunting rifles alone and en masse, despite the mounds of
corpses, and their fury defies description." The historian
Mikhail Kubanin calculated that in Tambov province 25 to
30 percent of the population took part in the uprising. He
concluded that "undoubtedly, 25 to 30 percent of the rural
population means that all of the adult male population had
joined the army of Antonov."[2] According to archival
documents published in 1962, the peasant army in the
Tambov uprising included eighteen well-armed regiments.
The regular forces commanded by Mikhail Tukhachevsky[3]
had to wage a real war no less intense than the one they
waged against Kolchak. Lenin himself stated directly that
the petty bourgeois [peasant] element had proved to be more
dangerous than all of the White armies put together.[4]

It is easy, however, to grasp that military means alone
could not provide a final solution to the peasant problem.
The goal was to eliminate commercial production in the
country, and the strongest commercial producers were the
kulak farms, which employed hired labor. By Lenin's
definition, the *kulaks* were "the most beastly, crudest, and
most savage exploiters." "And if the *kulak* remains
untouched," Lenin stated, "and if we do not defeat the
bloodsuckers, the czar and the capitalist will inevitably

---

[2] Alexander Antonov was the leader of a peasant uprising against the
Bolsheviks.

[3] Mikhail Tukhachevsky was a Bolshevik military leader during the
civil war.

[4] After the October Revolution, the Bolshevik party consisted of
several thousand members and a proletarian support base of less than 5
percent of the population. The "petty bourgeois" peasant element
accounted for nearly 95 percent of the country. Therefore, violent
uprisings against the Bolsheviks, such as the 1918 Tambov revolt led by
Antonov, exacerbated the leadership's anxieties.

return." He sent a directive to agitators dispatched to the provinces: "*Kulaks* and bloodsuckers must be cut down to size." To do this the authorities could rely only on the poor peasants, who constituted a negligible minority of the rural population (let us not forget that the peasants had received land as a result of the revolution). In June 1918 the committees of the poor were organized. They assisted in taking 50 million hectares of land from the *kulaks*. This was approximately one third of all the land in cultivation at the time. Thus, the material infrastructure of *kulak* production was destroyed. The facts irrefutably demonstrate that the *kulaks* were eliminated in the years of War Communism, rather than in the late 1920s and early 1930s.[5]

The middle peasant, after all, wanted to trade the products of his labor, and trade (according to the notions of the time) would lead directly to capitalism. It was believed that grain not turned over to the requisitioning authorities, even if it had been cultivated by the peasant's own hands, had been appropriated by him and thus turned him into a class enemy. "If a peasant sits on his own tract of land," Lenin stated, "and appropriates for himself surplus grain—that is, grain that neither he nor his livestock needs—and everyone else remains without grain, the peasant is already turning into an exploiter. The more grain he leaves for himself, the better it is for him: Let others go hungry, because the hungrier they are, the better the price I can get for this grain. We need to have everyone working according to one general plan on common land and at common factories and plants according to a common routine" (*Lenin* 41:310–11).

Consequently, the real solution to the problems of the socialist revolution was perceived to be the enticement of the peasantry to work on common land. This was a fundamental point of the Bolshevik party's program. As early as 1902 Lenin wrote: "A social democrat should propagandize nationalization of land as a transition to large-scale Communist farming rather than to small individual farming" (*Lenin* 6:339). Shortly after the

---

[5] War Communism (1918–1921) was the Bolshevik policy designed to win the civil war. It was characterized by martial law and the concentration of all economic resources.

revolution he took on the matter of "a gradual though unswerving transition from small one-man farms to common farming." In January of 1918, Lenin took part in drafting "The Fundamental Law on the Socialization of Land." A member of the preparatory commission, S. Ivanov, reminisced that "only Comrade Lenin did any work on the commission, while we, the others, simply voted." In discussing the draft, a dispute arose concerning gentry-owned land, as distinct from *kulak*-owned land. The Socialist Revolutionaries[6] insisted on dividing it up among the peasants, which would have strengthened the economic foundations of the petty bourgeois element. Lenin called for the creation of collective farms on gentry lands. Lenin's proposal passed.[7]

Despite the obvious benefits of better land and free implements, most peasants did not join these associations. Nonetheless, more than 5,000 state farms and about 6,000 collective farms were created in a very short time. But, as Lenin acknowledged, "the collective farms are still so disorganized and in such a sad condition that they deserve to be called poorhouses."

The best minds of that day tried to explain why such a good cause as collectivization proved to be a complete failure. The discussions proceeded as follows: Simply combining land and primitive implements could not yet ensure qualitative changes in the growth of production. If we had been able to provide the country with 100,000 tractors, then any peasant would have said, "I'm for the commune." But this equipment was not yet available and, according to their calculations, would not be available for at least another ten years.

From our vantage point, we cannot consider this explanation to be good enough. Mechanization, the use of agricultural chemicals, land improvement and

---

[6] The Socialist Revolutionaries (*esery*) were a Russian revolutionary party representing the aspirations of the peasants. Like other parties, it was crushed by the Bolsheviks.

[7] Although in 1917 the Bolsheviks usurped the program of the Socialist Revolutionary party ("all land to the peasants"), Lenin and other Bolsheviks still viewed collective farming as an essential component of Marxist thought.

reclamation, and intensive technologies are not sufficient to ensure success. Even Leo Tolstoy understood that the most important thing is "not the nitrogen and oxygen in the soil and in the air and not special plows or fertilizers, but the primary means by which nitrogen and oxygen, fertilizer and plow operate: that is, the peasant." Tolstoy's insight was ignored, however, and the primary emphasis was placed on brute force. It seems to me that here lie the deep roots of the many difficulties our country has experienced.

Violence, as we can see, spread like wildfire. Initially it was used to suppress enemies of the revolution, then it was extended to potential enemies (the Red Terror), and finally it became a means of resolving purely economic problems. In 1920, Leon Trotsky proposed placing it on a firm and long-term footing by turning the country into a gigantic concentration camp—more precisely, a system of camps. At the 9th Party Congress he set forth a program never seen before: Workers and peasants should be treated like mobilized soldiers and should be organized into "labor units similar to military units. Everyone will be obliged to consider himself a soldier of labor, of which he cannot freely dispose. If the order is given to transfer him, he must carry it out; if he does not, he will be a deserter, subject to punishment."

Would such labor have been efficient? Capitalism prevailed over the social formation that preceded it because it replaced the cudgel, serfdom, and the will of the master with a more effective work incentive, namely personal gain and the right to sell one's labor. Trotsky resolutely objected: "If we take seriously the old bourgeois prejudice, or rather the old bourgeois axiom, that forced labor is unproductive, then this applies not only to labor armies, but to labor obligations as a whole, to the foundation of our economic construction, and, needless to say, to socialist organization in general." (How blatant can he be, to state that forced labor is the foundation of socialist organization!) According to Trotsky, this "bourgeois axiom" applied only to the past: "We say that it is not true that forced labor is unproductive under any circumstances or under any conditions" (*9th Congress of the RKP(b). Protocols*, Moscow, 1960, pp. 97–98).

Modern historians assert that the 9th Party Congress rejected Trotsky's military bureaucratic approach to economic development. But this is clearly a whitewash of history by no means unusual in Russia; Herzen[8] pointed out that the "Russian government, in its hindsight, tries to make the past look good rather than the future." Let us turn to a fundamental resolution of the congress, namely, "On the Forthcoming Tasks of Economic Development":

In approving the propositions of the Central Committee of the Russian Communist party concerning the mobilization of the industrial proletariat, labor obligations, the militarization of the economy, and the use of military units for economic needs, the congress resolves that:

An accounting should be made of all skilled workers for the purpose of assigning them to productive work with the same thoroughness and rigor as has been done and is being done by commanders for the needs of the army.

Every skilled worker should return to work in his occupation.

Mass labor mobilizations must be conducted properly from the very beginning; that is, an exact correspondence between the number mobilized, their places of assignment, the scale of the task, and the number of tools required should be established as much as is possible in every case. It is just as important to provide the labor units formed from those mobilized with a technically competent and politically reliable instructor staff and Communist labor cells selected by party mobilization; that is, we should follow the same path as we did in creating the Red Army (*Resolutions of the Congresses of the CPSU*, vol. 2, *1917–24*, Moscow, 1970, p. 153).

The resolution also recommended the "use of a system of classes, which if not attended would cause a reduction in rations." And because a "significant number of workers, looking for better food and sometimes for the purpose of speculation, quite frequently abandon their places of employment and move from place to place, which does

---

[8]Alexander Herzen was a nineteenth-century Russian writer and revolutionary.

further damage to production," this practice should be stopped in a "fierce struggle against labor desertion, in particular, by means of publishing penalty lists, forming punitive labor teams from the ranks of the deserters, and if all else fails, confining them in concentration camps."

Don't even think that they were talking about temporary measures. In their resolution entitled "The Transition to a Militia System" they explained that, since the civil war was coming to an end and the international situation of Soviet Russia was favorable, a militia system for the economy would be introduced in the future, "perhaps on a long-term basis." The essence of this system would be "to involve the army to the greatest extent possible in the production process, so that the manpower of certain economic regions would at the same time be the personnel of certain military units."

These documents are even more instructive because they reveal the relationship between the economic mechanism and the rights of the individual. Commercial capitalist production means that someone who has money is free to undertake a profitable venture, acquire property, take risks, and bear economic responsibility for his actions. Any individual has the right to dispose of his own property, even if it only consists of a pair of working hands. There is no doubt that this system is harsh, but there is no need to make people work with threats and police supervision. The state has no need to break strikes, because the losses will be borne by the private entrepreneur. Although the state does not guarantee employment, it is obliged to provide a man with the complete freedom to get wealthy or freeze to death, whichever he can do. Human rights are the flip side of merciless economic freedoms. On the other hand, a total state monopoly on the means of production means the art of expropriating the individual himself and his physical and spiritual strengths in order to coordinate work within a single plan and routine. Under these conditions one may consider a human being to be a screw in a gigantic machine manufacturing future happiness for all. It would be strange to talk about the individual rights and civil liberties of a screw, and it would be equally ridiculous to talk about the individual rights and civil liberties of the screwdriver driving him into the proper place.

On March 1, 1921, the sailors of Kronstadt[9] rebelled. At the same time workers in Petrograd [St. Petersburg] went on strike, and they weren't the only ones. "This is something new," Lenin reflected. "This situation, juxtaposed with all our crises, must be given a great deal of consideration in a political sense and analyzed very thoroughly. This is a manifestation of the petty bourgeois, anarchist element, with its slogans of free trade, which is always aimed against the dictatorship of the proletariat. And this attitude is quite common among the proletariat. It has been expressed at plants in Moscow and at plants in a large number of locations around the province." The political demands made by the strikers were particularly alarming. "There is no doubt that there has been ferment and dissatisfaction among nonparty workers. When nonparty meetings were held in Moscow, it was clear that they put forward a slogan of democracy and freedom which would lead to the overthrow of Soviet power" (*Lenin* 43:241, 331).

Lenin expressed these thoughts in March of 1921 at the 10th Party Congress. At his insistence, the congress adopted a vital resolution calling for the replacement of requisitioning with taxation of the peasants. This did not yet constitute a price system. The measure was considered temporary. It was no accident that it was put into effect in March, before the spring planting, in order to convey the message to the peasants to plant more, because there would be no requisitions this year. At the same time, the resolution made no provision for the free sale of grain left after taxes. "Freedom of trade," Lenin emphasized, "even if it is initially not associated with the White Guards, as Kronstadt was, will nevertheless inevitably lead to White Guardism and to the victory of capitalism and its full restoration." But these were already rearguard battles. Taxes accounted for only half of the previously planned requisitions. It was clear that most of the food could be

---

[9]Kronstadt is the site of a naval base on the Gulf of Finland near Leningrad. The previous official interpretation of the sailors' rebellion against the government highlighted the Red Army's heroism in suppressing the revolt. Historian Roy Medvedev ("Kronstadt Was a Tragedy," *Yunost*, no. 11, 1988) criticizes past interpretations of the Kronstadt rebellion.

provided only by free sales of the products of agricultural labor. Only two months later, in May 1921, a party conference defined the system of measures known as New Economic Policy (NEP) as a serious and long-term course. Within one year the entire economic mechanism of War Communism had been dismantled and replaced with NEP, which in its main features was similar to the new economic mechanism taking shape today.

In this first lesson I see a basis for our current restructuring. We are faced with changes that are no less revolutionary: workers don't want to live as they did before, and the administrative *apparat* cannot govern in the way it did before. In general the direction of radical reform is clear, but even the fervent proponents of *perestroika* talk as if the democratization of public life and economic innovations must be introduced gradually, over the course of years. Most likely this won't get us anywhere; there is simply no time to spare, as it all has been used up and lost in decades of stagnation. According to forecasts, if there are no radical changes, by the mid-1990s our economy will fall apart with all the resultant social, foreign policy, and military consequences. Then it will be too late to worry about democracy, because dictatorships are better suited to periods of economic collapse. Until recently, we could only observe with sadness and alarm the facts indicating this trend in the development of our country. In April 1985 we got our chance for salvation.[10] Now our chances have improved, and it would be criminal to let them slip away. Another good thing about the experience of the early 1920s is that it demonstrated the possibility of revolutionary changes from the top in a matter of months.

Our second lesson is the impressive effect of the initial signals transmitted to the economy. It was because the changes were so fast and radical that the old economic mechanism did not interfere with the new. The bad harvest of 1921 had nothing to do with it; it was a natural disaster and in many respects a result of the experiments of War Communism. The most important point was that peasant revolts ceased during the terrible famine; there was no reason to rebel as long as the well-being of one's family

---

[10] April 1985 is the date of the first Communist party *plenum* with Mikhail Gorbachev as general secretary.

depended on one's own work. Economic measures were able to reduce social tension much better than executions, and as early as 1922 there was a good harvest. The 12th Party Congress demanded that efforts should be made to find foreign markets for grain (isn't it nice that we once had such things in our recent history!). It took only four to five years to reach prewar levels of industrial and agricultural production. In 1928 the prewar level of industrial production had been exceeded by 32 percent, while the prewar level of agricultural production had been exceeded by 24 percent. In comparison with 1921, the GNP was 3.3 times higher and industrial production had risen by a factor of 4.2, in heavy industry by a factor of 7.2. Wages in real terms had risen above the prewar level. It has been calculated that in 1924 people were eating better than they ever had before. The average Soviet worker consumed seventy-two kilograms of meat per year, an impressive figure even by today's standards.

Economic successes went hand in hand with the democratization of public life. (This is a burning topic today.) The limits of violence were sharply narrowed and legality was strengthened. Lenin justified it in this way: "The more we come into conditions that comprise the basis for a firm and solid authority and the further the development of civil life proceeds, the greater the need will be to advance greater revolutionary legality and the narrower the scope of the institutions that respond to any conspiratorial blows with countering blows will become." The country received criminal and civil laws. Revolutionary tribunals were replaced with courts, and prosecutors and defense attorneys were appointed.

It is true that the small urban entrepreneur sensed the instability of the legal situation and was hesitant to invest his profits in industrial enterprises. Anyone who did take the risk would try to "eat up" his profits or turn them into gold for a "rainy day." Retail trade was the sector in which a private entrepreneur indeed showed himself off: The initial investment was minimal, the payoff was quick, he took the profits, and then who cares if they shut down the business? The peasant, the man who fed the country, also felt inconvenient restrictions. But what if the obstacles had been removed? This was the idea proposed by Nikolai Bukharin, a strange fellow if there ever was one. A "left-wing Communist" during War Communism, the author of the first noncapitalist conceptions of economic development in the Soviet Union, and a proponent of the abolition of money, he underwent a rapid evolution as he searched for answers to the main questions of the day in life itself.

In a speech at a meeting of Moscow party activists on April 17, 1925, Bukharin explained NEP in this way:

> We still have certain residues of relations of the War Communism period to this day which are inhibiting our further growth. The wealthy upper stratum of the peasantry and the middle-class peasant, who is also trying to become wealthy, are now afraid to accumulate. A situation has come into being in which a peasant is afraid to put a tin roof on his house because he fears people will brand him a *kulak*, and if he buys a piece of machinery he does it in a way so that Communists won't see it. Higher technology is becoming a conspiracy.
>
> On the whole, we should tell all the peasants and all strata of the peasantry: Get richer, accumulate, develop your farms.

(Subsequently this appeal would come back to haunt him.)

But what sort of good would this do for industrialization? According to Bukharin, it would bring two benefits. First of all, a wealthier countryside would increase the demand for industrial goods, which would lead to the rapid growth of industry. Peasants' bank deposits also would become an additional resource for the development of the economy.

At that time many restrictions were removed. Commercial production inevitably led to property stratification in the countryside; some farms fell apart, while others got stronger. In early 1925 the authorities permitted leasing of land and hiring of labor, and all obstacles to free trade were removed. Ultimately, this resulted in the establishment of very efficient farms similar to American farms.

According to Bukharin, economic freedom was not only useful for the countryside: "We must learn how to manage in a sophisticated way under the complex conditions of the reconstruction period. We must activate and mobilize the maximum number of economic factors working in favor of socialism. This presupposes a very complex combination of individual, group, public, and state initiatives. We are entirely overcentralized. Shouldn't we take several steps in the direction of Lenin's communal state?" This passage was taken from "Notes of an Economist," which was published in *Pravda* on September 30, 1928, literally on the eve of the first day of the first five-year plan. (At that time the fiscal year began on October 1, and the program of accelerated industrialization was beginning.) By publishing "Notes," Bukharin was still attempting to influence events.

Thus, we have a coherent plan for socialist construction. With all its practical value, Bukharin's concept had one debatable point: How viable is the aforementioned "complex combination"? How could private farms and state-owned industry coexist? Would it be at all thinkable to include private property owners in socialism? Obviously, the author of the plan recognized this problem very clearly. He saw a solution to the conflict in the transition of the countryside to socialism through the gradual and voluntary cooperation of peasant farms. In this case he relied on Lenin's last works, on the idea that under the conditions of Soviet power a simple growth of cooperation would be equivalent to the growth of socialism.

By the way, NEP faced fierce opposition from the very beginning. Trotsky, the theoretician of barracks socialism, tried to frighten the 12th Party Congress in this way: "An era of growth and development of the capitalist element is beginning. And who knows, perhaps there will come a time in the next few years for us to defend every inch of our socialist ground, that is, every piece of our state economy, tooth and nail."

In the 1920s the unforgettable Stalin, a man who knew the price of power, concentrated unlimited power in his own hands. Disputes at conferences and meetings bothered him very little. He understood what was most important, that the country is governed by the people who truly control the executive *apparat* of the state. He also understood that the best model for a hierarchical *apparat* is military organization, with its discipline and chain of command. In 1921, in a rough draft of the brochure "On the Political Strategy and Tactics of Russian Communists," he noted with rare candor that "the Communist party is a sort of Order of the Knights of the Sword within the Soviet state, directing the agencies of the latter and inspiring their activity."[11] Of course, any kind of conflict of opinions was unthinkable, and factions were positively criminal.

The 10th Party Congress decided that belonging to any faction entailed "unconditional and immediate expulsion from the party." Many honorable party members lamented that a hierarchy of secretaries that resolved all questions had come into being, congresses and conferences had become executive assemblies, and party and public opinion had been stifled. At the 13th Party Congress, in January 1924, Stalin responded that the party cannot be an alliance of groups and factions and should become "a monolithic organization cut from a single block of granite."

In another speech Stalin referred to all other institutions (the soviets, trade unions, Young Communists, women's organizations, and so forth) as transmission belts, as "tentacles in the hands of the party by which it transmits its will to the working class, and the working class is being transformed from an atomized mass into the army of the party." That is, the soviets do not embody power but are merely a transmission belt. "The dictatorship of the proletariat," Stalin taught, "consists of the guiding instructions of the party, plus the mass organizations of the proletariat carrying out these instructions, plus the population putting them into practice."

What sort of "guiding instructions"? Whose specifically? All one has to do is ask these questions in order to make it clear that the party itself was also being transformed into a transmission belt, the primary belt in the entire transmission. The mechanism of power described by Stalin presupposes one single operator to control the entire machine.

The turn toward industrialization began with a clear break with NEP. In 1929 the *apparat* suppressed all forms of private enterprise. The entrepreneur was denied access to credit, he was stifled with taxes, and he paid the highest freight rates. Those in charge either requisitioned or

---

[11] The Order of the Knights of the Sword was a German Catholic order known for its strict military discipline.

simply shut down private factories and broke many contracts for leasing state-owned enterprises.

The *apparat* methodically and purposefully ground their heels into the peasantry, resurrecting the typical techniques of War Communism. Given the clearly unequal exchange of goods and intentionally paltry prices for grain, meat, milk, and other commodities, it was understandable that the peasant didn't want to sell the fruits of his labor to the state. Stalin personally led the charge. In early 1928 he sent a directive to local authorities ordering them to confiscate grain from peasants "by any means possible." Stalin himself went to Siberia, and at meetings with local authorities he accused the peasantry of disrupting supplies and demanded trials for speculation. The property of anyone convicted was to be confiscated. Similar to the practice during War Communism, Stalin proposed giving a quarter of the confiscated grain to poor peasants (in practice, to informers). Stalin ordered the dismissal of any party or soviet employee who did not carry out these repressive measures.

A wave of general searches swept the country, as had been common under War Communism. The authorities prohibited sales of grain at the markets, and armed roadblocks were set up in many places.

Forcible collectivization completed the destruction of commercial farming.

A series of energetic measures was used to destroy the commercial model for state industry. In 1932 the 17th Party Conference emphasized "the complete incompatibility between bourgeois-NEP perversions of the principle of self-financing expressed in the squandering of common state-owned resources and the disruption of established economic plans, on the one hand, and the policies of the party and the interests of the working class, on the other hand." Wholesale trade and economic responsibility for the results of one's work were called perversions and squandering. This was when the system of budgeted distribution of resources took root, a system which continues to have a deadly effect on the economy to this day.

The economist Grigory Khanin recently used new techniques to calculate the most important indicators of economic development from 1928 to 1941. It turned out that during this period the GNP rose only 50 percent rather than by a factor of 5.5, as the official statistics indicate, while labor productivity rose only 36 percent instead of by a factor of 4.3, and so forth. During this period, industrial plants were built at breakneck speed and new industrial sectors came into being. The fixed industrial capital in the economy almost doubled, but at the same time the rate of return on capital dropped 25 percent. The expenditure of materials per unit of final product increased by 25 to 30 percent, which essentially made the increase in the production of raw materials worthless. It was during this time that the disproportions and imbalances that are still tormenting our economy came into being, namely those between heavy and light industry, between transportation and other material industries, and between monetary income and the goods that it can purchase.

The destruction of commercial production objectively necessitated the replacement of economic labor incentives with brute force and greatly strengthened, as the magazine *Bolshevik* has written, that aspect of the dictatorship [of the proletariat] "expressed in the use of legally unrestricted violence, including the use of terror against class enemies when necessary." A great deal has already been written about the violent nature of collectivization. In March 1930, when it had become clear that the collective farms would disrupt the planting, Stalin came out with his article "Dizziness from Success." As usual, Stalin placed the blame for "excesses" on the persons carrying out the plan, and he authorized peasants to leave collective farms. However, peasants leaving the collective farms did not get their livestock and implements back, and the land they received was the worst available. In the summer of 1930, Stalin announced that "there is no turning back. The *kulaks* have been condemned and will be eliminated. There is only one way left, and that is the collective farm." Years later, in a conversation, he stated that millions of peasants were exterminated in the collectivization process. The actual number is still unknown.

As one wise man has noted, 1929 was justifiably known as the year of the great break, but no one ever said exactly what was broken. It was the backbone of the nation.

In economic development the methods of War Communism were essentially restored. The choice of specific methods was undoubtedly affected by the personality of the leader. Stalin instinctively mistrusted innovation and had no desire to implement Trotsky's splendid plan for militarizing labor. A classic form of force, namely the work of prisoners under guard, was closer to his heart. Prisoners opened up Kolyma and the Arctic region of the Urals, Siberia, and Kazakhstan, built Norilsk, Vorkuta, and Magadan, constructed canals, built roads in the north; there is no end to the projects they worked on. In one of my journalistic trips to the north, an eyewitness who had miraculously survived told me how they built the Kotlas-to-Vorkuta road. In the Arctic a worker must at least be given a quilted jacket, felt boots, and mittens. But there were not enough to go around. A prisoner was used for two weeks, because experience had shown that was how long he could work in the clothes in which he had been arrested. Then the frozen prisoner was sent to rot in a camp, and new "virgins" were brought to replace him. Until recently, it was forbidden even to mention this. Now, fortunately, times have changed. The dam of silence has been broken. In remembering the tragedies of Sergei Mironovich [Kirov] and Nikolai Ivanovich [Bukharin], however, we should not forget the sufferings of Ivan Denisovich.[12] A nation that forgets its history is condemned to repeat it.

---

[12] Sergei Mironovich Kirov, head of the Leningrad party organization, was murdered in 1934. Kirov's murder, allegedly on Stalin's orders, was a pretext for unleashing mass repressions. Nikolai Ivanovich Bukharin was executed after the "show trials" of 1937. Ivan Denisovich is the title character of Alexander Solzhenitsyn's novel, *A Day in the Life of Ivan Denisovich*, which describes the harsh daily routine in prison camps under Stalin.

The Stalin Phenomenon

Dmitry Volkogonov

Literaturnaya Gazeta
December 9, 1987

Does Stalinism equal socialism? In this analysis of the Stalin period, General Dmitry Volkogonov sharply criticizes Stalin for unforgivable crimes, but he also credits the Soviet leader with building socialism through the policies of industrialization and collectivization. In another contribution to the current debate about Stalin, reform historian Yuri Afanasiev condemns such a "hybrid image" of Stalin and the view that "on the one hand, mass repressions and crimes; on the other, daily happiness and record setting . . . there was also a record in terms of killing one's own people which it seems to me has been exceeded only by Pol Pot."[1] Some Soviet press articles have also criticized Volkogonov for commemorating the "more than 20,000 honest people" of the NKVD who died during the purges; NKVD officers arrested and tortured millions of people during the purges.

Volkogonov's views, while generally conservative, are more sophisticated and analytical than are most treatments of the Stalin era. Although it is unusual for a high-ranking military officer to write political history, General Volkogonov is also a professor of philosophy and has parlayed his military status into unprecedented access to the archives of the Ministry of Defense. He is the author of the first Gorbachev-period biography of Stalin, and this article is adapted from that book's foreword.

We cannot fail to rejoice that an active process is now taking place, not only a renewal of the present, but also a "restoration" of the past. And probably the intellectual and emotional epicenter of the public's interest in the past is the figure of Stalin. I think there has not been a more contradictory figure in our history (Russian or Soviet). The praise and abuse that have fallen upon him are enough for a whole legion of historical personalities.

---

[1]Yuri Afanasiev, *"Perestroika* and Historical Knowledge," *Literaturnaya Rossiya*, no. 2, June 17, 1988.

Traveling into the future is a difficult, rocky journey. Traveling into the past is no easier. It always, as Feuerbach[2] so aptly put it, "pierces the heart"; it is moving and disturbing. Stalin is one of the most complex of all personalities in history. Such people, whether we like it or not, belong not only to the past, but also to the present and future. Their lives are eternal philosophical "food" for thought about life, times, and conscience. One conclusion that becomes apparent as soon as you start studying Stalin is that the history of that individual is a crystallization of the highly complex dialectics of his age. To the extent to which the conditions of the times were complex, the personality at the head of the people and the party was equally complex. If we are honest about the truth, honest about history, we cannot help but admit Joseph Stalin's indisputable contribution to the struggle for socialism and its defense, as well as his unforgivable political errors and crimes, which took the form of an unjustified repression of many thousands of innocent people. Stalin and the leading nucleus of the party, while upholding and defending Leninism in the political and ideological struggle, created favorable conditions for accelerated socialist building. When it seemed that the most difficult time (in terms of the struggle within the party) was past and major successes were apparent in many spheres of new, creative work, a profoundly erroneous political thesis was born and "consecrated" by Stalin concerning the exacerbation of the class struggle as progress takes place. This thesis proposed that the dictatorship of the proletariat for the common cause increasingly turned toward not the constructive, but the punitive side. It is therefore no accident that assessments of Stalin's personality have undergone radical changes as the historical truth has emerged. If you compare, for instance, the greetings of the All-Union Communist Party (Bolsheviks) Central Committee and the USSR Council of Ministers on Stalin's seventieth birthday in 1949 with the provisions of Nikita Khrushchev's dramatic report delivered at the 20th Party Congress on the night of February 24, 1956, the assessments of Stalin as party leader are practically at opposite poles. Only a few

---

[2] Ludwig Feuerbach was a radical German philosopher whose writings influenced Karl Marx.

years lie between these assessments, which were made, for the most part, by the very same people. What followed was a kind of moratorium phase regarding public enlightenment.

When the name of Stalin is pronounced, what springs to many minds first of all is the repression, and the violation of humanity. Invisible Valkyries sprang into being in the atmosphere of society, and they, it is well known, have the power of life and death over people. Yes, all of this happened. There is no forgiveness for those guilty of these crimes. But we remember that during those same years Dneproges and Magnitka also sprang up, and there were Papanin, Angelina, Stakhanov, Busygin.[3] In those years the foundations of all that we build on today were created. Those were the times of the supreme flight of the human spirit of the Soviet people, who stood firm and conquered fascism in the Great Patriotic War.[4] It is therefore politically erroneous and morally dishonest, in condemning Stalin for his crimes, to call into question the real achievements of socialism and its basic potential. It is wrong, when assessing Stalin or the people in his immediate entourage, mechanically to transfer these assessments to the party and to the millions of ordinary people whose faith in the rightness of revolutionary ideals was not shaken.

You cannot evaluate the past on the basis of arithmetic: Which did Stalin have more of, merits or crimes? The very formulation of this question is immoral, because no merits can justify inhumanity. The question is considerably more complex. You have to comprehend the origins, the causes of the deformation of the machinery of power. How could it happen that the great coexisted with the base, evil was camouflaged by good? Why did the social degeneration of many individuals take place? Was tragedy inevitable? Why

---

[3] Dneproges is a hydroelectric plant built on the Dnieper River. Magnitka is a steel mill built at Magnitogorsk in the Urals. Sergei Papanin was a Soviet polar explorer. Pasha Angelina was the first woman tractor operator. Alexei Stakhanov was an advanced worker in the coal mines whose labor records were cited by Stalin and others as targets for Soviet workers. Alexander Busygin was a blacksmith at the automobile plant and an initiator of the Stakhanov movement in the automobile industry.

[4] World War II is called the Great Patriotic War in the USSR.

did the institutions of social defense not "work"? These and many other questions are often raised in our press, reflecting the rapid rise in the Soviet people's level of political and historical awareness which we have seen since the 27th Party Congress. In a number of cases, especially among young people who have only a sketchy knowledge of history, diametrically contradictory judgments and subjectivist assessments have caused intellectual confusion capable of generating social nihilism and disrespect for our values. The best way to quench the thirst for knowledge is to learn the truth.

The Leninist methodology of analysis of the October Socialist Revolution and its prospects and the assessment of the political and human qualities of its leaders—that is the starting point for creating a philosophical and political portrait. Stalin remembered all his life that Vladimir Lenin, in his notes for the congress in December 1922, called him and Leon Trotsky "outstanding leaders," but he also never forgot Lenin's searingly frank and profound assessment of his complex nature, his difficult character. Nor could he tolerate the fact that Lenin called Nikolai Bukharin the "darling of the whole party." A study of Stalin's speeches shows that he repeatedly, but extremely cautiously, in a rhetorical and roundabout way, disputed Lenin's assessments. For instance, as though he were polemicizing with Lenin, he said in one of his speeches that "we love Bukharin, but we love the truth, the party, the Comintern even more." That sentence contains practically the whole of Stalin: devoted to the doctrine, but cunning and subtle. Lenin's opinion that "Stalin is too rude" was interpreted by the general secretary in one of his speeches as meaning that he was "rude only to enemies." In turning to Lenin to analyze the Stalin phenomenon, you see again and again that Lenin's lightning thoughts are, as before, ahead of us. This is the quality not simply of wise, profound truths, but of prophetic truths.

Stalin knew, for instance, of Lenin's warm attitude toward Bukharin. Stalin himself for many years maintained friendly personal relations with Bukharin and his family. Bukharin played a role of considerable importance in helping Stalin in the struggle against Trotsky and Trotskyism. Stalin could not help but see that accusations of, for instance, espionage, conspiracy, and so forth against Bukharin looked utterly ridiculous. Bukharin, with his highly developed intellect, knew how to respect valid arguments. When he became convinced that his program of leisurely socialist development might lead to failure because history had not allowed our country time for a "slow start," he honestly admitted his mistakes. And he not only admitted them, but also became actively involved in the implementation of the party's instructions. But that did not prevent Stalin from sanctioning, in effect, reprisals against this most popular party figure, this close party comrade. How can we explain or understand that?

A few years ago, while preparing to write a philosophical and biographical essay on Joseph Stalin, I found myself taking an interest in literature about Alexander the Great, Caesar, Cromwell, Ivan the Terrible, and Peter the Great. I was interested in the psychology of "great leaders," dictators, sovereigns, and other absolutist leaders. Although I realize that all historical analogies are risky here, I would like to express one preliminary opinion. People with unlimited power outside democratic control usually develop feelings of infallibility, unlimited personal superiority, and omnipotence as well as exaggerated views of their own capabilities and potential. As a rule these individuals, although they live among people, are eternally alone. Stalin, as has been established, only very rarely talked with anyone one-on-one. Although he always had Viacheslav Molotov or Lazar Kaganovich, Kliment Voroshilov or Georgy Malenkov, Lavrenty Beria or someone else with him, he was eternally alone in his heart. He had nobody to relate to, nobody to justify himself to. Loneliness at the top and the chilling reality of unlimited power dried up his feelings and turned his intellect into a cold calculating machine. Every step instantly becoming "historic," "fateful," and "decisive" gradually kills the human being in the man.

I read the works of Stalin's political and ideological opponents within the country: Leon Trotsky, Grigory Zinoviev, Lev Kamenev, Nikolai Bukharin, Alexei Rykov, Mikhail Tomsky, and others. They were all both comrades in arms and pupils of Lenin. None of them considered himself a "protégé" of Stalin, whereas Lazar Kaganovich, Viacheslav Molotov, Kliment Voroshilov, and other new figures who took their place later spoke of themselves openly as such protégés.[5] In this case Stalin acted in accordance with the ancient law of dictators: The people they promote are notable for their greater devotion and do not lay claim to the prime roles. Trotsky, Zinoviev, Kamenev, and a number of other figures in the 1920s were better known to the party than was Stalin. It must be said that some of them were very prolific; for instance, Leon Trotsky had published seventeen volumes of his own works by 1927. This politician, who was full of energy and not without his share of literary talent, in creating his own "works" invariably showed off before the mirror of history, trying to justify his claims to party leadership.

On that tragic day of January 21, 1924, Stalin dictated a telegram stating the following: "To be conveyed to comrade Trotsky. Comrade Lenin died suddenly at 0650 on 21 January. Death followed paralysis of the respiratory center. Funeral Saturday 26 January. Stalin." As he signed the dispatch, Stalin realized that now he had to face a tough, merciless struggle with Trotsky for the leadership. But did Stalin know that when he overcame Trotsky he still would not have "got rid" of him, although he himself would not suspect it? The methods of the bureaucratic decree, violence, and "turning the screw," for which Trotsky was the apologist, were adopted by Stalin. Was this not one of the sources of the tragedy to come? And what were the others? I will mention only this:

There is a reason of a private nature, so to speak. After the 11th Party Congress, at the April 3, 1922, Central Committee *plenum*, the post of general secretary was instituted. At that time this post was not regarded as the main, key post, or else the first general secretary would obviously have been Lenin. The general secretary was to conduct the current work of the Secretariat. Lenin was already sick. Following Kamenev's recommendation (and obviously with Lenin's approval), Stalin was appointed to this post, having demonstrated his inclination for *apparat* work even earlier. Less than a year after this appointment, on January 4, 1923, in his appendix to the "Letter to the Congress," Lenin proposed to the comrades in the Central Committee that they "consider a means" of removing Stalin from that post. It had taken Vladimir Illyich [Lenin] only a

---

[5] Kaganovich, Molotov, and Voroshilov were Stalin's close associates.

few months to study the man in the post of general secretary and see in him something that could become dangerous in the future. The leader's death prevented the implementation of this intention. But another, special reason for the tragedy arises from this: the nonfulfillment of Lenin's will. The members of the Central Committee and delegates to the 13th Party Congress were inconsistent on this question. The concession to Stalin by the well-wishing (at that time!) Zinoviev and Kamenev later cost the party dearly. Stalin, learning of Lenin's letter, by some accounts even tried to resign. For the sake of objectivity it should be said that in 1924, Stalin was only one of many leaders, and nobody saw him as a future demon.

However, the main reason for the later tragedies lies elsewhere. It, too, is in the sphere of instructions given by Lenin that were not fulfilled by his heirs. In his last letters (and all of this in the unique Volume 45!) the leader returns repeatedly to the idea of democratizing the party's life, improving the *apparat*'s work, swelling the membership of the Central Committee with workers and peasants, and systematically renewing it. Unfortunately, these democratic foundations were merely laid, and not developed. After all, if Stalin's tenure in the newly instituted post had been limited to a specified term, the cult of deformation might have been prevented. In Lenin's proposal to the 12th Party Congress, "How We Should Reorganize the Workers' and Peasants' Inspectorate," we can glimpse the idea of a necessary renewal of leading party organs and the elimination of the functions of the Central Committee and soviets. The first green sprouts of democracy were not tended. They were gradually choked out by the stronger growth of dogmatism, bureaucracy, and administrative management. The cult of the "great leader" was no mere accident.

Throughout history, one man's triumph has often resulted in tragedy for a whole people. Nikita Khrushchev, delivering his report at the 20th Party Congress, placed the emphasis in the following way: "We cannot say," he noted, "that his actions were the actions of a mad despot. He believed that it was necessary to act in that way in the interests of the party and the working people's masses, for the sake of the defense of the revolutionary gains. Therein lies the tragedy!" I do not think the emphasis is quite right.

Mikhail Gorbachev's report of November 2, 1987, says that the documents that exist allow us to assume that Stalin knew about the scale of the repressions and their mass nature. Yes, he knew, and he knew precisely. For instance, Deputy Chairman of the Supreme Court Vasily Ulrikh regularly, with Andrei Vyshinsky,[6] reported to Stalin (and usually to Molotov and Yezhov[7] at the same time) on the trials and verdicts. In 1937, Ulrikh submitted a "report" every month on the total number of people convicted of "espionage, terrorist, and subversive activity." Stalin read all the reports, those on the harvest, on the quantity of coal extracted, and, terrible to say, on the number of people deprived of their lives.

Stalin rapidly grew accustomed to violence as a necessary attribute of unlimited power. Most likely—this is derived from logical assumptions—the punitive machine, set in full motion by Stalin, seized the imagination not only of low-level functionaries, but also of Stalin himself. Perhaps the downward progress toward the idea of violence as a universal solution evolved in a number of stages. First was the struggle against real enemies (and they did exist); then came the elimination of personal adversaries; after that, the terrible inertia of violence was already in force; finally, violence began to be regarded as an indicator of devotion and orthodoxy. For instance, even Stalin's closest aides, Molotov and Kaganovich, greeted without a murmur the reports that the former's wife and the latter's brother had been arrested as "enemies of the people."

Sometimes Stalin regarded society as a human zoo. Everything was in his power. "Sabotage," spy mania, and tilting at the windmills of "double dealing" became the shameful attributes of orthodoxy, blind faith, and devotion to the leader. For instance, it could hardly even be imagined that among the Politburo members and candidate members elected at the 14th All-Union Communist Party (Bolsheviks) Congress, six would turn out to be enemies! Stalin destroyed the "enemies," but the waves spread further and further. It was the force of evil. And who knows: Was there not, alongside the cruelty, a

---

[6] Andrei Vyshinsky was the state prosecutor during the famous show trials of the 1930s.

[7] Alexander Yezhov was head of the NKVD during the 1930s.

mental illness in Stalin that was never recognized? Otherwise it is hard to explain why, after eliminating his rivals, he needed to continue to "cut down" the best people in the party and state on the eve of dreadful tribulations. Incidentally, within the NKVD organs themselves, many Bolsheviks saw, earlier than others, the danger of hysterical universal suspicion and repressions. Among the NKVD workers alone, more than 20,000 honest people fell victims to this orgy of lawlessness.

However, no scowls on the face of history could ultimately take away the achievement of the people who created the "first land of socialism"; despite the tragedy, we preserved our devotion to our ideals. The dialectics of triumph and tragedy themselves contain the eternal complexity of our life, in which, while the decisive role belongs (ultimately!) to the masses, so much depends on historical individuals. As Hegel[8] said, a man's destiny is not his alone, it represents the general moral, tragic destiny. And the tragedy lay precisely in the fact that at a certain stage Stalin was perceived by millions of people not as a man of flesh and blood, but as a symbol of socialism, its living personification. After all, a lie repeated many times can look like the truth. The deification of the leader took on the highest meaning; it justified any negative phenomena, in the people's eyes, as being the result of intrigues by "enemies." Conversely, it attributed every success to the mind and will of one man alone. In adopting and promulgating this or that decision, especially at large forums, Stalin liked to quote the classics. Here he showed a common human weakness. People like to have patrons. Even such a powerful man as Stalin was not averse to hiding in the shadow of the authority of a theory, ideological clichés, his great predecessor. Triumph and tragedy were expressed in the Soviet people's lofty patriotism and internationalism, and at the same time in the dogmatism and bureaucracy of many institutions, in the genuine devotion and heroism of the millions, and in the omnipotence of the *apparat* and the imposition of the "cog" mentality.

---

[8]Georg Wilhelm Friedrich Hegel was a German philosopher from whom Marx borrowed the theory of the historical dialectic.

Looking back from the heights of the present it seems that after the death of Lenin, whom even the party's oppositionists admired, both Trotsky and Bukharin had a real chance to become head of the party. Today it can be affirmed that if Trotsky had taken the helm of the party even graver trials would have lain in store for it, trials fraught with the danger of losing socialist gains, especially because Trotsky did not have a clear, scientific program for building socialism in the USSR. Bukharin did have such a program, he had his vision of party-wide goals. But Bukharin, for all his attractiveness as a personality, his lofty intellect, gentleness, and humanity, for a long time failed to recognize the historical necessity for the country to undergo a rapid spurt in its buildup of economic might.

Of course, there were also Yanis Rudzutak, Mikhail Frunze, and Alexei Rykov. But it seems that, after Lenin's death and almost until the beginning of the 1930s, among the leaders of the revolution Stalin was probably the most consistent and strong-willed defender of the party's course of founding and strengthening the world's first socialist state. True, he did not have the qualities to replace Lenin. Nobody did. Of course, Stalin did not have Lenin's brilliant spiritual might, Plekhanov's theoretical profundity, or Lunacharsky's culture.[9] He was neither a major theorist, nor an orator, nor an attractive personality. Intellectually and morally he was inferior to many. And he became first! In the time of struggle for the survival of the new system, the leader's purposefulness and political will were exceptionally significant. And here perhaps Stalin had, after Lenin, no equals. In the words of Shakespeare's Hamlet, "with all his imperfections on his head," he still had something important that others did not have. Not the least important factor here was Stalin's ability to make maximum use of the party *apparat* to achieve his goals. And many of those who remained alongside Stalin after Lenin's death were not up to the task. Under these conditions the alternative of another leader was unlikely.

---

[9]Vladimir Plekhanov was the leader of the Menshevik party and is considered to have been the first Marxist in Russia. Anatoly Lunacharsky was people's commissar for culture after the October Revolution.

Ultimately it is not a matter of personalities, but the fact that the democratic potential that Lenin had begun to create was not preserved. That is the whole point. If the democratic attributes of social protection against the phenomena of change had been created, it would not have mattered crucially whether the leader was outstanding or less outstanding. Without these democratic attributes, however, the country's fate becomes excessively dependent on the historical choice of who is at the helm of power. Stalin, who did so much to establish socialism in our country and never so much as veered in the direction of any opposition, did not withstand the test of power. First and foremost, concerning his attitude toward common human moral values: Stalin was not simply merciless toward political adversaries. He regarded any other viewpoint as opportunist. He who was not with him was regarded as an enemy. For Stalin the notion of duty, which he interpreted as an expression of unfailing fulfillment of instructions, prevailed over the concept of human rights.

To outlive one's times is given only to a few. One such is Stalin. But his immortality is troubled. It will be a long time before the disputes about his role in our history die down, disputes accompanied by epithets tinged with reverence, hatred, bitterness, and eternal perplexity. One way or another, we are still learning from Stalin's life: that the power of great ideas is ultimately stronger than the power of men, and that the tragic catalog of Stalin's abuses could not, of course, undermine the tremendous attractive force of the ideals put forward by the leading lights of Marxism.

The judgment of men can be illusory. The judgment of history is eternal.

Khrushchev: Sketches for a Political Portrait

Fyodor Burlatsky

Literaturnaya Gazeta
February 24, 1988

Fyodor Burlatsky writes that for decades the Khrushchev period has been treated "as if someone's hand had torn a whole chapter clean out" of Soviet history books. This revisionist article represents the first attempt since his removal in 1964 to analyze objectively Khrushchev's rule. The author, a former Khrushchev speech writer, calls him a courageous pioneer who made mistakes but genuinely sought to change Soviet society for the better.

Burlatsky sometimes diminishes Khrushchev's vicissitudes, particularly concerning the intelligentsia (for example, he excuses Khrushchev for depriving writer Boris Pasternak of the Nobel Prize). Some also would question the assertion that Khrushchev was a "natural" successor to the Nikolai Bukharin reform wing of the party.

Burlatsky, however, justifiably calls Khrushchev's speech denouncing Joseph Stalin at the 20th Party Congress a "courageous decision." This denunciation of Stalin helped make the current era of historical revisionism possible. Khrushchev did not delve further into the Stalin era both because of his personal involvement in persecutions and because even the limited scope of his speech politically mobilized his conservative opponents. Burlatsky's article points to important parallels between the Khrushchev period and the current reform era.

Khrushchev and his times: an indisputably important period, and perhaps one of the most complex in our history. Important, because it has close echoes in the *perestroika* now taking place in this country and in the present process of democratization. Complex, because it is a decade that was at first called "glorious" but was later censured as a period of voluntarism and subjectivism. It was the time of the 20th and 22nd Party Congresses, reflections of the bitter political struggles that determined the country's new course. Under Nikita Khrushchev the first steps were taken toward reviving Leninist principles and purifying the ideals of socialism. Then, too, the transition began from the Cold War to peaceful coexistence, and a window on the modern world was once again opened. At that abrupt turning point in history our society took a deep breath of the air of renewal—and choked, either from too much oxygen, or from not enough.

For a long time, a very long time, it was customary not to speak of those stormy years, as if someone's hand had torn a whole chapter clean out of our annals. For nearly twenty years the name Khrushchev was taboo. But life will come into its own. In the report on the seventieth anniversary of October delivered by Mikhail Gorbachev, we heard long-awaited words about those times: what was done then, what was not done or done wrongly, what survived into the 1980s, and what was swept away and lost in the period of stagnation.

So what are the complex and contradictory features of this individual with whom we associate a turning point in our recent history? I do not seek to answer all the questions that have accumulated; I merely wish to share my personal reminiscences and a few opinions suggested by comparing the present and the past.

How did it come about that, after Stalin, it was Khrushchev who came to lead the country? Stalin appeared to have done everything possible to "purge" the party of all his opponents, real and imagined, "right" and "left." In the 1950s an aphorism attributed to him was passed from mouth to mouth: "If you have a man, you have a problem; no man—no problem." As a result it seemed that the most loyal, the most reliable survived. How did Stalin fail to see in Khrushchev the man who would dig a grave for his cult?

An old man's blindness? Probably not. Niccolò Machiavelli, that brilliant denouncer of tyranny, once said: "Brutus would have become caesar, if he had pretended to be a fool." I think that Khrushchev somehow managed to pretend to be a very pliable person without any special ambitions. It was said that during the endless all-night parties at the nearby dacha in Kuntsevo [near Moscow] where Stalin lived for the last thirty years, Khrushchev used to dance the *gopak* [a Ukrainian folk dance]. At that time he went about in a Ukrainian smock, playing the "genuine cossack," remote from any claims to power, a reliable performer of another's will. But evidently

Khrushchev even then was harboring protests deep within himself. This surfaced immediately after Stalin's death.

It was not by chance that Khrushchev came to power, yet at the same time it was by chance. It was not by chance in that he expressed the current in the party that, in different conditions and probably in different ways, was represented by such dissimilar figures as Felix Dzerzhinsky, Nikolai Bukharin, Alexei Rykov, Yanis Rudzutak, and Sergei Kirov.[1] They were the advocates of the development of NEP [New Economic Policy] and democratization, the opponents of coercive measures in industry, in agriculture, and even more so in culture. Despite the cruel Stalinist repressions, this current never dried up. In this sense Khrushchev's arrival on the scene was only natural.

But, of course, there was also a large element of chance here. If Malenkov had come to an agreement with Beria,[2] if the "Stalinist guard" had rallied in 1953 rather than in 1957, Khrushchev would not have been the leader. Our entire history could have followed a rather different course. It is hard for us to admit, but in fact everything hung by a thread.

All the same, history made the right choice. It was a response to the real problems of our life. The countryside increasingly reduced to poverty and basically half-ruined, the technologically backward industry, the acute housing shortage, the population's low living standard, millions of people held in prisons and camps, the country's isolation from the outside world—all of this required a new policy

---

[1] Felix Dzerzhinsky was head of the Cheka, the secret police in the years after the October Revolution. Nikolai Bukharin, one of the most popular early party leaders, strongly supported NEP. He was executed in 1938 after a show trial. Alexei Rykov was the first Soviet prime minister, from 1924 to 1929. Yanis Rudzutak was a party leader active in trade unions and a supporter of Stalin, who nevertheless was also executed in 1938. Sergei Kirov, who replaced Zinoviev as the head of the Leningrad party organization, was another Stalin supporter who was murdered, in 1934. His death signalled the beginning of the wave of Stalin's mass repressions.

[2] Lavrenty Beria was head of the NKVD (precursor of the KGB) during the 1940s and early 1950s. Georgy Malenkov was Stalin's closest aide during the last decade of Stalin's rule.

and radical changes. And Khrushchev arrived precisely as the people's hope, the precursor of a new age.

At that time everything associated with the 20th Party Congress deeply moved us. How did Khrushchev dare to deliver the report on Stalin, knowing that the vast majority of delegates would be against the revelations? Where did he find the courage and the confidence in eventual success? This was one of the very rare cases in history when a political leader put his personal power, and even his life, on the line for the sake of higher social objectives. Not a single figure in the post-Stalin leadership would have dared to deliver such a report on the personality cult. Khrushchev, and only Khrushchev, in my view, could do it—so boldly, so emotionally, and in many respects with so little contemplation. It took someone with Khrushchev's personality, his desperation to the point of adventurism. It took someone who had passed through the trials of suffering, fear, and time-serving to take such a step. His own assessment of the moment, heard during a meeting with foreign guests, is certainly interesting:

> I am often asked how I dared to deliver that report at the 20th Congress. We trusted that man for so many years! We raised him up. We created the cult. And then to take that risk. But since I was elected first secretary, I had to tell the truth about the past, whatever it cost me and whatever risk it entailed for me. It was Lenin who taught us that a party that is not afraid to tell the truth will never perish. We learned the lessons of the past, and we wanted the other fraternal parties to learn those lessons too, and then our common victory would be ensured.

But, of course, it was not only a matter of the sense of duty that the first secretary spoke of. I often heard Khrushchev reminisce about Stalin in lengthy, reflective monologues, often lasting many hours, a kind of conversation with himself, with his conscience. He was deeply wounded by Stalinism. There was a mixture of everything here: mystical fear of Stalin, who was capable of destroying anyone for one false step, gesture, or look, and horror at the shedding of innocent blood. There was a sense of personal guilt and a longing to protest, built up over decades, which burst out like steam from a cauldron.

I have heard Khrushchev describe his understanding of his role in our country's history. He used to say that Lenin was the organizer of the revolution and founder of the party and state and that Stalin, despite his errors, was the man who ensured victory in the bloody war against fascism. Khrushchev saw it as his own mission to give the Soviet people peace and prosperity. He spoke of this repeatedly as the main aim of his activity.

The problem, however, was that he was unclear about the means of fulfilling these goals. For all his radicalism, he rejected criticism from Palmiro Togliatti,[3] who advised him to seek the roots of the personality cult in the system that had grown up. Togliatti did not, of course, raise the question of replacing socialism with capitalism; instead, he had in mind a change in the regime of personal power itself.

Khrushchev attached the main significance to the ideological aspect of the matter, the need to expose the personality cult in full and tell the truth about the crimes of the 1930s and of other periods. But, alas, this truth was itself incomplete. From the first, Khrushchev came up against the problem of personal responsibility, because many people in the party knew about the role he himself had played in the persecution of cadres both in the Ukraine and in the Moscow party organization. Without telling the truth about himself, he could not tell the whole truth about others. Therefore, information about the responsibility of various individuals, not to mention Stalin's own responsibility, for the crimes committed was one-sided and often equivocal. It was dependent on political expediency. For instance, while exposing Viacheslav Molotov and Lazar Kaganovich at the 22nd Party Congress for their roles in the massacre of cadres in the 1930s, Khrushchev kept quiet about the participation of Anastas Mikoyan,[4] who subsequently became his reliable ally. In speaking of the 1930s, Khrushchev carefully avoided the period of

---

[3] Palmiro Togliatti served as general secretary of the Italian Communist party and is considered to have been the founder of Eurocommunism.

[4] Anastas Mikoyan was a close associate of Stalin and Khrushchev and is credited with political adroitness.

collectivization, because he personally was involved in the excesses of that time.

Khrushchev tried to form a common attitude toward the Stalin cult in all the members of the Central Committee Presidium.[5] On his instructions, each representative of the leadership who spoke at the 22nd Party Congress had to define his attitude toward this matter of principle. After the congress, however, it turned out that many of those who had fulminated against the personality cult found it easy to revise their positions and return, basically, to their former views.

The problem of guarantees against a regime of personal power met with an insuperable obstacle: the limited political sophistication of Khrushchev himself and of his generation of leaders. Theirs was a largely patriarchal culture, drawn from traditional ideas about leadership within the framework of the peasant household. Paternalism, interference in all kinds of affairs and relations, the infallibility of the patriarch, intolerance of differing opinions—all this made up the typical set of age-old ideas about power in Russia.

In this respect, the events that followed the June 1957 *plenum* were characteristic. At this *plenum*, as is known, the representatives of the old "Stalinist guard" sought Khrushchev's expulsion by means of a so-called "arithmetical majority." As a result of a vote by the CPSU Central Committee Presidium, a decision was approved to relieve him of the post of first secretary. This decision was overturned, however, thanks to the efforts of ardent Khrushchev supporters. Marshal Georgy Zhukov played an outstanding role in defeating the Stalinists. It was said at the time that during the CPSU Central Committee Presidium session Zhukov flung in their faces the historic remark: "The army is against this decision, and not one tank will move from the spot without my orders." This remark eventually cost him his political career. Soon after the June *plenum* Khrushchev managed to relieve Georgy Zhukov of his posts as member of the CPSU Central Committee Presidium and USSR defense minister.

Khrushchev's relations with the intelligentsia were affected by his haste, his desire to intervene in every issue

---

[5] The Presidium was the equivalent of today's Politburo.

and resolve it quickly. In this respect he was often the plaything of self-interested advisers and sometimes even of covert opponents who were planning his downfall. I remember well that his visit to the art exhibition at the Manege [Moscow exhibit hall] was provoked by a specially prepared catalog. It said little about the problems of art, but it cited genuine or invented remarks by writers and artists about Khrushchev, calling him the "jester on the throne," the "corn man," the "chatterbox." Driven to his wits' end, Khrushchev set off for the Manege to give the artists a piece of his mind. By the same method Khrushchev's covert opponents inveighed against him in the Pasternak episode, secured through him Alexander Nesmeyanov's removal from the post of president of the USSR Academy of Sciences in favor of Trofim Lysenko,[6] and set him against many representatives of literature, art, and science.

Economic policy was one of his most vulnerable areas. He saw the task mainly as changing the methods of economic leadership at the *apparat* level (in the Gosplan, the regional economic councils, and the ministries), but he did not recognize the significance of profound structural reforms that change working and living conditions for the actual producers, the workers, peasants, and scientific and technical intelligentsia.

Matters were even worse when it came to transformations in the sphere of state administration and the structure of party leadership. Who "fed" Khrushchev the idea of dividing party *obkoms* and *raikoms* into industrial and agricultural ones? Intuitively, I am convinced that it was not done without malice, it was done to decisively undermine his prestige among party leaders.

These errors were laid at Khrushchev's door at the CPSU Central Committee October (1964) *plenum*. At this *plenum* a strange symbiosis of political forces was formed. From advocates of consistent progress along the path of the 20th Party Congress to conservatives and crypto-Stalinists, they all rallied against the leader who had helped the majority of them "to the top." Subsequent events left no room for doubt that Khrushchev was removed not so much

---

[6]Khrushchev supported Trofim Lysenko, a biologist whose belligerence in advocating his bizarre scientific theories ruined the careers of many Soviet scientists.

for voluntarism as for his insatiable thirst for change. The slogan of "stability" put forward by his successors delayed urgently needed reforms for a long time. The very word "reform," as well as any mention of the 20th Party Congress, became dangerous and cost many supporters of this course their political careers.

Now, nearly a quarter of a century later, in comparing the periods before and after October 1964, we can see more clearly Khrushchev's strengths and weaknesses. His main merit was that he crushed Stalin's personality cult. This proved irreversible, despite all the cowardly attempts to set up the pedestal in its former place. That they did not work means that the plowman did not labor in vain. The courageous decision to rehabilitate many Communists and nonparty people who had been subjected to repressions and executions in the period of the personality cult restored justice, truth, and honor in the life of the party and the state. A mighty blow, if not in every respect an effective and bold one, was struck against overcentralism, bureaucracy, and bureaucratic arrogance.

In Khrushchev's time the foundations were laid for a breakthrough in the development of agriculture. Purchase prices were increased, the tax burden was reduced drastically, and new technologies began to be used. The opening up of the virgin lands, for all its shortcomings, played a part in providing the population with food. Khrushchev tried to point the countryside toward making use of foreign experience and the first agricultural revolution. Even his enthusiasm for corn was dictated by good intentions, although it was accompanied by naive extremes. Gigantism in the countryside and the reduction of farmstead plots also had a bad effect.

Let us recall that Khrushchev's name is associated with major achievements in science and technology that made it possible to lay the foundations for achieving strategic parity. To this day everyone can still remember the meeting between Yuri Gagarin[7] and Khrushchev, which marked our country's breakthrough into space. The peaceful coexistence proclaimed at the 20th Party Congress, after undergoing a shock during the Caribbean

---

[7] Yuri Gagarin was the first Soviet cosmonaut.

crisis,[8] became an increasingly firm platform for agreements and businesslike compromises with the West. The Helsinki Final Act, which consolidated the results of World War II and proclaimed new international relations, economic cooperation, and the exchange of information, ideas, and people, has its roots in the era of the "thaw."

At that time the party embarked on the solution of many social problems. The living standard of the population in the cities and in the countryside began to improve gradually. However, the planned economic and social reforms misfired. A serious blow was struck against the reformers' hopes by the tragic events in Hungary in 1956.[9] But not the least important part was played by Nikita Sergeyevich's self-confidence, his lack of concern for questions of theory and political strategy. "Khrushchevism" as a prospectus for the renewal of socialism did not work. To use the favorite metaphor of Mao Tse-tung, Khrushchev walked on two feet: One was stepping boldly into a new era, while the other was inextricably bogged down in the quagmire of the past.

In answer to the question of why the reforms suffered defeat in the 1960s, one could also say that conservative forces were able to prevail over reformers because the administrative *apparat* and the entire society were not ready for radical changes. But that answer is too general. It is necessary to try to clarify what the conservatives took advantage of.

In my view, one of the mistakes was basing the quest for a prospectus for reforms and the means of implementing them on traditional administrative and even bureaucratic methods. First, Khrushchev usually issued instructions to "study" particular problems (economic, cultural, political) to the ministries and departments—that is, to the administrative *apparat* itself, which was asked to limit its own power. But the *apparat* always found a way to protect itself against control, through direct, indirect, or ambiguous decisions.

More or less successful reforms, in both socialist and capitalist countries, have usually been planned by a group of experts, chiefly by scientists and public figures, working

---

[8] The Cuban missile crisis.

[9] Soviet tanks crushed the Hungarian revolt in October 1956.

under the leadership of the country's leader. This was the case, for instance, in Hungary, Yugoslavia, and China. In Japan, I met with Professor Saburo Okita, who is regarded as the author of the Japanese "miracle." In West Germany a plan of reforms was drawn up at one time by Professor Ludwig Erhard, who subsequently became the country's chancellor.

Second, the "people were silent." Now, based on the experience of *glasnost*, we can see particularly clearly how little was done to inform people about the past, about the real problems, about the planned solutions, to say nothing of involving the broadest strata of the public in the struggle for reforms. How many times, recently, have I heard: "But in what way was Khrushchev better than Stalin? Under Stalin at least there was order; they jailed the bureaucrats, and the prices came down." It was no accident that at the time of the CPSU Central Committee October (1964) *plenum* virtually a majority throughout society heaved a sigh of relief and hopefully awaited changes for the better.

One last lesson. It concerns Khrushchev himself. This man of keen, innate political intelligence, bold and energetic, could not resist the charms of praise of his own personality. "Our Nikita Sergeyevich!" Was not this the beginning of the fall from grace for the acknowledged fighter against the cult? The limpets drowned him in a sea of flattery and praise, receiving in return high posts, the top awards, bonuses, and titles. And it is no accident that the worse matters were in the country, the louder and more triumphant grew the chorus of limpets and flatterers lauding the successes of the "great decade."

The ancients used to say that "character is a man's guiding destiny." Nikita Khrushchev was the victim of his own character, not just the victim of the environment. Haste, rashness, and emotionalism were unconquerable characteristics of his.

One of Khrushchev's assistants told me about an amazing conversation that his boss had with Winston Churchill. It took place during the visit to Britain by Khrushchev and Bulganin[10] in 1956. They met with

---

[10]Nikolai Bulganin was minister of defense under Stalin and Khrushchev.

Churchill, as I recall it, at a reception at the Soviet embassy. This is what the old British lion said: "Mr. Khrushchev, you are launching great reforms, and that is good! I would only like to advise you not to be in too much of a hurry. It is not easy to cross an abyss in two jumps. You might fall in." I would venture to add on my own account: Nor can you cross an abyss when you do not know onto which bank you are trying to jump.

Brezhnev and the End of the Thaw: Reflections on the Nature of Political Leadership

Fyodor Burlatsky

Literaturnaya Gazeta
September 14, 1988

Fyodor Burlatsky's article characterizes the Brezhnev years as two decades of wasted opportunities. He argues that technological innovation did not occur during the Brezhnev era because government policies inhibited the rise of enterprising, free, and creative people. And, in a rare criticism of the enormous military expenditures incurred under Brezhnev, Burlatsky asserts that the burden of achieving military parity with the United States starved all other spheres of the economy and kept Soviet living standards low. Another unusual aspect of Burlatsky's article is the blame he assigns to Brezhnev for poor U.S.-Soviet relations.

With rare candor, Burlatsky discusses the difficulty of introducing democracy into Russian political culture, which has never tolerated much pluralism or freedom of speech. He hopes that the rise of the new leadership will be a "safe guarantee against a recurrence of Stalinist and Brezhnevian traditions." Burlatsky's article marks the birth of political science in the Soviet Union, a previously forbidden field of study. He is among the first writers to analyze the mechanics of the political processes in the Soviet Union: the system of succession, the style of leadership, and the politics of transition.

Above all else, what we perhaps particularly need at present is a clear and accurate evaluation of the age of stagnation. We should, we must understand what happened in nearly two decades of Leonid Brezhnev's leadership of the country, with his entourage and the whole administrative *apparat*. We must understand not, of course, in order to forgive, nor in order to curse. We must understand in order to evaluate the experience of the past for the sake of a better future. Because, as has often been said, peoples are at least partially rewarded for their great trials by the great lessons they learn from them.

The concept of stagnation itself requires further study. It can hardly be doubted that in some spheres (first and foremost the economy) a trend toward stagnation [*zastoi*] did indeed come increasingly to the fore, while in other spheres, such as those of politics and morality, there was an actual regression in comparison with the ten-year period of Khrushchevian thaw. The abandonment of reforms (and in many respects the return to the command-and-administer system of the Stalinist era), the freeze of living standards, the general delay of absolutely self-evident decisions and the substitution of trite political verbiage in their place, the corruption and degeneration of power in which whole strata of the people became increasingly involved, the loss of moral values and the universal decline in morality—if that is stagnation, what is a crisis? Foreign policy in particular fully reflected the contradictory nature of Brezhnev's time, when every step forward along the path of détente was followed by two steps back. Only a few years separate two events of such disparate nature, the Final Act in Helsinki and the war in Afghanistan.

Out of all the multifaceted aspects of stagnation, I would like to touch on just one: How did it come about that in such a difficult period in the history of our motherland, and indeed in world history, the man at the helm of the country's government was the weakest of all the leaders who had held that position in Soviet times, and perhaps even in prerevolutionary times? I am very anxious to avoid giving way to the temptation to ridicule this man who set up with almost childlike simplicity the accessories of his own cult: four times Hero of the Soviet Union, Hero of Socialist Labor, Marshal of the Soviet Union, International Lenin Prize, a bronze bust in his birthplace, the Lenin Prize for Literature, the Karl Marx Gold Medal. All that was lacking was the title of generalissimo: His life was cut short too soon. Ridicule is too easy a way; it is the way, moreover, that accords with what is probably the most persistent Russian tradition, alas. It was Vasily Klyuchevsky, I think, who observed that each new Russian czar began his career by repudiating his predecessor. There is a saying in the West: Speak no ill of the dead. With us, it is the other way round: Make immoderate litanies in praise of the living and endless abuse of the dead. Clearly this is a sublimation to make up for the lack of opportunity to criticize current leaders.

Out of all the leaders of the Soviet period, the only exception was Lenin. And how far was he an exception, given that Stalin repudiated Lenin's testament[1] in all his activity while preserving the hypocritical ritual of reverence toward Lenin personally? As for criticism of Stalin himself, only now is it developing into serious analysis of the political and ideological regime he established.

Is it not time to take this same reasonable step with regard to Brezhnev? Of course, detailed descriptions of the intimate secrets of his corrupt family tickle the sensibilities of some readers. Although it cannot be denied that their children have often been the bane of political leaders. It is probably more useful to reflect not so much on Brezhnev as on his regime, on Brezhnevism, on the style of political leadership that has, alas, not yet entirely died out, and here we need guarantees equally as strong as those we need against Stalinism. It was not for nothing that the radical reform of the political system outlined by the 19th Party Conference was necessary.[2]

Power was thrust upon Brezhnev as a gift of fate. In order to turn the post of party Central Committee general secretary, at that time a modest post, into the office of "master" of our country, Stalin "had to" eliminate virtually every member of Lenin's Politburo (except himself, naturally) as well as a huge portion of the party *aktiv*. After Stalin's death Khrushchev was second in line and not first, as many people think, because Malenkov[3] was regarded as first at the time. Khrushchev won the struggle against mighty and influential rivals, including such people as Viacheslav Molotov, who had formed the basis of the state practically since Lenin's time. Perhaps that was why the

---

[1] Lenin's testament, also known as his letter to the 12th Party Congress, recommended removing Stalin from his position as general secretary of the party.

[2] The 19th Party Conference was held in June 1988. See Chapter 6.

[3] Since the 1940s, Georgy Malenkov had been a close associate of Joseph Stalin.

Stalin and Khrushchev eras, each in its own way, were filled with dramatic changes, major reformations, disturbance, and instability.

Nothing of the kind happened with Brezhnev. He assumed power as smoothly as if someone had tried the crown of Monomakh[4] on various heads well in advance and settled on this one. And this crown fitted him so well that he wore it for eighteen years without fears, cataclysms, or conflicts of any kind. And the people closest to him longed for only one thing: for this man to live forever, it would be so good for them. Brezhnev himself, at a meeting with people from his regiment, showing off his new marshal's uniform, said, "You see? Service rewarded at last." This phrase is also very appropriate to describe the process by which he succeeded to the "office" of party and state leader: "service rewarded."

Brezhnev embodied the exact opposite of Khrushchev's boldness, willingness to take risks, adventurous spirit, and hunger for novelty and change. If we knew Nikita Sergeyevich less well, we might find it a mystery that Khrushchev so patronized a man of the opposite cast of mind and temperament. As an authoritarian personality not inclined to share power and influence with other people, he surrounded himself mainly with the kind of leaders who hung on his every word, said yes to everything, and willingly fulfilled his every instruction. He had no need for comrades in arms, and still less for captains [vozhdi]. He had had enough of them after Stalin's death, when Malenkov, Molotov, and [Lazar] Kaganovich tried to expel him from the political Olympus and perhaps let him rot in a faraway province.

It must be observed that Brezhnev did indeed owe his entire career to Khrushchev. He graduated from the land use surveyors' technical school in Kursk and only joined the party at the age of twenty-five. Then, after graduating from the institute, he began his political career. In May 1937 (!) Brezhnev became deputy chairman of Dneprodzerzhinsk municipality, and a year later he was

---

[4]Vladimir Monomakh was an early Russian ruler. "To wear Monomakh's crown" is a proverbial expression for bearing the burden of state responsibilities.

working in the party *obkom* in Dnepropetrovsk. It is hard to say whether Khrushchev assisted Brezhnev in these first steps, but his entire subsequent career had the most active support of the then first secretary of the Ukrainian Communist Party Central Committee, later secretary of the All-Union Communist party (Bolsheviks). When Brezhnev was appointed to the post of first secretary of the Moldavian Communist Party Central Committee, he took along many of his friends from Dnepropetrovsk, and there he also acquired as a close colleague the then chief of the republic's Communist Party Central Committee's Propaganda and Agitation Department, Konstantin Chernenko.[5]

After the 19th Party Congress (1952) Brezhnev became a candidate member of the Central Committee Presidium, and after Stalin's death he was at the Soviet Army and Navy Main Political Directorate. The stronger Khrushchev grew, the higher Brezhnev rose. By the October 1964 *plenum* he was second secretary of the Central Committee. Thus Khrushchev built his successor's pedestal with his own hands.

The most dramatic problem very soon became clear: Brezhnev was entirely unprepared for the role that unexpectedly fell upon him. He became first secretary of the party Central Committee as a result of a complex, multifaceted, and even bizarre symbiosis of forces. It involved a little of everything: dissatisfaction with Khrushchev's scornful attitude toward his colleagues; fear arising from the unrestrained extremes of his policy and the adventurist actions that played a part in the escalation of the Caribbean missile crisis; illusions about the "personality" basis of the conflict with China; and particularly the annoyance felt by the conservative section of the government *apparat* with the constant instability, jolts, changes, and reforms that were impossible to foresee. An important part was played by the struggle between different generations of leaders: the 1937 generation, to which Leonid Brezhnev, Mikhail Suslov,[6] and Alexei

---

[5] Konstantin Chernenko became general secretary of the CPSU in 1984 after Yuri Andropov's death.

[6] Mikhail Suslov was the most rigidly ideological Politburo member immediately after World War II. He played an important role in Nikita

Kosygin belonged, and the postwar generation, including Alexander Shelepin, Gennady Voronov, Dmitry Polyansky, and Yuri Andropov.[7] Brezhnev was in the center, at the intersection of all these roads. So in the initial stage he suited nearly everyone. Or, at any rate, no one protested. His very incompetence was a blessing: It offered the *apparat* workers plenty of opportunities. The only person made to look a fool was Shelepin, who thought he was the smartest. He did not advance a single step in his career, because not only Brezhnev but also Suslov and the other leaders detected his authoritarian ambitions.

Meanwhile, a fierce struggle broke out over the choice of the country's path of development. One person, as was mentioned above, unequivocally proposed a return to Stalinist methods. Another path was proposed to the leadership by Andropov, who submitted a detailed program based more consistently on the decisions of the anti-Stalinist 20th Party Congress than had been done in Khrushchev's time. It is not difficult to reconstruct these ideas today, because they were set forth in a more general form in an editorial article prepared at the time for *Pravda* ("State of the Entire Country," December 6, 1964). They are: (1) economic reform, (2) the transition to modern, scientific management, (3) the development of democracy and self-management, (4) the party's concentration on political leadership, (5) the ending of the nuclear missile race, which had become senseless, and (6) the USSR's entry into the world market with a goal of acquiring new technology.

Andropov expounded this program to Brezhnev and Kosygin during a trip to Poland in 1965. Some elements of it found support, but as a whole it did not meet with sympathy from either Brezhnev or Kosygin, although for

---

Khrushchev's overthrow. Alexei Kosygin was chairman of the Council of Ministers under Brezhnev. Shelepin, Polyansky, and Voronov were all members of the Politburo under Brezhnev.

[7] The late Soviet leader Yuri Andropov aided Gorbachev's rise to power and is generally viewed as a positive figure by the Soviet press. Burlatsky's article, for example, does not point out that, as head of the KGB for nearly fifteen years, Andropov was responsible for the persecution of dissidents and the strengthening of the security *apparat*.

different reasons. Kosygin supported economic transformations, but he insisted on the restoration of relations
with China at the cost of conceding to China by renouncing
the "extremes" of the 20th Party Congress.

As for Brezhnev, he was in no hurry to define his
position, because he was keeping an eye on the correlation
of forces inside the CPSU Central Committee Presidium
and in the party Central Committee.

Thus Brezhnev's main feature as a political leader was
immediately revealed. Being an extremely cautious man
who had not taken a single rash step during his rise to
power, being what is known as a "weathercock leader,"
Brezhnev adopted a centrist position from the beginning.
He did not accept one extreme or the other, neither the
program of reform in the spirit of the 20th Congress, nor
neo-Stalinism. Incidentally, here he was following a
tradition that became established after Lenin. Probably not
everyone knows that Stalin also came to power as a
centrist. He formed a bloc with Lev Kamenev and Grigory
Zinoviev against the "leftist" Leon Trotsky, and later with
Viacheslav Molotov, Anastas Mikoyan, and others against
the "rightist" Nikolai Bukharin. And only at the end of the
1920s, and then primarily with a view to strengthening his
personal power, did he begin to implement the leftist
program of "revolution from above" and terror.
Khrushchev, who began by stripping himself of his own
shirt in the secret report to the 20th Party Congress, also
began to shift toward the center after the events in Hungary
in 1956. Speaking at the Chinese embassy in Moscow, he
called Stalin a "great Marxist-Leninist," then quarreled
with representatives of the intelligentsia who ardently
supported the criticism of the personality cult, and so forth.
True, he was constantly getting carried away in the
direction of extreme decisions. He, too, paid the full price
for his inconsistency and thoughtless mistakes in October
1964.

Brezhnev was another matter. By his very nature, his
type of education, and his career, he was a typical *oblast*-
level *apparatchik*: not a bad executor of orders, but no
leader [*vozhd*]. He therefore took a good deal from Stalin,
but a little from Khrushchev, too.

At first after coming to power, Brezhnev began his
working day in an unconventional way, devoting a

minimum of two hours to telephone calls to other members of the top leadership and to many powerful secretaries of union republic Central Committees and *obkoms*. As a rule he always talked in the same way: "Look, Ivan Ivanovich,[8] we are studying this matter. I wanted to consult you, to hear your opinion." You can imagine the sense of pride that filled Ivan Ivanovich's heart at that moment. That is how Brezhnev's prestige grew stronger. He created the impression of an impartial, calm, tactful leader who would not take a single step without consulting with other comrades and receiving the full approval of his colleagues.

When questions were discussed at sessions of the Central Committee Secretariat or the Presidium he almost never spoke first. He allowed everyone to have a say, listened attentively, and if there was no consensus he preferred to postpone the matter, do some more work, agree it with everyone, and submit it for examination again. It was under him that very complicated agreements flourished, requiring dozens of signatures on documents, bringing the decisions to be adopted to a standstill or entirely distorting their meaning.

As for the Brezhnevian style, this was perhaps precisely of what it consisted. People with that style are not very competent at resolving substantive questions of the economy, culture, or policy. But they do understand very well whom to appoint to what post, whom to reward, when, and how. Leonid Illyich worked hard to install in leadership posts (in the party organizations and in the economy, science, and culture) exponents of this style, "little Brezhnevs" who were not hasty, not incisive, not outstanding, and not particularly concerned about their jobs, but well able to handle valuables.

The people of the 20th Party Congress or those who were simply bold innovators were not shot, as they might have been in the 1930s. They were quietly pushed aside, pushed out, hampered, suppressed. More and more "mediocrities" triumphed everywhere, people who were not exactly stupid or entirely incompetent, but who were patently untalented, who lacked fighting qualities and principles. They gradually filled posts in the party and state *apparat*, in the

---

[8] A figure of speech, like "John Doe."

leadership of the economy, and even in science and culture. Everything grew dull and went into a decline. The underlings increasingly resembled the boss.

Here is a curious fact. After Nikolai Yegorychev's removal from the post of secretary of the Moscow party organization, Leonid Illyich called him and said something like this: "Forgive me, these things happen. Do you have any problems at all, family problems or anything else?" Yegorychev, whose daughter had married not long before and was struggling with a husband and child without an apartment, was weak enough to tell Brezhnev about this. And guess what? A few days later the young family had an apartment. Brezhnev did not want anyone to bear a grudge. If he had been a connoisseur of art, he would probably have preferred diluted pastels, with no bright colors, whether white or red, green or orange. He often presented his entourage with apartments himself. How about that? Can you imagine a U.S. president handing out apartments?

Brezhnev arrived without his own program for the country's development. This is a rare case in modern political history of a person taking power as such, with no specific plans. But it cannot be said, in Mao Tse-tung's expression, that he was a clean sheet of paper on which any characters could be written. A deeply traditional and conservative man by nature, he was most afraid of abrupt movements, sharp turns, major changes. Condemning Khrushchev for voluntarism and subjectivism, he was concerned most of all with erasing his radical initiatives and restoring what had been approved in Stalin's day. First of all, the regional economic councils and the division of party organs into industrial and agricultural bodies (a form of Khrushchevian pluralism?) which had so annoyed the government *apparat* were abolished. Major leaders who had been sent off against their will to the periphery, near and far, returned to their old places in Moscow. The idea of cadre rotation was quietly and almost unnoticeably nullified. As a counterweight to it, the slogan of stability— the cherished dream of every *apparatchik*—was put forward. Brezhnev did not return to the Stalinist repressions, but he dealt summarily with dissidents.

People in the *apparat* used to recount Brezhnev's words on the subject of Kosygin's report at the September *plenum*:

"What is he thinking of? Reform, reform. Who needs it, and who can understand it? We need to work better, that is the only problem."

What I really cannot agree with is the concept of "two Brezhnevs" (before and after the mid-1970s), the assertion that at the beginning of his time in office he was a supporter of economic and other reforms. People cite a lengthy quotation from Brezhnev's speech at the September 1965 *plenum* that is supposedly particularly characteristic of his position. But even then it was known for sure that Brezhnev was an active opponent of the reform proposed by Kosygin and that it was first and foremost his fault that it had failed.

Brezhnev's rule was twenty years of wasted opportunities. The technological revolution that had begun in the rest of the world passed us by. We did not even notice it, but instead we continued to talk about the traditional sort of scientific and technical progress. During that time Japan became the world's second industrial power, South Korea was hot on the heels of Japan, Brazil joined the ranks of the new centers of industrial might. True, we achieved military parity with the biggest industrial power of the modern world. But at what cost? At the cost of an increasing technological laggardness in all other spheres of the economy, a further disruption of agriculture, a failure to create a modern service sphere, and a freezing of the people's living standard at a low level.

The situation was complicated by the fact that any endeavor to modernize the model of socialism itself was rejected. On the contrary, faith in organizational and bureaucratic decisions grew stronger. No sooner had a problem arisen than the country's leadership reacted with one voice: Whose responsibility is it? We must set up a new ministry or some analogous organ.

Agriculture and the food problem were still the Achilles' heel of our economy. But decisions were sought according to the traditional patterns, which had already demonstrated their ineffectiveness in the preceding era. The policy of converting collective farms into state farms, that is, further state control, continued.

The wide use of [agricultural] chemicals did not yield the expected results. Despite the fact that in the 1970s the USSR was ahead of the United States in fertilizer production, labor productivity in agriculture was several times lower. One fourth of the working population of the USSR was unable to feed the country, while 3 percent of the U.S. population, the farmers, produced so much that they sold a significant portion of it abroad.

There was only one reason for the economic and technological laggardness: incomprehension and fear in the face of urgently needed structural reforms; that is, the transition to economic accountability in industry, cooperativization of the service sphere, and team and family contracts in the countryside. And the most dreadful thing of all, for the regime of those years, would have been to agree to democratization and the restriction of the power of Brezhnev's main power base—the bureaucracy.

All attempts to progress along the path of reform and show economic independence or independence of thought were mercilessly clamped down.

The first lesson of the Brezhnev era is the collapse of the command-administrative system that grew up under Stalin. The state not only failed to ensure progress, it acted increasingly as a brake on society's economic, cultural, and moral development. Brezhnev and his entourage accumulated, in one respect, experience that is not entirely useless, although unfortunately it took nearly twenty years. There is no going back! Even if Brezhnev had decided to shore up the decaying edifice by regressing into Stalinist repressions, he would have been unable to make that system effective. Because the technological revolution demands free labor, personal initiative and commitment, creativity, continuous endeavor, rivalry. Structural reforms and restructuring were the essential, logical way out of stagnation.

The second lesson is that it is time to put an end forever to a system whereby people become the country's leaders not as a result of the normal democratic procedure and public activity in the party and state, but by means of backstage deals or, worse, conspiracies and bloody purges. Experience has already shown sufficiently that in this situation those who come to power are by no means the most capable leaders, the most committed Leninists, or those who are most devoted to the people; instead, they are the most cunning Ulysses types, the masters of infighting, intrigues, and even common corruption.

The most important guarantee against a recurrence of Brezhnevism is socialist pluralism, which the party has hit upon and is now implementing. It has its model in the Lenin period. At the same time we have the potential to go considerably further. Exaggerated fears about the extremes of *glasnost*—and such extremes undoubtedly do accompany the generally healthy flow—do not reflect concern for socialism, they are generated by an authoritarian political culture.

Here what we are up against most of all is the conservative tradition. Russian political culture has not tolerated pluralism of opinions or freedom to criticize government activity. It was only after the 1905 revolution that a small breach was made. But even then it was basically impossible to criticize the czar, czarism, or the existing system.

Guarantees of minority rights are associated with our pluralism, and have we not seen from our own experience how important that is? The revolutionary restructuring, at least in its initial stage, was based on the ideas, views, and will not of the majority, but of a minority. This has nearly always been the case when it comes to a struggle between the new and the old. The most virginal and graceful of all democracies, that of Athens, decided through the mouth of the majority that Socrates must drink poison. Drink it, Socrates, drink it, because the majority demands it! And in our country, did Stalin not draw on the will of the majority in the 1930s? We will say nothing of his comrades in arms; of them no questions were asked. Even Khrushchev, the mighty destroyer of the personality cult, sincerely and selflessly took part in slaughter by the will of the majority. The majority thought Bukharin was wrong. Go then, Nikolai Ivanovich [Bukharin], don't look back, the bullet will find its hole.

And most recently, Brezhnev—surely he was not alone? The vast majority in the government *apparat* idolized him and received everything from him, titles, prizes, academy money, dacha buildings, bribes. He was also supported by those social strata that lived fearlessly, and still live now, on unearned income.

How can one provide guarantees for the minority, for its will, its interests, its views? The minority, which today is apparently wrong, but which tomorrow could become the main champion of progress? Only by means of personal rights in the party, in the state, and in other institutions of the political system: freedom to think, speak, write, seek the truth, and strive for its recognition—there is no other way.

In the sphere of science and culture guarantees of minority rights are commonplace, although even here we have suffered from considerable bureaucratic coercion. It has not yet been erased from our memory how the majority persecuted geneticists, anathematized the theory of relativity and cybernetics, rejected jazz and still more rock and roll, wiped out abstract art, and rejected sociology and political science. Now it seems to be accepted that he who murders thought is three times a murderer. But there are other spheres that touch more closely on power and politics, where it is hard to guarantee the autonomy of the minority in the name of alternative solutions. Here we need particularly fine and accurate work by the legislator's chisel, to carve out the balance between the views and interests of the majority and the minority, true socialist pluralism.

And finally, down with flatterers in political life! Doubtless all political leaders from all peoples like flattery. But in our own time Stalin and Brezhnev liked flattery of the most exaggerated variety, the cult variety. And not because they believed such praise, but because the humiliation of the flatterer, his trampled, flattened demeanor, pleased them. Some of our homegrown Fouchés and Talleyrands have gone through all the political regimes as easily as a knife through butter, and are now bustling feverishly in the struggle for self-preservation.

Fortunately people who have a clear program for the country's development and regard radical political reform as paramount have come and are coming to power in our country. Let us hope that the formation of a new school of political leadership and a new democratic culture of the whole people has begun. This will be a guarantee against a recurrence of Stalinist and Brezhnevian traditions.

Bibliography

POSTREVOLUTIONARY PERIOD

Gerasimenko, Obichkin, and Popov. "Only the Truth Is Not on Trial." *Pravda*, February 15, 1988.

This conservative article attacks Mikhail Shatrov's play *Onward, Onward, Onward*. It accuses Shatrov of implying that Stalin's methods had roots in Leninism.

Kapustin, Mikhail. "To Which Heritage Are We Waiving Our Claims?" *Oktiabr*, no. 4, 1988.

The author asserts that Stalin based his repression on Trotsky's writings. He also declares that both Trotsky and Stalin are "alien" to Russia.

Mikoyan, Sergei. "The Servant." *Komsomolskaya Pravda*, February 21, 1988.

While many articles in the Soviet press now discuss the victims of Stalin's purges, this one describes the actions of Stalin's chief executioner, Lavrenty Beria. Written by Anastas Mikoyan's son, this article is controversial because the author's father also was involved in repressive policies.

STALIN

Afanasiev, A. "Victor." *Komsomolskaya Pravda*, January 15, 1988.

This article praises Leningrad party chief Alexei Kuznetsov, who was executed by Stalin during the "Leningrad affair" of 1950.

Afanasiev, Yuri. "*Perestroika* and Historical Knowledge." *Literaturnaya Rossiya*, no. 24, June 17, 1988.

The article rejects the evaluation of Stalinism as the result of Stalin's personality flaws. Afanasiev addresses all the major issues in the historical debate, including a reevaluation of Leon Trotsky, Lev Kamenev, and Grigory Zinoviev.

Bestuzhev-Lada, Igor. "Return to the Truth." *Nedelya*, no. 15, 1988.

The article analyzes letters from people who defend Stalin's policies.

Kirsanov, A., and Lisochkin, I. "The Leningrad Affair." *Leningradskaya Pravda*, May 18, 1988.

This article is the most detailed and analytical description of Stalin's postwar destruction of the Leningrad party organization.

WORLD WAR II

Dorizo, Nikolai. "Yakov Dzhugashvili." *Moskva*, nos. 2 and 3, 1988.

The main theme of this poem is the heroic behavior of Stalin's son Yakov as a POW in German hands. Yakov is portrayed as someone who remained loyal to his father and committed suicide to avoid bringing shame to his country and to Stalin.

Filatov, Colonel Victor. "Order No. 227." *Krasnaya Zvezda*, March 26, 1988.

Filatov justifies Stalin's order of "not one step back," which was signed on July 28, 1942. The order called for penal units to enforce discipline as well as special units to shoot soldiers and officers who tried to retreat.

———. "Whites, Greys, Blacks." *Krasnaya Zvezda*, January 16, 1988.

This conservative military historian criticizes the "emotionalism" surrounding the history of Stalin's repressions of 1937 and his actions during the initial period of World War II. Colonel Filatov asserts that many articles have not been based on a study of the documents from the period.

Kanevskii, Boris. "History in Search of the Truth." *Komsomolskaya Pravda*, March 6, 1988.

This defense of the Soviet military advocates patriotic education. The author also notes that millions of files on World War II soldiers declared "missing in action" have never even been opened.

Khor'kov, A. "From Positions of Historical Truth." *Kommunist Vooruzhennykh Sil*, no. 7, April 1988.

Khor'kov argues that Stalin's role as supreme commander during World War II cannot be properly evaluated without access to archival documents.

Kondratiev, Viacheslav. "On the Fresh Trail of Memory and Truth." *Nedelya*, no. 50, 1987.

A participant in World War II refutes many of the stereotypes about the war presented by veterans and in Soviet propaganda, and he criticizes those who defend Stalin's wartime policies.

LITERATURE

Barabanov, Y. "Prediction or Warning?" *Moscow News*, February 28, 1988.

This is an analysis of the antiutopian novel *We* and its author Yevgeny Zamyatin. The book, an allegory warning against extreme state power over the individual, was banned in the USSR for seventy years.

Editorial. " 'Crazily Surpassing One's Strength' in B. Pasternak's Novel *Doctor Zhivago*." *Pravda*, April 27, 1988.

Pravda reviews the novel *Dr. Zhivago*, published in the USSR after being banned for three decades.

Zalygin, Sergei P. (editor in chief of *Novy Mir*). "About George Orwell and His Novel." *Literaturnaya Gazeta*, May 11, 1988.

Zalygin discusses the historical significance of George Orwell's antitotalitarian novel *1984*.

Chapter Two

Economic Reforms

Concern about the damage inflicted by seven decades of the party's economic mismanagement is the engine propelling Mikhail Gorbachev's *perestroika*. Seventy-two years after the Bolshevik Revolution, Soviet citizens daily wait in ever-lengthening lines for meat, soap, sugar, and butter. The contradictory nature of the Soviet economy is striking: The military and space industries are virtually world leaders, while the consumer and agricultural sectors barely rival those of the Third World. A sleeping bear awakened in the mid-1980s and was embarrassed to find itself economically inferior not only to the West, but also to countries like South Korea, and potentially to China. As the articles in this section illustrate, the current state of affairs cannot continue without the further deterioration of daily living standards and the related political repercussions. Both conservatives and reformers agree that the Soviet economy must be reformed; however, achieving a consensus on which reforms to choose and how to implement them has proved to be a far more contentious undertaking.

Western and Soviet economists generally agree on the six key problems that plague the Soviet economy: (1) the constant shortages of consumer goods and good-quality food, (2) the low quality of industrial goods needed for export markets, (3) a serious diminution in Soviet technology vis-à-vis the rest of the world, (4) an economic structure that is overcentralized and rigidly bureaucratic, (5) a system that permits Communist party officials to interfere in both micro and macro management of the economy, and (6) the lack of an incentive-based system to improve industrial and agricultural productivity.

Although economic shortcomings have long plagued the Soviet Union, *glasnost* has erupted into increasingly candid public discussion about the economy. Soviet newspapers have printed analytical articles about the illegal black market and even have published letters from citizens complaining that the shortages have grown even more acute under *perestroika*. Ed Hewitt, a senior fellow at the Brookings Institution, asserts that by exposing how bad the economy really is, "*glasnost* gives Gorbachev a tool in order to continue pushing for the reforms, a tool that is quite useful for him now."[1]

During Gorbachev's first year and a half as general secretary, he displayed no inclination for radical economic reform. Harvard Professor Marshall Goldman writes,

> Taking a leaf from his mentor Yuri Andropov, Gorbachev, too, called for more discipline and a crackdown on alcoholism. Typically he also ordered some increased centralization, some decentralization, an economic speed-up (*uskorenie* or acceleration), more technological growth and more investment in the machine-tool industry. Just as with Andropov, this prescription brought some short-run improvement, but in no way addressed any of the basic needs of the society for far-reaching reforms.[2]

Gorbachev's early policies proved unsuccessful, because "accelerating" industrial growth did nothing to improve the quality of goods and services in the economy. Furthermore, the government's administrative approach to the alcoholism problem inspired more anti-Gorbachev jokes than sobriety. Soviet economists note that the loss of tax revenues to *samogon* producers substantially contributed to the state's 100-billion ruble ($163 billion) budget deficit.

Glasnost pushed Gorbachev in the direction of fundamental economic reforms by allowing average citizens to vent their frustrations directly and with unprecedented frankness. Since he came to office without a preconceived manifesto for change, Gorbachev has displayed a willingness to listen to the ideas of others. He broke precedent with previous leaders by going directly to the people in gatherings filmed for television. Marshall Goldman points out that "instead of Gorbachev convincing the crowds to adapt to his traditional set of panaceas, they managed to convince him that conditions were much graver than Gorbachev had originally anticipated and that reform would have to be much more far-reaching than Gorbachev had thought."[3] Moreover, the dire predictions of advisers like Abel Aganbegyan and Leonid Abalkin greatly influenced Gorbachev's redirection of the reform effort.

A pivotal debate over economic reform has developed in the press between "cavalrymen" and "merchants." "Cavalrymen" hope to change the economy by state decisions from above; this approach would continue the tradition of managing the economy by decrees from the Council of Ministers and the Central Committee. The "cavalry-

---

[1] U.S. Congress, House, Testimony of Ed Hewitt, Hearings before the Subcommittee on Europe and the Middle East of the Committee on Foreign Affairs, *U.S.-Soviet Relations*, 100th Cong., 2d sess., 1988, 1:92.

[2] Ibid., testimony of Marshall Goldman, p. 82.

[3] Ibid.

men" want to preserve ideological purity and argue against the free play of market forces which, in their view, leads to capitalism, private property, and the "exploitation of man by man." The exaggerated fear of capitalist values and exploitation is very widespread even among pro-reform party leaders such as Gorbachev. The connection between socialism and Russian nationalism is important for many conservatives. For example, conservative writer Mikhail Antonov (Document #7) argues that "the essential cause of stagnation is not in the economic mechanism and the management methods, but in those people who have lost the feeling of being privy to the motherland's historical fate."[4]

"Merchants," such as Abel Aganbegyan and Nikolai Shmelyov, reject quibbling over socialist morality and believe that market forces and competition can lead to quality work, individual initiative, and a revived Soviet economy. Shmelyov (Document #11) argues that "we must teach our people to understand that everything that is economically inefficient is immoral, as well as the reverse—that efficiency is morality."[5] However, the Soviet economy lacks the millions of knowledgeable and dedicated managers and workers needed to improve economic efficiency and to take advantage of market incentives. For political reasons, Gorbachev has not fully adopted the "merchant" approach and has staked out a middle ground on economic issues.

A key issue for Soviet reformers is how to inspire workers to increase their productivity. Increasing wages and dangling the promise of bonuses is ineffective, as there is almost nothing of value to purchase. Abel Aganbegyan (Document #6), an economic adviser to Mikhail Gorbachev, asserts that if the necessary food and other consumer goods are plentiful in Soviet stores, "then your well-being will be determined by your earnings, and you will work with more energy so that those earnings will be increased."[6] But Russian nationalist Mikhail Antonov (Document #7) retorts that "yes, most of our people now require many things, including good food, consumer goods, comfortable housing, and gardens. However, as soon as the first needs are satisfied, everyone will see how little material incentives mean to us."[7]

To improve industrial performance, reformers want to grant the managers of enterprises independence from party officials and from the central ministries. As Abel Aganbegyan (Document #6) points out, not all individuals in management are in favor of increased

[4]Mikhail Antonov, "At the Turning Point," *Moskva*, no. 3, 1988.

[5]Nikolai Shmelyov, "New Worries," *Novy Mir*, no. 5, 1988.

[6]Abel Aganbegyan, "People and Economics," an interview in *Ogonyok*, July 18–25, 1987.

[7]Antonov, "At the Turning Point."

independence. He writes that for " 'backward people in the economy'. . . it is easier to work in the command and administrative system . . . than in an atmosphere where independent decisions must be made. Independence is a very heavy load of responsibility. Rights go with responsibilities. Not everyone wants that."[8]

Preventing party interference in the daily managing of the economy is a key objective of Gorbachev's reforms. Glasgow University's Professor Alec Nove writes that "in a country in which no other party has been tolerated, every interest group finds expression in the party, including those groups which would benefit from reform. However, the full-time party officials, especially in the localities but also central committee officials, exercise very considerable powers. They appoint, they dismiss, they allocate and reallocate, they interfere in current affairs, they adjudicate."[9]

In his *Novy Mir* essay "New Worries" (Document #11), Nikolai Shmelyov warns that *perestroika* is facing a "conspiracy" in both agriculture and industry. He writes that "open opposition to *perestroika* is growing . . . among many local party, soviet, and economic organizations. It is also becoming obvious that many central ministries which claim to support *perestroika* are trying to cripple it."[10] Several years earlier Alec Nove correctly asserted that "reform of the market type is inconsistent with the exercise of power by officials of the party at all levels, at least in the arbitrary form in which they are accustomed to exercise it. The same is true of many state planning and finance officials."[11]

At the apex of the Soviet Union's centralized economy is Gosplan, which formulates plans and sets prices for nearly every enterprise and product in the economy. For years Gosplan and the central ministries (which Gosplan has jurisdiction over) have ignored the laws of supply and demand. Approximately one hundred ministries determine the prices and quantities of the goods produced by more than 100,000 enterprises. To provide information to the central ministries and to carry out orders from Moscow a bureaucracy employing 18 million people in state, party, and ministry jobs has been created. Alec Nove writes that "the bureaucratic problems that arise are common to any large organization, including the Western corporation. They show themselves in acute form in the USSR because of its size and also the vast range of the activities which it covers; it is not only a super-corporation but a super-conglomerate."[12] Bureaucracy, of course, is a

---

[8]Aganbegyan, "People and Economics."

[9]Alec Nove, *The Soviet Economic System* (London: Allen and Unwin, 1982), p. 317.

[10]Shmelyov, "New Worries."

[11]Nove, *The Soviet Economic System*, p. 317.

[12]Ibid., p. 48.

fact of modern society and government, but the entire American economy is not run by the Department of Commerce. Furthermore, in the Soviet Union enterprises operate more like the U.S. Postal Service than IBM or General Motors. In the United States if a corporation consistently loses money it goes out of business, but in the Soviet Union unsuccessful enterprises have always received more money from the state.

The Soviet construction industry is in an especially catastrophic state. Poor quality and the slow pace of work have resulted in the astronomical amount of 150 billion rubles' worth of unfinished construction, much of which will be abandoned.

The first measure introduced by Mikhail Gorbachev to improve industrial performance was Gospriemka (the State Quality Control Commission). Its objective was to improve the quality of goods, to raise them to world standards. In 1987 the government introduced Gospriemka to 1,500 of the best-equipped Soviet enterprises. But unrealistic demands for quality resulted in massive disruptions in deliveries and a shortfall in production quotas. Because meeting quotas determines the salaries of workers and managers, it was unreasonable to expect products of both higher quality and equal quantity. Because a large-scale introduction of such a system could be disastrous, through 1988 Gospriemka functioned in only 2,200 out of 46,000 selected enterprises.

A second and most important industrial initiative, the Law on State Enterprises, was introduced on January 1, 1988. This law was designed as a step toward decentralization and as a means to provide more incentives for managers and workers by increasing the independence of enterprises from central control. Prior to this law, enterprises depended completely on the ministries for guidance on all production and marketing goals. Gorbachev supporters hoped that, if enterprises were allowed to sell on the open market those products they produced above the "state contract," they would produce higher quality goods. Although the term *khozraschet* (cost accountability) has been used previously, Gorbachev's reforms have been intended to make enterprises truly independent and self-reliant.

Thus far the Law on State Enterprises has failed to bear fruit. Bureaucrats from the ministries did not want enterprise managers to gain freedom and resources by selling their goods on the open market. Therefore, these bureaucrats ensured that state contracts often exceeded the production possibilities of the plants. As these enterprises still have no goods to sell on their own, the concept of decentralization has so far been defeated. Of course, many enterprise managers whose products are not competitive or who do not wish to become preoccupied with marketing to consumers are pleased with the law's results.

Price reform remains a key issue for improving economic performance. For seven decades, prices on Soviet products have not reflected market forces; state policies have determined the price ratio between different goods and services. For example, in the 1930s the state set the price for industrial goods artificially high in order to siphon money from the peasantry to fund industrialization. Today, industrial goods such as cars and television sets remain artificially high-priced, while food prices are artificially low.[13] Many economists, such as Abel Aganbegyan and Leonid Abalkin, recommended starting *perestroika* with a price reform. But based on what occurred in Poland, where price increases sparked mass rioting, Gorbachev believed that introducing radical price reform would entail considerable political risks. Given the poor state of the consumer sector and the fear of rampant inflation (as in Yugoslavia), even radical reform economists now agree that it will be necessary to delay introducing fundamental price reform.

In an effort to encourage individual initiative and improve the service sector, in 1987 the Soviet government permitted the development of cooperatives and ITD (Individual Labor Activity). ITD allows people to work in their off-hours at such tasks as taxi driving, carpentry, and language teaching with the permission of the state. Many individuals had previously worked at these jobs on the black market, but now the state can regulate and tax these activities. More importantly, ITD can help to improve the overall quality and quantity of services available. According to government statistics, at the beginning of 1989 two million Soviets were engaged in work related to cooperatives and ITD.[14]

The Soviet press has devoted considerable coverage, not all of it positive, to the cooperative movement. Many Soviets oppose cooperatives on ideological grounds and resent the high prices charged by them and the high incomes received by cooperative members. This is possibly the most controversial aspect of Gorbachev's economic reforms. Cafés are the most visible type of cooperative, but others have sprung up that sell clothes, make furniture, and engage in other activities. State bureaucrats whose fiefdoms are threatened by this unsupervised activity consistently have interpreted the laws to the detriment of cooperative managers.

Many cooperatives charge high prices, but this money is often needed to meet bank loans, which must be repaid fully within six months. The citizens who resent the high prices have generated calls for considerable state pressure against cooperative managers. Another problem cooperatives must confront is racketeering. Joseph

---

[13]The average worker's monthly salary is 200 rubles ($350), yet a color television set costs approximately 700 rubles ($1200).

[14]*Ekonomicheskaya Gazeta*, no. 5, 1989.

Perezovsky, the manager of the Moscow café At Joseph's (Document #9), keeps a rifle to defend himself against the mafia extortionists who increasingly demand protection money from cooperatives.[15]

There are now 60,000 cooperatives in the Soviet Union (7,000 in Moscow), but the bureaucratic impediments to them continue to mount. Revised regulations in 1988 restrict cooperative activity in book publishing, medical care, and a host of other areas. Even more troubling, local authorities, who generally oppose cooperatives, have been granted additional authority to regulate prices and other activities. However, a new type of cooperative has been introduced—one that takes control of a liquidated plant and has the right to hire and fire. Although in the long run the initiative of cooperative managers might prevail, in the immediate future it appears that cooperatives will not be full-fledged competitors to the state sector. Reformers had hoped that cooperatives would spur an increase in efficiency among state enterprises, but this has not been the case.

Reforms to allow joint enterprises with Western firms have been instituted under Gorbachev for three primary reasons: (1) the success of joint ventures in improving the Chinese and Hungarian economies, (2) the Soviet Union's failure to improve its economy in the 1970s by the simple purchase of Western machines and technology, and (3) the idea that joint ventures can teach Soviet workers and managers how to become more productive and innovative. Gorbachev hopes that joint ventures and greater freedom to travel will both improve the work habits of Soviet citizens and make them more cognizant of their country's declining status. But, by 1988, only 189 joint ventures had been established in the USSR, far fewer than in China.[16] By mid-1989, 360 joint venture agreements had been reached, with only 110 of them actually in operation. Total foreign investment in these ventures had reached only several tens of millions of dollars—a disappointing amount from the Soviet point of view. If problems such as ruble convertibility and the Soviet bureaucracy can be surmounted, and if an increase in world oil prices increases Soviet hard currency reserves, then foreign trade and joint ventures could work to substantially improve the Soviet economy.

The most intransigent problem Gorbachev's economic reforms face in agriculture, as in industry, is the old bureaucratic and party structure of the economy. It is difficult to make new wine in broken Soviet bottles. Collective farms continue to take up 80 percent of the country's arable land, as compared to 17 percent for state farms and only 3 percent for the highly productive private plots. Yet every conceivable effort to improve collective farm productivity under

---

[15] See also Peter Galuszka, "And You Think Western Capitalists Have Problems," *Business Week*, January 30, 1989.

[16] *Ekonomicheskaya Gazeta*, no. 5, 1989.

Khrushchev and Brezhnev proved unsuccessful. *Glasnost* has contributed to agriculture by permitting the first sincere Soviet denunciation of the horrors of collectivization. Soviet writers now deplore the atrocities perpetrated against the peasantry and debate how many millions died during collectivization and the ensuing famine. Reformers hoped that these denunciations would set the stage for dismantling the collective and state farm system; however, this has not occurred.

The maintenance of the collective and state farms severely impedes the progress of two key agricultural reforms: family and lease farming. Soviet television and the printed media have featured success stories of Russian farming families (see Document #8). The official point of view is that family farming is not capitalist in nature, as the land and machines used by these families belong to the socialist state. While traditionally Soviet writers have labeled farmers victims of capitalist exploitation, the term "farmer" is now developing a more positive connotation.

Family farming generally begins with the head of the family signing a contract with a collective farm for a five- to ten-year period. But, because many collective farm directors view family farms as an unwelcome intrusion, they often provide families with abandoned livestock farms or an unprofitable piece of land. Moreover, collective farms have sometimes reneged on the contracts of successful family farms and generally provide no firm guarantees for family farmers that they will be able to keep their farms for a long period of time. Family farms are totally dependent on collective and state farm officials for resources, land, and machinery, and it is hard to foresee the success of family farms while the existing state and collective farm system remains intact.

Another reform development in agriculture is lease farming. This initiative allows families, groups within collective farms, or even city dwellers to lease land from collective farms for several years. Lease farmers enjoy more freedom than farmers engaged in family or team contracts.

Still, it is widely believed that few members of the collective farms today have the capacity and desire to work very hard. As Vasily Belov writes in *Pravda*, "If private ownership of land were now introduced, then it seems to me that there would be few in the motherland who would agree to take it. A generation has grown up that doesn't need anything—not land, not livestock farming, not their own home."[17] Collectivization, famines, and purges robbed Russia of its most abundant natural resource—the resourcefulness of its peasantry.

---

[17] Vasily Belov, "To Recreate a Peasant in the Peasantry," *Pravda*, April 15, 1988.

More than four years after Gorbachev came to power, the Soviet economy is in dire straits. Shortages of all basic goods persist, the budget deficit is at least $160 billion, and there is an imbalance in the money supply. A temporary retreat to a rigid, centralized economy for the sake of the public welfare should not be precluded.

At the beginning of 1989, Gorbachev's chief economic adviser, Leonid Abalkin, declared that only by 1995 will the average Soviet citizen begin to reap tangible benefits from the economic reforms. The further deterioration of the food and consumer goods market has become increasingly disconcerting to radical reformers. Nikolai Shmelyov, for example, has urged that gold reserves be used to inspire citizen support for *perestroika* through purchases of imported consumer goods. Although the passivity of the Soviet population remains a major stumbling block to radical reform, Mikhail Gorbachev for a time rejected this solution and urged patience. Finally the Soviet government had to agree, at the beginning of 1989, to spend $8 billion for imported consumer goods.

The overall prospects for a successful economic reform are uncertain for several reasons. First, the need to make political compromises with conservatives has led to numerous half-measures (for example, compromises on cooperatives and on the Law on State Enterprises) which frustrate reform aspirations. These half-measures make the transition to a more market-oriented economic system longer and more arduous. Second, low world oil prices combined with the costly war in Afghanistan, the Chernobyl nuclear accidents, and the earthquakes in Armenia and Tadzhikistan have limited the resources that can be allocated to improving the economy. Third, and most important, the main impediment to reforms is still the interference of the party and bureaucratic *apparat*. Although in 1988 a step in the right direction was made in an attempt to eliminate 600,000 jobs in the bureaucracy,[18] this was simply the first salvo in what promises to be a war of attrition between reformers and conservatives. Further progress on reform of the political system could provide the needed boost to minimize the conservative opposition's inhibition of the economic reforms.

Economic reform under Gorbachev is likely to be unsuccessful if the existing economic structures remain intact. Georgetown University's Professor Thane Gustafson attributes previous Soviet reform failures to efforts "to impose new priorities on old structures."[19] It is clear that to improve the economy dramatic steps must be taken,

---

[18]*Ekonomicheskaya Gazeta*, no. 5, 1989.

[19]Thane Gustafson, "Lessons of the Brezhnev Policies on Land and Water and the Future of Reform," in Erik P. Hoffman and Robbin F. Laird, eds., *The Soviet Polity in the Modern Era* (New York: Aldine, 1984), p. 520.

including the dismantling of the collective farm apparatus, abolishing or severely limiting the power of the central ministries, and introducing price reforms. Soviet leaders who for years have been concerned with quantitative growth must now redirect the nation's energy toward technological innovation. Gorbachev and his allies need to press forward and endure a period of political uncertainty to ensure the emergence of a modernized Soviet economy in the twenty-first century.

Advances and Debts

Nikolai Shmelyov

Novy Mir, no. 6, 1987

In an interview with *Nedelya* (September 26-October 2, 1988) Nikolai Shmelyov discussed why he wrote this landmark article published in *Novy Mir*: "I thought to myself, why not beat the internal censor and pour out everything that has built up, everything that we have discussed among professionals? I would not have taken this step on my own accord; I was persuaded [by a friend]. I did not expect the storm that it caused." No article did more to accelerate the debate about economic reforms than this spring 1987 essay.

Shmelyov presents a ruthless, straightforward analysis of what ails the Soviet economy, arguing that the problems go beyond military expenditures and foreign policy commitments. Rather, he sees the problems as being caused by a failure to provide incentives for workers and by the economy's continued inability to observe the laws of supply and demand.

Shmelyov makes a number of innovative suggestions for improving the economy. Ahead of his colleagues he has advocated the creation of "free zones," in which joint enterprises with foreign companies could operate without restrictions, and permission for Soviet enterprises to sell stock to obtain increased investment. In essence, Shmelyov blames the centralized planning system for preventing economic, scientific, and technical progress.

The state of our economy does not satisfy anyone. It is too central, built-in, as they say. Its defects are certainly clear to everyone: the producer's monopoly in general deficit conditions and the absence of incentives for an enterprise to make scientific-technological progress. But how can we get rid of these defects, and what is to be done, not in theory, but in practice? Anybody who would dare to assert that he knew a fully suitable prescription for life can be assured that today there are no such sages, either above or below. Now we and everyone else have many more questions than answers. And we still have much talking, arguing, proposing, and rejecting to do before we and the rest of the world discover the answers that are so necessary to us.

The basic reasons for the atherosclerosis and restriction of the blood circulation of our country's economy have already been revealed. A principle has been raised, "from a surplus-appropriation system to a tax-in-kind," signifying that the administrative methods of controlling the economy should be exchanged for economic stimuli and levers not sponsored by the state. It is certainly possible to say that the road to common sense, at least in the ideological-theoretical sphere, has been opened. It is evident, however, that *perestroika* of such dimensions cannot be brought about at one stroke, however much we might want it to be. For too long, the command instead of the ruble has predominated in our economy, for so long that it seems we have already forgotten that there was—there truly was—a time when the predominant factor in our economy was the ruble and not the command, that is, common sense and not impractical, speculative, arbitrary rule.

I understand what kind of reproaches I am inviting, but the question is far too serious and vitally important for me to soften my language and resort to silence. If we do not acknowledge that the repudiation of Lenin's New Economic Policy [NEP] gravely complicated socialist construction in the USSR, we again, as in 1953 and 1965,[1] condemn ourselves to halfway measures, and it is well known that a halfway policy is often worse than inertia. NEP, with its economic stimuli and levers, was replaced by an administrative system of rule. Such a system by its very nature was unable to concern itself with improving production quality, increasing the effectiveness of manufacturing, or achieving the highest result at the lowest expense. This system achieved the necessary quantities—in gross output—not in accord with the objective laws of economics, but in defiance of them. And because it was done in defiance of economic laws, it was done at the price of inconceivably high expenditures of material and, above all, human resources.

We must clearly understand that the cause of our difficulties lies not only, and not even very much, in the

---

[1] Previous attempts at economic reform were made starting in 1953 under Khrushchev and in 1965 at the beginning of Brezhnev's rule.

heavy burden of military expenditures and the very expensive scope of the country's global responsibilities. Responsible expenditure of the remaining material and human resources would be fully sufficient to maintain a balanced economy oriented toward technical progress and to satisfy the traditionally modest social needs of our population. However, the persistent, protracted attempts to overcome the objective laws of economic life and to suppress the stimuli to work that have been formed over centuries in response to human nature have, in the final analysis, led to results diametrically opposed to what we intended. Today we have an economy in deficit, unbalanced in practically all aspects and unmanageable in many, and—if we are to be completely honest—we have an unyielding planned economy that still does not accept technological progress. Industry today rejects up to 80 percent of newly approved technical solutions and inventions! Our labor productivity rate is one of the lowest among industrialized countries, especially in agriculture and construction; during the years of stagnation the working masses displayed a nearly complete lack of interest in full-blooded, honest labor.

However, the results of the "administrative economy" that are most difficult to cure lie in the economic sphere.

A purely administrative view of economic problems has deeply implanted itself in the system—an almost religious "belief in organization" and a reluctance and an inability to see that nothing sensible can be made through force, pressure, conscription, or urging on the economy. As both our own experience and world experience show, the main conditions for the viability and effectiveness of intricate social systems are an independent superstructure, self-regulation, and self-development. Attempts to subordinate the socioeconomic "Brownian movement" (with its inescapable, but consequently acceptable, expenses) to some central point of administration were largely abortive, and the farther we get away from this system the more evident this becomes.

Apathy and indifference, stealing, and disrespect for honest work have all become commonplace along with an aggressive envy for those who earn a lot, even if they earn it honestly. Indications of an almost physical degradation have appeared in a significant part of the nation because of drunkenness and idleness. And, finally, there is a skepticism toward aims and intentions that declare that a more reasonable organization of economic and social life is possible. According to the impartial observation of the academician Tatyana Zaslavskaya in the journal *Kommunist* (1986, no. 13), "frequent collisions with various forms of social injustice, along with the futility of attempts at individual struggles with its manifestations, became one of the principal reasons for the alienation of some workers from social goals and values."

It would evidently be unrealistic to think that all of this could be overcome quickly—it will require years, and perhaps even generations. To construct a completely self-financing socialism will entail far more than simply eliminating separate, cumbersome bureaucratic structures. This does not mean, however, that one ought to sit with folded arms. Considering today's internal and international realities, we cannot return to "administrative socialism." But we don't have any time for marching in place or for halfway policies.

What alarms us more than anything today is indecisiveness in the movement toward common sense. Slogans can't change the world view of many leading cadres, those who possess only the skills of bare administration and the *apparatchik* craft. In the same way, no explanations can overcome the obvious distrust that people have for claims that leaders have taken matters seriously and carried through contemplated changes, or that after this halfstep forward there will not again be two steps backward. It is possible to convince only by deeds. In order to instill belief in the normalization of the economy, it is necessary to have immediate success and tangible indications, indications that are apparent to all, that life is improving. First of all, the market must be satiated as soon as possible. This is not simple, but with the proper resolve it is possible. It is possible, however, only by means of self-financing socialism, by developing the market itself.

We must call things by their true names: stupidity is stupidity, incompetence is incompetence, and active Stalinism is active Stalinism. Life demands that we be prepared to do anything to secure our food market within the next few years. Otherwise, all calculations of activating the human factor will be up in the air; people will not respond to them. Let us lose our ideological virginity which, incidentally, exists only in newspaper fairy-tale editorials. People are stealing and becoming rich by exploiting this virginity more than ever before, people who make a living not by creating anything and who neither want nor know how to create anything. Let only those people prosper who are willing and able to give society real products and services, things of real value. Only when we have solved the problem of providing our daily bread, and not before, will it be possible to think about preventing the largest profits of the most work-loving people and enterprising proprietors from resulting in the formation of threatening capital. For this there are simple, effective means: taxes and the corresponding powers of the revenue inspector (reasonable ones, of course, so as not to kill the goose that has just begun to lay golden eggs for the good of everyone).

Tax levers can and should provide reasonable control and, moreover, one means of satiating the consumer market, a means that does not require great capital investment: personal, family, and cooperative production in the sphere of services and small industry. Certainly, only today can we fully evaluate the significance of Lenin's thoughts about the formation of civilized cooperatives, for this is all that we need for the triumph of socialism.

The expansion of the individual-cooperative sector in the cities will provide benefits beyond the physical satiation of the market. Our light industry, trade, and service sectors currently operate under inadmissibly favorable conditions that encourage inertia. No one competes with them, and import of consumer goods is still too small to stir them from their inertia. The appearance of a competitor such as the individual-cooperative sector could quickly change the conditions of the market. State industrial, trade, and domestic enterprises must either improve their work sharply or yield a substantial portion of their profits to other producers, resulting in the reduction of wages and expenditures on social needs, and even the curtailment of personnel to the extent of dissolving collectives of bad workers and closing enterprises.

Today's system of material incentives for conscientious work acts weakly, and not just because it is a thoroughly bad one. Wages and bonuses don't work either, as there is nothing for a person to buy with the money he receives. To revitalize the consumer sector of the national economy, to satiate the market and to give choices to the masses of buyers, means to make it possible for wages to finally work at full strength, so that our citizens could actually wish to be paid well for honest, scrupulous labor.

The material preconditions for development of the individual-cooperative sector undoubtedly exist in this country. In the cities there are enough empty accommodations. In the stocks of state enterprises is any amount—up to a billion rubles' worth!—of unnecessary or obsolete equipment; raw and other types of materials are stored, just in case. Although it would be called a gamble, by offering this equipment and material for open sale it might be possible to meet the initial basic requirements of small individual and cooperative enterprises. Of course, with such a turn of events, violence, theft, and corruption might be escaped only if two conditions are met: First, free wholesale trade of the means of production, raw and other materials, must be allowed. Second, the individual-cooperative sector must be fully equal (as both buyer and seller) to the state enterprises and organizations in legal and economic conditions.

A decisive general introduction of the well-known "Shchekino formula"[2] could also produce a very quick effect. If one judges by the past, by the ruinous ministerial experience, this formula permits the number of workers to be reduced by 25 to 30 percent over two and one half years, without great investment. This is especially important today, when the productive capacity of many branches is underloaded by 20 to 40 percent, when the majority of machines are used during only one shift, and when working hands are acutely insufficient for the construction of the country. Exaggerations have been presented so forcefully that there are apprehensions that a general dissemination of the "Shchekino formula" will give rise to unemployment.

---

[2]An initiative by the Shchekino chemical plant managers to significantly reduce the number of employees without reducing output by utilizing additional wage payments as an incentive.

First of all, natural unemployment among people who are seeking work or changing their place of work exists even today; at any given moment it is scarcely less than 2 percent of the work force, and if one counts vagrants who are not registered anywhere, unemployment undoubtedly approaches 3 percent. It is one thing to discuss the problem while pretending that we have no unemployment at all, but it is an entirely different matter to realize calmly that there is some sort of unemployment and that it is not possible not to have unemployment. Second, there are millions of unoccupied positions, and new work places are opening constantly. We could quickly reduce the scale of temporary unemployment to a minimum. Naturally, this will require considerable additional state efforts to retrain the displaced work force, to convert it to other professions in other regions, to stimulate an organized migration, etc. Third, we shall not close our eyes to the economic damage caused by our parasitic certitude about guaranteed work. Today it seems clear to all that, for the most part, we owe agitation, drunkenness, and shoddy workmanship to excessively full employment. We must consider, fearlessly and in a businesslike manner, what can be gained by us from a comparatively small reserve army of labor which would, of course, not be left entirely to the mercy of fate by the state. This is a discussion about replacing administrative coercion with economic coercion. The real danger of losing work, of turning to temporary means or being obliged to work where one is sent, isn't bad medicine at all for laziness, drunkenness, and irresponsibility. Many experts believe that it would be cheaper to pay temporarily unemployed workers an allowance sufficient for a few months than it is to keep in the factory a mass of loafers who don't fear anything, loafers by whom any profitable enterprise, any attempts to raise the quality and effectiveness of general labor, can (and will) be crushed.

"Socialism," emphasizes the well-known Soviet economist Stanislav Shatalin, "has yet to create a mechanism that does not simply provide full employment for the population (this is a passing stage of extensive development of our economy), but employment that is socially and economically effective, rational, full of significance. The principles of socialism are not principles of philanthropy that automatically guarantee every worker a position that he is not capable of fulfilling" (*Kommunist*, 1986, no. 14).

A definite review of all our policies of economic assistance to socialist and developing states has become urgent. In the final analysis we are talking about billions. Too many objectives which are being carried out with our participation are not being used practically by us or our partners. Specific examples are the construction of the gigantic GES [hydroelectric station]—the means being devoured are huge, but the return is expected no sooner than the next millennium—and wasteful metallurgical plants; a general example is the emphasis on heavy industry in places where attention is needed most by small and medium-sized enterprises for the production of mass-demand products.

We have dared to begin the creation of enterprises with foreign participants on our territory. It would have been worth it, possibly, to think also about creating "free economic zones." This business is very difficult politically as well as economically. To attract significant amounts of foreign capital is hard. It is even harder to reach the point at which joint enterprises easily get along under our conditions, the point at which foreigners willingly place in our industry the profits received from us (reinvestment). If we were to achieve apparent success here, we could not only accelerate the satiation of our domestic market, but also noticeably strengthen the country's export position. Interesting propositions are already being made to us today. However, we are keenly aware of the provisions of the new law, specifically the 45 percent tax it stipulates on profits from foreign partnerships, which is considered unattractive abroad. It seems that the usual little-justified economic stereotypes are playing a role here, and it is inescapably necessary to change them.[3]

For all the importance of the question of the initial satiation of our domestic market, we must at the same time realize that this is only the sharpest, most urgent part of all

---

[3] The joint enterprise law has since been revised so that foreign firms are permitted to hold a 51 percent controlling interest, and the 45 percent tax on foreign profits has been reduced to 30 percent.

the problems of cost accounting, of self-financing socialism.

The most difficult problem we have today in the organization of a fully self-financed economic structure is the equalization of basic price proportions in the domestic economy. The arbitrary price decisions accumulated since the end of the 1920s are indeed a frightening legacy. If we do not eliminate this legacy, we will never have objective reference points for an indisputable evaluation of the expenditures and results of production independent of arbitrary human rule. Consequently, we will never have genuine nonstate financing. In theoretical discussions today, various plans to reform the price system are being put forth. Most of these plans, however, contain one common and, judging by our experience, extraordinarily dangerous defect: the supposition that prices will again be designed in offices, speculatively, in isolation from life and from the real processes in both ours and the world's economy.

Roughly equal price proportions function today, not only in capitalist countries, but also in many socialist ones. They have taken shape under the objective influence of general tendencies in the development of productive forces. Of course national differences in price levels and proportions exist, but as a rule the basic correlation remains. For the quick, safe normalization of our economic structure, a gradual equalization is necessary, first of the wholesale, and then of the retail price proportions, in balance with what is taking place in the rest of the world. We now have sharply declining prices for fuel, minerals, and agricultural raw materials and increasing prices for mechanically engineered products. We have unjustifiably sharply declining prices for food and public utilities and unjustifiably increasing prices for all industrial consumer goods. Soviet prices should correspond with world prices as closely as possible. The next question is: Who will be in charge of price formation, the State Committee on Prices, the Industrial Ministry, or the enterprise/producer itself? First, it is necessary to make the initial step and equalize the proportions.

The equalization of prices is an exceptionally delicate matter, particularly because it calls for a noticeable rise in prices for food products and public utilities. It is necessary to be prepared for anything by persistent, methodical, and—most important—honest and open preparatory work.

Today the Soviet consumer receives more than $50 billion per year from the treasury in the form of subsidies of unprofitable prices for basic food products and services. And why should he not receive the same money in the form of an increase in his basic wages and, possibly, also in his savings bank deposit? In the final analysis, why underpay for meat and at the same time overpay for fabric and shoes; why not buy both at real prices? Of course, in order for people to get used to this, the stereotypes they have formed must be broken, but to break them will be difficult. Only honest, understandable attempts to normalize our economy can convince the average consumer to change his habits. It is necessary to begin talking with the people, essentially as it was done in Hungary, where extensive explanations in 1976 paved the way for the smooth introduction of new prices. And we shouldn't forget the sad experience of Poland, where in that same year of 1976 they tried to change the prices in one fell swoop and then were forced to rescind the changes.

There is still another prejudice: rejection of the joint-stock structure. Why is it prohibited to attract the free means of our citizens and enterprises for the purpose of creating new manufacturing facilities and expanding the old? This position defies all sensible explanations. It is simply blindness or open unwillingness to implement what for the time being lies dormant but can be of very useful service to the whole country. Our famous economists Pavel Bunich and Vladimir Moskalenko correctly state the point: Today's lack of invested means "can be filled, specifically by having suitable enterprises sell their bonds to enterprises that have free resources." Only one thing needs to be added—to sell to private individuals as well. Or is it better for the state if these means lie dormant?

6

People and Economics

Abel Aganbegyan

An interview in *Ogonyok*
nos. 29 and 30
July and August 1987

Along with Tatyana Zaslavskaya and other influential members of the Novosibirsk Academy, Abel G. Aganbegyan realized in the early 1980s that the Soviet Union required radical economic reform. When Gorbachev came to power many of Aganbegyan's ideas became politically viable, and he has become both a Gorbachev adviser and a leading proponent of economic reform. Aganbegyan's interviews and articles have been widely published both in the Soviet Union and abroad, and they are particularly valuable for their numerous revealing statistics. Although Aganbegyan advises Mikhail Gorbachev on economic policy, many of his ideas for a truly radical reform of the system have yet to be implemented.

In these important interviews with *Ogonyok* correspondent Leonid Pleshakov, Aganbegyan spares no details in describing the severe state of the Soviet economy. He argues that, in order for the economy to excel in technological progress, the country requires democratization to help create a new type of worker. He also notes that the current command-administrative approach impedes innovation, as all resources and directions come from the center. And because enterprises in the Soviet Union are paid for nearly everything they produce, there is little concern for the quality of their products. This problem of the dictatorial power of the producer over the consumer in the Soviet economic system is also addressed by Aganbegyan.

Pleshakov: Abel Gezevich, we would like to move directly to the role of the human factor in acceleration and *perestroika*, which you have called one of the main problems of the present stage of our country's economic development. Why?

Aganbegyan: In order to answer your question I must dwell in a bit more detail on the terms themselves: "acceleration" and "*perestroika*." It is no exaggeration to say that the fate of our state, its future in the broadest sense of the word, depends on carrying out the party's scientific-economic strategy, at the heart of which is the concept of acceleration of the country's socioeconomic development. It is for the sake of acceleration that the large-scale restructuring of our entire national economy was conceived.[1]

The concept of acceleration cannot be understood in mechanical terms, in terms of mere quantity: First, there is speed, and then additional speed for every unit of time. Of course, the quantitative aspect is also important here, but it is not the main thing. During the 11th Five-Year Plan, for example, our national income, as has already been stated, grew barely more than 3 percent per year. In the 12th we would like it to rise to 4 percent. In the 1990s, 5 percent. As we see, the rates are rising substantially. But far more important than the rise in the rates is the new quality of the growth. What do these 3, 4, and 5 percents embody, what kinds of products, from what source, for what purpose? For acceleration itself, as the pivot of our scientific-economic strategy, was not conceived in order to expand the scale of the quantitative growth of production: mining more coal, extracting more petroleum, smelting more metal, and so on. We must get the national economy on the track of intensification. The rise of labor productivity must be increased by half over the 11th Five-Year Plan even during the 12th; there must be a larger saving on fuel and raw materials, and the growth rate of the output-capital ratio must be tripled.[2]

So, the principal purpose of acceleration is to boost our entire society to a higher qualitative state. To do this we must build a material and technical base that meets the requirements of the technological revolution so that we may enter the twenty-first century with updated productive forces. We must, as has already been said, update all of our economic forms and production relations, the entire system of management, and the economic mechanism. It is clear that the worker must also meet the new conditions. He must possess more thorough vocational and general knowledge, an inner sense of discipline in the broad sense,

---

[1] The term "acceleration" is no longer used to describe an economic goal of the reforms.

[2] The 11th Five-Year Plan lasted from 1981 to 1985. The 12th Five-Year Plan encompasses the years 1986 to 1990.

and the ability to work as part of a team. He must be active in a social sense and in the workplace, he must have a higher level of sophistication. In short, this must be a new man—our principal productive force.

We must raise our entire state of prosperity to a new level by expanding uniquely socialist achievements. But life does not come down to economics alone. We must renew all of our public institutions: solve the problems of openness, democracy, self-management, and many, many other things consistently and thoroughly, and this also can come under the heading of "acceleration."

Pleshakov: Abel Gezevich, so far we have been talking mainly about how our economy, our society as a whole, must be raised to a new level as a result of *perestroika* and acceleration. But what does man specifically obtain as a result of the performance of all these measures? What sort of goals are we setting for ourselves in this regard? How realistically can we expect their fulfillment? After all, in the end man is not only the protagonist and creator of *perestroika* and acceleration, but also, if it can be put this way, their object. It is on his behalf, in his interests, that they were conceived. And our slogan "everything for man" will remain only a slogan until we back it up with specific deeds and content. What goals are we setting for ourselves in this regard, what tasks do we have to perform in the immediate and more distant future?

Aganbegyan: The change of direction that we must accomplish in the sphere of social welfare is equivalent in scale to the qualitative leap outlined for the economy. Strictly speaking, it is not possible to separate one from the other. After all, we want to raise the country's economy to a new and higher level not for the sake of the economy itself, but in order to satisfy people's growing needs at a higher level. So that their prosperity rises, they have greater opportunities for comprehensive development, and the socialist way of life also rises to a higher level. The efficiency of the economy that we want to achieve must ultimately redound to the benefit of man and bring about the highest level of living in the world. Moreover, this would not be the kind of standard of living that exists in other countries, but rather a qualitatively new one that would include our socialist advantages. To be specific, even now there are certain examples and certain aspects of life with which we can demonstrate and prove what we have achieved: full employment, the absence of unemployment, no discrimination, no exploitation of man by man, a regulated and rather short workday (and this has been done at a level of labor productivity that is still low compared to other advanced countries), social consumption funds, and achievements in the domain of social welfare benefits and priorities. But there are other spheres in which we lag seriously behind the advanced countries: in the level of real income, the supply and comfort and convenience of housing, average lifespan, average level of education, and certain other aspects where we still have a great deal to do.

Pleshakov: It is no secret that there are quite a few problems involved in raising the level of well-being and comprehensive development of all members of our society. Which of them, Abel Gezevich, are in your view the most important ones, the ones that need to be solved first?

Aganbegyan: That is a complicated question, because everything concerning man has to be examined in the entire context, and it is very difficult to separate one or several problems from the entire group and say that this is the main thing. So I will rank the problems now being discussed in order of acuteness.

The problem of food has not been solved. For an advanced country, and that is what we are, in the last quarter of the twentieth century in which we are living, we have been eating poorly, particularly from the qualitative standpoint. First of all, we need to meet the population's need for the products of animal husbandry. There is a chronic shortage of animal protein and fat. It is not even so much a matter of quantity, of wanting to have a per capita meat consumption of eighty kilograms when we eat only sixty-one kilograms at present. That is not the point. It is the quality and the variety of the products consumed that are important in nutrition. We mainly eat frozen meat that has lost half of its nutrients. We eat fish that has been refrozen, in which once again there is little benefit left.

The second problem in the area of food concerns fruits and vegetables. This is where we have the largest lag, as our consumption of fruits and vegetables (which, like our meat, have lost their nutrients) is only one third of the standard. We are not talking about the global and summary figures, but about uniform supply throughout the year. All of our summary indicators smooth out and distort the true state of affairs; they say nothing about the seasonal nature of the supply of these products. We are living in the year of the seventieth anniversary of the October Revolution, forty-two years after the victorious end of the Great Patriotic War, and yet you go into a store [and find nothing].

Solving the food problem is one of our key tasks in the remaining years of the twentieth century. There are large plans to be implemented in this area even during the 12th Five-Year Plan, when the growth rate of agricultural production is to exceed by almost 2.5-fold the rates achieved in the previous five-year planning period: not 6 percent, which is what it was, but 14.4 percent. In large part this will allow us to give up imports of those foods that we can (and must) produce ourselves as we improve the supply to the public: grain, meat, and butter.

In 1985 we produced 788 million pairs of leather footwear, and the United States produced only 300 million. If this is put on a per capita basis, this would be 2.8 pairs per person in our country and only 1.3 pairs for the Americans. There are heaps of relatively inexpensive shoes in their stores to meet every taste. We can also be said to have heaps of shoes, the shelves are loaded. But, to put it in crude terms, there is "nothing" to buy. These shoes have been left on the shelf because they are not very comfortable, they are not stylish, and they are not good-looking. If in fact they are purchased, this is only because there is nothing else. And even when they are purchased, they are not always worn. But when at the end of the month or quarter some import is "thrown on the market" to "fulfill the plan," then you cannot get to the counter. To speak frankly, our footwear industry is to a large extent doing nothing more than converting the leather and other materials.

Pleshakov: Again the notorious cost-intensive character of production and the dictate of the producer over that of the consumer?

Aganbegyan: When such principles lie at the base of our economy, all sectors are treated the same—those that melt metal and those that sew women's boots. But let us get back to quality. In many cases it is horrible in our country. Year after year we are losing the advantages and positions we once had in this respect. Just think back to the 1950s. True, our things were not so beautiful or so stylish as those abroad, but still any of our things was more durable. The ugly domestic radios played for decades. Our automobile, the Pobeda [Victory] (you feel a thrill when you see one on the street), was not so stylish or speedy even for its time, but it was distinguished in its strength and its reliability.

In the mid-1950s, immediately after I graduated from the institute, I bought my mother a television set in the GUM.[3] Black-and-white, with a small screen. It worked for twenty years or so—and nothing went wrong with it. And our first refrigerators, the Saratov and the ZIL? After all, earlier we did not even know that there was such a thing as a household appliance repairman. We never called one because nothing ever broke.

And now? It is a terrible thing: Every year in Moscow alone more than two thousand color television sets catch fire. Houses go up in flames along with them. That is exactly what caused the last fire in the Rossiya Hotel. Is it not a crime to develop and manufacture a television designed so that it causes a higher risk of fire?

And our Volgas? These cars are in such need of modernization and of updating to a new model that many countries have prohibited their import. They do not meet any of the safety requirements that an up-to-date automobile must meet. Nor, at the same time, do they meet the ecological requirements that are now being applied to motor vehicles. They pollute the environment to a considerably greater extent than is allowable for models in their class. Gasoline and oil consumption of our Volgas are extremely high. They lack comfort and features; in this respect they are inferior to foreign automobiles even in the small class. It is quite clear why many states do not allow them to be imported.

Pleshakov: Let us assume that our market is saturated to sufficiency with all the necessary industrial goods, foodstuffs, and also services—what then?

Aganbegyan: Then your well-being will be determined by your earnings, and you will work with more energy so

---

[3] The GUM, located on Red Square, near the Kremlin, is the largest department store in the country.

that those earnings will be increased. Then every additional ten rubles that you earn will be important, because it will have its value.

Pleshakov: Two years have passed since the April *plenum* of the party's Central Committee and a year since the 12th Party Congress. A turn for the better is noticeable, but still things are going more slowly than might be wished. It has proven to be more difficult than anticipated. This was, in fact, discussed at the party *plenum* in June of this year, as the mass media have been constantly reporting. One gets the feeling that our acceleration is being deliberately held back, that brakes are being applied to the wheel of *perestroika*. In words, to be sure, everyone is unanimously in favor. Tell us, Abel Gezevich, in your view, in the view of an economist, who finds *perestroika* undesirable? I am thinking not of individuals, but of groups of people, and to some extent even strata of society. The term "group egoism" has even emerged now.

Aganbegyan: You see, something new is always a struggle, something has to be overcome. New things are always difficult in and of themselves. Even when you go into the water, no one is standing in your way, but you feel resistance: a new medium. The restructuring which we have begun to carry out is not simply a new medium, but new economic relations, new methods of management. There are, of course, some sort of forces behind them, and they infringe upon someone's interests. The main thing is what we intend to do in the restructuring of management: to broaden the rights of enterprises, collectives, and state farms. And if someone's rights are broadened, that means someone else's are being diminished. In taking away the rights from some tier of management, we are taking away its power, some of its privileges, and often we're generally casting doubt on the advisability of its existence. And there are people behind that entire management apparatus. Just imagine a man who has become accustomed to issuing orders for holding meetings, discussing things, having things cleared by him, and he suddenly realizes that his job and he himself are no longer necessary to anyone. It is difficult to go through that. Of course, there are people who will cling to the old out of inertia, and they will behave passively toward the new things.

There is also another very interesting group (I refer to them as the "backward people in the economy") for whom it is easier to work in the command and administrative system of management and appointments than in a system of elections by work collectives, in an atmosphere where independent decisions must be made. Independence is a very heavy load of responsibility. Rights go with responsibilities. Not everyone wants that.

A third group consists of people who are living on money that they have not earned. I am not thinking of pilferers, *nesuny*, those who take bribes, speculators, not even those who repair their own automobiles in the state motor pool without paying. I am not talking about them. We have millions of people who receive wages that do not correspond to the contribution they make in their work. Often they are paid for doing nothing at all. Go to any plant and any institution, and how many people are on endless cigarette breaks and tea breaks? They are counted as being at work. In a formal sense this is so, but actually they do little, their participation is only a token of work. The number of superfluous people is especially great in our scientific research and project-planning institutes.

Pleshakov: Recently *Pravda* reported that in Moscow alone there are 1,087 scientific research and project-planning and design collectives with a total work force of 933,000.

Aganbegyan: A huge army, but sometimes the results are tiny. And there are a great many people who receive more than they give to society in various spheres of our life. Under the conditions of *perestroika*, more is being demanded of those people, they are being called upon to "earn" their keep. Some of them are resisting this.

7

At the Turning Point

Mikhail Antonov

Moskva, no. 3, 1988

Russian nationalist Mikhail Antonov's article in the conservative journal *Moskva* illustrates the lively nature of the *glasnost*-inspired debate about Soviet economic policy. Many conservative Russian thinkers, like Antonov, combine an affinity for their heritage with loyalty to the Communist party. However, in emphasizing Russian national traditions, Antonov and others ignore or underplay the fact that the Soviet Union consists of over one hundred diverse nationalities, with Russians comprising only 53 percent of the population.

Antonov harshly criticizes reform economist Abel Aganbegyan for failing to appreciate the nature of the Russian soul when advocating economic reforms. Antonov blames Aganbegyan and other such scholars for the poor state of the economy. He writes that, while party doctrines have been excellent over the years, the economists have not supplied the proper advice to carry out the party's programs. Antonov accuses Aganbegyan of "economism," a political charge often levied in the 1930s which connotes placing economic reasoning ahead of ideology. Although Aganbegyan is one of the architects of the economic reforms, Antonov accuses him of being an enemy of *perestroika*. Antonov displays the conservative views of the Brezhnev period. He believes that to improve the economy, it is necessary to inspire people with high ideals and values.

Abel Aganbegyan has criticized the stagnation that prevailed in the economy until the mid-1980s and defined plans for a *perestroika* in order to ensure the acceleration of socioeconomic development for the country. How does he view stagnation and its causes?

Stagnation is a drop in the pace of growth of national income, a reduction of the quality of production, etc. It is caused by the outmoded economic mechanism and predominantly administrative methods of management that took shape in the 1930s and suited the conditions of that time but absolutely do not correspond to the reality of our time. While reading this I thought, aren't we taking an oversimplified approach to the most complex socioeconomic problems, and aren't we confusing causes with effects? Indeed, it is impossible to solve complex problems by oversimplified methods. It is possible, for example, to attempt to eliminate drunkenness and alcoholism by prohibiting the sale of alcoholic beverages, but this would lead, alas, to the drunk consuming moonshine of the highest quality while I, who do not need alcohol, would not be able to purchase cologne for the proper price to freshen up my face after shaving. In order to overcome drunkenness we must also give people something else, something more important and attractive; more precisely, we must give people high ideals and values. Without this necessary change in their life-style, many people would feel that their life had suddenly become boring and that holidays had disappeared. Therefore the battle against drunkenness requires not so much economic, propagandistic, and administrative measures as it does social, moral, and spiritual measures.

The cause of stagnation should be analyzed in a similar manner. I confess that I was confused by the data from numerous sociological studies that showed that only one quarter to one third of workers perform to their full potential. Does the reason for this reduction in the people's work activity lie much deeper than in the economic mechanism and management methods?

According to the academician Abel Aganbegyan, the solution to this problem lies in increasing the material incentive of workers and saturating the market with goods so that there would be merchandise for each ruble. Then, according to his thinking, "your well-being would be determined by your salary, and so that your salary will be bigger you will work with more energy. Saturating the market with goods will ensure an absolutely different quality of life. Let's presume that you receive more than I do, but thanks to the variety of goods and services I will be able to dress as well as you. Simply put, I will have a set of clothes slightly cheaper, but it will look as good as your suit."

Such reasoning probably seems convincing to many people. But it seems to me that people who make the following remarks are closer to the truth: First of all, I will remind you of the words of Mikhail Vagin: "Village (and not only the village—M.A.) is flooded with money." Second, as Vagin remarked, many people do not strive for more money if they have to earn it (naturally they would not refuse free money). Third, is it not rare when a person receives twice as much money for half as much work? In short, the reflections of the scholar are based on the "economic man," who lives according to the principle that "you work more, you earn more, and you will live better," but a living person quite often does not at all resemble such a "theoretical model." In other words, the conclusions of the scholar turn out to be very debatable. The model of the economic man even allows the following interpretation: "The higher the contribution of the individual, the more money he is paid. That is, if I have more money I must be more valuable to society. Therefore, I need as much money as possible and then I will be a hero of our time." Many people think and act in this way, and many are convinced that this is the essence of the "skill of living." That's why they look with contempt on those who do not have other sources of income except for a modest salary (and almost all of us receive a very modest salary), especially those whose leisure is built on some type of "spiritual life."

And why shouldn't every worker want to work at full strength and take full responsibility for his job? Why, on the contrary, during the first five-year plans, did people who were sometimes hungry and, to say the least, were not dressed according to the latest fashion, build Turksib and Magnitka, Kuznetsk and Komsomolsk-on-Amur with such "equipment" as spades, crowbars, and wheelbarrows?[1] They built at a speed which seems simply fantastic even to our contemporaries, who are armed with powerful excavators and bulldozers.

These men did not work just for food. They were creating a new world, a world seen not only in their dreams but almost tangible to them, a world that would arrive at any moment. This was the inspiration that diminished the burden of their labor.

So I think that the essential cause of stagnation is not in the economic mechanism and the management methods, but in those people who have lost the feeling of being privy to the motherland's historical fate, of being the master of

---

[1] The Turksib railroad, Magnitka and Kuznetsk metallurgy complexes, and Komsomolsk-on-Amur, a city in the Far East, were the biggest construction projects of the early 1930s.

the production, the master of the country. Our respected academician-sociologists[2] should have thought about this earlier, and their main contribution to our party should have been to design the strategy for acceleration.

Should we be surprised that the academician Abel Aganbegyan describes acceleration as the increase in the national income's rate of annual growth from 3 percent in the last five-year plan, to 4 percent in the current one, and even up to 5 percent (imagine that!) in the future? Isn't it clear that with such "acceleration" we would not "catch up and overtake" the foremost capitalist countries until at least the middle of the third millennium? Meanwhile, we continue to make declarations about the advantages of socialism. It has been noted more than once in the party documents that we do not yet truly understand, in scientific terms, the society in which we live. We have not found the mainspring for its true takeoff, as well as the increased efficiency of production, measured not in percentages, but in times. And we have not found this mainspring because our leading scholars, our sociologists, who formed their views during the period of stagnation and themselves contributed to this stagnation, continue to be prisoners of the ideology of "economism"[3] and to contaminate us with it.

Academician Abel Aganbegyan has already taught leaders for a long time, and *Literaturnaya Gazeta* reported on June 3, 1987, about his "business games" and other classes in the Academy of the National Economy of the Council of Ministers of the USSR. It was reported in the most optimistic vein: "In one month, this first graduating class, armed with the latest word in economics, will return to its enterprises. Scientists will return to their work and research knowing about the newest facts and problems." But half a year has already passed, and there are no joyous changes either in practice (look at the results of the plan for the socioeconomic development of the country for 1987) or in theory (look at the interviews with Abel Aganbegyan in the

---

[2] The term "sociologist" is used here in a pejorative sense.

[3] "Economism," which was criticized by the Bolsheviks, is a political theory from the early 1900s which emphasized the struggle for economic demands, for a constitution, and for Western liberties. Lenin ferociously attacked the main document of the Economists, "Credo."

August 24, 1987, *Izvestiya* and in the popular publication *Argumenty i Facty*, 1987, no. 44).

It is necessary to change the very philosophy of education, to promote the moral education of the personality, the noble idea, the contemporary understanding of the meaning of life—in short, to promote what we have expected in vain from our sociologists for many decades. Until now, the quality of spiritual nourishment suggested to our rising generation has remained very low, and if this situation persists it will be hard to expect a real modernization of schools.

At literally every step the "economism" of Abel Aganbegyan is felt. The scholar starts a conversation about culture and mentions such facts as the 130-ruble salary of the workers in this area. What labor exploits can we expect from a person with such a salary?

On the other hand, it is hard not to notice that the leading sociologists materially are provided for incredibly better than ordinary workers of culture; nevertheless, nobody has heard about the labor exploits of these leading scholars for quite some time. Of course, nobody would feel that money is superfluous, but you cannot resolve the problem only with money, and money would not inspire people to do great work. This touches upon the Russian national character, in which the merchant ideal is not inherent. Yes, most of our people now require many things, including good food, consumer goods, comfortable housing, and gardens. However, as soon as the first needs are satisfied, everyone will see how little material incentives mean to us, those incentives on which the proponents of "economism" have put such great hopes.

Only naive people and wretched economic science could conclude that if we create a new economic mechanism and appoint literate managers everywhere, everything will be okay and His Majesty the Ruble will take care of the rest. The Soviet people, for the most part, will respond to the party's appeal if it is necessary to save the motherland or to turn it into a blossoming garden, setting an example for all peoples on earth, accomplishing the historical endeavor understood by all, an endeavor which surpasses the magnitude of daily life. But to think that they will rise as one to fight for an increase in the rate of return or to exchange the chandelier in their apartment for a more elegant one, this would be unforgivably harebrained economic scheming. The leading sociologists should have been able to understand this themselves and to show this to the leadership and the public. Instead, they are preoccupied with speculative constructions based on the "economic man." In light of this, the very first phrase of Abel Aganbegyan's interview, that the essential in *perestroika* is the man, seems odd.

Therefore, to the three categories of the enemies of *perestroika* that Aganbegyan enumerates (leaders used to the command style of management, regressive managers without initiative, and people who like to get money without working for it) I would add a fourth category, possibly the most dangerous today: sociologists, proponents of "economism."

The danger posed by the advocates of these backward theoretical views is multiplied many times if they are advisers to the high leadership or in charge of the scientific councils that advise the leadership.

Let's take, for example, the theory of the economic exploitation of Siberia. Many prominent scholars and writers say in one voice that this is not economic exploitation, but rather an orgy of favoritism and a complete neglect of the people's needs and the environment's requirements for protection. In general, investing huge sums for the extraction and sale abroad of oil and gas while at the same time leaving metallurgy, machine building, transport, and other branches of industry without investment hardly can be called a smart decision. Or, for another example, take the settling of the territory of the Baikal-Amur main line. It is now apparent that this grandiose construction, which required many billions of rubles, was not sufficiently thought through and was badly organized.[4] In order to complete it, an equal amount of additional investment will be required. At the same time the construction of the railroad, which is vitally important to the country, has been postponed due to a

---

[4] The Baikal-Amur mainline, the redirection of the northern rivers, and other industrial projects became rallying cries for Russian nationalists. Although they were approved by predominately Russian leaders, nationalists view these projects as sacrifices imposed on Russia for the sake of other nationalities.

shortage of resources. And how about scientific research into the problems of the Caspian lowlands? Here as well a less-than-optimal solution was adopted: Canals were dug that would leave the lower Volga without water and would resurrect the idea, already rejected once by the people, of diverting the flow of northern rivers and destroying the last natural spawning places of sturgeon.

Are these random mistakes? I don't think so. Today, backward theoretical views and loyalty to the ideas of economism inevitably bring the sociologist into an impasse. It is even possible to agree with the opinion of the pedagogue V. Svirsky: "Some academicians of the social sciences caused the society as much damage as those who in their time were destroying genetics" (*Izvestiya*, July 20, 1987).

The predominance of backward views among the leading sociologists of our time can be explained by various reasons. One reason is the break with cultural tradition caused by ignorance of the ideas of Russian thinkers who are distinguished by a wholesome outlook on the world (A. Pushkin, I. Kireevsky, A. Khomyakov, and others).[5] Although it is not possible to adequately address this question within the framework of this article, it is necessary to mention it, as the search for the solution to the difficult problems of our economy inevitably will result in the creation of a new thinking based to a greater extent on the national tradition.

----

[5] Alexander Pushkin is a famous Russian poet. Ivan Kireevsky and Alexei Khomyakov are Russian intellectuals belonging to the Slavophile movement.

8

The Family Farm of the Shaposhnikovs

V. Letov

Izvestiya, March 30, 1988

This article presents a very positive portrait of a fairly rare phenomenon in the Soviet Union: a family farm. Despite unfavorable conditions, the Shaposhnikov family cultivated sugar beets at one sixth the cost of those produced by state farms. The success of this family, however, should be viewed as an exceptional achievement rather than the rule in the Soviet Union. It was unusual in that the head of the state farm in this area provided a great deal of assistance to the Shaposhnikov family. In many cases, state farm chairmen provide land of poor quality and no assistance to family farms. The press also reports many cases of vandalism against family farms committed by jealous or intolerant state farm workers.

They showed the farmers of Smolensk what it's like to work efficiently.

In the Smolensk province, under the auspices of the Mankovsky cattle factory of the Krasninsky district, the Shaposhnikovs' academy has been operating since last fall, a permanent seminar on advanced family farming run by the provincial agro-industrial department. This seminar might not be in existence if it weren't for two brave individuals who got together in Mankovo a year ago. Nikolai Shaposhnikov, a mechanic, approached the factory director Ivan Salygin with a risky idea. Nikolai Yakovlevich and his wife offered to grow and collect a harvest of 500 to 600 centners [one centner = one hundred kilos] of fodder beet from each of forty assigned hectares. Of course if this family is confirmed as a production unit, the field will be assigned. Throughout the years, beet fields of the cattle factory have been the primary responsibility of the citizens of Mankovo. This has demanded a lot of time, work, and money, but yielded only one quarter to one third of what Shaposhnikov proposed.

Of course the proposal made by the mechanic, a respected citizen in the village, was followed by an arrangement. The Shaposhnikovs had never worked with beets; they had studied the technology from books, but forty hectares is not forty acres of a garden. Furthermore, the family has six children, but only one son is old enough to help. There seemed to be two obvious risks: The Mankovsky factory could end up without fodder for its cattle, and this big family could end up without its pay.

The story of the Shaposhnikov family has been in the papers and has been talked about. Last fall, specialists from all areas came down to see how the family was collecting the harvest. They did not meet their goal; they only collected 430 centners of fodder beet from each of thirty-two hectares. Why didn't they collect from all forty hectares? The chief agriculturalist of the factory thought that the family's experiment would be a failure, so only a rough estimate of the field was given to the family. Of course the cold summer and the very rainy fall damaged the harvest, but more damage was done by the hearsay and disbelief in the family's work. Nevertheless, the cost of beets from the Shaposhnikovs' field was one sixth of what is standard cost in Mankovsky. Hard work, dedication, the desire to learn agriculture, and the ability to make dreams come true can be learned from this family. It is not disastrous that the Shaposhnikov family has not yet broken a production record. They broke a record in something else. In Smolensk, they were one of the first pioneers to disprove the axiom that one person in a battlefield does not make up an army. He can be a soldier in a field if he does not fear the job, but works with all his heart. When it became time to harvest, the family was joined by Nikolai Yakovlevich's brother, Valery, and his wife. The field is not at all small. This region has never seen a harvest of a field of this size without the participation of students and workers.

"Nothing successful would have come out of this if it were not for the assistance of the director," Shaposhnikov insists. "The necessary technology was not available. The equipment that we used was assembled from what we had available, and sometimes we had to invent things. For instance the equipment for flocking roots, an idea that the director came up with, also can be used in other collective farms of the *oblast*."

Distinguished Mechanic of the Republic Ivan Salygin is also the inventor of several other types of equipment which are used in the factory but not, unfortunately, on other farms. "There is no time to take care of promotion," said Ivan Vasilievich while waving his hand. "Ideas must work and not wait for reviews." For the director a real accomplishment is not that the factory possesses one more piece of equipment, but the fact that people's attitude toward work is more positive. "The key is," he said, repeating the thoughts of his fellow countryman Alexander Engelgardt, who said this over a hundred years ago, "when the peasants don't just plow the fields, but are enjoying the fruits of their labor."

Last year the Mankovsky cattle factory had an average yield of over three thousand kilograms of milk per cow. This year it expects to increase this amount by four hundred kilograms. And, again, the hope to accomplish this increase is tied to the Shaposhnikovs' team. They have almost been called the beet team, but not anymore.

The Shaposhnikov family already has made new plans. First of all, the two brothers, Nikolai and Valery, will combine their resources. The two brothers themselves measured and prepared a field of sixty hectares for spring. About one fourth of the field will be used to raise sugar beet, not fodder beet. Sugar beet is twice as nutritious as fodder beet. This makes a difference. After estimating their increased opportunities, the Shaposhnikovs decided to start a pig-feeding farm. They began with three hundred pigs, and now there are a thousand and a half. After increasing the number of pigs, the brothers intend to decrease the actual costs of feeding the pigs by at least by one and a half times. So it is difficult to say whether the Shaposhnikovs are in the fodder beet business or the livestock business.

"These are good peasants," the director told me. "They are the way they should be. They are the people of the land."

The specialists keep on coming to Mankovo. They write down numbers from presentations, examine technology, and ask about the profits that the Shaposhnikovs make. Nikolai Yakovlevich admits that all his life he has wanted to make a big ruble. Finally he has begun to enjoy what he has long craved. A big family has many expenses. As it turned out, it was possible for him to make good money without going far from home. Last year, Shaposhnikov's monthly salary was seven hundred rubles.

"The secret to success," he maintains, "is hard work. How much one works is how much one will get paid."

9

New in Town: A Jewish Café, At Joseph's

B. Yakovlev

Vechernyaya Moskva
May 24, 1988

This article displays *glasnost* by discussing a café that serves Jewish cuisine. Russians continue to display conflicting attitudes toward Jews. For example, the film *Commissar*, which depicts a Bolshevik woman housed by a Jewish family during the civil war, was released in the fall of 1988 only after a two-decade suppression.

The article's positive portrayal of this cooperative café discusses how its founder, a war veteran, attracts customers by decorating the walls and providing orchestra music for dinner. The article also notes that actors from the Moscow Jewish Chamber Theater will soon perform at the café.

The members of this cooperative prepare gefilte fish, stuffed chicken neck, sweet and sour meat with plums, borscht, strudel, and other dishes of Jewish cuisine.

The curious public gathered today for the opening of the Jewish cooperative café, At Joseph's. It is located not far from the Paveletskaya metro station, on Dubininskaya Street, 11.

The café belongs to the Moskvorechie cooperative, headed by the Perezovsky family. The cooperative has nine members, and twelve more work under contract. Among them are veterans of World War II, women, and some who have miraculously survived Kiev's and Minsk's fascist ghettos.

After a two-day trial period followed by an official and festive opening, the cooperative café, which seats forty people, is now open from 11:00 A.M. to 11:00 P.M. Until 3:00 P.M. full dinners are offered that cost from two rubles to two-and-a-half rubles. To war veterans, regardless of their nationality, a 50 percent discount is offered.

The walls of At Joseph's are decorated with paintings by young artists, which soon will be available for purchase. Performances by the actors of the Moscow Jewish

Chamber Theater are anticipated, and a small orchestra plays every evening.

"We found Muscovites who knew the best recipes of Jewish cuisine and who could cook superbly, and they were many," explained Joseph Maksovich, after whom the café was named. "Most of our menu consists of national [Jewish] food, and we plan to prepare other dishes as well."

In the near future, a small additional room will open to serve kosher foods prepared from specifically designated fish and meat with special kitchen equipment. By the way, the word "kosher" is found in *The Explanatory Dictionary of the Great Living Russian Language* from 1882 by Vladimir Dal', but I could not find it in *The Dictionary of the Russian Language* published a hundred years later, in 1981, edited by A. Evgenieva.

Our city, the capital of a heterogeneous country in which people of numerous nationalities live, will be happy to see the reemergence of the Jewish café, which used to exist some time ago. People say they were located on the first of Meshchanskaya, along the prospect of Peace, and in other places. They have almost been forgotten by everyone except the very elderly.

The time has come for At Joseph's to join the diverse family that treats Muscovites to Russian and Ukrainian, Georgian and Uzbek, Korean and Chinese varieties of food. It is also time for it to take the colorful place that it deserves among the enterprises that cater to Moscow's needs and fancies.

There is one more piece of information to add: At Joseph's intends to feed the night shift workers of nearby enterprises, including the mailmen, and to provide the passengers of the Paveletskaya station with hot food for a price not to exceed one ruble.

10

Black Market: People, Goods, Facts

Galina Belikova and Alexander Shokhin

Ogonyok, no. 36
September 1987

The black market was never analyzed in the Soviet press prior to *glasnost*. This illegal second economy enables Soviet citizens to purchase goods unavailable in state stores. The chronic shortage of consumer goods has led to the proliferation of individual operators, some syndicates, and many average citizens who sell scarce products. The article, written by a sociologist and an economist, praises the ingenuity of some black marketeers.

The black market is different in the Soviet Union from that in many other countries, because black market participants hold legitimate jobs and in some cases are members of the elite. The perpetual seller's market in the USSR means that high prices can be charged for Western products like radios and clothes and for other sought-after goods or services, such as car repairs. The black market serves a social purpose by alleviating some of the consumer anxiety in the country.

This article charges that Communist party officials are active participants in the illegal market. The authors also criticize the inequality of the legally sanctioned system, which allows members of the elite who hold special pink tickets to purchase goods at subsidized prices from restricted-access distribution stores.

In the last year or two we have all read, heard, and talked about the shortcomings of our existing system of management by fiat. This journal recently published a detailed analysis of these shortcomings (and by the way, they cannot properly be called shortcomings, because they are definitive characteristics of this system of management) by the academician Abel Aganbegyan [Document #6]. Rigid quotas and "rationing" of resources, shortages of practically all resources, goods, and services, extreme wastefulness, the dictatorship of the producer over the consumer, low quality of goods, the decline in the growth rate and the quality level as well make up merely a partial list of the negative aspects of our socioeconomic system that the steps planned by the June *plenum* of the Central Committee were designed to overcome.

But objective laws do exist, notwithstanding the will and conscience of men. That is why, of course, certain elementary forms of doing business and decentralized decision-making mechanisms have come into being in our economic life. These forms have not been adequately studied, and economists, sociologists, and jurists have not provided an unambiguous interpretation of them. They use the terms "the second economy," "the shadow economy," "the black (or gray or pink) market," and, in general, the "colored" economy.

Where to Look!

Everything's there and everyone knows it. Anything from a 4-kopeck nut to a 40,000-ruble Toyota.

And there are people who have everything. People who have no supply privileges and who do not work in the retail business but nonetheless have "it": Swedish chandeliers and Indian tea in English teapots, Panasonics and Macintoshes, books by Boris Pasternak and Osip Mandelstam. They've never gone abroad, yet even their dogs are imported—with pedigrees from the time of Elizabeth II [*sic*]. All of it comes from the black market.

"But where the hell is the black market?" ask ordinary, out-of-touch citizens who have saved up some money but can't do business. They're still looking.

But they're not looking in the right way. The petty street pushers disappeared a long time ago; the black market has taken on quite civilized forms. People look for a high-handed hag with an impudent mug, a repulsive figure with shifty eyes, but a major black market operator fits into society and looks good.

He doesn't mess around, he does business in a smooth and measured way. He doesn't haggle over his goods. He meets his customers halfway, and he does favors. He might do you a favor, or he might do someone else a favor, and quite often he's considered a benefactor. In most cases you couldn't legally call him a speculator, but even if you could, even the most ungrateful customer wouldn't.

Old-fashioned notions about the black market keep prospective customers on the surface of the business, near goods of doubtful value, and keep them from getting to the heart of the matter. Where the really good stuff is.

On the surface is the stuff that usually floats on the surface—the usual scum and trash, such as "Moldavanka gypsies" with bad cosmetics, men standing around bookstores hawking potboiling rubbish, peddlers with worn-out rags, a noisy, common crowd, an eyesore trying to give the impression that it is our black market, but which in fact is only a very small part of it.

There are three basic tracks in the black market: haulers, importers, and governmental commercial agencies.

In addition to the black market in goods, there is also a black market in services that encompasses practically the entire service sector.

You don't just walk into the real black market. You won't start living the good life right away; you have to make contacts, connections, and the right friends and cultivate businesslike and solid acquaintances.

This is where the vast "gray" market has come from, the direct exchange of goods and services that bypasses the "paper money" and works on the principle of "You scratch my back, and I'll scratch yours."

Importers

We all know what can be imported and from where. We're not talking about Soviet consumer goods from Buzuluk or Krivoi Rog. We're talking about high-quality "brand name" goods from the capitalist, socialist, and developing countries that have been imported by someone who's been abroad on assignment. As they say, what makes you rich makes you happy. People import for themselves, for their home, for their families, or for anyone their heart desires. For their craving countrymen, they will import anything that will bring a maximum profit at resale.

Of course, the meaning of "maximum" has changed over time. It's hard to believe that twenty years ago humble women, their husbands' wives, used to bring in mohair sweaters in their purses for "selling," and they were satisfied. Now the resale of two expensive stereo systems (let's say an Akai or a Sony) produces enough money for a down payment on a two-room cooperative apartment.

There is a unique division of labor among the different categories of employees who make regular trips abroad, such as sailors and railroad men, who import different kinds of "trifles." For example Provotorov, an electrician on the Estonian ship *Rapla*, supplied with hard currency by Baykov, an electrician who had never left the Soviet Union, purchased 2,900 silver chains in Antwerp (each chain cost about 20 francs, that is 3 rubles and 30 kopecks, and fetched 38 rubles). At the time he was detained, Provotorov had already made more than 1 million rubles. Speculation by sailors in the early 1980s led to a number of complaints by the courts to the Soviet Ministry of the Merchant Marine, where they had the opinion that such business dealings constituted a common and necessary kind of self-compensation; as they say, our salaries aren't worth a damn, and the temptation is great. People in better positions such as foreign trade officials and officials from other agencies usually bring in electronics, while athletes and artists import clothes. We know of no cases in which a major speculator caught red-handed has led the authorities to his source. The stock phrase used in this situation is "purchased from person(s) unknown." Hence these channels and connections have not been investigated.

The most money is made in electronic goods (tape recorders, dictaphones, VCRs, stereo and quad systems), computers, cameras, musical instruments, clothing, and footwear. They may be imported legally and illegally.

Walking On Water, But Not Getting Wet

In almost every corner of the country there are two retail and two service sectors: one for the general public, and the other for "our" people. According to sociological studies, 83 percent of the public overpays for goods and services in one way or another: people have their "own meatmen," their "own barbers," connections for shoes, and so forth.

In the service sector, no favor exists which cannot be overpaid for. People pay speculative prices for "special attention" (in essence, just for the worker doing his job), for their barber to give them a haircut that they won't be ashamed to walk outside with, for the faucet not to start leaking after the plumbers leave, and so forth. They also pay excessively for such illegal services as getting their names moved up on the list for an apartment against existing regulations or buying a plot at a restricted cemetery. Speculation in grief is currently the rage; cemeteries are far ahead of the pack in extortions, followed by cab drivers, hospital attendants, TV repairmen, barbers, auto mechanics, doormen, and doctors. A cemetery director holds the record for the most money extorted at one time: 3,000 rubles. (For purposes of comparison, the smallest sum extorted for which criminal charges were brought was 60 kopecks. The accused was a cab driver.) Shortages in all categories of goods (furniture, household appliances, and more) account for some of the overpayments. There are some towns, primarily small ones, where no halfway decent goods ever make it to the shelves. This explains both the massive pilgrimages to Moscow for "shopping" and the provincial's lack of discrimination which Muscovites cannot comprehend: "Boy, these rubes buy anything!"

But food is the most popular item in the country as a whole. According to approximate data, the public overpays 1.5 billion rubles every year just for sausage.

Among retailers the opinion that you can't make an honest living in the business has become an axiom. Swindling and cheating the customer is assumed to be an indisputable fact of life which has taken root in the "feeding" system existing in the overwhelming majority of food stores. The "food chain" runs from the salesman to the department head to the director to the warehouse. Under this system, people who are basically honest or who simply don't know how to swindle are naturally squeezed out of business: If you don't pay the director, the director "can't deliver" to the warehouse, and if there are no goods, he can't meet his quotas. Your salary is from 80 to 100 rubles a month, and you'll have to give half of it away in the form of deductions, which every salesman has to pay, for shrinkage and spillage, errors not in one's favor, a "slight" (say, 50 kilos out of a ton) shortage in a shipment delivered from the warehouse, and so forth. You have to pay this out of your own pocket, which would be quite painful if you weren't making money "on the side."

One cannot always separate crimes of greed from the "shadow" economy in the retail business, where kickbacks from rank-and-file salesmen to the bosses are considered a "normal" characteristic of a "normally" functioning process of selling goods. Recently a number of criminal cases from the big Tregubov scandal in Moscow were reopened for investigation. Why? Several of the accused managed to paint a convincing picture of a situation in which "they, not out of greed, but only due to prevailing procedures, violated retail regulations and engaged in financial abuses."

Nevertheless, operating on the black market generally produces good results. Retail workers in the Soviet Union spend an average of 60 percent more than they officially make, and retail and service workers own 70 percent of the foreign cars in the country (Renaults, Pontiacs, Mercedes, Volvos, and others).

They are also the most active participants in the "gray market." A touching friendship based on a perfect "fit" between goods and services binds together individuals and entire groups, the cobblers and the fish sellers, the antique dealers and the auto mechanics. These ties form an extraordinarily strong network of "pull" which reliably protects its members from the problems and difficulties of life.

"Socialization" is yet another current feature of the "gray market": goods or services that satisfy social or spiritual needs are increasingly used to pay for goods in short supply. Teachers, for example, may give more attention to the children of retail workers by tutoring them at home (this is probably why there is a high percentage of medal winners among this category of students). The holders of goods in short supply "make friends" with doctors, lawyers, and instructors. Providing "gray" services may conflict with the law (for example, showing favoritism in school admissions) or with certain regulations (such as finding a bed in a "special hospital").

Nevertheless, the most unpleasant and repulsive aspect of this matter is not the material application of the principles of "You scratch my back, and I'll scratch yours," but rather its introduction into the moral and psychological realm as both incentive and standard behavior (in the form of the spiritual poverty increasingly becoming a burden for mankind).

Here we have already touched on the subject of the "pink market." By this we mean the establishment of supply priorities for certain segments of the public and residents of certain locales. This is the order system at factories, the system of special distribution outlets for elite employees, and the unevenness of the distribution of consumer goods by regions. The problem is not only that the existence of such "pink markets" (which are justified by the need to maximize the output of leading groups of workers or industries under conditions of scarcity) has created conditions allowing the leakage of scarce goods to the black market. Their existence, by giving certain groups the right to possess scarce, high-quality goods, also sets a precedent both for the unjustified expansion of special distribution systems (let us use the example of Kazakhstan, where up to 30 percent of meat and meat products have gone to illegally organized distribution outlets) and for persons who have access to scarce goods because of their occupations. In addition, the multiplicity of official markets leads to a situation in which the less well-off segments of the public are forced to go to the "commercial" markets (farmers' markets, coop markets), while the better-off segments are able to buy goods at low, subsidized prices through a system of special orders.

Haulers

A great deal has been written regarding the haulers, about both what they haul and from where they haul it. There has even been a description of a city, Michurinsk, whose residents practically all lived on the money they made from what they carried off.

Such massive operations by haulers are good in that one cannot help but notice them, and thus one cannot help but reduce them. More dangerous is the quiet hauler who works steadily, one step at a time, and who sells exclusively to a reliable clientele.

It would seem that any one particular hauler could do very little harm, but that's only the way it seems. Despite the formal crackdown, the number of haulers has not decreased: At a number of food-processing plants every third worker has been detained during inspections. Put together they constitute a major force and a well-established channel of the black market. Isak, a mechanic at the Kalev confectionery in Tallinn, was caught red-handed committing petty theft. A search turned up a total of 100,000 rubles (retail value) worth of such stolen goods as cognac, liquor, chewing gum, and chocolate.

The practice of "retail" law (with punishments as severe as the death penalty) has proved that there has been no radical improvement in the situation (let us also remember the press articles on the situation in Rostov-on-the-Don after the notorious "Rostov case"). Consequently we have to get at the root of the problem.

What Can Be Done?

The black market has had many negative consequences in the economic, social, and moral realms. Hence it is understood that one of the results of the current reforms must be the disappearance of this phenomenon from our lives.

One of the most important directions of the reform is providing more goods and services for the market by expanding production, radically improving quality, and becoming consumer-oriented. Reform of the consumer goods sector is a top priority. The first steps have already been taken in agriculture, light industry, retail trade, and services. But it is still too early to talk about noticeable improvements. We need to take additional steps: limiting administrative methods of controlling businesses in this sector, switching to wholesale trade in capital goods, and eliminating elements of monopolism.

The goal of eliminating the monopoly of the producer and strengthening the influence of the consumer on the formulation of production programs and the amount, quality, and variety of products will also be furthered by the development of individual labor and new forms of cooperation in services, public dining, and the production of goods from the wastes of large-scale production. These kinds of activity should be encouraged not just because they will "plug the gaps" that government-owned enterprises and organizations cannot fill, but primarily because this way of organizing labor and production is quite efficient in a number of consumer goods and service sectors. They should be able to offer real competition to government-owned operations in meeting the needs of the public.

We must use price formation both to stimulate the production of goods that best meet the demands of the public and to apply economic sanctions against the production of unnecessary goods. A comprehensive reform of retail prices will be required to solve these problems. This issue was considered at the June 1987 *plenum* of the Central Committee.

Retail price reform will make it possible to eliminate the black market, because it should establish a stable relationship between monetary income, public demand, and their consumption equivalent. The economic foundations of speculation will be undermined, such motives for theft and "hauling" as the lack of goods for sale will be weakened, and the multiplicity of consumer markets which makes it possible to manipulate shortages will be eliminated.

It would be worth examining the subject of eliminating the numerous official consumer markets, particularly the special distribution outlets. Abolition of the inherent privileges of elite employees should be compensated by a corresponding increase in their salaries, but of course this increase should be linked to the functions actually performed by these administrators.

True, getting more than merely verbal participation of the workers in managing their enterprises would be an effective way of combating "hauling." A sense of ownership will not appear, regardless of how many times we call for it, outside of its vital context.

The most important aspect of these and all other similar steps is the legalization of truly economic methods of management, which will make it possible to eliminate the "shadow" economy, including the black market in consumer goods.

11

New Worries

Nikolai Shmelyov

Novy Mir, no. 4, April 1988

Approximately one year after his first devastating critique of the Soviet economy (Document #5), Shmelyov presented another influential article, "New Worries," summarizing the successes and failures of *perestroika*. Shmelyov believes that the Soviet economy is at an impasse and that supporters of reforms are under attack.

In this article, Shmelyov provides a more incisive analysis of the progress of reforms than Mikhail Gorbachev has delivered in his speeches. In fact, the article is a severe criticism of Gorbachev's inability to put local leaders in line and to establish control over the central ministries. He argues that initiatives like the state contracts have become a farce and that bureaucrats have sabotaged the 1988 Law on State Enterprises. According to Shmelyov, party and state management represent both hidden and open resistance to *perestroika*. Many provincial and district officials oppose giving land to peasants. Party and state bureaucrats have also interfered with the growth of ITD (Individual Work Initiative) and cooperatives.

Shmelyov advocates dramatically increasing imports of consumer goods and believes that the goods shortage is so critical that gold reserves should be sold to pay for imports. He argues that unless dramatic changes are introduced and effectively implemented the nation will be "left on the curbside of history."

As it becomes more evident that restructuring of our social life is by no means a momentary, tactical maneuver, that it is serious, concern for its fate increases. Today there is concern among the most active part of our population, and there is a definite lack of faith among the masses. On the one hand, they fear that attempts to revitalize the political and socioeconomic life of our country will, in the end, turn out to be insincere; on the other hand, they fear the possible social consequences of *perestroika*.

A series of recently aggravated negative influences cause particular concern.

First, it is impossible not to see that a more open opposition to *perestroika* is growing in the districts and in the provinces among many local party, soviet, and economic organizations. It is also becoming obvious that many central ministries which claim to support *perestroika* are trying to cripple it. Attempts to use administrative methods to paralyze implementation of the Central Committee's line of full *khozraschet*, independence, self-compensation, and self-financing of enterprises have also become more obvious.[1]

A thought suggests itself: A kind of quiet conspiracy against *perestroika* has been established, in which the interests of a certain part of the local leadership and central ministries are drawn together. Especially worrisome is the fact that the positions of several leading periodicals actually support this opposition, sometimes by not speaking out against it. As our famous publicist Ivan Vasiliev noted, "A really worrying situation is emerging in society. A colossal administrative pyramid, which has been attacked with increasing forcefulness by the masses who are being roused to action, is shifting from its initial disorder to a counteroffensive" (*Sovetskaya Rossiya*, April 10, 1987).

Second, acceleration has been achieved largely through growth in the production of unnecessary goods. In the words of the author of the article entitled "The Soviet Economy at a Turning Point," published in the journal *Kommunist* (1987, no. 12), in the 12th Five-Year Plan "the planned growth for many types of production was higher than real demand." Really, it was growth without analysis, growth in the production of everything, growth for the sake of growth. Is that really what we need today?

Meanwhile the situation of many industrial enterprises has noticeably deteriorated, as they find themselves crushed between two mutually exclusive demands. On the one hand they must stress output (really, goods production) regardless of everything, and on the other hand they must

---

[1] *Khozraschet*, or cost-accounting, refers to a system in which economic enterprises are evaluated in terms of their net earnings rather than their gross output. "Self-financing," the most far-reaching form of financial autonomy, requires enterprises to cover all of their costs out of receipts and permits them autonomy in the distribution or reinvestment of profits. The 1988 Law on State Enterprises attempts to convert Soviet economic enterprises to a system of self-financing.

adjust the enterprise to Gospriemka[2] and ensure the high quality to which they are still unaccustomed. This has created a bad series of mutually defeating situations as enterprises have not been resupplied with the necessary amounts of manufactured goods and have been unable to fulfill their delivery obligations to the consumers of their own products. Results for those enterprises that converted to self-financing in 1987 are scarcely better; in fact, in some places, they have been worse than before. These factories went into a fever; idle time increased, wages declined, and the voices of both directors and workers called for the return of a "firm hand." At the same time unsold stocks of products that no one needs have begun to grow again, only now they are not only a few popular consumption goods, but also such means of production as tractors and combines.

Third, a growing number of people believe that the situation in the market of foodstuffs and general consumption goods has not only not improved, but has become even worse. This is perhaps connected with rising expectations. As before, there are lines in stores and empty shelves. There has been an insignificant increase in the state production of resources, the quality of domestic consumer goods is unchanged, and imports of even such goods of primary necessity as tea and coffee have noticeably declined.

Fourth, fears that few of the proposed economic measures would directly affect the social sphere are gaining strength among the public.

Fifth, our recent successes and failures in the struggle against the real national tragedy of alcoholism have attracted heightened attention.

Although we have made definite progress in this struggle, particularly in the decline of industrial accidents and "drunken" crimes, it is impossible not to see that this is only the beginning. Overall, the first stage of this struggle has gone successfully. But there are concerns that alcoholism is beginning to adapt to the new conditions and today is taking a new, more hideous form, that of the

---

[2] Gospriemka is the State Quality Control body, introduced in 1987.

consumption of chemical and cleaning solutions and other toxins.

Administrative measures in the struggle against alcoholism have apparently already accomplished all that they can. The struggle has entered a new stage, and it is important not to overlook this change. Today it is necessary to move the struggle onto the economic and social planes. Many are disappointed with the ineffectiveness of the measures that have already been taken. It must be asked: What did we expect? Did we really believe in quick results? The population's drinking habits have not changed in sixty years. Can we really hope to break down, in two years, the existing psychology and life-style of the entire people?

According to my evaluation, if at the beginning of the 1980s the government received two thirds of the receipts from the sale of alcohol and the *samogon* producers received one third, then today, given the same general per capita level of alcohol consumption, we have managed to directly invert this proportion. But, having given up the income from alcohol to the *samogon* producers, over the past two years the government has run up a budgetary imbalance. Today this budget deficit is financed by such highly dangerous and unhealthy means as the printing press.

One should emphasize that, speaking from a purely financial point of view, such an absurdity—to actually and voluntarily give up legal state income to the *samogon* producers—has happened only a few times in history, beginning with the ancient Mesopotamian state of Sumer. For America, in particular, the dry law was a moral experiment that ended in total failure after having damaged the profits of the private companies that had produced alcohol. Excise taxes on alcohol played a relatively small role in the American federal budget at that time.

It is reassuring, however, that credit for the new course among the people, and particularly among the intelligentsia, is still generally quite high. But when we take into account that the policy of *perestroika* began more than two years ago, the question of how long this credit will last naturally arises. Apparently, we can expect that sometime after two years there will be a reversal in the mood of the masses and a display of disappointment, apathy, and increasing distrust in the planned course.

We need a visible success, not "sometime" but in the near future. We could have achieved this success last year had not the conscious or subconscious opposition (both types have the same impact) to *perestroika*, especially in the countryside, paralyzed such a possibility. If we do not succeed in achieving something substantial in the next two years, we can expect that the future of *perestroika* will be threatened.

It seems to me that we now must take a series of decisive steps inside the country which, in aggregate, could have a positive effect and could reinforce the population's faith that *perestroika* is both justified and beneficial.

I think that several strong actions are absolutely necessary to break down the increasingly popular belief that the localities are stronger than Moscow and that some central ministries are now stronger than the Central Committee of the CPSU.

The crisis in our agricultural economy is obvious to everyone. The reasons for this condition do not lie in insufficient capital investment. Over the last fifteen years, more than enough capital investment has been directed toward agriculture, but it has not really accomplished anything. This current crisis is our return for over five years of violence against common sense and against everything that compels an individual to perform normal and conscientious labor. Today few doubt that the basic reason for the disastrous condition of our agricultural economy lies in the undivided power of the bureaucracy over everyone who lives in the countryside.

We cannot continue to be indifferent to the fact that several ministries use administrative instructions to inhibit reform. Before we can resolve the main questions about what would be the most expedient number of ministries, the proper size of their staffs, and the limits of their competency, we must publicly point out the antistate character of these ministries. Some set norms of 90 percent deductions from enterprise profits for their own use and impede the right of enterprises to distribute their own funds. We cannot underrate the political significance of the high leadership's interference in this area, even if it is reduced to only a few instances. Both the workers and the ministerial apparatus must know that the strength here lies not in the "bureaucratic swamp" but in *perestroika* and the central leadership organs.

Theoretically, after January 1 of this year [1988], roughly 60 percent of all industrial production should be produced on the basis of full *khozraschet*, according to the new Law on State Enterprises. This, of course, is a good and just law. But what is left of it in practice today? Will the fact that only a little bit remains not undermine the faith of enterprise directors and labor collectives in *perestroika* and real *khozraschet*? We are all tired of good papers and good words. Today, only actions mean anything.

Of course, as long as price reform is not being implemented, it would be unrealistic, for example, to count on the introduction of a single tax on profits throughout industry; that is, a single norm for deductions from enterprise profits for the budget and the use of ministries. But is that really grounds to take more than 90 percent of the profits from enterprises, as is now done in light and foodstuff industries? What kind of political, economic, and simply human right do the responsible ministries have to do that? Are we again taking from those who work well, in order to support those who do not? And the budget? Light and foodstuff industries secure the budget's income anyway, through turnover taxes. And if working well and working badly are all the same, then what kind of independence and initiative, what kind of stimulation of entrepreneurship, what kind of quality and technical progress, and, finally, what kind of struggle on behalf of the consumer can we expect?

Today, too much of *perestroika* depends not only on economic factors, but also on the psychology of those who are in charge of restructuring and of those toward whom it is directed. Without decisiveness and a fierce struggle we will not overcome the bureaucratism that Mikhail Gorbachev recently and justly called "the most evil and dangerous enemy of revolutionary *perestroika*."

One of the most serious questions concerning our current economic situation is where to get the money for *perestroika*. Traditional budgetary means are apparently insufficient, even if we decide to liquidate today's gaps in the budget (and we must liquidate them). We need new, nontraditional sources of financing.

The possibility of a real reduction in military expenditures is a question independent of this discussion. Here, I would want to draw attention to two other poorly used, but potentially significant, sources of financing.

We have an extremely underdeveloped internal credit market. The savings that we have in our country are insufficiently exploited for productive purposes. About 260 billion rubles are kept in savings banks, and that is a lot compared to the existing mass of commodities. These savings weigh on the market and intensify the problem of goods hunger in the country. In the long run, we must put them to work (without the threat of their owners withdrawing them if they change their minds) financing the investment needs of the country. But we can do this only if clear and tangible profits from these funds are secured for their owners. In this case, it is advisable to remember that much of the population's money is kept not in savings banks but in stockings.

If we permit enterprises to issue and sell and we allow people to buy stocks and bonds with a high rate of return, then industrial associations, collectives, and state farms will be able to mobilize tens of billions of rubles to supplement their own resources. Many potential creditors will willingly put their funds into circulation for a high return (7 to 10 percent). In the political sense that return will, in principle, be no different from that which any depositor in a savings bank receives.

In almost every country of the world, including socialist ones, normal credit (that is, credit repayable according to commercial principles) long ago became a powerful driving force of the economy. In this, we are still in infancy. Why, for example, can enterprises not provide their available means of production to each other on credit? Why can cooperatives not form a bank? Why does the government, which pays such low rates on the people's deposits in savings banks, more readily encourage people to waste their income than to save it? Today, hardly anyone can give an intelligent answer to these questions.

Another source of financing is long-term external borrowing. Our net debt at the beginning of 1987 is, by Western evaluations, at a level of slightly over $20 billion. In regard to our volume of external per capita borrowing, we are noticeably behind all the European socialist countries. In general, our position in the world, taking into account all types and all geographic orientations of borrowing, is still the position of a creditor, not a debtor.

In international practice the growth of external borrowing, as long as it does not exceed determined limits, is regarded as an absolutely normal phenomenon. Moreover, for many countries, growth in borrowing is characteristic of precisely those historical periods during which a radical structural reform of their economies is under way.

Apparently, we could borrow several tens of billions of dollars on the international credit market in the near future and remain solvent; that is, we could stay within the danger limits. It stands to reason that most of the money borrowed for the long term should be set aside for the purchase of advanced imported equipment for the organization of export production in machine construction and other promising branches of industry, so that after five to seven years we could begin to use these products to repay the credit that we have received. We must not repeat the error of the 1970s, when a noticeable portion of long-term foreign credits was actually spent on food. These long-term credits could also be converted into stocks and bonds of joint enterprises (given that we will make the required efforts). This has already become a widespread international practice, and we ought not to be left by the wayside.

It is impossible not to see that economic reform is only a part, and maybe not even the most important part, of all the problems of *perestroika*. It has already been emphasized several times from high places that the economic reforms of the 1950s and 1960s were choked because the political structure of society did not change. Today, we fully realize the need for democratization, *glasnost*, and the development of social initiative. But it seems to me that the moral atmosphere of the country is equally important. This is an inexhaustible theme. Here, I want to emphasize only two things. First, we must teach our people to understand that everything that is economically inefficient is immoral, as well as the reverse—that efficiency is morality. I am deeply convinced that the economically inefficient situation of general deficit is the fundamental reason for theft, bribery, and double-dyed bureaucratism, for every kind of secret, immoral lie, and for human maliciousness. The economically inefficient and wasteful mechanism of planning has engendered a thoughtless plundering of our national resources, while an amoral attitude toward our natural wealth and the absence of rent payments for land and water have led to such wild consequences as the degradation of entire regions of the country (for example, the Aral region). The economically inefficient containment of the activity and entrepreneurship of the population, *uravnilovka* [excessive wage leveling] in production, and a prolonged campaign against all forms of individual and cooperative labor—these, I am sure, are the main reasons for the increase in such social problems as idleness and drunkenness, which threaten our national future.

Second, I am convinced that the main moral flaw of the "administrative economy" is a blind and burning envy of one's neighbor's successes. This envy, found on nearly all levels, is the strongest brake on the ideas and practices of *perestroika*. And as long as we do not choke this envy, the success of *perestroika* will always be in doubt.

A revolutionary situation has truly been created in our country. The "heights" can no longer rule, and the "lower parts" do not want to live as before. But a revolution means a revolution. We have already embarked on its path. The decisions of the June *plenum* of the Central Committee CPSU truly have potentially revolutionary significance for the fate of our country. But a revolution from above is by no means easier than a revolution from below. Like any revolution, its success depends above all on the tenacity and resoluteness of the revolutionary forces and their ability to break down an opposition that has outlived the mood and structure of society.

Bibliography

Druzenko, Anatoly. "Transformation of the Apparatus." *Izvestiya*, April 4, 1988.
A scathing criticism of the bureaucracy and the ministries.

Kuzmin, A. "Wounded Roots." *Novy Mir*, no. 3, 1988.
A desperate cry to prevent the disappearance of small villages.

Selyunin, Vasily, and Khanin, Grigory. "Do Statistics Know Everything?" *Novy Mir*, no. 12, December 1987.
The writers argue that official statistics continue to provide Soviet policymakers with an unrealistic portrayal of economic problems such as inadequate housing and inflation.

Semyonov, B. "Plan and Spontaneity." *Novy Mir*, no. 12, 1987.
Semyonov argues that the central planning system has developed a "dictatorial" character, resulting in numerous economic problems.

Simonyan, R. "Corporation: From Needle to Missile." *Sotsialisticheskaya Industriya*, January 8, 1988.
An analysis of the advantages of American corporations as compared to the Soviet ministries.

Slutsky, Anatoly. "The Peasant from Arkhangelsk." *Literaturnaya Rossiya*, April 29, 1988.
A persuasive conservative argument against transforming Soviet villages into individual farms.

Totsky, Ivan. "Land Near the House." *Pravda*, May 5, 1988.
Discusses the decline of private plots under Brezhnev.

Vitaliev, V. "Without Ruble and without Shop Windows." *Krokodil*, no. 6, February 1988.
This criticizes the special *beryozka* stores, which sell high-quality goods to foreigners while Soviet stores are barren.

During the course of the reforms it
may be necessary for us to go beyond
the strictures of the one-party system.

Yuri Afanasiev

Chapter Three

Unofficial Groups and
Soviet Youth

Environmental activists demanding justice, screaming rock fans
seeking a social reformation, and right-wing groups fighting liberal-
democratic groups for their political-ideological place: these are all a
part of the winds of change sweeping through Mikhail Gorbachev's
Russia. The freshest breeze in recent times is the burgeoning of more
than 30,000 "informal" groups. Informal groups, organizations outside
of the formal structure of the Communist party, represent the hopes of
reformers, average citizens, and Soviet youth. As the articles in this
section indicate, however, with these hopes comes the fear that a
conservative backlash and the appearance of groups like Pamyat will
diminish rather than expand freedom in the USSR.

The first informal groups appeared in the 1970s. They consisted
primarily of sports fans, bodybuilders, rock music lovers, and people
studying yoga. In the 1980s reformers have legitimized unofficial
associations under the banner of "socialist pluralism," a theory which
states that various opinions and organizations are permitted to flourish
under socialism, so long as group members acknowledge the leading
role of the Communist party.

Gorbachev and his supporters understand that they must enlist
the average Soviet citizen in the battle against the regional party
bureaucracy and middle management. In the short term, together with
glasnost in the media, the unofficial groups distract people from the
country's intractable economic problems. In the long term informal
groups can serve Gorbachev's aims by counterbalancing the
pervasive conservative traditions of Soviet society. Political and
economic reforms cannot be achieved without citizen support. But
when, for example, Gorbachev urged a group of citizens in Kiev to
fight against local politicians, an old woman responded with the
consensus of the crowd: "People are still afraid."[1]

---

[1]"A Rude Dose of Reality for Gorbachev," *New York Times*, February
21, 1989.

To engage in public demonstrations and other protest activities, the informal groups must overcome considerable resistance by party and state officials. Local authorities in cities all across the nation do not yet accept *glasnost*. After years of breaking up protests and arresting demonstrations, provincial leaders need to learn tolerance. Local authorities are waging a relentless war of attrition against the entire unofficial movement. Petty harassment and impeding job advancement are two of the many tools at the disposal of officials. Militiamen (local police forces) often permit or refuse to permit demonstrations, depending on the political orientation of the informal group. According to *Moscow News*, Moscow authorities refused to allow 644 demonstrations to take place during the first eleven months of 1988.[2]

Three major factors have given rise to the informal movement during Gorbachev's tenure. First, under Brezhnev, Yuri Andropov, and Konstantin Chernenko, the party leadership neglected serious ecological concerns. Industrial development has led to such extreme cumulative pollution of air and water that many people have been forced to leave their homes. The industrial pollution in Nizhni Tagil (see Document #12) has been blamed for miscarriages and other medical problems.

The central press generally supported environmental issues even in the years before *glasnost*; the apolitical nature of environmental awareness gave legitimacy to the protests. In the 1970s party bureaucrats disregarded the criticism of Soviet writers and built paper mills that polluted Lake Baikal, the largest freshwater lake in Eurasia. Although the bureaucrats won the battle, the writers correctly predicted the ultimately catastrophic results of industrial overdevelopment.

Second, the official Communist youth group (Komsomol) and other official Soviet organizations have been thoroughly discredited in the eyes of Soviet youth. Gorbachev supporters realize that, to promulgate deep-rooted reforms, they must change the attitudes of the younger generation. The Komsomol (ages fourteen to twenty-eight) has experienced difficulties in the era of *glasnost*. Komsomol membership has declined by more than four million between 1985 and 1988, both as a protest against official strictures and because there is less pressure exerted on youth to join the organization.[3] A dramatic critique of the Komsomol appeared in Mikhail Shatrov's play *Dictatorship of Conscience*. Komsomol members are portrayed as hypocrites who say whatever is necessary to please their superiors. Moreover, Komsomol members in the play not only smoke marijuana

---

[2]Natalya Gevorkyan, "644 Unsanctioned Attempts to Hold Rallies or Demonstrations," *Moscow News*, no. 46, November 27, 1988.

[3]*New York Times*, February 7, 1988.

and shoot up heroin, but also nearly gang rape a young woman. Articles have appeared arguing that the organizational framework of the Komsomol encourages the rise of "careerists"—future conservative bureaucrats.

To combat declining membership, some leading reformers have encouraged Komsomol leaders to organize rock festivals and to support the growing environmental movement. *Komsomolskaya Pravda* (Document #12) noted with surprise and approval that local Komsomol leaders organized protests of more than 10,000 young people against air pollution in Nizhni Tagil. Komsomol groups are trying to find their place alongside the informal movement. As sociologist Mikhail Malyutin points out, Soviet young people disappointed with official ideology are taking initiatives. He notes that "in many large cities, 30 to 40 percent of youth belong to informal groups; it's becoming prestigious to be an informal."[4]

The third major reason for the rise of informal groups is that, under the newly liberalized conditions, people may now organize without so much fear of repression. Tens of thousands of people mobilized by their convictions contradict the traditional notion that the Soviet people are inherently docile and apathetic. The group Memorial, first organized by prominent intellectuals, is dedicated to commemorating the victims of Stalin's repression. The bureaucratic obstacles inhibiting Memorial's attempt to build a museum and research center have come to symbolize the difficulties of political change.

Organizations fighting for the environment and the preservation of historical monuments are one distinct category of informal groups. Many individuals belong to both causes, indicating the symbiotic relationship between protecting the past and ensuring the future. In 1986 the nuclear power plant disaster at Chernobyl proved to the Soviet public that party officials could not be trusted to protect the environment. The explosion also demonstrated the limits of man's control over nuclear power and led to increased press freedom to cover the environment. In the wake of Chernobyl, *glasnost* provided the impetus for the first concrete example of public opinion changing a political decision in the Soviet Union. A national protest movement brought about cancellation of a proposed project to divert the northern rivers to the southern regions. Conservative intellectuals and environmentalists successfully argued that such a massive redirection of water could lead to an ecological nightmare.

The most prominent figure in the fight for the environment and the preservation of historic monuments is the renowned linguist and academician Dmitry Likhachev, who serves as chairman of the Soviet Cultural Foundation and enjoys the support of Raisa Gorbachev.

---

[4]Mikhail Malyutin, "Informal Groups and Restructuring: Experience and Perspectives," *Inovo Ne Dano* [There is no other way], 1988.

Likhachev revealed the attempted cover-up of the 1988 fire in the Leningrad Library of the Academy of Sciences. This blaze destroyed tens of thousands of historically valuable books and became a rallying cry against bureaucratic neglect of the artifacts of Russian art and culture.

Another type of informal organization, represented by the group Pamyat and its fraternal organizations Motherland, Fatherland, Young Russia, and Patriot, is inspired by Russian nationalist fervor. Pamyat was originally founded to preserve monuments in the Russian republic, but it quietly evolved into an outlet for right-wing nationalism. Pamyat's creed of protecting the Russian people struck a responsive chord among influential party officials who are disturbed that the Russian republic is poorer than the republics of Transcaucasia and the Baltic region.

Pamyat arose as an extreme reaction against the nationalism of other Soviet peoples. The group employs nationalistic and anti-Semitic slogans that exploit the official Soviet propaganda about the state of Israel and the emigration of Soviet Jews. Pamyat bases its philosophy on an extremist interpretation of nineteenth-century Slavophile literature. In essence, the group blames Russia's ills on the introduction of Marxism and other Western influences.

The group originally received positive press coverage for its efforts to protect national monuments. But, by 1987, Pamyat began to be vilified in the press. The group's appeal is considered a special threat because chauvinism, xenophobia, and anti-Semitism have long been dangerous and powerful influences in Russia. Pamyat especially frightens Jews, the Baltic peoples, and other minorities. The Pamyat manifesto released in 1989 blames Jews and homosexuals for many of Russia's problems, criticizes the Western orientation of Soviet foreign policy under Gorbachev, and complains about the lack of Russian representation in the government and culture, although the Politburo is predominately composed of ethnic Russians.[5] Oddly enough, Gorbachev has not mentioned Pamyat in his numerous speeches. Citing freedom of speech, the militiamen do not interfere with the group's demonstrations and meetings. There is some sympathy toward Pamyat among party officials and the military.

Yet another type of informal group has a distinctly different political orientation. Press articles vehemently attack these groups for their radical political demands and for their alleged contact with Western media. Some observers believe that these groups damage their own cause by making unrealistic political demands that provide conservatives with ammunition to attack Gorbachev and *glasnost.*

---

[5]"Russian Nationalists' Manifesto Assails the West," *Washington Post,* February 19, 1989.

The press regularly castigates the Democratic Union, a coalition of political groups which seeks to become a political party. A May 1988 article in *Moskovskaya Pravda* applauded informal groups that "oppose the forces of inertia and bureaucracy" but argued that the Democratic Union "is our ideological adversary."[6] In another article, the military newspaper *Krasnaya Zvezda* questioned aspects of the unofficial movement in general and excoriated the Democratic Union in particular for opposing "military-patriotic education."[7]

Sergei Grigoryants, a former political prisoner released in an amnesty proclaimed by Gorbachev, publishes the independent journal *Glasnost*, which reports on human rights abuses and news like the ethnic riots in Armenia and Azerbaijan. Authorities frequently harass Grigoryants and on several occasions have confiscated his printing press and returned it in damaged condition. Under previous regimes, however, the government would have imprisoned him for his activities and would not have permitted him to continue publishing.

Rock music fans formed their own informal groups in the days before *glasnost*. But the musicians did not fare well in establishing their careers in those days, primarily because conservatives viewed rock music as a corrupting Western influence on youth. The intolerance to rock which still permeates Soviet society is concentrated in members of the older generation, especially war veterans, who become incensed at the sight of unorthodox behavior. V. S. Ovchinsky notes (in Document #14) that one can still hear statements such as: "Today you listen to rock, tomorrow you will betray your motherland."

Soviet rock musicians and their fans believe that they are experiencing what American youth lived through in the 1960s, proving that social and cultural changes never bypass Russia but merely lag a decade or two behind the West. This idea is reflected in the lyrics of a song by the popular Leningrad group Alisa. In the movie *Burglar*, Alisa's lead singer, Kostya Kinchev, plays a disaffected rock performer disturbed by family difficulties. The film features Alisa's song "My Generation" (the title of a Who song in the 1960s), which pointedly criticizes Soviet youth for its lack of courage:

My generation is silent in the corner
My generation is feeling death
My generation is feeling pain
My generation looks down
My generation is afraid of the day.

---

[6]Yu Shabanov, *Moskovskaya Pravda*, May 14, 1988.

[7]Lt. Col. V. Kosarev, "Social Viewpoint: Informal Groups—Who Are They?" *Krasnaya Zvezda*, January 21, 1989.

Rock groups have attained semiofficial status due to the new tolerance of some state and party officials. Communist party officials who sincerely favor reform understand the larger implications of youth involvement with rock music. They recognize the parallels between rock and the rapid transformation Soviet society is undergoing. And, most important for reformers, rock represents a rejection of the past. Although for generational reasons Gorbachev's Politburo ally Alexander Yakovlev detests hard rock music, he still argues that "we must counter it with better music and songs that are more humanistic" rather than ban it.[8]

Only by transforming the attitudes of Soviet youth can Gorbachev and his allies initiate lasting reforms. The nonconformity rock music has long represented in the Soviet Union is transforming into a bold message for change in the lyrics of groups such as DDT and Alisa, as well as in films such as *Assa* and *Rock*. The aspirations of Soviet youth are evident, but it remains the reformers' task to activate this potential source of political support. The film *Assa* reflects this potential for youth activism, but the lyrics of the group Kino, with their emphasis on waiting for change, display ambivalence:

They demand our hearts
They demand our eyes
Change—we're waiting for change.

The environmental movement and rock songs criticizing political decisions such as the war in Afghanistan are just two manifestations of the growing political activity of the new generation. The majority of informal group members are between twenty-five and thirty years of age, and *glasnost* has provided them with the opportunity to express their dissatisfaction with Soviet society. Most important, the flourishing of the unofficial movement is an effective rejection of the official dogma that only one party, the Communist party, and its affiliate organizations represent all of the hopes and wishes of Soviet citizens. The existence of independent groups and youth involvement in politics can help in the battle to make *perestroika* irreversible.

An important element of the unofficial movement is located in the non-Russian republics, most notably Estonia and Lithuania, and it carries a political and distinctly nationalist imprint. The "national fronts" were ostensibly organized to defend Gorbachev's policy of *perestroika*, but they quickly turned into the most powerful political influence in the Baltic republics. The Popular Fronts in Estonia and Latvia and the Sajudis movement in Lithuania are taking part directly in

---

[8]"Moscow's Other Mastermind," *New York Times Magazine*, February 19, 1989.

political activities such as organizing protests for greater autonomy. For all practical purposes the national fronts are political parties, as they influence all spheres of life in the republics, they supported candidates for the people's deputies election in March 1989, and their work led to the proclamations of Latvian, Lithuanian, and Estonian as the official languages of their respective republics. The Russians living in these republics have organized, likely with the help of the KGB, their own informal groups (Unity in Lithuania and the International Front in Estonia).

The organizational skills that informal group members acquire and the support their activities generate within many segments of the Soviet population is leading them to a greater political role. The national fronts in the Baltic republics are prototypes of alternative political parties. The nationalist character of Pamyat parallels groups in other countries, such as the followers of Jean-Marie Le Pen in France. The anti-Semitic tendencies of Pamyat parallel the racism of the Ku Klux Klan. Similarly, some environmental groups in the Soviet Union now call themselves Greens, after the Green party in West Germany. Hungary, the most liberal and Western-oriented country in the Soviet bloc, has announced plans to permit by the mid-1990s a genuine multiparty system with a restricted role for the Communist party. While the changes taking place in the USSR are not developing as quickly as in Hungary, in the coming decade far greater pluralism within the Communist party may well occur as the seeds planted for a multiparty system take root.

12

Smog over the City

V. Sanatin

Komsomolskaya Pravda
April 6, 1988

Citizens in Nizhni Tagil, one of the country's major industrial centers, have organized to protest the health hazards of living in their city. Huge clouds of dust have filled the air with pollutants harsh enough to burn a child's face. In addition to pointing out Nizhni Tagil's alarming health situation, Sanatin notes a startling development: the organizing of the protest by the local Komsomol. In a rare event, the Komsomol leaders fought off interference from the local party leaders and industrial plant managers and organized the protest against their wishes.

Although Vadim Dudarenko, leader (first secretary) of the Nizhni Tagil Komsomol, showed courage and initiative in helping to organize the demonstration, he did not wish to antagonize the city's leaders. In major industrial towns the plant management is often a dominating political force that works with local party leaders to meet their productivity goals.

Ten thousand people demonstrated on the square and the Komsomol leaders were the organizers of the gathering.

Smog is a regular phenomenon for Nizhni Tagil, but this time a special misfortune befell. On the eve of the demonstration, the forecast reported no wind. This proved to be correct. The city was surrounded by an abundance of smog. Every hour, the smog thickened. Around dinner time, cars passing by the Nizhni Tagil Metallurgy Industrial Plant [NTMK] were forced to use their headlights. By evening the city was covered with a heavy, suffocating fog. The neighborhood of Dzerzhinsky suffered the most. The next morning, the Urals citizens experienced headaches and nausea. The influence of the damaging industrial waste accumulating in the air was so powerful that, on the way to kindergarten, children's faces were distinctively burned.

After a few days, when a mass of protests against the pollution had arisen in Nizhni Tagil, some doctors asserted that the local children suffer from fruit allergies because their parents overfeed them with oranges. Not believing my own ears, I went to every fruit market. As it turned out, I could not find even one orange and was told that "they are never sold."

Here are the statistics. In my possession I have one of the 150 copies of an informational bulletin distributed by the industrial-transportation department of the city committee of the CPSU. It states:

> Nizhni Tagil is among fifty cities in the USSR where the level of pollution exceeds the healthful norm. The main contributor to this pollution is the metallurgy industry. Their industrial waste totals over 629,000 tons a year. The industrial toxic waste from the complex Uralvagonzavod [railroad car plant] by itself is 18,600 tons a year. The waste of the cement plant equals 12,000 tons a year, and the waste of the copper-radiator plant is 10,700 tons a year.

The list goes on. There are countless enterprises in Nizhni Tagil, one of the largest industrial centers in the Sverdlovsk region. They are numerous enough even for a city of several million people. Nizhni Tagil could not sustain this enormous chemical pressure, and it suffocated. The dramatic events did not occur in one day. The quantity of dangerous toxic waste has been building up for a long time: 1.5 tons per citizen per year.

An explosion finally occurred, an explosion in the public conscience. Surprisingly, the city committee of the Komsomol turned out to be at the center of these events.

Soon after those dreadful and suffocating days the Komsomol organizers of the Uralvagonzavod, Viacheslav Ogarkov, Vadim Beloglazov, and others, appeared on the doorsteps of the city committee of the Komsomol. They were determined. "We propose to have a protest demonstration. We demand that the decision to arrange this demonstration be authorized by the bureau of the city committee of the Komsomol. The demonstration must be organized, and it must have detailed demands."

What should be demanded? The initiating group and the bureau of the city committee of the Komsomol answered this question immediately. The first demand was to close the first and the second coke units of the Nizhni Tagil Metallurgy Industrial Plant. Those units had served for forty-five years, or two and a half times their expected technological life span. They had served their time. The units were not equipped with contemporary technology for the dry extinguishment of coke, and they pollute the atmosphere by producing thousands of tons of toxic waste a year, most often in the form of benzene and carbon monoxide.

The administration of the metallurgy plant notes that the old coke units' production contributes only 1 percent of the damaging waste. Therefore, they say, there is no hurry to dismantle the coke plants. There is an odd contradiction in this argument. It is known that carbon monoxide is invisible, dangerous, and poisonous. It is two hundred times more active than oxygen. It combines with the hemoglobin in human blood to create a carboxyhemoglobin. This results in the organism starving for oxygen, causing irreversible change in the tissues of the blood vessels, heart, lungs, and brain. Consequently, anything can be expected: allergies, bronchial asthma, tachycardia, strokes, atherosclerosis, and insulin shock.

Before they dared to demonstrate and to demand the permission to do it from the bureau of the city committee of the Komsomol, the Komsomol organizers looked through tens of volumes of medical and chemical textbooks, dictionaries, and encyclopedias. They verified the well-known fact that to kill a living organism, a milligram of poison is enough. A civilized society, if it strives to flourish and not head toward destruction, needs to fight for every gram of clean air. Otherwise the future generations, with an asinine rather than a bureaucratic stupidity, will produce hundreds of thousands of tons of poison in hundreds of thousands of cubic meters of atmosphere, then happily applaud and shout, "There is PDK."

PDK is the limit for the allowed concentration of harmful substances in the air and in the water. It is inconceivable, but nonetheless a fact, that the administration of the unified industries known as Uralkhimplast [plant of chemical plastics], like little children, are delighted by the fact that they exceed PDK only by 4.5 times, unlike other cities which exceed it by 5 to 7 times. What a blasphemous celebration! The blind happiness of self-justification cannot understand that the first word in the abbreviation PDK is "limited." This is the critical difference, the boundary between the healthy and the sick, the living and the dying.

Some time ago, I had the privilege of participating in a festive celebration of the early opening of the ninth coke plant. I clearly remember the oath that the plant specialists and administration took. They vowed that this would be the first plant in the Soviet Union with ecologically clean coke production. That is hard to believe now.

The "harmlessness" of the ninth coke production plant was calculated in comparison with the amount of pollution per manufactured unit of the aged units. This picture appears to be acceptable: for every ton of production the waste would be reduced by half. Unfortunately, the specialists hid the other side of the story. The new plant, unlike the older version, would produce 1 million tons of coke a year, not 400,000 tons. In other words, the plant was designed to pollute the atmosphere with 3,500 tons of toxic waste. This waste is 500 tons more than that of the first and second plants combined. This is just according to the blueprint. Furthermore, the hundreds of large and small mistakes in the production of the unit resulted in the ninth coke plant producing twice the projected amount of toxic waste. The secretary of the party committee of the plant, Nikolai Sharov, was not himself during those days. The actions of the members of the Komsomol, including young workers of the plant, were considered by Sharov to be "sabotage." Unfortunately, Sharov obtained the letters of the second graders from School #55 of the Dzerzhinsky neighborhood. Enclosed were some drawings of smoking pipes and the smog that covered the whole city, with "I don't want to die!" written under the drawings. After seeing that, Nikolai Dmitrievich accused the Komsomol of all the deadly sins: instigation, provocation, and blackmail.

In the offices of the leading managers of the plant, a version of the socioeconomic "bankruptcy" of the huge enterprise was urgently being invented. Through the factory newspaper, the following statement was released:

> If the Ministry of Ferrous Metallurgy requires the new plant alone to complete the delivery of the coke and iron, after the closing of the two old plants the losses in

production would increase to 74 million rubles. The financial losses from employees' salaries would amount to 2.6 million rubles. The loss of profits would reach 33 million rubles, and the loss of funds for economical stimulation of up to 17 million rubles would result in irreparable material and social repercussions for several thousands of metallurgists.

As a result, if the workers of the city achieve the closing of the old plants, the metallurgy workers will not get paid, will have no retirement fund, will have nowhere to live, and will have no vacations. The newspaper article should have made the readers more nervous than the innocent drawings of the second graders. Why is there no mention in the article about the 260 million rubles of annual profits? That is an enormous sum! Who is in charge of that sum, when metallurgy workers have to wait for ten to fifteen years for a residence?

The local authorities attempted to stop the wave of protests against the pollution. Four days prior to the demonstration planned by the city committee of the Komsomol, workers of the Dzerzhinsky neighborhood were invited to the I. Okunev House of Culture, but an agreement was not reached. Half of the speakers began by addressing the problems of defending the environment, and instantly the subject was changed to the problems of public health services, leisure, tourism, and the supply of food to the city.

People assembled on the square between the local Komsomol office and the Sovremenik movie theater. Buses had been previously obtained by the organizers. The drivers of the buses disregarded orders from the administration and went to the Ural bus depot. They were told that this was a mistake. The administration of the bus depot ordered a general *subbotnik* [volunteer work] on the day of the meeting. Nevertheless, after lunch, the drivers left the depot on their own initiative and got on the designated buses.

On the square, the demonstrators were determined to unfold protest signs. Vadim Dudarenko got authorization for the texts of the signs from the city committee of the CPSU. In front of me, he called to the factory committee of Komsomol and dictated to them what should be done. Now looking at the signs instinctively, the tragedies and people's tears had to be divided between approved and disapproved texts. Towering above all the others was a sign that read, "What could you have done so there would be no smog?" Two huge steelworkers proudly carried signs, and a woman in tears literally tied a sign to herself that said, "Who is responsible for 54 miscarriages in 1987?" This question is still unanswered.

N. Duzenko, a war veteran, walked to the microphone on the tall steps of the movie theater and said,

> Dear comrades and members of the Komsomol! Thank you very much for today's meeting. Thank you for your courage and your ability to face the problem. We protested at other times, but we could never really criticize anything or anyone. At the tank armor produced by us we could hardly stand on our feet. If you scream, "Comrade, give me a light" and suddenly you see the comrade has been carried away, and next to you there is the chief engineer, giving you a light. At this meeting, for four hours we have been heard. Still, we have not heard from the leaders of our town. Not one of them has stepped in front of the microphone. Therefore, I will again ask, in front of all the people: Who are you, our ruling guard? Where are you? Why did you forget to "give us a light"?

It was apparent that Vadim Dudarenko, the first secretary of the city committee of the Komsomol, who had not stepped away from the speakers, was embarrassed. The meeting was not going according to the scenario. The speakers stubbornly contrasted the initiative of the members of the Komsomol to the behavior of the city leaders. The day before the event, Dudarenko had visited the city committee of the CPSU as well as its bureau. Their position had been strongly expressed: Anyone who is interested in learning the position of the city committee of the CPSU and of the executive committee of the City Soviet of People's Deputies must go to the Stroitel House of Culture. There, E. Sushilov, the first secretary of the city committee of the party, and V. Cherdyntsev, the chairman of the executive committee of the City Soviet of People's Deputies, would talk to them.

That day the theory of democracy of the pompous schoolteacher who claimed, "You are still too immature," was not functioning. At the meeting there were more than 10,000 people, from the cheerful fifth grader Andrei Zakoryuchkin, to senior citizens suffering from bronchial asthma.

At the meeting was everything from personal suffering to the pain felt for other people. To the surprise of the authorities, people were stubbornly uniting and reasoning together, compatibly and abundantly.

Boris Belous, who is a worker at the Uralvagonzavod, said,

> For me, today's meeting is a holiday. This meeting is the first piece of evidence that *perestroika* is occurring in my town. I suggest that we hold meetings like this every three months, right here, in front of the city committee of the Komsomol. I also suggest the creation of expert ecological groups, not just here, but in all industrial cities. Today, the leaders of the city did not step in front of the microphone, but I think that in their hearts they are with us. Therefore, I strongly hope that next time, not only the city committee of the Komsomol, but also the city committee of the CPSU will learn to answer to the people. Great thanks to the Komsomol for this brave step!

If Belous had only known whom to thank, he would have named the members of the bureau of the city committee, secretary Alexei Skomorokhov, secretary Alexander Kushkov, student Galina Ignatieva, and a member of the Central Committee of the Komsomol, steelworker Andrei Trubin.

Let's look at the results. Soon after the meeting, a second NTMK coke plant was stopped. An order for its stoppage was signed by the minister of the ferrous metals industry, Sergei Kolpakov, right on the spot in Nizhni Tagil. However, the first coke plant is still polluting the city.

Fortunately, after the meeting a new ecological commission was established. It includes the workers of the city committee and the district committee of the CPSU, public prosecutors, and an expert on the preservation of air and water purity. Vadim Dudarenko represents the Komsomol on the committee, but he is going to move to Sverdlovsk to work in the regional committee of the Komsomol. The demonstration's initiators, however, did not get to be in the committee. Furthermore, the administration completely disbanded the initiative group of the Uralvagonzavod. Natalya Ovcharenko, instructor for the plant committee of the Komsomol, was transferred as the technologist to the shop, and soon after that she left the plant.

An attempt has been made to slow down the ecological movement of the youth at the NTMK. Viacheslav Solovyev, an expert in fireproofing and until recently an active fighter against air pollution, told me while working at his coke plant that "it is said that there are no laws regarding an establishment of expert ecological groups among the workers. At least that is what our supervisors are telling us."

It became necessary to remind someone about the law concerning labor collectives, and also that Solovyev, himself, is the deputy of the city soviet.

The installation of the second plant and a discussion with V. Solovyev will occur later. Standing next to Vadim Dudarenko on the steps of the theater, I was joyful about an unusual event: In Nizhni Tagil, there was an organized ecological meeting. As provided for in the framework of the constitution, and as time has proven, democratic action is necessary for the sake of human development.

At the demonstration I bravely signed a petition to the Council of Ministers of the USSR on which, above my name, 85,000 people have also signed their names.

13

Pamyat and Others

Vladimir Petrov

Pravda, February 1, 1988

This article favors the overall growth of the unofficial movement but criticizes what the author considers to be extreme tendencies, specifically the Russian nationalist group Pamyat and Sergei Grigoryants's journal *Glasnost*. It contains many interesting details about Pamyat including its origin, the views of its leader, and the group's activities. Some would argue with Petrov's statement that Pamyat's anti-Semitic and chauvinist feelings are alien to Russia. The article, however, reveals that the group's leader, Dmitry Vasiliev, is allowed to visit factories and to speak with workers, which shows support for Pamyat within the Communist party. Party officials certainly could prevent any unofficial group from propagating its views in factories and certainly would not grant these privileges to Sergei Grigoryants.

The publication *Glasnost*, edited by Grigoryants, is often vilified in the official press, particularly for reporting on human rights abuses. This article shows that, despite improved relations with the West, the charge of Western connections sometimes still is employed as a smear tactic. Pamyat is the primary target of the article, and it is likely that Petrov criticized Grigoryants as well in large part to show balance. The article also raises a serious general question about *glasnost*: What limits, if any, should be placed on political viewpoints?

The radio station "Voice of America" recently drew its listeners' attention to the *Pravda* editorial "Democracy and Initiative" published on December 27, 1987. According to VOA, many American journalists saw the article as an attempt to limit and control those new, so-called informal (or more precisely, independent) groups and associations whose activities, "from the point of view of the party authorities," are reprehensible. Exactly which groups do they have in mind? We asked *Pravda* correspondents working in capitalist countries and heard the same names: "Pamyat," "*glasnost*," and several others.

But for now we will put VOA aside and turn to the judgment of our readers, to their voices, and to what is happening in our own country.

Here, the difficult work of *perestroika* is in progress. Many new things, including independent associations, are appearing in public life. These associations are beginning to play more active roles, and that is good. Here, we are talking about democratization and *glasnost*. We are aware of them in everyday life, and that is also good. But judging by the letters to the editor, people are beginning to be surprised that extremist speeches are being delivered in certain auditoriums and that nationalistic hostilities are being rekindled. And all of this appears under the guise of *glasnost*.

Such surprise and, at times, alarm is justified. What is the matter?

Today there are more than thirty thousand independent groups and associations in our country. We can examine their development only in the single stream of *perestroika*. In earlier years, any noticeable initiative had to undergo the scrutiny of the ministries before it could express itself in words and deeds; but now, after the April 1985 *plenum* of the Central Committee of the CPSU and the 27th Party Congress, everything has fundamentally changed. It is no accident that in various regions, especially the large urban centers, all kinds of social clubs, including youth groups, have appeared. They attract dynamic people who are excited by the changes taking place in our life. These people support restructuring with their knowledge, experience, and energy. Their opinions often become those of the public, and local and central organs of power are listening to them.

For example, it is a well-known fact that, despite the resistance and disapproval of certain distinguished officials, it was public alarm that motivated the decision to stop work on the diversion of part of the flow of the northern rivers. And there is this fact that *Pravda* has reported: For its subsidiary agricultural farm, the Tula collective's V. Riabnikov machine-building plant received the neglected lands of the state farm Kultura near the village of Plotnitsyno, where the remains of Leo Tolstoy's patrimonial estate are located. This was one of the great writer's favorite places, and it was here that he wrote many chapters of *War and Peace*. So the machine builders and the community of the Chernskii region together decided to restore the great author's home. They had to knock on the doors of many ministries, including the Gosplan of the USSR, and they had to secure the support of the academician Dmitry Likhachev.

In the end, thanks to the efforts of the enthusiasts who gave their free time to this restoration, our country was given yet another cultural center. The Children's Fund and the Cultural Fund, the upheavals over the monument on Poklonnaya Hill, the hostility toward drunkenness and bureaucracy, the military-patriotic and international clubs, the research groups who are adding new facts to the war chronicles, the organizations striving for the preservation of historical and cultural monuments, youth studios—this is, of course, a far-from-complete list of the positive developments in our country.

One can only be happy about this. Indeed, the main theme of *perestroika* is to give our lives more socialism and democracy. This means more initiative. It is well known that, above all, Lenin valued the initiative of the masses, the desire to perform revolutionary work, and that he taught people to foster change.

Nevertheless, why do the letters to the editor express such agitation? It would seem that people speaking aloud, openly, and without fear should be a welcome change. Instead, people display irritation. Why?

Though a definitive answer cannot be found, one conclusion can be made. The provinces and even the urban centers were poorly prepared, both practically and theoretically, to comprehend the explosion of societal activity. They are just now becoming accustomed to it, although they still find themselves believing that "something bad could happen" and have difficulty ridding themselves of the strict regimentation and petty control of initiative.

Today, we all study democracy. The party, the local soviet, and the Komsomol must profoundly explore the processes taking place at different levels of society. They are learning to respond quickly and efficiently to the mood of the people, neither fearing nor avoiding the new, but meeting it halfway. However, it is one thing to desire change in theory and quite another to accept it in actual practice, when life sometimes creates nontypical situations. For example, an independent club might criticize local shortcomings regarding the town's alarming ecological situation. What should be done here? Local leaders, relying on the strictures of the old thinking, frequently react prohibitively.

In one of his works Lenin observed that "there is nothing to fear from the people." What, then, motivates fear of the unusual and atypical? In this case it seems to occur not because of the groups and associations that pursue the useful work of *perestroika* without demagoguery, but because those groups with ambitions, aspirations, and hostility to Soviet power and party policy attract the attention of the public with the help of the mass media, including the foreign press. Whether purposely or not, these groups become the yardstick by which other associations are measured.

In general, passions are boiling over Pamyat. "White-hot" letters are still coming to the editor. Some believe that Pamyat preaches anti-Semitism and advocates "great-Russian chauvinism." Another opinion is: "We know the goals that Pamyat pursues. They are the preservation of cultural monuments and the struggle for sobriety. Stop persecuting Pamyat."

To better understand the situation, we should return to the days of Pamyat's emergence. Incidentally, what does emergence mean? After all, we aren't "Ivans" of unknown ancestry. Our memory preserves all that is dear to our people. To consign our history and cultural legacy to oblivion is impossible. This memory has always survived, and there have always been enthusiasts possessed (in the best sense of the word) by a concern for its preservation.

Sometime in the early 1980s, Moscow historians, scholars, engineers, workers, and students gathered under the auspices of the ministry of the aviation industry. Some chose not to remain, others joined and gathered to work. With shovels and trowels in hand, they helped to restore historic buildings. They spoke out far and wide for the protection of ancient and cultural monuments. They protested the demolition of a historic section of Moscow and sent letters about it to the responsible authorities. It cannot be said that people supported them in all they did, nor did their efforts receive the value they deserved, but one cannot deny that they acted honestly and unselfishly.

They were disturbed by the demographic situation in Russia and by the declaration that many Russian villages had no future, and they were grieved and angered by the plight of the nonblack-soil lands, which evoked their heartfelt protest.[1] These people are still alive and healthy. They regret that their Pamyat has now acquired a different reputation.

About two years ago radical changes took place. New people, very different than their predecessors, declared themselves to be the leaders of Pamyat. One cannot use another word: They stole it. This small extremist group, led by [Dmitry] Vasiliev, is acting in the name of Pamyat and has compromised it in everyone's eyes.

We do not always stop to think about the origins of the leaders of independent groups. Obviously, there are different paths. Life chooses some of them; others advance themselves as leaders and pursue various goals. Some suffer from the revenge syndrome, saying, "They didn't recognize my talents earlier, so now I'm getting back at my former 'persecutors' by making them talk about me." Others dream of becoming political authorities and "bravely" uncover those of society's shortcomings that our press has already loudly decried. But they all pretend to support *glasnost*.

Vasiliev, with his eighth-grade education, appears before audiences with his friends in various disguises. Those who have attended these meetings, such as the one at the Dynamo plant's House of Culture, have left feeling that they had been drowned in a stream of spiteful stories. Judge for yourself:

Scientists have established that there is 1.5 percent alcohol in kefir. That means that someone is benefiting by making our children accustomed to drink.

The year 1941 has come into our lives, and we are still scratching our heads.[2]

---

[1]The plight of the rural areas of central and northern Russia (nonblack-soil areas) is viewed by Russian nationalists as a sacrifice of the Russian people for the sake of the common welfare of the USSR.

[2] Pamyat mentions the year 1941 (when the USSR was attacked by Nazi Germany) as an indication that an invasion is now taking place in Russia, and it is necessary to organize resistance.

The metro lines are arranged so that one could easily blow up the most important government buildings.

A bar and grill was built on the premises of the old church on Khavskaya Street. In a short time a brothel will be opened, which will use our wives and daughters as prostitutes.

Pamyat's current leaders openly call for extremism. In their so-called "Appeal to the Russian People" we read: "Be brave in discovering and naming the hostile conspiratorial asylums. Look for and advance the true leaders in our midst. Conduct demonstrations and referenda throughout the country. Establish control over the mass media, expose the corrupt journalists and deal with them. The motherland is in danger!"

Who exactly threatens the motherland? Zionists and "cosmopolites," assert Vasiliev and his supporters, who are trying to arouse anti-Semitism in the Soviet people. However, anti-Semitism and chauvinism have always been alien to our people and to the very nature of socialism.

Is this ignorance or intentional incitement? These questions immediately arise: Whose interests do these people express? What idea do they serve, wrapping themselves in the flag of *perestroika*? Today honest people do not linger around Vasiliev and his associates. They listen for a while, then go away. Such thoughts have nothing in common with those with which the patriotic movement began.

Incidentally, we called V. Tolmachev, the vice president of VOOPIK (All-Union Society for the Preservation of Historical and Cultural Monuments), and asked if Vasiliev and his friends participate in work connected with the restoration of historical monuments. This is the reply we received:

"We do not have that information."

Readers may ask how the name of Pamyat became the hostage of a small group of people. The answer is not a simple one. The responsibility for this lies with the members of that society who said nothing when the "artist-photographer-journalist," as Vasiliev's friends sometimes introduce him, formed a self-styled council which elevated to the rank of president a man who is registered in the psychiatric hospital. Vasiliev likes to try to arouse interest in his own personality. For example, he likes to say that one day he, the warrior of *glasnost*, will be found with his skull split, and so he is forced to hide himself and disguise his appearance.

Of course, the problem is not solely with Vasiliev. There is another, more serious, concern. Because we do not wish to seem old-fashioned or supportive of the stagnant period, we have stopped calling things by their names. And this leads to no good. An extremist is an extremist. Some newspaper pieces have not only been unable to clarify the situation, they have confused things even more. The names of Russian and Soviet writers were used in some of Vasiliev's slogans, giving the impression that they were acting in concert with the extremists.

People feel that something is wrong, and they write about it in their letters to the editor. These letters are written not only by Russians, but by people of other nationalities. "Some of us have understood the development of democracy and *glasnost* as an opportunity for open attack on the achievements of socialism," observe Odessa party members V. Kurdyukov and B. Zlotko. "Vasiliev and his friends threaten that which is most sacred to us: revolution and the friendship of peoples."

"We have never experienced anything like this," reads a letter from I. Zhukov. "We do not need such openness and broadening of democracy. This is demagoguery and speculation under the guise of patriotism."

"It is perfectly clear," we read in letters from a group of authors, "that the activity of some people should be considered from the angle of criminal law. Why then, instead of making them account for their actions, are they amiably given conference halls in various cities?"

"The main tasks of this society are the preservation of historical and cultural monuments and the struggle for sobriety," writes seventeen-year-old A. Kunenkov. "That would be fine, but why do the people who act in its name love to chatter about *perestroika*? I think the phrase-mongers and chatterers should be turned out of Pamyat. Cleansing it of everything superfluous would only do good."

Here is a letter from Khabarovsk: "We are for memory. For the memory of Alexander Nevsky, Kuzma Minin, and Dmitry Pozharsky, Alexander Suvorov and Mikhail

Kutuzov, Mikhail Lomonosov, Pyotr Tchaikovsky, of those who gave their lives following Lenin in the war against czarism and brought the revolution. We are for the memory of those millions of Soviet people who gave their lives in the Great War of the Fatherland. So can we really allow the blackening of our memory, the mockery of the memory of our great ancestors and of the whole nation? A thousand times no!"

As has already been reported in the press, the workers of the Likhachev's auto plant in Moscow who met with Vasiliev expressed similar thoughts. Other readers suggest separating Pamyat from the small group of leaders who haven't the right to represent the organization. Readers advise party organizations and workers' collectives to act more vigorously against provocateurs. It is necessary to attract scholars and propagandists and to not avoid discussion.

Vasiliev is not the only one compromising the good, patriotic work of independent groups and associations in our country.

For some time, the West has admired the typewritten bulletin *Glasnost*. Sergei Grigoryants, who considers himself to be its "father," has recently been tried for crimes including anti-Soviet activity.[3] As we look through several issues, we are surprised to see that Western publications about human rights "violations" and "political prisoners" are known in the USSR. It is as if these bulletins are reprints from the Western press. For instance, it cries about the fate of a "prisoner of freedom" who is guilty of misappropriation of Soviet property or, more accurately, theft. The bulletin publishes an "open letter," ostensibly from unemployed Soviet citizens who have suffered because of their principles and their criticism of and struggle against the bureaucracy. But these "sufferers" are out-and-out loafers and destroyers of discipline.

For whose benefit is this bulletin published? A Western commentator gave a precise answer, calling it a

---

[3] Sergei Grigoryants, like many dissidents before him, was tried and sentenced for anti-Soviet propaganda.

supplement to the White newspaper *Ruskaya Mysl*.[4] And then, from an anti-Soviet center in Frankfort on the Main comes a letter: "Dear (space for name), If you need help, we will offer it without question. If problems arise, write or call. We would be happy to base our department in Moscow."

Recently, on lampposts, in dark alleys, and in mailboxes, Muscovites have been finding a four-page pamphlet signed by the seminar known as "Democracy and Humanism" calling on those who "support democratic reforms" to attend a demonstration. What is this seminar's goal? It does not accept the constitution of the USSR and demands its revision; it demands the abolition of the articles of criminal law that oblige Soviet citizens to work. In addition, this seminar calls for the complete de-ideologization of the USSR. And what does it propose? Its members say that the seventy-year path taken by the Soviet people has been wrong and that they must find a way out of this deadend. In the pamphlet, which was timed to coincide with the anniversary of the October Revolution, one reads: "The physical destruction of dissidents began in the first months after the October Revolution. Detachments were assigned to rob and kill peasants, to arrest and shoot striking workers. War Communism raged."

Nothing sacred to the people is truly sacred to these associations. True, they love to repeat the words "fatherland," "nation," *"perestroika."* They claim to stand for *glasnost* and for the people when, in fact, those are the very things they fear. So they hide in dark corners.

What exactly do they all want? Prompting comes from the West: You should unite, create a unified political platform, and seize the initiative. There have been attempts at unification, such as the events of August of last year. Of course, the organizers of the Social Initiatives club and other groups produced nothing. Their conference ended in scandal. Throughout, ambitions to "win first place" raged, as they tore the microphone from one another on stage. Even those who had been fascinated by their "idols" saw

---

[4] *Ruskaya Mysl* is a Russian-language newspaper published in Paris by Russian émigrés.

their true colors. One sober voice was heard to say, "They've fooled all of us."

Such deception has become the rule here. They are fooling each other and their listeners, who applaud the "revelations" of the fledgling leaders. They are deceiving their friends overseas by representing themselves as a political force. Alas, several foreign diplomats and journalists have swallowed their stories, even those who used to enjoy digging through trash cans. But, as is said, times change. Now those journalists and diplomats prefer various "seminars." About whom are we talking? The undersecretaries of the political department in the U.S. embassy in Moscow, Susan Wagner and Richard Stephenson, and the correspondents Hartwig Nathe and Kauffman from the DPA and Agence France-Presse respectively. We will not argue personal tastes here; we will only list these names by way of mention.

Several groups have been named here. It is possible that some have received the impression that the ranks of the enemies of our way of life and the anti-Soviets are growing. But that is not the case. Each of the groups mentioned above have about ten or fifteen members. One can add to that small number several citizens who call themselves representatives of the "Union of People's Workers" (NTS), with which these groups maintain a connection.

We would like to repeat that there are more than thirty thousand independent groups and associations in our country. The great majority of those support *perestroika* with their initiative, practical suggestions, just criticism, and hard work. But, as they say, our family is not without its political freaks. Should we close our eyes to them and pretend that nothing is happening? Readers justly think that our principles will guide us in judging the new, that we will recognize where there is genuine social activity in the interests of the Soviet people and where there are political extremism, affectation, petty-bourgeois tendencies, and anti-Sovietism.

We must use the energy of the independent groups for good works in the interest of our society. It is important to provide patriotic, international education and to show the propriety of our social ideals by using the strength of social opinion and, when necessary, the law.

As for the VOA's treatment of *Pravda*'s editorial, one would like to ask its contributors, "Why the sudden worry?" We are calmly putting our affairs in order, and no doubt we will see where unselfishness and provocation exist.

14

Rock: Music? Subculture? Life-style?

Editorial Roundtable Discussion

Sotsiologicheskie Issledovaniya
June 1987

In the years before *glasnost*, the press featured vitriolic attacks against the Western influence presented in rock music. Few attempted to analyze seriously the reasons for rock music's appeal to Soviet youth. This roundtable discussion published in the country's leading sociological research journal displays the higher level of debate rock music is now eliciting.

While attitudes toward rock music continue to change in the Soviet Union, in some respects the debate is reminiscent of the controversy this music catalyzed in America two to three decades ago. V. S. Ovchinsky, for example, rejects prohibitions against rock music. He advocates this, however, out of fear that bans have promoted criminal and uncivilized behavior in the rock "underground." The rock underground that developed in the 1970s includes few criminal elements, but consists primarily of informal groups who enjoy the Beatles, punk and heavy metal fans, and musicians who wish to remain independent of official control.

M. A. Manuilsky takes a more positive approach to rock than does Ovchinsky. Manuilsky dismisses simplistic perceptions of rock music as a harmful influence and asserts that official restrictions and repressive cultural policies are more harmful to youth and to the rest of society. He expresses strong support for rock as an outlet for the individual aspirations of Soviet youth.

Rock music is thirty-five years old. For quite a long time it was held back by all sorts of official cultural prohibitions, but can one really establish any reliable obstacles against something that stirs the interest of millions? Regardless of all bans, rock music increasingly defines the music scene in our country. In the 1970s in the pages of newspapers and magazines the following words began to appear: "rock ensemble," "rock group," "rock star," and "rock opera." Among the musical preferences of the young, this movement became dominant. It continues to remain so to this day. For example, according to the data of the Estonian sociologist N. Meinert, of nine genres of music the most popular with young people is rock music: 79 percent of those polled liked it (statistics are from 1984).

Experts state that the attraction to rock is declining. However, for a dozen years it was a mass phenomenon, and so it deserves the serious attention of sociologists. By the way, the music community has repeatedly addressed such bothersome questions to sociologists. For example, in a conversation with an *Izvestiya* correspondent, A. Rybnikov, author of the famous operas *Yunona* and *Avos*, proposed to investigate such questions as "Do we need rock or not?" and "Do we need classical music or not?" The lack of sociological interpretations for the process of the formation of the musical tastes of the young is obvious. This is a professional "debt" that sociologists owe to the readers of this magazine and to the society as a whole. We have decided to present the theme of rock culture as a social phenomenon at this "round table" discussion.

N. D. Sarkitov: Rock music exists in the USSR in two forms, foreign and indigenous. The audience that accepts this music is also heterogeneous. The fans of indigenous amateur rock music are, as a rule, highly educated connoisseurs. In sharp contrast to them are the fans of foreign "metal" music. Among the latter one doesn't find intellectuals. Many of the functions of Western and Soviet rock music do not correspond.

It is necessary to elaborate one point: Rock music has experienced three stages of development and is now beginning a fourth. The first stage lasted from the mid-1960s to the mid-1970s. In the beginning, the majority of ensembles followed the best Western rock groups and performers, more often than not faithfully reproducing their best compositions. That was natural. At the beginning of the last century a very similar period was experienced in the development of Russian classical music.

At the end of this period, for many of the indigenous ensembles, very popular British "hard rock" groups became the examples to be followed here, as they were in the West. (For example, Stas Namin's group, Flowers, followed Uriah Heep.) These ensembles were representative of indigenous "heavy" rock music during this period.

The completion of the first stage coincided in time with and was closely linked to the appearance of different kinds of prohibition which, in the long run, brought rock groups (Time Machine, Leap Summer, Ruby Attack, and Tin Soldiers) into a bitter struggle for survival and brought about the second stage of the development of our rock music. The struggle was prolonged; most of the rock groups did not survive it and disappeared. Only those who fought their way to the professional scene could survive (Alexander Gradsky's Time Machine and Stas Namin's group, Leap Summer, which eventually became Autograph). Survive they did, but meanwhile they lost much of their "rockness."

The second stage was also characterized by the formation of a new kind of rock within the youth music culture. By the beginning of the 1980s so-called amateur rock music had been born, in contrast to the "commercial" professional rock.

The third stage began in the late 1970s and early 1980s and has continued to this day. It is differentiated from the first two stages first, by rock's sharp divergence by 1983 into two ideologically distinct entities (professional and amateur) and, second, by the unusually successful blossoming of "heavy metal" on both the amateur and the professional stage. (Amateur groups worked during this period in rock clubs and rock laboratories.) The second half of this stage has been marked by the formation of a third center of Soviet rock music, in the Urals (Yuri Shevchuk and DDT, Urfin Juice, Nautilus). These groups have defined the philosophical and aesthetic positions of Soviet rock music.

Now, the third period is finished (by 1986). A new time has arrived, and it is too early to discern its characteristic features. Nonetheless, certain peculiarities can be noted even today. The first noticeable aspect is the ongoing diversification of style within rock. For example, in the Moscow rock laboratory the following trends have taken shape: "Heavy metal," "mainstream," avant garde, and "electronic romanticism." The second aspect is the formation within amateur rock of an extremely radical wing, which is in opposition to the rock laboratories and rock clubs, and in which one can discern vivid elements of counterculture (for example, the Moscow group Pig). The third aspect is the absolute domination of the professional scene by "heavy metal," which has supplanted the vocal-and-instrumental ensembles.

I cannot agree with Yuri Davydov that rock music is undergoing a conflict between center and periphery. Conflict is apparent, but it is of a different nature; it is a conflict inside the centers of culture. This arises when a city becomes a megalopolis in which conflicts form between strata and age groups, when new relations develop between youth and older people. Out of this conflict between generations living in a large city, between the young and the "older society," rock music arises. When it becomes a sufficiently powerful entity, it then comes into conflict with other cultural or social phenomena. Rock music starts out as an event of social life, not aesthetic life.

V. Ovchinsky: Along with the creation of genuine musical masterpieces, a "rock underground" was formed. One cannot hide from the facts. Even in the 1950s, in the very beginning of the victorious march of rock music. In both the United States and Europe, fanatics or "rockers" appeared (in other parlance, "teddy boys," *"pizhons,"* *"stilyagas"* ["beatniks"]). Frenzy at the concerts of Elvis Presley and other youth idols often turned to violence, group violations of social order, and vandalism. The 1960s and 1970s "enriched" rock music with overt drug use. The mass media hurried to vividly paint rock stars' addictions to various drugs. In those years, because of this type of "advertisement," marijuana became one of the characteristics of Western youth subculture. In other words, along with the development of rock music as a new musical movement, along with the creation of genuine masterpieces of popular music (the works of the Beatles, Deep Purple, the rock operas of Andrew Lloyd Weber and others), the so-called rock underground was being formed. It included not only the fanatical adoration of rock groups, but also various forms of social pathology. With the passage of time, this formation of the underground gathered momentum. Its apogee was reached in 1977–78 with the creation of the punk movement around the rock group Sex Pistols and others. In this situation the underground ceased to be "under" and openly advocated violence, aggression, sex, sexual perversity, and drug abuse as well as crime, occultism, fascism, anticommunism, and anti-Sovietism.

Soviet youth does not live in an isolated world. The broadening of contacts with foreigners has intensified the exchange of information. Rock rather quickly entered our lives through unofficial channels. The makers of Soviet music policy simply ignored the real situation. Four generations of youth (1950s, 1960s, 1970s, and the 1980s) confronted the mass media's angry condemnation of any variety of rock music. The fear of the further spread of "rock mania" as a source of antisocial phenomena brought forth a "forbid-o-mania." Even now you can occasionally hear authoritative statements such as: "Today you listen to rock, tomorrow you will betray your motherland." As a result, our youth has had to decide alone (or with the aid of Western radio broadcasts) whom to select as a musical idol. Thus the homemade "rock underground" was brought to life with all its negative aspects: fashionable violence, sexual promiscuity, drunkenness, and drug abuse.

Sweet is the forbidden fruit, and prohibition removes the situation from any kind of social control. This happened with "heavy metal." Barriers placed in front of this rock movement brought about a "natural" market for "metallists" where speculation in albums and video and tape recordings flourishes, and "*samizdat*" hand-typed rock magazines such as *Urlait* and *Ucho* [Ear] are disseminated. All sorts of "bunkers" (attics and basements so named by teenagers) have appeared, where they listen to "metal rock." Often this listening is accompanied by the use of toxic substances and misdemeanors. Outside of the professional stage several rock groups, devotees of "heavy metal," strut their semi-legal condition, actively promoting the worst examples of punk rock. The media have reported the hooliganism and pornographic escapades of the group Chudo-yudo [Miracle] at the festival of the Moscow rock laboratory in the spring of 1987.

Such are the results of the "forbid-o-mania" of new varieties of rock. It is perfectly understandable that the organs of justice have to react appropriately to excesses and violations of law. As a result, an impression is created that rock is the source of antisocial behavior. But this is a great mistake. Not rock by itself, but its incorrect cultivation creates an explosive situation. A situation has developed in which young people have come to identify all rock art with the "rock underground." Meanwhile, as has been noted, not all modern rock is punk rock.

Now it is important to decide how to help the young to separate the wheat from the chaff. What needs to be done is to prevent rock from becoming a symbol of deviant behavior, from turning into a countercultural means of destroying aesthetic and moral values. The answer, in my opinion, is the following: We must decisively reject bans, by all means popularize the best examples of rock music, and draw the youth out of the "underground." In other words, we must remove the tension in the situation—I state it directly—which is crime-fostering and antihuman.

M. Manuilsky: If we wish to have a serious discussion about rock music, then it is essential to abandon the long-cultivated "syndrome of unanimity." For many years only one evaluation of any new phenomenon was acceptable, based on whether the phenomenon was in accordance with certain principles or not. Even the thought that a phenomenon could be heterogeneous or controversial was considered heretical, considered a revision of the dominant views, or a yielding to foreign ideology. Echoes of this approach are still heard. The majority of mass media reports describe the achievements and drawbacks of rock music in general. That the traditional (wholly negative) evaluation is counterbalanced with a positive opinion does not change the nature of the situation. Nor do the attempts to draw out the positive and negative aspects of rock.

Of course, one must know what constitutes the essence of rock music, what is its social content. This is the most important problem. Its resolution begins simply with a detailed analysis of its nuances, facets, and directions. It is time once and for all to make clear that the multiplicity of social manifestations is inseparable from its diverseness and uniqueness. The initial tendency toward oversimplification contrasts with any objective analysis, particularly regarding modern rock music.

It is thought that the young have become obsessed with rock. The results of sociological investigations have refuted this popular view. As has already been noted, according to the statistics of N. Meinert, rock music is popular in Estonia with 79 percent of those polled. And almost as many express interest in other popular modern music. The latter, according to indications of preference, falls behind rock by .12 (on a scale of 5.0). This agrees with the results of polls conducted by the laboratory of youth problems of *Sotsiologicheskie Issledovaniya* and *Literaturnaya Gazeta*, which show that rock music is popular with 47 to 73 percent of teenagers.

What do these facts tell us? Rock music is not the only passion of the young. Many young men and women, following fashion, consider themselves fans of "heavy metal" without fearing ostracism, especially since the official ban has been lifted. In reality, a considerable part of the youth (exactly what part remains to be determined) associates rock with any composition that is performed with a heavy beat on ultramodern instruments.

Rock music is quite heterogenous and controversial. It encompasses commercial music, *shlyager* [coarse popular tunes], and *razvlekashki* [empty entertainment]. There are musicians and music oriented toward "getting high" and being shocking. Distorted faces, wild whistling and screaming, torn clothing, shattered furniture, and doses of drugs—all of this has happened and still occurs right here in the performance hall. This is not somewhere in California, but in Moscow or in Ufa. But this is foam, whipped up first of all by the prolonged objection to rock culture by the official system of values. This is "official" in the worst meaning of the word, implying bureaucratic, "over-rationalized," lacking any emotional attraction, and not allowing the slightest deviation from the principles supposedly canonized in the name of history and the people. No, it is not that the young have found an area for the expression of their dissent which, lacking any kind of meaningful idea, turns into a disgusting orgy. Blind guidance and cultural dicta, by completely shutting the doors of philosophical and moral search, are themselves guilty of bringing to life this monster of counterculture. But nowadays we drop our jaws in bewilderment and ask, where did this come from?

To a great extent, the situation described above explains the unusualness, the "differentness" of rock music. With a relative sparseness of musical means of expression, its works are distinguished by complex emotional images and the broad use of symbols and metaphors. It is not simply a search for "one's own values," but rather an attempt to uncover the diversity and polyphony of humanitarian ideals and bring them to everyday life. Polysemy is the fundamental feature of rock music. In contrast to the cheap stylized rock tunes, rock refutes standards. The world is diverse. Every young person is bothered by the eternal problems (love, friendship, obligation) in his own way. Rock music provides an opportunity to grapple with the depth and breadth of life, to develop a unique perception. This is the attraction of rock.

Rock music is a position. To enter the world and affirm yourself, to discover one's "self" and present it to other people—this is the highest goal of rock culture.

15

Lucky Ticket: A Few Meetings with Yuri Shevchuk

Ilya Smirnov

Selskaya Molodyozh, no. 6, 1988

This article published in the youth newspaper *Selskaya Molodyozh* provides many insights into the recent history of Soviet rock music, the travails of a nonconformist's life in a provincial town, and the political message rock groups send to their fans. In a *Yunost* (no. 5, 1987) survey, readers selected DDT as the country's third most popular band (Aquarium and Mashina Vremeni were more popular). A third-place finish for DDT was significant because the group had never released a record album and never appeared on national television. Smirnov's article briefly mentions the "tape recording industry" by which bands like DDT have gained popularity: fans make copies of their songs and spread the music throughout the country.

Smirnov's article displays *glasnost* by describing DDT's lead singer and songwriter Yuri Shevchuk's battles with local authorities in Ufa, a large industrial town in the Urals. His controversial lyrics elicited attacks in the press and attempts to coerce him to end his unofficial status as a musician. Shevchuk found more hospitable terrain in Leningrad, the Soviet Union's most progressive city for rock music and other forms of cultural expression. Smirnov believes that artists like Shevchuk, who suffer official harassment, avoid bureaucratic control, and cope with minimal financial rewards, are heroes who have maintained their integrity in the face of adversity.

An artist from Ufa, Yuri Shevchuk, began his musical career as a bard, giving performances with his guitar in clubs. After one of these concerts he met Vladimir Sigachev, who played the organ in a local club. This is how the group was born. It was named for the place they first rehearsed, the Home of Children's Creativity, with the initials meaning the "poisonous" DDT. In a short time the group became well known, and in 1982 *Komsomolskaya Pravda* nominated DDT for the all-union *Zolotoi Kamerton* [Golden Tuning Fork] competition for their song "Don't Shoot!"

"Don't Shoot" became DDT's first well-known hit in the country. It was different from other songs of these years, because it was not written by request. The hero of this song does not live overseas but rather side by side with us; it is the same guy that we saw in the movie *Is It Easy To Be Young?*,[1] or his friend, brother, or school buddy:

> And when someone was remembering the war
> He was drowning his conscience in wine:
> Before him stood alive again
> A man who asked him only one thing:
> Don't shoot!

It is strange that the jury of the competition did not notice these words. Nevertheless, DDT now had a career opportunity to follow what some people see as the natural path of development for young musicians: from "amateur" to "professional." This brings collaboration with a composer, a salary with the philharmonic, an author's honorarium (if you behave well),[2] and in the future trips abroad (clothing plus stereo equipment).

> And after receiving all benefits of life
> I sang a sweet tune
> Shouting stupid words from the stage
> But making very good money.

Ignoring the inducements of this "natural" way, the boys isolated themselves in their Home of Children's Creativity and began to record albums. The songs "Bashkir Honey," "They Play Hard Rock," and "Compromise" were sounding from microphones all over the country while avoiding the cultural councils and the salary commission.

---

[1] *Is It Easy To Be Young?*, a documentary released in 1986, was controversial for its portrayal of punk rockers, hippies, and other members of the counterculture.

[2] An "author's honorarium" refers to the money awarded to songwriters by the official composers' and songwriters' union. These composers implore bands to play their music, because they receive royalties every time their songs are performed. Today, rock bands are permitted additional freedom to earn money through cooperatives, but nearly all Soviet rock artists must continue to work at full-time jobs.

And I am not afraid to say that "Periphery" (1984) remains an unsurpassed work of art. I don't want to repeat compliments about the satirist Shevchuk; Natalya Zimyanina in *Yunost* (1987, no. 2) has already compared him, justifiably, and his picture of provincial reality in the beginning of the 1980s with the well-known stories of Mikhail Saltykov-Shchedrin and Andrei Platonov.

I will only say that "Lucky Ticket" sounded like a revelation to us, a requiem for all of our contemporaries and friends who suffocated in the poisonous atmosphere of those years: "I received this role, I got the lucky ticket." Indeed, this was a very honorable task for DDT, to speak the truth in the name of a whole generation, but at the same time it was tragic as well. The previous leadership of the autonomous republic Bashkiria (since fired for scandalous abuses) considered the song "Periphery" to be a slander against the Soviet village. Shevchuk also was labeled a Vatican agent, because in another of his songs Christ is mentioned. From the "laureate" and the "pride of the Ufa art scene," he instantaneously became a pariah. He was fired from his job and persecuted by such mercenary writers as the authors of the libelous "Minstrel with the Alien Voice," "When the Masks Are Removed," and other similar works of art in the local press.

He stubbornly refused to promise in writing that from now on "he will not write and perform his own songs" (an interesting judicial innovation?). Then late one evening two sober, well-dressed men approached him on the street. One asked him a question, and the other hit him over the head. This encounter could have had a much worse ending if some passersby had not appeared. But the first thing Yuri did after recovering was gather his team together and go to Moscow to record the new album "DDT-85," also known by the name *"Vremya."* How strange that the album turned out to be very optimistic! You feel in it a breath of the fresh wind of changes.

> It's okay, my friend,
> We will beat you up
> And history will throw you away.

These words turned out to be prophetic. Although Shevchuk and Sigachev had to leave Ufa, Yuri went on to

Leningrad, where he immediately became a center of gravity for all who opposed the empty-headed "major chord" rock in the style of Manufactura, which dominated the rock club on Rubinstein Street from 1984 to 1986. DDT includes the drummer Igor Dotsenko, the guitarist Andrei Vasiliev, sound technician Yevgeny Mochulov, bassist Vadim Kurilev, and Nikita Zaitsev, who seems to play any instrument known to musicians. In addition there is Gennady Zaitsev, one of the founders and leaders of the Leningrad rock club. At the Chernogolovykh festival, DDT was selected the most popular group in a survey of listeners there. And among the listeners' three favorite songs, two were written by Shevchuk.

A significant number of young people, however, still form their tastes with the help of a "shallow screen" (a term used by Alexander Gradsky), and their idols are still Modern Talking (natural and in translation),[3] ex-rocker and now lyricist Vladimir Kuzmin, and the group Forum. This will continue until our mass media plow under the musical mafia and the bureaucracy of countless art councils who have appropriated for themselves the right to decide for people which songs they need.[4] It is simply terrible to imagine what would have happened to us without the "tape recording industry," but no matter how inventive the modern "left-handed" writers are (those who write music in independent studios),[5] it is hard for them to compete with the powerful musical monopolies.

> We don't have dashing bandits—they all live in America.
> We don't have drunks—that stuff is sold abroad.
> We don't have conceited bosses, nor thieves and *blat*.[6]
> We don't have private property, and everyone is young and healthy.
> Everyone is working very hard, the whole country without exception.

---

[3] "Natural and in translation" refers to in English and in Russian.

[4] The "mafia" refers to the Union of Composers and their supporters, who control the radio, television, and recording industry.

[5] The term "left-handed" here means nonconformist.

[6] *Blat* is a Russian word describing an informal exchange of goods and services.

We don't have good-for-nothing artists—each is a genius of the Renaissance.

It would be possible to call the boys from DDT the heroes of our time. But why such loftiness? We've had more than enough of it. These are simply people who do their job honestly, like the chairman of the collective farm who took good care of his villagers and for that was demoted to night watchman. Like the judge who refused to condemn the innocent and for that lost his job. Like the writer who wrote truth that was inconvenient for the bosses, "for the drawer."[7] But despite DDT's noisy success at the festival, Shevchuk was not particularly happy with his program. I doubt that I have the right to disclose our nightly conversations in the kitchen over tea, but it seems to me (without going into details) that his is the only possible promising position. Dissatisfaction with yourself is the professional sickness of a true artist. And the artist who is happy with himself very quickly comes to resemble the unsympathetic statue that Pantagruel observed on the island belonging to Gaster.[8]

The discussion between those in the ruins continues: By the way, do the rockers have a positive program? Why should this question be addressed only to rockers? Didn't you notice that in Anna Akhmatova's work *Plakha* all positive heroes are doomed?

Indeed, this question is addressed to all, to writers, rockers, bards, politicians. This is the question for all people: How do we get out of the mess we've got ourselves into? On this Shevchuk is silent, but he has already expressed his opinion in song:

And only love can help us to remain people.
Remain people.
Remain people.

---

[7] The phrase "for the drawer" is used in the USSR to describe works written to be published when the political climate improves.

[8] The hero of the French novel *Gargantua and Pantagruel*, by François Rabelais.

16

Letter about Brezhnev's Portrait in Art Rock Parade

Sovetskaya Kultura
April 30, 1988

This letter to the editor complains about a report in the newspaper *Vechernaya Moskva* that young people danced on a portrait of Leonid Brezhnev during a rock show performed in conjunction with the film *Assa*. The director of *Assa* denied that this incident occurred, but the letter illustrates public sensitivity about rock music crossing the line into politics.

"It can be explained by the desire to surprise the viewer, the unusual form of decorating this evening," writes *Vechernaya Moskva*, April 18, 1988.

The portrait of Leonid Brezhnev spread over the floor indeed was surprising. Any person would agree that to walk or dance on anyone's portrait is not nice. Even if it is the "portrait of the man with whose name the years of stagnation are associated."

I by no means justify and defend the years of stagnation. Wasn't it enough that during this period our souls were walked all over? Why emulate?!

N. Chuvashova Mytishchi
Moscow *oblast*

Bibliography

Kanev, C. "Where Would the Club Go?" *Leningradskaya Pravda*, June 4, 1988.

A Leningrad historian analyzes *samizdat* documents of the informal group Democratization of Trade Unions and points out their theoretical misconceptions.

Losoto, Yelena. "Reflections on the Mail: Too Similar." *Komsomolskaya Pravda*, December 19, 1988.

Losoto reprints letters to make the case that the nationalistic and anti-Semitic views of Pamyat are analogous to those of the leaders of Nazi Germany.

Milovsky, Alexander. "Who Protects Monuments, and from Whom?" *Sovetskaya Kultura*, March 3, 1988.

This article argues that unofficial organizations are not preventing authorities in Moscow, Pskov, and other Russian towns from destroying or allowing the deterioration of historical monuments and landmark buildings.

Panov, E. " 'Delta' and Others." *Sotsialisticheskaya Industriya*, June 21, 1988.

Discusses an informal environmental group in Leningrad which opposes a project to build a dam at the Finnish Gulf.

Pustov, Vasily. "Without a Fly and without an Elephant." *Krasnaya Zvezda*, May 7, 1988.

This article viciously attacks informal groups, particularly the group Doverie for its alleged anti-Sovietism.

Sidorov, I. " 'DC': Face to Face." *Leningradskaya Pravda*, August 5, 1988.

This article criticizes the group Democratic Union for proclaiming political goals.

Timasheva, M., and Sokolyansky, A. "Images of Russian Rock." *Sovetskaya Kultura*, December 24, 1988.

The authors describe various rock groups and their stars in the context of the social and political role of Soviet rock music.

Chapter Four
National, Religious, and Social Issues

I. Relations among Nationalities in the Soviet Union

The nationality conflicts that have exploded under *glasnost* surprised no one more than Mikhail Gorbachev and the Communist party leadership. The 1986 Communist party program proclaimed that the "nationalities question inherited from the past has been successfully solved in the Soviet Union." As recent events in the Baltic republics, Armenia, Azerbaijan, and Georgia reveal, the nationalities issue is far from solved. The discussion between historians Leokadiya Drobizheva and Yuri Polyakov (Document #17) provides a historical and political framework for examining this pivotal issue.

The process of forming the Union of Soviet Socialist Republics as a multinational state took place in two stages, the Lenin period and the Stalin era. In founding the Soviet state, Lenin was heavily influenced by the belief that distinct national cultures were the product of a precapitalist past. After the October Revolution, the Bolsheviks dismissed the issue of cultural autonomy for nationalities; they deemed the concept of national culture unnecessary, superseded by internationalism, equality, and socialism. The end of the civil war led to the official proclamation of nationhood for the Soviet Union in 1922.

Joseph Stalin, who often ruled his country as mercilessly as the Russian czars before him, employed cruel repressions which spared no part of the population. However, the oppressive policies carried the most lasting impact for small minorities such as the Jews and Crimean Tatars, who were deported from their homeland. Two tendencies emerged in the 1920s to dominate the nationality question: (1) the determination of the party to achieve the victory of socialism by any means, and (2) the process of Russification in the republics. Side by side with such positive phenomena as the first written alphabet and textbooks for some nationalities, a socialist cultural content was imposed by coercion and persecution.

Centralization and industrialization became crucial features of nation building in the Soviet Union, leading to mass forced migrations of labor which altered the demographic composition of the republics and severely limited their sovereignty. To this day Russian engineers and workers play significant roles in industrial development in every republic. Stalin's decision to exterminate the leaders of the republics and local intelligentsia, often under the guise of fighting "bourgeois nationalism," both strengthened central control and weakened the ability of nationalities to resist Russification. The process of Russification became especially powerful after World War II, as the government abolished many national schools and prohibited the teaching of more than one hundred minority languages.

The Soviet Union is a multinational state whose fifteen republics include one hundred sizable nationalities. Russians dominate the political and economic decision making of the entire country, with the Ukrainians holding second place. Russians constitute approximately 53 percent of the population of the USSR, but the overall Slavic population (including Ukrainians and Byelorussians) accounts for nearly 75 percent. In the next fifty years, however, these numbers are expected to change dramatically because of the demographic explosion of central Asian peoples, the Uzbeks, Tadzhiks, Kirghiz, and Turkmens. Although diversity can be a country's strength, rigid centralization, economic inequality, national chauvinism, and centuries-old prejudices have prevented the USSR from becoming a socialist melting pot. Since Gorbachev has come to power, and since the onset of *glasnost*, one can observe a genuine explosion of nationalist sentiments in the country.

Three primary reasons can be cited for the depth of the current nationalities crisis. First, throughout Soviet history the government has displayed a willingness to respond with force to any perceived threat to the integrity of the Soviet state. Second, the anticorruption campaigns initiated in the republics by Yuri Andropov and Gorbachev weakened party and state control over the local populations by removing experienced and ruthless national cadres. Moreover, the ousted local leadership of various republics in all likelihood has assumed an active role in the nationalist movements. Third, *glasnost* and political liberalization have allowed thousands of people to organize, publish, and demonstrate without fear of persecution.

Soviet nationality issues fall into two main categories: relations between Russians and other nationalities, and conflicts between non-Russian nationalities. The two most prominent demonstrations of anti-Russian sentiments have emerged in Kazakhstan and the Baltic republics. The first nationalist issue to confront Mikhail Gorbachev came in the summer of 1985 in Alma-Ata, the capital of Kazakhstan. Riots erupted in Alma-Ata when the Soviet leadership replaced a corrupt Communist party boss, Dinmukhamed Kunaev (a Kazakh), with Gennady Kolbin (an ethnic Russian). Kazakhstan, like the Baltic republics of Estonia and Lithuania, has experienced industrial development resulting in a rapid growth in the Russian and Russian-speaking population, and Kazakhs view this as threatening their cultural heritage.

In Gorbachev's quest for economic efficiency, he violated the Soviet practice of allowing the Communist leader of a republic to be a representative of the republic's major ethnic group. Seweryn Bialer writes that "it is the formation of native elites, of the political and social mobility that it represents, of the opportunity and satisfaction of indigenous cadres that it reflects, which forms . . . a key element of the explanation for the stability of nationality relations in the past decade."[1] Gorbachev showed a real lack of understanding of the delicate balance of power between the imperial authority in Moscow and the local ruling elites in Kazakhstan.

The explosion of nationalist sentiments in the Baltic republics shows a skillful utilization of *glasnost* to address grievances that have accumulated for nearly half a century. The increasing pace of Russian immigration to the more prosperous Baltic republics has fueled long-simmering nationalism. In Latvia and Estonia the indigenous population has become increasingly vocal as the number of Russians working in the republics has grown to half of all residents. In Latvia only 53 percent of the residents are natives, and in Riga, the capital of the Latvian republic, 78 percent of the population consists of Russians or other nonnatives.[2] Another issue that unites the local populations against the central Russian authorities is the harmful ecological impact of rapid industrialization.

Citizens in the Baltic republics have held massive protest rallies, have proclaimed their national languages official for business and government, and have restored their national flags. While political independence for the Baltic republics is an unrealistic prognosis for the foreseeable future, the central government has made significant concessions on language, flags, and political representation. Furthermore, the Soviet government may grant greater economic autonomy and allow the republics to retain a larger share of the wealth they produce.

The outbreak of ethnic violence between Armenia and Azerbaijan is unprecedented in the Soviet Union and represents a different type of nationality problem. The conflict between Armenians and Azerbaijanis has far more to do with religious and historical grievances than with Russian control. In fact, Soviet troops have played a peacekeeping role in the region. Both republics have adopted clear nationalist platforms that oppose each other on the issue of Nagorno-Karabakh, a territory located inside Azerbaijan in which 80 percent of

---

[1] Seweryn Bialer, *Stalin's Successors* (New York: Cambridge University Press, 1980), p. 216.

[2] In Latvia only 6 percent of the police are Latvians. Alla Kallas, "Permanent Contacts Are Necessary," *Tallin*, no. 3, 1988, p. 127.

the population is Armenian. Historically Nagorno-Karabakh was a Moslem khanate which later became part of Azerbaijan.

Gorbachev's vacillation in formulating a policy toward this ethnic conflict might have exacerbated tensions. The June 1988 rioting in Sumgait, in which at least thirty were killed and hundreds wounded, reminded the world more of events in Lebanon than in a resolute Soviet state. As in the Baltic republics, the most striking feature of the conflict has been the helplessness of the local party and state leadership to control events.

The events in Tbilisi on April 9, 1989, were even more shocking to the Soviet people than the riots in Sumgait. Army units and troops from the Ministry of Internal Affairs viciously attacked a crowd of eight thousand demonstrators with poison gases and shovels. Twenty people, mostly women and children, were killed and hundreds were hospitalized. A strong wave of anti-Russian sentiment swept the entire republic of Georgia.

The current situation in the republics poses a great challenge for Mikhail Gorbachev and his reforms. The appearance of anarchy and the helplessness of the central authorities in managing the nationality crises could become a factor provoking conservative elements of the Communist party to overthrow Gorbachev. This would lead to the end of *glasnost*. If the Soviet Union is to engage in successful economic modernization and the democratization of its political system, it will be necessary to introduce a new approach toward managing nationality relations.

II. Religious Issues

Unlike the nationalities problem where the situation gets more complicated daily, or the economy where the dire necessity to make ideological concessions is understandable, religious issues have not presented any pressing problems to the Soviet leadership. For this reason a more tolerant attitude toward religion since Gorbachev took power has surprised everyone. The national celebration of the millennium of the Baptism of Rus', the establishment of friendly relations with the Vatican, and the opening of the Jewish Cultural Center are the most notable changes in this officially atheist country. The change is also striking because there has not been a considerable internal pressure for change.

The Russian Orthodox church is the only significant organization preserved from the old czarist regime. Acceptance of this organized alien philosophy, albeit a grudging acceptance, proves that the Soviet system possesses a certain amount of flexibility. Until now coexistence with the church was a necessity that rarely required a significant digression from the official policies of distrust and pressure.

Thus Stalin, after the severe persecutions of the 1920s and 1930s, in 1943 restored the patriarchate in exchange for the assistance of the church in stirring up patriotism and national feelings in the fight against the Germans in World War II.

The Soviet educational system instills in the young a militant atheism. Religious beliefs are considered to belong to elderly uneducated people or people who are striving for personal gains. Soviet theoreticians had hoped that religion eventually would become extinct.

A new religion was supposed to take the church's place in human hearts. For seventy years the Soviet brand of communism has been an all-embracing system of beliefs, a de facto state religion with such features as infallibility of the Marxist-Leninist prophets, their iconization, and legends about their incredible powers and personal qualities. They were judged to be authorities in all spheres of life, especially the spiritual sphere. To compete with the religious ceremonies, new rituals and traditions were created.

Thirty years of Stalin's rule brought a glorification of the leader that reached incredible proportions rivaling any other example in human history. Khrushchev called it a cult of personality. An impatient leader and a passionate believer in communism, Khrushchev speeded up the closing of the churches and allowed vicious antireligious propaganda. Instead of Stalin, Lenin became the main personage in the Soviet pantheon.

Mikhail Gorbachev, by allowing the celebrations of the millennium of the Baptism of Rus', surpassed expectations and showed that the limits of *glasnost* are expandable. As the metropolitan of Leningrad and Novgorod Alexiy admitted:

> To be honest not long ago it was impossible to imagine that via television the whole country would be able to hear the hymn "How the Russian Land Faces God" performed in the Bolshoi Theater by the joint chorus of Trinity Sergy Monastery and of the Moscow Theological Academy and Seminary; that millions of people would watch *The Cathedral*, a TV documentary on their screen. That Andrei Gromyko, Chairman of the USSR Presidium of the Supreme Soviet, would meet the participants in the Jubilee festivities of the Russian Orthodox Church in the Kremlin and would pointedly speak about the prominent role of Christianity in the destiny of our fatherland.[3]

The Russian Orthodox church was rewarded beyond anyone's expectations for not supporting lonely religious dissidents (in contrast to the Polish church) and for actively participating in the Soviet-sponsored international peace movement. In return Gorbachev might expect the support of 70 million believers for his *perestroika* as well as

---

[3]Abel Aganbegyan, *Perestroika 1989* (New York: Scribner's, 1988), p. 303.

participation in the antialcoholism campaign and in strengthening family values. Gorbachev has also deprived the Russian nationalist extremists of a monopoly on the topic. Chairman of the State Committee Konstantin Kharchev, according to his interview with writer Alexander Nezhny (Document #18), is an ardent supporter of returning full citizenship to the believers—a revolutionary idea for the Soviet Union.

III. Social Issues

For years the mass media have made Soviet citizens virtual experts on the social vices of Western capitalist countries. Information about Soviet social problems, however, was considered to be a state secret. But under Gorbachev Soviet citizens have been informed that crime, corruption, drugs, and alcoholism are at least as serious a problem in the world's first socialist country as they are anywhere else. Stories about Soviet shortcomings have shocked average citizens and alarmed conservative stalwarts. Gorbachev and his supporters, in their quest to improve economic performance, have placed great emphasis on solving social ills.

An antialcohol campaign was the first major program initiated by Mikhail Gorbachev. The new Soviet leader's style became apparent as he directed the entire state *apparat* to wage an all-out attack on the problem. There had been antialcohol campaigns in the past, but never at this level of intensity. Vineyards were destroyed, plants dismantled, thousands of stores closed, vodka prices doubled, and punishments for public drunkenness became strictly enforced. Police confiscated more than 1 million moonshine stills and 4 million liters of raw brandy. Sixty percent of those apprehended were women, and half of them were elderly.[4] The mass media also became involved as television and the press presented revealing exposés and analytical reports on this social crisis (see Document #19).

Gorbachev's antialcohol campaign was a failure. He attempted to solve a social problem with roots in prerevolutionary Russia by purely administrative methods. A special bureaucracy was created, the All-Union Voluntary Society of Sobriety. These seven thousand "sobercrats" became the subject of cartoons rather than effective problem solvers. A sugar shortage resulted from the widespread production of *samogon*, and in 1987 more than ten thousand people poisoned themselves trying to get drunk on various liquids.[5] Gorbachev admitted that the decline in the sale of alcoholic beverages

---

[4]*Izvestiya*, November 29, 1987.

[5]In 1986, 785,000 more tons of sugar were sold than in 1985. *Nedelya*, no. 25, 1988.

resulted in an enormous budget loss of 49 billion rubles. Although undoubtedly some lives were saved as a result of this well-intentioned campaign, the use of administrative methods to solve a societal disease proved to be ill advised. Recently, in response to public outcry, several of the antialcohol provisions have been rescinded.

While there is no hard evidence linking the antialcohol campaign to a rise in drug use, narcotics have developed into a serious issue in the Soviet Union. Lieutenant General Pankin of the Soviet militia (police force) cited the antialcohol campaign and increased contacts with the West as two reasons for the rise in drug abuse. Thirty thousand drug-related court cases were reported in 1986 and 1987. In 1987 the militia confiscated forty-two tons of narcotics and recorded five hundred drug-related crimes.[6] While the drug problem in the USSR seems miniscule compared to the situation in the United States, public concern is growing. Blaming the government's refusal to acknowledge this social problem, Nina Fokina writes, "I am certain that drug addiction would not have begun to spread if we, the drug experts, had been able to study it and cut it off from the very beginning" (Document #20).

Mikhail Gorbachev continued the drive against corruption begun by Yuri Andropov. Although corruption always has been a reality of Russian life, corrupt practices reached new heights during the Brezhnev years. In exchange for political loyalty, Brezhnev granted virtual fiefdoms to his supporters in the republics. The 1988 trial of Brezhnev's son-in-law, Yuri Churbanov, for his involvement in the notorious Uzbekistan cotton affair was widely viewed as a general indictment of Brezhnev's corrupt political system. The most revealing element of the trial proved to be the complete collusion of party, state, police, KGB, and criminal elements in controlling the entire republic. Georgy Ovcharenko (Document #21) reports that the mafia in Uzbekistan stole more than 4 billion rubles from the state. The famous trial of those implicated in the Uzbek affair revealed the depth of the political crisis, and it can be used by Gorbachev as a justification for fundamental changes.

Glasnost and democratization have proved to be effective tools for combatting corruption and exposing social ills. To achieve significant results against these vices, however, a radical transformation of the country's political situation must be achieved. In a one-party state with a great concentration of power in the hands of local and central leaders, corruption cannot be rooted out. A strong

[6]Andrei Illesh and Yevgeny Shestinsky, "Drug Abuse: A Report from the Militia," *Izvestiya*, February 29, 1988, an interview with Lieutenant General of Militia Viacheslav Pankin, chief of MVD Main Administration for Criminal Investigations.

and independent press can be a weapon against corruption and can also educate the Soviet public about the dangers of alcoholism and drug abuse.

17

There Were No Previous Models for the Development of National Relations

Georgy Melikyants, Leokadiya Drobizheva, and Yuri Polyakov

Izvestiya, March 22, 1988

The sensitive nature of nationality issues has limited the openness of the official press on this topic. This *Izvestiya* article reflects a scholarly, almost detached approach to the subject, but it acknowledges the complexity of the nationality situation in the Soviet Union. Historians Drobizheva and Polyakov address the controversial issue of national languages and education and agree that the recruiting of nationalities for the *apparat* has been unsuccessful.

In placing the nationalities situation in a historical context, Drobizheva and Polyakov note that the recent achievement by other nationalities of cultural equality with Russians has resulted in difficulties for all concerned. Equality and competition have replaced the concept of the Russian people as providers of assistance. Drobizheva notes that some people believe that further democratization could further exacerbate the nationality question.

Among the important values of our society we rightfully list the friendships among the peoples of the USSR, which is comprised of hundreds of large and small nations. But we well know that the national processes are complex and not without difficulties.

What is the value of the Soviet government's experience in national relations? What can one learn from it? What kind of new problems arise? This was the subject of our discussion with Leokadiya Mikhailovna Drobizheva, a doctor of historical science and the well-known director of the Institute of Ethnography of the Academy of Sciences of the USSR, and Yuri Alexandrovich Polyakov, an associate member of the Academy of Sciences of the USSR and a chairman of the Scientific Council of the Soviet Academy of Sciences of the USSR in historical geography and demography.

Melikyants: Apparently the problem now is to precisely and scientifically determine what is complicated about the national question and where are the origins of this complexity. The friendship of our peoples has not vanished into thin air; it is actively forged in daily interaction, work, and struggle. But in the distressing events of recent times, it would seem that we have forgotten about this.

Polyakov: Where there is growth, there is opposition. It is important to remember that even the most confused issues are resolvable. We inherited quite a few problems between nationalities. After the revolution, we resolved a significant number of them. The creation of national republics and regions—and I am not afraid of exaggerating—was an act of tremendous importance. The majority of today's republics and regions were formed in six to seven years. And what years of war and starvation those were! We were not prepared for this endeavor. Most of the peoples establishing their republics had never before had their own government. What then was the principle of their formation? For example, at first the mountainous Gorskaya ASSR absorbed several peoples from Northern Caucasia. It quickly became clear that the inclusion of many nationalities in one republic was pointless. Several autonomous republics replaced this single one.

Melikyants: However, in Dagestan, where there are more than ten nations and nationalities. . . .

Polyakov: That's quite an interesting experiment! Dagestan has such a multinational community that the autonomy of the separate peoples is practically impossible. The national divisions in Central Asia are also unique. Look at the map: How crooked these borders are in some cases! But it is a reflection of the "crooked" pattern of the population's resettlement.

Melikyants: Lenin wrote that hundreds of thousands of people spread from one end of Russia to another; the national composition of the population fluctuates, so isolation and national backwardness must fade away.

Polyakov: Today, for example, 66 percent of the Armenians in our country live in Armenia (according to the 1979 census), 11.5 percent of them live in Azerbaijan, almost 11 percent in Georgia, and around 9 percent in the Russian republic. Twenty percent of the Tadzhiks live outside the borders of their republic. Only 26 percent of the Tatars live in their republic. Apparently the process of liquidation of isolation and backwardness has been more prolonged than we might have wished.

If we are to talk about the historical experience, a very important stage of that experience was when the national republics were unified, having declared their desire to live as one family. This unification took place voluntarily, according to the Leninist principle of self-determination including secession. Incidentally, Lenin especially emphasized "including secession," asserting that although secession is not obligatory, the right to secede is.

Melikyants: Yuri Alexandrovich, this short excursion into history shows us that, in the unique process of multinational building, questions were raised that had never before received attention. And we began to truly examine them. But has everything been accomplished as it was envisaged, as it was planned? For example, let's look at the recruitment of native populations into the administrative apparatus. How would we look on this today?

Polyakov: Where the natural path was followed (that is, the children of native nationalities finished school and received education), it was wholesome and good. But when we lowered our standards to allow a certain percentage of local nationalities into some institutions, the results were damaging. In trying to do something faster, we sometimes did it worse. Soon a new-fledged specialist was a bad specialist, and a new-fledged intellectual was not at all intelligent.

Melikyants: But let's ask the question this way: If the formation of national cadres in all branches had not been controlled, even with the help of planning it would have stretched out over a long period of time.

Drobizheva: The encouragement of all those who did not possess a sufficient educational background was a reasonable step. In order for a new authority to consolidate itself there should be leaders who are familiar with local conditions, who understand the mood, and who have command of the national language. Necessities, such as teachers and doctors familiar with the local populations, should be provided. However, temporary cadres in these jobs do not suffice. It is important that people who go to the so-called border lands strive to learn the language, history, and culture of their "new home." This is considered a nice touch.

Melikyants: We remember the celebrated Lenin's Train,[1] which founded Tashkent University. . . .

Drobizheva: This touches upon a serious problem, which scientists call adaptive migration. For example, Estonia needs to increase the extraction of natural resources and secure order in the work force of its growing economy. To what social consequences has this led? Were we prepared for the pluralism of opinions? Some of our Estonian colleagues believe that the influx of outside specialists should be stopped, because it suppresses the spark of the Estonian population. This is especially alarming in the growth of material production. Others have decided that, in the interest of the development of the republic, it is impossible for this influx to stop. So, in Estonia and among specialists who are occupied with these problems beyond Estonian borders, we must have open discussions. Surely this question and many others are of concern to our country.

Polyakov: There are also two points of view on national schools. Why, for example, is the number of Byelorussian schools declining? The typical answer is: The number of students has reduced. There are no students, so there are no schools. Others say that in order for people to study in Byelorussian, there must be schools—the students exist already. What then comes first, schools or students?

Having made the basic point in concrete terms, we approach the question in this way: To have only one Kirgiz school in the capital of Kirgizia is, really, an odd occurrence. Where then is the Kirgiz language taught?

I studied in Uzbekistan in a Russian school, and there we had to study Uzbek. To study the language of the republic in which one lives is, in my view, the duty of all citizens of any nationality.

Melikyants: Everyone agrees with this. This discussion of national schools continues. If the study of Byelorussian is reserved for Russian schools, then soon only certain individuals will know Byelorussian.

---

[1] After the Bolsheviks established control over Central Asia, a train with Moscow and Leningrad professors came to Tashkent to organize a university at Lenin's request.

Drobizheva: All the same, there is a democratic principle of the will of the people. Such a question requires not emotion, but at least a poll of social opinion, a clarification of all sides of the problem.

Polyakov: You're right, Leokadiya Mikhailovna, willingness is absolutely necessary. But it is important to search for an answer. For example, could there be schools with parallel classes taught in different languages? To study the language of a given republic is absolutely necessary, and here there is no problem aside from this: There must be good teachers and better training.

I think that the state should turn its attention to the measures necessary to logically, scientifically, and rationally search for ways to improve matters.

Melikyants: But the comrades from those republics say that it is not just a matter of training children in the native language. The reduction of training in a language hinders its growth. It becomes poorer, and new scientific and technological terms are no longer introduced into it. The language withers away; not only is it spoken less, but also it is written even more infrequently.

Drobizheva: Once again, the language in which [something] is written is an especially personal matter. Oles Gonchar writes in Ukrainian, but Fasil Iskander writes in Russian.[2] Whom does this affect?

Melikyants: The development of our national languages and our national cultures is a governmental concern, do not forget this.

Polyakov: We acknowledge the problems. Ambivalence on the part of the state does not resolve them. And other problems flare up from time to time in any number of places. This still-smoldering problem has been noticed by writers, sociologists, and historians. Since it has not yet turned into something insurmountable, we must search for the best way to approach it.

Drobizheva: At the same time, we must study the historical experience. The struggle for any national-cultural symbols (for example, language) has always reflected the social interests of a definite group. At present, it seems that it is more important to see not only one's own

---

[2] Oles Gonchar is a Ukrainian and Fasil Iskander is an Abkhazian.

national interests but also the general ones of the entire country. If we do not emphasize socioeconomic acceleration, we base the resolution of national problems only on the clarification of linguistic and cultural-historical questions. These are undoubtedly important; it is impossible to avoid their resolution. But it is even more important that national factors (for example, language and territorial issues) do not obscure the resolution of the economic and social problems of our society.

Melikyants: The pressures of national life are directly connected with unique national behavior. While this area is new to us, it directs necessary attention to the interrelations of nations and their, so to speak, compatible coexistence.

Drobizheva: Yes, we have only poorly studied the vital worth of people, their orientations, and their interests. All of these things are related to ethnic psychology. It is possible to raise the people's level of education in a short time, but it is impossible to alter human psychology quickly. However, it is high time to study this issue and to use the results of this study.

Polyakov: This has practical applications. For example, the Japanese have discovered which industrial habits are especially typical of the Japanese in general and of inhabitants of certain regions in particular. Can we scientifically explain anything similar? This does not mean that we must restrict the participation of any people in any activity, but wouldn't it be better to know their preferences, skills, and traditions? We cannot escape the fact that they are all different. Let's utilize all of the traditional forms that motivate different peoples in their quests for public achievement.

In every republic there are economic "riddles." For example, in Uzbekistan they have a surplus of labor resources [more people than jobs]. How is this problem to be resolved? Within the framework of the republic? Within the framework of the entire state? By exporting labor resources? Attempts at moving people without specific preparations have not always been successful. But when there were construction detachments (for example, on the BAM [Baikal-Magistral Railroad]) comprised of different parts of the multinational community, things have gone well.

Drobizheva: But the resettlement of the nonblack-soil region did not bring the anticipated results.[3] The same number of Uzbeks left as arrived there. Generally, the regulation of migration is a delicate point. For a long time we thought that if use of the Russian language spread in labor-surplus regions, then the migration from these republics would increase. The majority of Kabardinians, Checheny, Ingushy, and Balkarians spoke Russian as if it were their native tongue; all the same, their representatives who received education in other regions went home to the lands of their ancestors. Such is their tradition.

Polyakov: It is important that national traditions are harmonized with international traditions. They were naturally born, not forced or invented, and thus they have gained mighty strength. These are not mere words; this is reality.

Drobizheva: For a long time, we have set aside the resolution of current national problems, but now this is simply impossible. Sometimes there are problems between neighboring ethnic groups; in other cases, it is necessary to satisfy the social, cultural, and domestic demands of nationality for those living among the natives of a different national republic. Part of the concern about the retreat from Leninist national politics has reached us; many of these concerns were created by the economic and moral deformations of the years of stagnation. This is why we expect a dedication to national relations from the *plenum* of the Central Committee of the CPSU.[4]

Polyakov: Now we're talking about the political rights of nonnative nationalities, their representation in the soviets, in the governmental organs of the republics.

Drobizheva: But concerning the satisfaction of their cultural, social, and everyday interests we should see nothing bad. Let's say that the Tatars in Moscow began to celebrate the Sabantui [a Tatar national-religious holiday]. People would listen to Tatar songs, dance, and converse in

---

[3] The population has abandoned thousands of villages under Soviet rule in the nonblack-soil lands of northern Russia for a variety of economic and social reasons.

[4] The *plenum* on the nationality question has been long delayed, and some people's expectations for it are perhaps too high.

their native language. Incidentally, the Sabantui has also attracted many Russians. Let there be national theaters, newspapers, cafés, and national holidays. This will arouse the interest of other nationalities, who will say: Why not examine this and try it ourselves?

Up until now all of our national politics have been founded on the attainment of true equality among nations. Until recently, steps in this direction have been taken. Peoples who are equally developed socially and culturally are regularly in contact with each other. But, having decided that this is the pinnacle of all endeavors, we then discovered that we are undergoing significant psychological reconstruction. For example, the Russians previously appeared in the role of "helpers." Today we should understand that they [Russians] live and work in equality with peoples who already have their own working class and intelligentsia and which fully realize that they, too, have achieved great successes. This means that psychological restructuring must occur also among those who were helped. (They must understand that they can no longer rely on their former helpers.) And, of course, those who helped should now understand that they are equal partners. The difficulty lies in the fact that complete psychological restructuring will take a long time. On the other hand, when people of equal sociocultural status come into contact, a competitive situation is created, and only business-like qualities have meaning relevant to occupying any position. But not every man is ready for this; we have yet to acknowledge the results of such "competitions of knowledge and ability." In multinational areas, however, any dissatisfaction is transferred to a national level.

In the beginning of *perestroika*, it was important to see how national relations were influenced by other factors such as, for example, the law, the existence of cultural traditions, and the interests of specific peoples. Our situation is favorable because we have government, law, and a moral ideology strengthening the friendship of peoples. It is no accident that all people took to heart the events in Kazakhstan and Yakutia,[5] and that they are still monitoring the events in Azerbaijan and Armenia.

---

[5] The autonomous republic of Yakutia experienced anti-Russian riots in 1987 which received little attention in the West.

Melikyants: In your opinion, why did the excesses in Alma-Ata and Sumgait occur?

Polyakov: National tensions were used by antisocial extremist elements. This led to violence and crime. And crime should always be punished.

But from where has this tension, for example in Karabakh, come? It is from the remote echoes of the discord unleashed here by nationalists in the most oppressive times of intervention and civil war, and from our present shortcomings in undertaking the socioeconomic and cultural development of an autonomous region. Under such conditions, grounds are created for tense, quickly fired, one-sided demands. Do not discount accounts of attempts to use the process of democratization to serve narrow self-interests. The results will be disorder, outbreaks of violence that are impossible to justify, and economic damage preventing people from working normally.

Many now demand improvement of the situation in Karabakh. I think, on the one hand, that it's a good idea to consider measures to accelerate social development of the region to satisfy not just individual groups, but the entire population.

Drobizheva: I also think that it's helpful to study all the facts when one forms an opinion about the causes of events. One of these causes is variation in the democratic tradition resulting from the various paces and types of development of different peoples. This also accentuates today's behavior in this critical situation. We practice only a few democratic forms of the expression of will. It is clear, however, that *glasnost*, calm discussions, and sober decisions can and must play a significant role in the improvement of the situation in Karabakh. No issue can be resolved without broad discussion among all the instruments of democracy and *glasnost*: the labor collectives, local soviets, and social organizations. It's important that ideological measures ensure the possibility for social and cultural growth of local populations that in the final result does not conflict with the interests of other nations.

Melikyants: We have discussed a small range of questions, but through this it has become evident that this multifaceted, difficult question requires serious long-range analysis for its resolution. Life reminds us that national processes go together with growth, and it is important to understand this in order to look ahead with optimism and the assurance of success.

18

Conscience Is Free

Alexander Nezhny and Konstantin Kharchev

Ogonyok, no. 21, 1988

In this article writer Alexander Nezhny and Konstantin Kharchev, chairman of the State Committee for Religious Affairs, compete with each other in exposing the oppressive authoritarian behavior of local officials toward religious believers and the church. Although these actions are described here as illegal, none of the local officials ever gets punished for abusing power. Konstantin Kharchev describes a new level of tolerance for religion as a significant achievement of the Gorbachev reforms. The tone of Kharchev's remarks is, by Soviet standards, extremely courageous and challenging. Nevertheless, the interview completely avoids discussion of other religions, such as Islam, Judaism, Catholicism, and their specific problems in the Soviet Union.

From ten o'clock on Saturday morning Konstantin Kharchev was receiving the believers. I sat nearby and took notes.

Three people arrived from the village of Mashanets of the Chernovtsy *oblast*: a middle-aged woman and two elderly men with rows of decorative ribbons. One man had only one leg.

"Where did you lose your leg?" asked Konstantin Mikhailovich.

"In 1944, near Tallinn," responded Vasily Shevchuk. His comrade had fought at the third Ukrainian front. The woman had lost her father. They delivered a letter signed by 572 people, Orthodox believers who were asking that the church that had been taken from them in the early 1960s be returned. Once it housed pictures of the best workers, and now grain is kept there.

Two women from Alushta [a city on the Crimean peninsula] requested, on behalf of the city's Orthodox believers, the registration of a religious community and the return of the temple of the Fyodor Stratilat Martyr, closed since 1963. "Why do I get letters with the word 'citizen' " asked one of them. "Just because I am a believer?" [The normal term of address is "comrade."]

A delegation from Cheboksary asked for the registration of a second Orthodox community and for the return of a temple. "It is getting ruined. It is used to store brooms and barrels."

Visitors from Gorky explained that this city of almost two million inhabitants has only three small Orthodox churches, located on the outskirts of town. The believers asked for permission to use the Spaso-Preobrazhensky Cathedral, where dismountable rostrums are stored.

Pyatidesyatniks [a religious sect] from Ternopol, Baptists from Chernovtsy *oblast*, the Orthodox from the Rostov *oblast*—altogether Kharchev received thirty-one delegations until nine o'clock in the evening.

Nezhny: "Konstantin Mikhailovich," I said at our next meeting with the chairman of the State Committee for Religious Affairs, "I would only need to be present at your reception to understand and feel the extreme gravity of the problem. In addition, I have at my disposal quite a few similar facts collected during my trips, from meetings with the believers, and from the mail. We should admit this with bitterness: In the localities, the constitutional rights of the believers[1] and the laws concerning religious cults are routinely violated."

Kharchev: "Routinely" is too categorical. We have a sufficient number of examples of a different kind, examples of the respectful attitude of local authorities toward the legitimate requests of our compatriots who practice religion. After the April 1985 *plenum* of the Central Committee of the CPSU, to my knowledge three hundred religious groupings of various denominations were registered. But, undoubtedly, there are still too many unresolved problems in this social sphere of our life. Some leaders who allow themselves to not follow the rule of law still exist. Being imprisoned by old perceptions, living by the customs of yesterday or even of time before yesterday, they apply administrative pressure, rejection, and the shameful bureaucratic red tape that was so instrumental

---

[1] Article 52 of the 1977 Soviet constitution, although it allows believers to practice any religion, restricts their contacts with the rest of Soviet society. In practice religious activities are tightly regulated by the state.

in the past—all this solely for the sake of not allowing "concessions" to the church, which would be inadmissible from their point of view!

Nezhny: The former secretary of the Kirov *oblast* party committee, Yu. Karacharov, who is now retired, told me straightforwardly, "Not one step back for the church!" He was talking about the legitimate right of the inhabitants of Kirov who were asking to register a second Orthodox community.

Kharchev: As you know, the State Committee for Religious Affairs of the Council of Ministers of the USSR has registered this community. Certainly we would not have had to interfere if the local officials had followed the stipulations of the laws. After all, this is their duty.

Nezhny: Any avoidance of executing the laws must be punished. Only under this condition is it possible to instill in people an unconditional respect for the laws, including the clauses that defend that principle most important for the public, the principle of freedom of conscience.

Kharchev: I completely agree with you. Moreover, I am profoundly convinced that the fate of *perestroika* is determined in many ways by the attitude of the believers. To whom will they give their hearts, who will they become: active, passionate supporters of *perestroika* or perhaps enemies of the changes taking place in the country? This will become one of the most significant dilemmas of our political life! Look, there are tens of millions of believers in our country, around seventy million people. Although the majority of the population consists of people who espouse the materialistic outlook, there are no grounds to speak of the abandonment of religion by the masses. Thus there are millions, tens of millions of believers. That politics begins where the millions are is a well-known fact. Therefore, the dilemma is extremely simple and clear. If the believers feel that *perestroika* is advancing and that it rejects the view that a believer is a second-rate person, that it demands on all levels of society a strict observation of the principle of freedom of conscience and following it to the letter of the law, then, I am sure, they all will become its consistent allies and participants.

At his meeting with the leadership of the Russian Orthodox church Mikhail Gorbachev emphasized that *perestroika*, democratization, and *glasnost* include the believers, without any reservations whatsoever.

We should reflect on something else as well. We are striving for trust between peoples, and this is the essence of our foreign policy. Indeed, what kind of life can there be on the small planet Earth without mutual trust between peoples, what universal human ideals can we discuss? But no less important than this is to restore the trust of the believers in the party and the state. The ability to trust has been lost to a considerable degree. If we restore the trust, we will reinforce the movement of *perestroika* by a multimillion human factor, and we will attract the believers to our side, as happened in the first years after the October Revolution.

Nezhny: Do you think, Konstantin Mikhailovich, that Soviet authorities succeeded in gaining the support of the believers in the first years of the Soviet Union's existence?

Kharchev: Undoubtedly! Such ideals of the October Revolution as justice, liberty, and equality were consonant with the ideals of Christianity so dear to its believers. The personal modesty of the Bolsheviks, their readiness to sacrifice themselves, their absence of thought for personal well-being—all of this could have led the believers (in other words, the majority of the population) to make spontaneous comparisons with the martyrs for faith who were always so respected in Russia. That is why, by the way, this lesson, or if you wish the legacy of the first years after the revolution, is so important to those of us who carry the heavy load of responsibility for spiritual renaissance. The purer the moral makeup of the Communist, the more people believe him.

Nezhny: I recently obtained an eloquent document from 1961, a document for which Mikhail Saltykov-Shchedrin [a well-known nineteenth-century Russian satirist] would have paid a lot, had he lived in our time. It is a decree from Slobodskoi municipality in the Kirov *oblast*. I quote:

> After considering the request of such public organizations as the movie theater Avrora, a preschool kindergarten, kindergarten no. 2, a children's school of sports, a police precinct and others to prohibit the ringing of bells, which interferes with the attentive watching of movies in the theaters and the normal relaxation of

children in kindergartens and citizens in their
apartments after their daily work, in accordance with the
regulation governing legislation on denominations the
municipality decides to forbid the ringing of the bells in
the church of St. Catherine.

You see, the ringing of the bells inhibits attentive viewing of
movies!

Kharchev: In essence, this is a rude violation of the
legislation on religious denominations. Unfortunately,
even today the ringing of bells is forbidden in a number of
cities and provinces, for example in Saransk, in
Arkhangelsk and Sverdlovsk provinces, and in many cities
of the Ukraine and Byelorussia. You were present at the
reception of the believers and must have noticed that, in
most cases, the subject of the discussion was religious
societies deprived of registration in the 1960s. The churches
were closed, but the believers did not disappear. This is the
most glaring example of voluntarism! [Nikita Khrushchev
was accused by the party leaders who overthrew him of
voluntarism; that is, that the actions taken by him were
based on his whims and not on the broad consensus.] The
question arises: Did this strengthen the trust of the people
in the Soviet authorities? Did it help to rally the society? Did
it strengthen conviction in the supremacy of the law and
the inescapable accountability for its violation? When
churches were closed (and, moreover, even destroyed
openly), did these good-for-nothing leaders reflect on the
fact that through their antidemocratic actions they sowed
the seeds of animosity in the people?

The consequences of this administrative itching to close
down, to close down by all means, are felt today as well.
Only last year the State Committee for Religious Affairs of
the Council of Ministers of the USSR received more than
three thousand complaints from the believers. We
encounter cases of the most savage bureaucratic behavior.
Instead of trying to ease to a greater extent the spiritual life
of the believers within the existing legislation (which for all
its shortcomings does allow such possibilities), some
officials would never miss an opportunity to place an
obstacle literally without a reason. For years disputes have
taken place concerning whether to build a new house of
prayer or to modernize an old one so that it will have a

dome. The believer cannot understand why erecting a building is allowed, yet constructing a dome over it is forbidden.

Nezhny: Even the convinced atheist with solid democratic views will consider this approach an encroachment on the freedom of conscience.

Kharchev: And it is known who is causing the trouble: the city's architect, the secretary of the municipality, other Soviet authorities—all, as a rule, party members. So what do they say to the believers? "You see, this cross can be seen from the windows of the school! It is impossible!" or "The dome will interfere with the architectural view!" or "This sign—Baptist House of Prayer—should be taken off." And some very zealous local officials will even establish for how many minutes the bells may ring and send this schedule to the church! The regulation that parents who intend to baptize their child must show their passports has been annulled; it was, by the way, illegal. Now there are reports from the localities that birth certificates and other documents are requested. So, either by hook or by crook.

Nezhny: All that follows then is no secret: the notice to the place of work, the deliberation in a meeting of coworkers, the caricature in the wall newspaper [wall newspapers are a propaganda tool for depicting how an enterprise or organization fulfills its duties in light of the latest party appeals], and even the administrative measures.

Kharchev: But baptism is the personal business of the believer; it is according to his conscience whose freedom is guaranteed by the constitution! One cannot manage the spiritual sphere by the fist. This is an indisputable, agonizing lesson of our history, but its incredible importance, it seems, is not quite fully understood.

Nezhny: The coincidence of topics is amazing. The struggle for the dome you mentioned took place in the Krasnodar territory (by the way, *Ogonyok* published this story). I recently visited Uzbekistan, however. There, in the city of Dzhizak, the Orthodox believers renovated their church and built up a dome, which is necessary for the ventilation of the interior in the hot climate of Central Asia. On a beautiful June night in 1986, the local authorities had the church surrounded and the dome destroyed. Since then, the believers have been demanding, so far in vain, the restoration of the dome. Had I been in their position, I would have gone to the courts. What do you think, Konstantin Mikhailovich?

Kharchev: The courts should exemplarily punish the guilty, based on the letter and spirit of the law.

Nezhny: From my notes of the same trip: In the settlement of Romanovka, near Frunze, evangelical Baptists built a new house of prayer several years ago after filing all of the necessary papers. One of the top officials of the republic of Kirgiz, after seeing this house, decided that it was too good for the Baptists and ordered that it be taken away and given to the Young Pioneers [the Communist organization for youth aged nine to fourteen]. The consequences of this and similar illegal and immoral actions you, Konstantin Mikhailovich, know very well.

Kharchev: People come to religion because of bureaucracy and our callousness. I would like to repeat again and again that it is impossible and unacceptable to oppose the church from the position of force. It is time to understand that to separate the church from the state does not at all mean to separate it from the society. The believers are our Soviet men and women, grown up and educated in the Soviet period. The church is the organization of the believers; it cannot be cut off from the processes taking place in society, from participating in the solutions to our internal problems, from the politics. Also, as the recent convocation of bishops of the Russian Orthodox church showed, the present clergy by an overwhelming majority actively support *perestroika* and resist resolutely all attempts to split the believers and prevent them from taking part in the democratic transformation of our life.

In the 1930s we developed an exclusively negative attitude toward religion and the believers. It is now necessary to change this attitude. We cannot advance by exploiting negative feelings. The time has come to restructure ourselves. The dialectics of the relations between the socialist state and the church are extremely delicate. Religion is a philosophy with which the Marxist ideology is waging and will continue to wage a constant struggle, but it is a different matter that the church is a public institution consisting of the clergy and the believers. We should not transfer contradictions from the first sphere into the second one, where the principle of mutual respect should be observed. Now, in the atmosphere of democratization, Lenin's tenet that to create a heaven on Earth is more important for us than the unanimity of opinions among the proletariat about heaven in the skies should be viewed as essential. After all, there are some goals whose achievement is a true priority and whose solution now takes on an enormous significance. Social and political problems of our society, the struggle for peace, ecology—these are areas in which it is necessary to unify all of the forces that are ready for sincere and active cooperation. If it is our fate to live in a mixed society consisting of both materialists and believers, then let's build socialism and carry out *perestroika* together with the believers and not separately from them!

The spiritual life of those whose world outlook is different from ours is taking its normal course in its own fashion. This currently cannot be eliminated, nor can it merge with our own ideology. But it is necessary to combine both the efforts and the aspirations of people for universal moral and spiritual values toward our common well-being and peace. It is possible and necessary to ensure this unity, even if we all must learn many things anew.

Nezhny: There is an apprehension that after the festivities on the occasion of the millennium of the Baptism of Rus' the "screws will be tightened."

Kharchev: There is no way that this can happen. During the meeting with the Patriarch Pimen of Moscow and All Russia and the members of the Holy Synod of the Russian Orthodox church, Mikhail Gorbachev said that "we are fully reconstructing the Leninist principles of the attitude toward religion, church, and believers. The attitude toward church and believers should be determined by the concern for strengthening the unity of all workers, all our people." We are considering the jubilee arrangements as a weighty step toward perfection of the relations between the church and state, perfection in the spirit of Lenin's decree on religion.

Nezhny: So that we could legitimately say that conscience is free!

Kharchev: Precisely so.

19

Impasses of Sobering Up

Lev Ovrutsky

Sovetskaya Kultura, July 16, 1988

Unlike most authors of articles on this subject, Ovrutsky believes that the antialcoholism campaign initiated in 1985 has been quite successful. As proof he cites significant decreases in the number of auto accidents, fewer dissolved marriages, and the reduction in the mortality rate. His explanation that the sugar boom is a result of such factors as fears of shortages and seasonal changes in demand seems reasonable and weighty. Ovrutsky believes that moonshining was widespread even before the new restrictions on the sale of alcoholic beverages were imposed, but he blames the policies of raising the price and further curtailing the amount of alcohol for sale for a substantial increase in moonshining.

Regardless of the role of the various factors affecting the distribution of sugar, it is now rationed throughout the whole country. Most observers consider the antialcoholism policies to be extreme, and even Mikhail Gorbachev has admitted that the state lost 49 billion rubles in two years by selling less alcohol, most of which money probably was taken in by the moonshiners.

Future historians take note: The first resolute step taken after April 1985 was to dismantle the old policy toward drinking. The general feeling at that time was that things could not continue in the same way. Something had to be done immediately. Drugged by vodka, the country had to be shaken up before a discussion could begin about this very serious matter.

After three years it became evident that some of the planned actions had succeeded and some had failed. This is the current focus of the discussion. Some of the strongest irritations today, according to public opinion, are wine and sugar lines and shortages of lotions, toothpaste, and tomato paste.

"In the embrace of the coil." "Green serpent in the slippers."[7] "Stop the moonshiner!" The tone of the newspaper headlines reminds one of reports from the war fronts. This is indeed a front, and the changes taking place

---

[7]The green serpent is a symbol of drunkenness in Russia.

here are alarming. The sale of sugar is increasing: In 1985 it reached 7,850,000 tons; in 1986, 8,635,000; in 1987, 9,280,000. The number of moonshiners caught is dramatically increasing: Last year's level was five times higher than the level of 1985. As the procurator general of the USSR noted, "the sale of alcoholic beverages is reduced by half, but this reduction is almost 'compensated' for by moonshine."

Some distressed people ask, who could have expected this?

We warned you, say others who are shining with the light of triumphant truth.

Just wait for what may still lie ahead, foretell others with gloom.

It is said that doubts are the bread of a researcher, so I invite the reader to this poor meal.

As is well known, the most important indicators of moonshining are the quantity of sugar sold to the public and the number of moonshiners uncovered. However, after delving only slightly into the depth of the statistics, one gets the impression that the phenomenon of moonshining is woven from paradoxes. It seems that the number of uncovered moonshiners is growing only in two cases: (a) when the sales of sugar are rising; (b) when sales are on the decline. So what indicator should be taken seriously, sugar sales or the "uncovering" of moonshiners? Sugar sales, it seems, is the correct answer. This indicator has the advantage of being more objective, and therefore it can be trusted more.

And what does the "uncovering" in this case disclose? At the very least, two things. First, the degree of activity of the police forces. If in the past, while appealing to the public to be vigilant, the police kept three kilometers away from the area of the moonshiner so as not to burden the crime statistics or to hinder the crime rate's gradual decline, now the producer of moonshine is caught much more often. How much more often is hard to say, but I have some information for reflection. *Izvestiya* published a curious piece on October 22, 1985, about the two-month campaign for the voluntary surrender of moonshine equipment in the Yantikovsky district of Chuvashiya. Without going into colorful details, here is the summary: In this district of 6,000 households there were 5,115 *samogon* apparatuses confiscated. Another 400 were found at the outskirts of the villages. That is wholesale moonshining (or almost wholesale). However, in 1984 there were only seven cases of moonshining uncovered.

Second, the "grimaces" of the police statistics are like a mirror reflecting the change in antimoonshine legislation. After July of 1987, when the responsibility for manufacturing substitute beverages was changed from criminal to administrative authorities, the second half of the year was marked by a jump in "disclosures" (they grew fourfold compared with the first half of the year). The new legislation considerably simplified the procedure of uncovering moonshiners and created a new legal basis for prosecuting the violators. According to the procurator general of the USSR this allowed authorities to "quickly process the cases in order to put an end to moonshining." It is hard to explain, but the improved functioning of the judicial organs began to be interpreted as an increase in the activities of moonshiners. It is the same as claiming, after installing a powerful pump on the well, that there is more oil underground.

As has already been mentioned the level of sugar sales is a more objective and trustworthy indicator, but it also demands a "delicate" treatment. In the article "Potholes on the Road to Sobriety," published in *Pravda* on October 19, 1987, A. Martynov writes that "it is not difficult to calculate that the million tons of sugar that the press calls 'superfluous,' which the population has consumed additionally since 1986, makes up a billion sugar packets weighing one kilo each. If they were all used to prepare the 'stuff,' they would make two billion bottles of moonshine."

This judgment is typical and clearly reflects the depth of analysis and knowledge of facts by the journalists. A. Martynov proceeds from the position, "if this sugar was used to manufacture the 'stuff.' " But what if it was used for something else? To prepare jam and similar items, for example. This hypothesis can be easily verified if one examines quarterly rather than yearly sugar sales. Thus, the first and second quarters of 1986 showed a reduction in sales compared to the corresponding quarters of 1985. But the third quarter gave the entire yearly addition in sugar sales. If one rejects the supposition that the moonshiners are people who are capable of being ascetic for the first six months of a year and then compensating for this abstention with a vengeance in the summer heat, one would have to conclude that it is precisely the harvest of fruits and berries that sets the amplitude of yearly oscillations in the demand for sugar. Indeed in 1986 there was a record fruit harvest, a million tons more than the average of the previous five years. This extra million required 843,000 tons of sugar that were not "superfluous."

To determine the current level of *samogon* production it is necessary to know what it was yesterday. This question is useful to ask but dangerous to respond to in conditions of information deficit.

To reflect on the level of *samogon* production during the 1970s and 1980s is only possible based on some scattered data. For example, in the late 1960s, V. Perevedentsev circulated a questionnaire among the "clients" of medical sobering stations. It appeared that every seventh client got drunk with the help of homemade brew. The author noted that this also happened in Moscow, where store shelves were filled with alcohol. In the small republic of Chuvashiya, 16,000 *samogon* apparatuses were voluntarily turned in. (Yantikovsky district was mentioned above. And how many such districts are there in Russia?) And in the Ukraine, as was reported by the television program "The Spotlight of *Perestroika*" on September 20, 1987, 500,000 apparatuses were surrendered! One can only guess whether every owner of an apparatus gave it up, or only every tenth owner.

There is one more witness to moonshining—the consequences. I remember that five or six years ago, during the heated and sometimes brutal discussions on the strategy of the antialcohol movement, forecasts were often made that the decrease in alcohol sales would inevitably be compensated for by illegal production and distribution. All negative phenomena will remain, it was predicted, and they will become even more aggravated. Were these forecasts true? Unfortunately, those who made them do not bother now to address these questions.

Let's turn to the facts. For the last three years crime accompanied by drinking has decreased by 40 percent, and the number of accidents involving drunk drivers has dropped by one third. Although the police are now much stricter about this, the number of people punished in connection with antialcohol legislation decreased from 14.4 million to 9.6 million in 1986 and further to 8.6 million in 1987. The number of failures to report to work has decreased by 40 percent, the number of divorces decreased, and life expectancy increased. Finally, the most important and "final" result of antialcohol policies: For the last two years there have been an average of two hundred thousand fewer deaths than in 1984.

The process of sobering up is especially apparent among youth. V. Morozov, a sociologist from Novosibirsk, followed the changes in drinking habits of students in 1984 to 1986 and established that among girls the number of those completely abstaining from alcohol rose from 2 to 8 percent, and among young men the number of those abstaining rose from 1 to 13 percent.

This author recently conducted a survey among "experts" on the problems of sobering up the young. These "experts" were the secretaries of district and city committees of the Komsomol. Fifty-five percent of those questioned agreed with the statement that "young workers are drinking less often." According to a quarter of the "experts," working youth drink with the same frequency as in the past. The rest declined to answer, but remarkably not one person claimed that drinking had increased. A similar distribution of replies was received concerning the drinking habits of students of professional schools. The Komsomol workers felt that the biggest positive changes had taken place among high-school students. Only one out of ten was asserting that schoolchildren drink as much as before, and the majority indicated considerable successes in school.

Could we have observed all of the signs of sobering up if moonshine had compensated for the reduction in the manufacturing and sale of alcohol? Prominent journalist S. Sheverdin formulated LID, the "law of the inescapability of damage" from the use of alcohol. Through this metaphorical construction a solid philosophical basis can be viewed: The energy of the evil encompassed in alcohol cannot dissolve without a trace. Alcohol of home or factory bottling equally explodes with crime, accidents, sickness, and the breaking up of the family. And if omniscient statistics report that there is less crime, accidents, deaths, and divorces, it should be taken into account.

"There are circumstances," wrote Marc Bloch when he encountered an insoluble problem, "when the researcher must first of all state what he did not find."

In compliance with the French historian, I did not find any proof that moonshining increased in 1985 and 1986. On the contrary; it seems to me that it decreased at this point. The tendency toward growth apparently revealed itself only in 1987. The State Committee on Prices long ago acquired a mystical ability to guess and meet the innermost wishes of the workers; however, the ability to calculate even the immediate aftereffects must still be learned. Meanwhile, ours and foreign experience unambiguously indicate that a price hike on alcohol (especially a dramatic one) provokes an increase of moonshining. It is sufficient to remember the first steps toward a consumer market made by the notorious *rykovka* [after Alexei Rykov, chairman of the Council of Ministers of the USSR in the 1920s]. The sale of vodka began in October 1925 at one ruble per bottle. Sales were so brisk that in December it was decided to raise the price by 50 percent. There was an immediate response; the villages stopped buying it. So in July 1926 there was no choice but to lower the price to one ruble and ten kopecks.

Police statistics indicate that the main producers and consumers of *samogon* and home-brewed beer are social outsiders: primarily low-income people such as retirees (often women), unqualified workers, etc. Let me add that the study of five hundred court cases of moonshining which I conducted together with the head of the public order department of the Tatar Autonomous Republic, V. Beliaev, showed that one in every ten moonshiners had been treated for alcohol addiction and one in every five had been tried.

Let's think: How would this social type respond to the price increase? Retired women are used to receiving payment for household services with a "bottle," so what should they do if the price for alcohol doubles? It is necessary to break the law, as the chauffeur, driver of the tractor, carpenter, and woodcutter are implacable.

What should a sick man or an alcoholic do? If he is accustomed to, figuratively speaking, spending all of his salary on alcohol, what would he do upon discovering that his salary is suddenly only sufficient for half of his "norm"? Naturally, the other half would be filled with a substitute.

By the way, it is a delusion to think that lines for wine encourage the *samogon* makers. The alcoholized consumer is prepared to stand in line but as a rule cannot pay double price. And he would rather abstain from alcohol than produce or consume *samogon*.

By sharply reducing the sales of alcoholic beverages in the fall of 1987, we crossed the line beyond which millions of drunkards and alcoholics were left without a choice. (It is significant that the reduction of sales occurred mostly at the expense of vodka and *bormotukha*, the sweet wine with a high content of alcohol especially valued by this group.) These people produce *samogon* for the simple reason that they cannot live without drinking.

One can hardly confine considerations regarding the sugar "boom" that struck the country in the fall of 1987, and which has only recently moderated, to the findings stated above. There are other considerations as well. First, due to weather the harvest of sugar beet was collected later than usual. Correspondingly, the entire technological process had to be moved up. As a result in September some regions received less sugar than was planned. Second, influenced by rumors about a sugar deficit, the hoarding of sugar is taking place. The principle of "snowballing" that is guiding the deficit "fever" has already been well described, so there is no need to reiterate. Incidentally, on May 22, the Leningrad "TV Courier" broadcast a story on the salt boom that has spread around this city on the Neva river. Is it those moonshiners again?

20

Who Will Pick the Red Flower?

Nina Fokina

Dalnii Vostok, no. 1, 1988

This article from *Dalnii Vostok* (the journal of the Far East) illustrates that the drug problem exists in all parts of the Soviet Union. Nina Fokina blames the deterioration of social problems and the lack of a public dialogue on the twenty-year period of stagnation under Brezhnev. She supports her point of view with several letters and interviews.

A letter printed here about a seventeen-year-old girl from a working family discusses a circle of people who regularly smoked pot. Her parents did not succeed in obtaining help from officials and the police. Since until recently there was no official recognition of a drug problem, the police would not make any attempts to intercede. One doctor cited in the article explains that, according to official Soviet thinking, there should be no social roots for drug addiction in the USSR. As a result, most schools and enterprises have never reported or sought help for drug addicts. The doctor finds this to be a dangerous attitude that has helped spread the use of drugs.

It so happens that there are more letters and fewer meetings. I can explain it, though: Drug addiction among youth remains a secret for us, although we speak about it today aloud and even loudly.

We do speak loudly about it, but only amongst ourselves. A dialogue with the "victims of the evil"—the teenagers, girls and boys, who have tasted the "forbidden fruit"—still has not occurred. They do not come out for direct contact, they do not hurry with confessions, and if they agree to spell out their point of view on the problem, then it is under the condition of anonymity.

However, the fact that they who have never before admitted adults into their tight and secret circle have now decided to start a correspondence with us, the adults, merits much consideration.

As a journalist, a newspaper writer covering youth problems, I see in drug addiction the same roots as I see in violence, infantilism, alcoholism, political indifference, prostitution—the diseases that we always ascribed to the "birthmarks" of the past, to the corrupting influence of the West, to what you will, so as not to renounce the noble concept that our society is intrinsically free of any factors that would give rise to these diseases.

Today we see that this is not so. We owe many of these abnormalities in our young generation to the twenty years called "the years of stagnation" at the 27th Party Congress, the years when the "second economy" nearly became the norm, when our children were told one thing in school and outside it they would see something else quite different, when their vocabulary was enriched with such short words as "pull," "protection," and "graft." With what thoughtlessness did we try to raise a healthy generation!

It is possible that people will object: "Do you think that young people are not at fault for their own errors?"

Of course they are guilty. Fyodor Dostoevsky noted that a human being answers first for his own actions, whatever external circumstances might be. But, first, in the contemporary world, with its powerful mass media and omnipresent temptations, the influence of surroundings on the inner world of a person has grown to an enormous extent. This has to be taken into account. Second, if we heap troubles on the young people and walk away "snow white," then what will happen to our conscience, both personal and civic? Dostoevsky also reminds us that only with the feeling of one's own guilt should one enter a courtroom. Only then will there be meaning and sense in the judgment.

This goes by way of introduction to this discussion. I will add also that the letters quoted here are the "originals." Only spelling mistakes, if there were any, have been corrected.

A Letter

The problem is that we have a daughter who is seventeen. She goes to a commercial school, but she is cruel to us and to herself. In October, she fell in with a sect or a group and did not come home for four days. She was not in class, and when she came home and we asked her where she had been, she answered, "If I tell, then someone in our family will die." I said, "I'd rather be dead than not know the truth." And I found out something unbelievable.

No longer, Tanya said, did she plan to work for the state. And she did not advise her brother—we have a younger son—to go into the army. And also, she said, people with Aryan blood in their veins will come and liberate us.

I began to question her about where she had heard this nonsense. With difficulty I got it out of her.

They gather somewhere in a three-room apartment. The host is about forty. The apartment has many rugs, there is no sofa, there are no chairs, and they sit on the floor. If you knew how I begged her to tell me the address! "No," she said, "if I tell, they will kill me." I answered that I'd rather have no daughter and go weep at the cemetery every day than know that someone is doggedly turning you into an idiot.

She objected absolutely calmly that there was nothing wrong with this group. They don't drink. Only the host smokes, but he fills the room with smoke that makes it impossible to think about anything. "And don't ask me, Mama," she said, "to tell you where this takes place, because we gave an oath." She showed me her finger, which was bandaged. They swore a blood oath. They mixed blood in a glass, diluted it with water, and passed it around the circle—to drink.

No, no, you cannot imagine my state! I said to my daughter, "You cannot do it. This is not our life. We are working people, we have a different ideology. Aryans have already come to our country." I will never forget that. Indeed, my childhood was spent "under the Germans." I am a native of Byelorussia. I said all that, but it was as if she did not hear. She got ready to go out again and left, no matter how I tried to block the door and how much I cried. Again three sleepless nights passed, and then she appeared in the morning and showed me a cap with a long peak of dark velvet. On it there was an ornament, some kind of American emblem. The embroidery was very skillfully done.

I don't blame anyone but myself for anything. But what are her father and I guilty of? We live on our wages. Modestly. We never spoiled Tanya with imported things. Besides a ruble for lunch, we never gave her any money. For almost thirty years both her father and I have been well regarded at the factory. But in the end we turned out to be powerless before this unknown preacher. I would pay dearly to know what swine perverted our Tanya. And probably not only Tanya.

The address was indicated on the envelope, and I decided to visit this family, although I didn't trust all of the facts laid out in the letter. Indeed, in those years we all thought that our way of life guaranteed us against the appearance of such calamities as drug addiction. My opinion was shared by many. Later I found out that, when Tanya's mother knocked on doors where Tanya studied, they looked at her as if she were crazy, and at the police station they told her, "It's not our problem."

In the end, rightly or wrongly, the mother placed Tanya under psychiatric observation, suspecting a psychological disorder. She soon learned that, as with every drug addict, Tanya's state of mind was, in fact, not in order.

I would like, of course, to tell here how the doctors sounded the alarm and roused the public and the police to search for the ringleader, and how the group was caught "red-handed" with all the proper consequences. But I promised to tell the truth. And the truth, alas, is different. If the spread of drug addiction is not officially recognized, what regional department of the police is going to complicate its life with a search for drug addicts? Indeed, these young people sit quietly on rugs, indulge in their folly, and make no trouble for anyone, no brawls in public parks. As for American caps and "alien" ideas, let some other department worry about it. And what are our teachers for? Let them improve their educational work. And the Komsomol? And the family, if you please?

Thus the circle is completed. Tanya's mother ran to Tanya's friends who might know where her daughter went, where the group gathered. No, they didn't know. And who would tell if he knew, anyway?

After the hospital, Tanya held out for almost half a year. One day, returning to the office from vacation, I found a letter on my desk. I was told it had been there for a long time. I opened it and read with alarm: "It is all pointless. Tanya has disappeared."

The Fruits of Silence

From an interview between a junior member of the Department of Psychiatry of Khabarovsk Medical Institute, candidate of medical sciences Vladimir Ivanovich Mikhailov, and *Tikhookeanskaya Zvezda* [*Pacific Star*, the main newspaper of the Khabarovsk territory] correspondent A. Izmailov:

Drug addiction began to spread in the country in the 1970s. By that time, in the Ministry of Health a style of leadership had formed that appealed to all of us to work, in essence, for "rosy" reports, and not to do our best.

I am certain that drug addiction would not have begun to spread if we, the drug experts, had been able to study it and cut it off from the very beginning. In 1975 an idea was formed, according to which the social roots of drug addiction do not exist here, and so drug addiction could not and did not exist. This meant that research on this subject was neither encouraged nor planned.

Under these conditions we, the drug specialists, could solve these problems only on the local level. We were much too late, since drug addiction had left the stage of individual cases and is now surrounded by a criminal network of drug dealers. While we remained silent, a drug market was being organized. With our silence we have made drug addiction a social phenomenon.

Once, in one of the districts of Khabarovsk, a drug specialist working with young people was being inspected. His report listed only three addicts. He was reprimanded. And what do you think happened? A little later the number in the report had grown a hundred times. Do you understand what that means? The statistics we have speak not so much of the number of addicts as of the firmness of our prejudice or our chronic fear of this work. We do not have knowledge about what we are fighting, and so drug addiction is stronger than drug enforcement.

A shocking event recently took place in our clinic. Pavel S. is one of our patients. He is twenty-seven, and for the past three years he has worked at the Ordzhonikidze oil refinery. He is an addict. So recently a representative of the administration of the refinery came to him and tried to convince him to sign and backdate a statement of voluntary resignation, so that the collective's record would show no absences and they would get a bonus.

No secondary or vocational school will ever release information on the number of addicts. In essence, they are mainly concerned with padding their educational reports. This is really terrible! In the hospital where I work, we have a certain addict. He was a normal, happy person, and now he is a clear-cut case of schizophrenia. He also suffers from persecution mania and delusions. He constantly discusses the mechanism of a perpetual motion machine comprising the universe, with himself as a cogwheel in this mechanism. The man has lost his mind. Nothing interests him except drugs and delusions.

As a physician I can say that there is no illusory world into which, as it is widely believed, the addict withdraws. Hashish contains neurotropic poison which acts on the complex chemical process in the head that we call thought.

Every "joint" is a step down to the animal state. Every hemp cigarette kills a hundred thousand brain cells. The effect is the same as banging a man's head against a wall for ten hours. The remaining cells work under increased pressure and quickly tire, and this already means a diminished life. Externally, this is expressed as fury, rage, pathological behavior. This is the only existence for a brain damaged by cannabis.

Therefore, I say that drug addiction is always a tragedy. It begins with foolishness and ends with insanity or death.

Yes, we must fight against this phenomenon. But what we must do first is love people more than reports on educational work. As long as we cover up drug addiction, it will (alas!) spread on.

21

Cobras over Gold

Georgy Ovcharenko

Pravda, January 23, 1988

This article details the high levels of corruption reached in the republic of Uzbekistan. Nearly the entire party and state leadership of the republic formed a mafia in order to enrich themselves and to control the population. The Uzbek leadership falsely reported high harvests of cotton in order to receive billions of rubles from Moscow. To uncover the cotton affair (*rashidovshchina*), Moscow investigators worked for five years under adverse conditions. This article does not address the issue of how many other corrupt party leaders remain in other regions of the country.

"**H**ere, now . . . here exactly." Said poked at a common elm shrub and suddenly turned pale. On the sand, expanding its hood ominously, a huge cobra raised its head. But their feet were faster than it was. In a split second they were at a safe distance from the snake. But raised there, the cobra was ready with lightning speed to punish anyone who would come closer.

"That's the last straw," Bakhtiyar Abdurakhimov muttered in Uzbek. He had something to be annoyed about: In preparing the retrieval operation for the valuables of the former first secretary of one of the party district committees of the Kashkadaryinskaya *oblast*, they had miscalculated. They believed that a small part of the missing amount, some 250,000 rubles taken in bribes, was hidden with his brother. And the three of them had set out to retrieve it.

The secretary's brother gave over the money with suspicious ease.

"That isn't much." Albert Kartashyan decided to pressure him. "Where's the rest?"

"Uh, there isn't." The man opened his hands. "Some people came from my brother; they took it."

Bakhtiyar exchanged glances with his comrades. A familiar picture: Hidden at the slightest danger, the money is divided up, distributed to relatives and trusted individuals. Like a needle in a haystack. All that remained was for them to regret that the criminologists from Vladimir Antonov's group were not with them. Their instruments literally can see beneath the ground and through walls. There were only three of them and each minute was indeed worth its weight in gold.

By the end of two days without food or sleep, they were able to retrieve about a million more. There was still a young fellow named Said who, according to the brother of the former first secretary of the district committee, had dragged away a heavy bag.

They were lying in ambush at Said's house. At dawn, when their eyes were still heavy with sleep, Bakhtiyar noticed a shadow noiselessly approaching the house from the foothills. It was Said returning on his motorcycle with the headlights and engine turned off. Later, he led them through the desert from one elm shrub to another. It began to seem that there would be no end, that they were only being led by the nose. They dug through cubic meters of sand before they reached the place that the cobra now guarded.

"I'll swear to it the snake was not here," Said assured them. "Obviously it was lured to the gold."

Somehow they chased off the snake. The valuables, some 300,000 rubles more, were in the bag. In the car, the other guys fell asleep right away, while Bakhtiyar was thinking about folk legends. It is said that gold attracts snakes and greedy, crafty people who, with those traits, are worse than snakes. That's just the way it is, he thought, and dozed off.

In the summer of 1983 the inspector of special affairs from the general procurator [attorney general] of the USSR, Telman Gdlyan, was instructed to assemble a group and fly to Bukhara. It was there that militia [police] Lieutenant Colonel A. Muzaffarov, head of the OBKhSS [department of the police against embezzlement of socialist property and speculation] of the regional UVD [department of internal affairs], was caught red-handed after accepting a bribe for 1,000 rubles by KGB agents. The resulting information revealed a network of bribe takers, interwoven like a tangle of snakes, operating in the Bukhara *oblast*. Upon the arrival of the investigating group, the head of the *oblast* department of internal affairs, A. Dustov, was arrested along with the director of the Bukhara city trade department, Sh. Kudratov, and the head of the *oblast* department of industrial supplies [Gossnab], D. Sharipov.

Telman Khorenovich Gdlyan and his colleagues were given the intricate task, not unusual for their work, of investigating to determine the bribe takers' criminal connections, to expose how the state's stolen resources were processed, to organize the evidence charging each one of the accused, and to submit the case before the court. Nobody guessed then that it was more complicated than that. The threads from Bukhara were spun over all of Uzbekistan, to the capital itself. At that time, the Uzbek republic was boasting in the press and on television about its hundreds of thousands of tons of above-plan production of cotton. The republic's leaders could not find enough spaces on their jackets for more and more awards.

The cotton affair in Uzbekistan cracked open loudly and unexpectedly, like a clap of thunder on a clear day. The newspapers published articles disclosing how the state paid Uzbekistan for cotton that did not exist. Nearly a million tons of it were registered on paper every year. The paradox was explainable: Cotton harvests increased on paper while fabric production decreased. Next came a huge case that ended in an exceptional degree of punishment for the former minister of the republic's cotton industry and for other organizers in the affair, while hundreds more were implicated.

Gdlyan followed the trail and grew angry: "Really, did nobody else in the republic, except for the organizers in the affair, see the exaggerated figures? The party workers, the soviets or law protection agencies didn't see it? And why were so many people involved? For the numbers? Surely it's clear that most of them had been placed in desperate circumstances. And the important thing: Where is the money, the valuables? Billions were stolen and only crumbs retrieved. It even offers grounds for new crimes!"

"I think that our group must answer those questions," said Nikolai Ivanov calmly. He was Gdlyan's deputy in the Bukhara investigation.

Nikolai Veniaminovich [Ivanov] had just returned from the arrest of Abduvakhid Karimov, former first secretary of the Bukhara Regional Committee of the Communist party of Uzbekistan. Even as deputy minister of land reclamation and water conservation, Karimov had never changed his habits. The first day of a business trip to Karshi was marked by a grand drinking and gift-taking spree in the ministry's "guest cottage." The investigating group waited until the guests dispersed. At six in the morning, they called the guardhouse:

"A personal delivery for Karimov," Ivanov said. The guard, who was used to guests coming at any time, let him in.

A half-drunk Karimov opened the door. Extending his hands toward the package, he felt the handcuffs lock on his wrists.

"What's this for?"

"You know yourself what for," said Ivanov reproachfully.

"Uh, I see, I see," Karimov admitted.

At the first turn, the investigators changed the license plates on the car, and it was not in vain. Surprised by a car leaving so early, the guard sounded the alarm: "They've taken Karimov!" He also notified the state automobile inspection with the license number of the car in which Ivanov drove off with the former secretary of the *oblast* committee. It is difficult to say how the affair would have ended had Karimov's henchmen caught up to the car with him in it.

These are not mere words. The situation in Uzbekistan actually was that way in those years. Without exaggerating, it is possible to talk about the regional and republican "leaders" as modern-day emirs, breaking away from socialism, transgressing all legal and moral standards. They lost their authority with the people while in pursuit of the golden calf, and the trough of power provided their personal income at the price of lawlessness. Through economic and moral corruption, these leaders led the republic into a slow and agonizing decay in which extortion and bribery became the norm. A large part of the workers from the legal, party, and soviet organs became involved in a world of crime.

It has now been proven that the cotton magnates stole more than four billion rubles from the state, half of which they stuffed into their own pockets. But if one takes into consideration the many millions embezzled from the sphere of the republic's trade and enterprises, from consumer services and silk production, all of which was under investigation by staff from the internal affairs organs together with Gdlyan's group, then it becomes clear that a well-planned system of organized crime was involved, that every stolen ruble had a subsequent destination. Most of the money went into bribing officials, another part of it is used in expanding the criminal trade. Year after year, like a cancerous growth, the number of the so-called "shop managers," those who own private underground companies, increases. Their extra money is spent on the "good life" and to replenish their caches with gold.

A racket involved in large-scale blackmail and extortion also surfaced in the republic. It thrived by means of threats and violence, just as it is stated in the encyclopedic dictionary. The racketeers shook the underground millionaires like autumn shakes nuts from a tree. In the end, they began to hire the bandits in their "shadowy" business, using them as personal bodyguards. Mercenaries in Uzbekistan are nothing new. Moreover, they strike at those who are trying to untie the knot of corruption. For example, it is now known for certain that one of the high-ranking workers was planning an attempt to kill Gdlyan, but it did not succeed. He committed suicide after his protectors warned him about his imminent arrest. That is why it was not a useless precaution to handcuff Karimov.

For the first months, the USSR procurator's investigation group worked in conditions that were more or less normal. They were met halfway as long as the group did not touch the mafia's "godfathers," who were attentively following the investigation's course. They were not protecting the "small fry." They even feigned strong indignation when, for example, they found out that the same Muzaffarov, head of the department against the embezzlement of socialist property and speculation (OBKhSS), was personally protecting employees of the Bukhara trade department who were selling goods at inflated prices. Or that the first secretary of one of the party's district committees forced *kolkhoz* representatives to make up figures and give bribes by forcing them to hold weights over their heads until they gave in or collapsed from fatigue. Or that Kudratov, head of the Bukhara trade department, unmercifully beat any of his subordinates who dared protest his blatant appropriation of a store's daily receipts.

There was a dramatic change in the situation after Karimov's arrest. It was clear that Gdlyan's group would get to the bottom of it. Numerous attempts to bribe the investigators did not work: "I'll give you a million so that only the Uzbek court examines my case." They also used threats of physical violence. But within five years a host of officials were taken into custody, including former secretaries of the Central Committee of the Uzbekistan Communist party, first secretaries of *oblast*, city, and district party committees, the chairman of the soviet Council of Ministers of the republic, the deputy of the chairman of the Presidium of the Uzbekistan Supreme Soviet, the party's Central Committee affairs manager, the first deputy minister of the USSR ministry of internal affairs, Uzbekistan's minister of internal affairs and three of his deputies, heads of the *oblast* departments of internal affairs, and state and industry officials.

It would seem that a heavy blow had been dealt to organized crime in Uzbekistan. Moreover, from the highest podium of the republic, Rashidov was condemned;[1] and it was stated that the Central Committee bureau was, as it were, under hypnosis and incapable of counteracting lawlessness, abuse, and violations of socialist morals. It is now said that a definite end allegedly will be put to all of this.

But the investigation led by Gdlyan, Ivanov, and their comrades under the direction of Herman Karakozov, head of the investigation unit, and Alexander Katusev, deputy to the general procurator, showed that the situation in the republic had changed very little. Just as before, the same great difficulties occurred with interrogating party officials, who would shield themselves from justice by claiming deputy inviolability. Just as before, the bribe takers and plunderers considered themselves unpunished. It reached a point where some of them were taking new bribes literally ten minutes after leaving an interrogation. But, most important, a "jesuitical" pressure began to be put on witnesses who had previously made statements about how bribes had been extorted from them, how they were

---

[1] Sharif Rashidov was a Politburo member and Uzbekistan's first secretary of the party during Brezhnev's rule.

forced to exaggerate figures and hide the loot of others. Despite the fact that the USSR procurator had exonerated these people from criminal penalty and asked that this fact be considered during party and administration punishment, it was the beginning of party expulsions and job dismissals for many in the Bukhara *oblast*. But those who did not give testimony to the investigators were left in safe security. Gdlyan and his fellow group workers had raced across the republic trying to convince people that admitting guilt would decrease the sentence. Actually, everything turned out differently.

Meanwhile, in the Central Committee of the Uzbekistan Communist party, questions started to resound: "What has that group been doing for five years? Isn't it time that they concluded their work?" It was being said that there had been enough "terrorizing of the people." Telman Khorenovich was tired of trying to prove that the republic's situation and moral microclimate could be corrected not by scraping the surface of criminality, but only by cutting it at its roots. It is questionable how this hostility would have ended had the Central Committee of the CPSU not supported the position of the investigation group. Today, the investigation is nearing an end, although many other matters lie ahead for the group.

Much remains for the Uzbekistan party organization to explain, to clarify how a small group of renegades could manage its wicked ball: Distortion of the principles of socialism for personal gain, economic destruction, derision of other people—even the criminals do not deny that that is how it was. Here is what they said about it during the investigation:

'In Uzbekistan, crimes such as bribery, distorting statistics and embezzlement have become the norm. There was no real struggle against them. Moreover, it was all justified and masked by traditional hospitality, by the necessity to fulfill the plan. Both *oblast* and republican leaders were involved in it.'

'Not one issue was resolved without a bribe. Whoever offered bribes had everything taken care of for him. It was a matter of either you quit your job or live by the rules of criminals. There was no objectivity, no party adherence or decency in the relationships and business affairs.'

'Greed abounded, and so did abuse of one's professional position for material gain. There was lack of control, amorality, mutual patronage and bribery, unscrupulousness, national chauvinism and nepotism. Subordinates' initiatives were suppressed, while leaders were fawned upon.'

'The mafia stopped at nothing right up to tacitly activating Islam, which advocates humility and subordination to elders based on their rank and age.'

Obviously, this "sincerity" issued from fear of punishment. When these scoundrels were not looking at life from behind bars, their thoughts were on something else, as well as their actions and ideas. Like any thieves or swindlers, they only cared about making money and gaining power, as power was for them the means of enrichment. Aiming to achieve this, they would go to the lowest level of degradation. For example, one of the former secretaries of the Central Committee of the Uzbekistan Communist party turned gifts into money by selling them through the republic's Council of Ministers store. He received 14,000 rubles by trading vodka, robes, and fur hats.

Today, the criminals are turning to their relatives and other trusted individuals, asking them to return the hidden money and valuables to the state, in hope of bailing themselves out. Of course, the admission of guilt and voluntary reimbursement for material damages can influence the court's verdict. But what about the rest? What about the economy of the republic, what about the people whose faith in social justice is devastated?

Bibliography

Afanasiev, A., et al. "With Pain and Hope." *Komsomolskaya Pravda*, March 27, 1988.

The authors discuss events in Nagorno-Karabakh in the aftermath of the Sumgait massacre.

Avotinsh, V. "Dignity." *Komsomolskaya Pravda*, March 3, 1988.

This article discusses the attitudes of Russians and Latvians living side by side in one republic.

Bromlei, Yuri. "We Live in One House." *Izvestiya*, April 23, 1988.

The author addresses the paradox of growing national tensions during a time of "internationalization of culture."

Khazin, M. "The Ninth Wave of *Samogon*." *Nedelya*, no. 25, 1988.

An alarming article on the dramatic increase of moonshine consumption in the Soviet Union.

Lebedeva, Marina. "A Glass for Two." *Izvestiya*, November 24, 1987.

Discusses the significant role played by women in producing homemade liquor.

Solntsev, V. "My Language Is My Friend." *Sovetskaya Kultura*, July 16, 1988.

The author proclaims the need to study a second language.

> You will not find even a single
> mention of the slightest mistake or
> error in books and articles about our
> foreign policy.
>
> Viacheslav Dashichev

Chapter Five

Foreign and Military Issues

When he came to power in 1985, Mikhail Gorbachev inherited numerous and unenviable foreign policy dilemmas. Soviet troops were fighting in Afghanistan, the Soviet delegation had walked out of arms control talks with the United States, world opinion continued to condemn the country for persecuting Jews and political dissidents, and anti-Soviet sentiments thrived in the United States and continued unabated in Western Europe. Within four years, however, Gorbachev overcame or at least made great progress on these and other seemingly intractable foreign and military problems. As the articles in this chapter illustrate, a reevaluation of previous Soviet foreign and military policy has allowed Gorbachev to dramatically transform the country's approach to international affairs.

It is a paradox that Gorbachev has achieved significant successes in foreign policy while his domestic programs have yet to bear fruit. This can be explained, in part, by the amount of political power a Soviet leader has in foreign compared to domestic policy. In foreign policy, Gorbachev essentially can control the decision making through the operations of one Moscow building—the Foreign Ministry. In domestic affairs, on the other hand, he must deal with countless power centers, including the party and state chiefs in the fifteen republics and the chairmen of over one hundred ministries in agriculture and industry. Appointing a foreign minister from outside the foreign affairs establishment, Georgian party chief Eduard Shevardnadze, signalled Gorbachev's intention to play a strong role in international affairs. Western policymakers view Shevardnadze as far easier to deal with than his predecessor, Andrei Gromyko, who had played a prominent role in Soviet foreign policy since the time of Joseph Stalin. Noting the improvement in U.S.-Soviet relations, Secretary of State George Shultz said that the United States and the

217

Soviet Union had "sparred at arm's length" when dealing with Gromyko as foreign minister.[1]

Gorbachev made progress on his international difficulties by promulgating a policy of "new thinking." In formulating this concept Gorbachev was aided by a group of "Americanist" advisers led by former Soviet ambassador to the United States Anatoly Dobrynin and Politburo ally Alexander Yakovlev, the former ambassador to Canada. These men influenced Gorbachev's perceptions of the outside world with their ability to vividly relate to him Western apprehensions of Soviet foreign and military policies.

Three primary factors—the military balance, Gorbachev's world view, and economic prerogatives—advanced the development of "new thinking" in foreign affairs. First, the years of established military parity with the United States have changed Soviet perceptions of security. Attaining strategic parity with the United States had long been a Soviet objective. While the military buildup in the 1970s satisfied the ambitions of the Kremlin leadership, it alarmed the West. The years of parity unquestionably have increased the Soviet Union's feeling of security. Colonel Lev Semeyko (Document #24) writes that the new Soviet military doctrine of "reasonable sufficiency" presupposes the presence of strategic parity. Gorbachev believes that the country is now negotiating from a position of strength, not weakness.

Second, Gorbachev believes that the nuclear disaster at Chernobyl was a gloomy portent of mankind's future if the conduct of international affairs is not radically changed. He often cites the Chernobyl disaster in speeches about the dangers of nuclear war. In his book *Perestroika and New Thinking*, Gorbachev warned that "we are speaking here only about one reactor! Chernobyl ruthlessly reminded what awaits all of us if the nuclear thunder will strike."[2]

The third and most important factor influencing "new thinking" is Gorbachev's desire for a stable international climate in which the Soviet Union will be able to concentrate on its economic problems and attract Western trade and financial credit. The expansion of Soviet influence abroad in the 1960s and 1970s increased international tensions and further burdened the country's economy. In the 1970s the Soviet Union gained allies in some of the world's poorest nations: Angola, Nicaragua, Mozambique, Vietnam, and Ethiopia. All of these allies required large sums of military and economic aid. These expenses, along with subsidies to Cuba, the war in Afghanistan, and troops in Eastern Europe and at the Chinese border extracted a heavy

---

[1]"Wrapping It Up: George Shultz Looks at His Tenure at State," *New York Times*, December 18, 1988.

[2]Mikhail S. Gorbachev, *Perestroika and New Thinking* (Moscow, 1987), p. 250.

price from the Soviet economy and aggravated relations with the United States, China, and other nations.

The military parity with the United States achieved in the 1970s also came at a heavy price. While concentrating on the military sector, the country neglected advances in technology and the consumer industry. Obtaining high technology from the West, both legally and illegally, alleviated transient military needs but did not solve endemic economic problems. Soviet academician Oleg Bogomolov wrote in *Literaturnaya Gazeta* that "while trying to achieve military-strategic parity, we became involved in an arms race which was beyond the means of our economy."[3]

The INF (Intermediate-range Nuclear Forces) treaty, signed in December 1987 at the Reagan-Gorbachev summit in Washington, represented a significant achievement for Gorbachev in international affairs. In 1979, responding to Soviet deployment of SS-20 missiles in Europe, NATO had adopted the dual-track policy of deploying U.S. missiles in Western Europe while attempting to negotiate with the Kremlin. But U.S.-Soviet arms control negotiations stalled over a variety of issues, including the American proposal to eliminate all of the Soviet missiles in Europe in exchange for forgoing the deployment of American missiles. In 1983 the Soviet Union responded to the American deployment by walking out of the negotiations in Geneva.

Mikhail Gorbachev played a decisive role in bringing about the new Soviet flexibility displayed during the INF negotiations. Lynn Davis writes in *Foreign Affairs*,

> After negotiations resumed in 1985, General Secretary Gorbachev—to most everyone's surprise—changed tactics and over the next years acquiesced, in turn, to American demands for an agreement covering missiles and not aircraft, to establishing equal ceilings, to eliminating all INF missiles in Europe, to excluding limits on British and French nuclear forces, to including collateral constraints on shorter-range missiles, to banning INF missiles in Asia, and to requiring on-site inspections.[4]

Although it has been generally overlooked in the West, it is unlikely that Gorbachev, without substantially weakening the role of the Soviet military in foreign policy decision making, could have successfully offered concessions so numerous and substantive in order to secure an arms control agreement.

The INF treaty negotiations set a number of important precedents. First, in the spirit of *glasnost* the Soviet Union matched the United

---

[3]Oleg Bogomolov, "From Balance of Forces to Balance of Interests" (round-table discussion), *Literaturnaya Gazeta*, June 29, 1988.

[4]Lynn Davis, "Lessons of the INF Treaty," *Foreign Affairs*, Spring 1988.

States by agreeing to on-site verification and other intrusive means to ensure compliance with the treaty. Second, the treaty was the first U.S.-Soviet agreement to eliminate an entire class of nuclear weapons. Third, the agreement showed the tangible results of the Soviet military doctrine of "reasonable sufficiency," which allows for asymmetrical cuts in weaponry to improve stability. The Soviet Union eliminated more than three times as many missiles as the United States to achieve the INF treaty.

For the United States, positive coverage in the Soviet press was a welcome by-product of the INF treaty. Prior to Gorbachev's visit to Washington in December 1987, the Soviet press consistently criticized American policies and society, albeit in a more stylish manner than had been done before Gorbachev came to power. In contrast, television coverage of Gorbachev's visit featured straightforward reporting on tourist attractions in the nation's capital and, most importantly, showed the Soviet leader being greeted warmly by Americans from all walks of life. Although press reporting on the United States always becomes more positive during periods of good relations, *glasnost* coverage of America is different. Numerous articles have appeared citing America as a positive example in such areas as restaurant service, individual initiative, and even democratic political traditions.

In general, as coverage of the war in Afghanistan illustrates, *glasnost* took time to develop in press coverage of foreign affairs. For the first two years of Gorbachev's rule the Soviet press continued to ignore the reality of the war in Afghanistan. The small amount of coverage that appeared glorified the actions of the "limited contingent." But Gorbachev and his advisers decided by the summer of 1987 to begin withdrawing Soviet troops within a few years. Therefore, a well-organized effort ensued to prepare the population for the withdrawal; the government encouraged reporters to portray the grim reality of war.

This signal from the top dramatically changed press coverage of Afghanistan. Stories began to appear in *Ogonyok* and *Literaturnaya Gazeta* that reported the war through the eyes of the young soldiers. Severely wounded soldiers related the horrors of battle and the psychological scars they would carry home. Articles also appeared discussing the plight of Soviet veterans of the Afghan war. Eighteen- and nineteen-year-old recruits told the nation about friends dying before their eyes. Still, press coverage never condemned the war as an imperialistic venture. Nor did stories appear (as they did in the United States during Vietnam) questioning the morality of the war. The Soviet intervention was portrayed as a mistake only because the war could not be won. As a frank interview with Major General Kim Tsagolov reveals (Document #23), some people publicly blame their Communist allies in Kabul for the debacle.

The vast improvement in reporting on Afghanistan notwithstanding, the Soviet press still carries a minimum of debate over foreign and military policies. Soviet Foreign Minister Eduard Shevardnadze has said that "bold, interesting, and questioning articles have appeared on . . . the economy, culture, art, and science. Yet there is nothing like this in the foreign policy sphere. Does this mean that everything here is correct and that there are no other options apart from the ones being implemented?"[5]

An important complement to Gorbachev's "new thinking" in foreign policy has been the military doctrine of "reasonable sufficiency." Mikhail Gorbachev first advanced this doctrine in two international settings, the February 1987 International Forum for a Non-Nuclear World and the April 1987 meeting of Soviet-Czechoslovak Friendship in Prague. This doctrine advocates that the Soviet Union not seek an increase in military strength, so as to prevent Western nations from perceiving a real or imagined Soviet threat. Moreover, the Soviet Union should strive to maintain no more than a sufficient level of forces and should seek to stabilize the present balance by gradually reducing Soviet and American armed forces and armaments.[6] The substantial asymmetrical cuts to be made by the Soviets in accordance with the INF treaty and Gorbachev's unilateral cut of 500,000 troops and 10,000 tanks announced during his United Nations speech (Document #33) are two significant manifestations of "reasonable sufficiency." This policy has carried an equally important political message inside the USSR. For seven decades, the government educated the Soviet military and general population about the permanent threat of imperialism. It would be difficult to cut military forces and expenditures without a theoretical justification. To carry out important and necessary changes in military policy has required a new military doctrine for domestic consumption.

The concept of "military trust" (rather than the old term "nonoffensive defense") is a complement to "reasonable sufficiency." This advocates the use of nonmilitary means to establish greater trust between the two blocs. Rear Admiral and Professor G. Kostev writes that "in the military sphere, as indicated at the 27th Congress of the CPSU, the Soviet Union intends in the future to act in a way that no one will have any reasons for fears, even imagined ones, for its security."[7]

There have been three significant examples of "military trust" in recent U.S.-Soviet relations: (1) permitting U.S. congressional staff

---

[5]See Document #22.

[6]Isaac Tarasulo and Stuart Anderson, "Gorbachev's Jitters about the Military," *Houston Post*, June 16, 1987.

[7]Rear Admiral G. Kostev, "Our Military Doctrine in Light of the New Political Thinking," *Kommunist Vooruzhenykh Sil*, no. 17, September 1987.

members to visit the disputed radar site at Krasnoyarsk, the location of which the Reagan administration had declared a violation of the 1972 ABM treaty; (2) allowing Western scientists to inspect a chemical weapons production site, thus improving the atmosphere for a treaty; and (3) Soviet readiness to agree to on-site verification of the INF treaty. In fact, the most significant manifestation of "military trust" is the Soviet Union's agreement to American proposals that on-site observers be stationed permanently to monitor the INF treaty.

Soviet willingness to discuss a greater role for foreign military observers figures prominently into the concept of military trust. The stationing of military observers in NATO and Warsaw Pact countries may be an important confidence-building measure included in the Conventional Stability Talks in Vienna. (These negotiations are designed to reduce troops and artillery in Europe.) Agreements on the quantity of conventional weaponry and manpower have consistently eluded NATO and Warsaw Pact negotiators. Current measures, such as preliminary warnings of military exercises and the dispatching of observers to troop maneuvers, already play a positive role in Europe. It is possible, however, that permanently stationing observers in airports, railroad stations, and areas where sizable military forces are present could help to solve previously intractable problems.

While changes in foreign and military policy have proceeded apace, reforming the Soviet military establishment has proved to be a far more difficult task. The military earned a special place in society by achieving parity with the United States and by saving the country during World War II. In terms of economic efficiency, by virtue of its access to superior technology and personnel Soviet military quality and production have contrasted sharply with the rest of the nation's industries. For two years Gorbachev did not attempt to interfere with military personnel decisions. While military leaders supported Gorbachev's call for revitalizing the Soviet economy, they believed themselves exempt from these changes. Exempt, that is, until May 1987.

On May 28, 1987, nineteen-year-old Mathias Rust landed his Cessna 172 in Red Square. Neither the air defense forces, naval aviation, nor the air forces in various military districts fulfilled their duties. This event was a major failure for the entire Soviet armed forces. After the golden years for the military establishment under Leonid Brezhnev, it took a West German teenager to bring *perestroika* to the military.

The aftermath of Mathias Rust's flight brought a new era in military-civilian relations. Gorbachev immediately fired two distinguished military leaders, Defense Minister Sergei Sokolov and the chief of the Air Defense Forces, Alexander Koldunov. For the first time in recent history, the Soviet military establishment was presented as an unsuccessful institution. This differed significantly from its portrayal after the Korean airliner was shot down in 1983 when, within the USSR, the military was glorified for fulfilling its patriotic duty.

Gorbachev intended the appointment of Defense Minister Dmitry Yazov to shake up the military. Removing prominent marshals and generals and replacing them with unknown men would allow Gorbachev to both conduct his own arms control policies and cut military expenditures with less resistance. But Gorbachev's problems with the military run deep. Prior to his ascent to power, his chief adversary on the Politburo was Leningrad party chief Grigory Romanov, a man with extensive ties to the military-industrial complex. In contrast to Romanov, Gorbachev, as a member of the Politburo responsible for agriculture, possessed no strong military allies and had little experience with military issues. Although Romanov was pushed out of the Politburo six months after Gorbachev became general secretary, there is little doubt that the Soviet leader rose to power viewing the military with apprehension. In sharp contrast to his predecessors, military men are rarely seen near Gorbachev at public appearances.

There are strong indications that the military is dissatisfied with Gorbachev's disarmament policies. In 1987, then Chief of the General Staff Marshal Sergei Akhromeyev and others questioned Gorbachev's efforts to continually renew the Soviet unilateral moratorium on nuclear testing despite the ongoing U.S. testing program. Moreover, Gorbachev's proposal of unilateral force reductions in his United Nations address (Document #33) caused Akhromeyev to resign. Supplanting Akhromeyev with the forty-nine-year-old Mikhail Moiseyev further alienated military men who were already disappointed with the unexpected designation of Dmitry Yazov as defense minister. Although there is no history of Soviet officers personally ousting a leader, their dissatisfaction could play a role in setting the stage for a future conservative coup d'état against Gorbachev.

Mathias Rust's flight made *glasnost* possible in military affairs by allowing Soviet civilians to criticize the military for the first time. Moreover, critical debate within the Soviet military began to emerge openly on several issues. The conflicts between different nationalities in the armed forces, the demographic time bomb of a shrinking proportion of ethnic Russians among Soviet military personnel, and the language barriers between Russian and other troops were all discussed in the press. A particularly surprising issue was the abuse of younger soldiers by older ones (see Document #27). Still, on the whole, *glasnost* in the military lags far behind the open reporting of economic, political, and historical issues. The military is the most conservative institution in Soviet society, and, accordingly, the military press is run by the country's most conservative editors. Nonetheless, numerous recently published articles criticizing the military and television reports on the use of army units to maintain order in Armenia, Azerbaijan, and Georgia have seriously eroded the prestige of the Soviet military.

Over the past four years an assertion of civilian over military priorities combined with the diminishing influence of orthodox Marxist ideology in Soviet foreign policy have led to significant achievements for Mikhail Gorbachev. Soviet troops have departed from the war in Afghanistan. A historic INF arms control treaty between the United States and the Soviet Union has eliminated all medium-range missiles in Europe and provided momentum for an agreement on long-range nuclear weapons. The Soviet government has addressed many of the international community's human rights complaints by freeing hundreds of political prisoners and allowing many Soviet Jews to emigrate. And perhaps most consequentially Mikhail Gorbachev is now hailed as a remarkable and trustworthy leader in both the United States and Western Europe. His May 1989 visit to China, publicly ending the long estrangement between the world's two great Communist giants, is further proof of his ability to achieve formidable foreign policy goals. Gorbachev hopes to use these foreign policy gains to allow the Soviet Union to turn inward to tackle the economic and social problems that accumulated under Stalin and Brezhnev.

The scholar George Kennan, author of America's "containment" policy after World War II, writes that "Gorbachev has given every evidence, for his part, of an intention to remove as many of the possible factors that have hampered Soviet-American relations in the past; and a number of bold steps he has taken in that direction do testimony to the sincerity of his effort. To the extent he is able to carry these efforts to conclusion (and that depends to some extent on the response from our side), they present the most favorable opportunity the United States has had in the last seventy years to develop a normal, constructive and hopeful relationship with the Soviet Union."[8]

---

[8]George Kennan, "After the Cold War," *New York Times Magazine*, February 5, 1989.

22

East-West Quest for New Relations: The Priorities of Soviet Foreign Policy

Viacheslav Dashichev

Literaturnaya Gazeta
May 18, 1988

Dashichev's article is the boldest critique of past foreign policy practices to appear in the Soviet press under *glasnost*. He frankly admits that the Western world has a negative view of Soviet policies not primarily because of anti-Soviet propaganda, but rather because of Soviet foreign and military practices. Although traditionally the West, particularly the United States, has been blamed for the decline of détente, Dashichev argues that Brezhnev's actions in the Third World were largely to blame. Moreover, he writes that Western leaders interpreted the Soviet military buildup as an attempt to exploit the positive atmosphere that détente engendered in East-West relations.

In examining the roots of the Cold War, Dashichev writes that, in the period following World War II, Soviet foreign policy was perceived (and not without cause) as distinctly hegemonic by nature. He hopes that in the nuclear age a "political modus vivendi" between the USSR and the West can be achieved through mutual trust.

The realities of the nuclear age and of the scientific and technical revolution demand new thinking and new approaches toward the completion of foreign policy tasks. Movement in this direction is only just beginning. It is obvious that any serious changes will take much longer. This is because the most difficult task of all is to effect a restructuring of minds, to overcome the stereotypes and the departmental, group, and personal interests that influence foreign policy decision making.

It is particularly important to rid ourselves of incorrect ideas on such a fundamental question as the correlation between war and politics. For decades our political thinking on this issue took positions that prevented us from finding the correct ways to solve the problems of peace and disarmament.

"There was a time," Foreign Minister Eduard Shevardnadze said, when controversial topics were not raised, and opinions different from official views, even when they were inoffensive, were not expressed. That time is now past. But just look at what is happening. Bold, interesting, and questioning articles have appeared on many basic questions of internal life in all its forms, of party and state building, and of the economy, culture, art, and science. Yet there is nothing like this in the foreign policy sphere. Does this mean that everything here is correct and that there are no other options apart from the ones being implemented?

Indeed, you will not find even a single mention of the slightest mistake or error in books and articles about our foreign policy. No matter what has been done, everything is depicted as infallible. Of course, Soviet foreign policy enjoys high esteem. It has always been marked by an anti-imperialist orientation aimed at ensuring the security of the USSR and its allies and at supporting the international workers' movement and national liberation struggles all over the world. But was everything done correctly? Is it possible to seriously believe that, while we were committing major mistakes in internal development, we managed to avoid them in the international arena in all those seventy years? This simply cannot be. To err is human. It is important to realize your mistakes and to learn from them. There were times when heated debates of foreign policy took place in our country also. Let us recall just the very tense struggle of opinions, openly and fearlessly expressed, about the Brest-Litovsk peace treaty.[1]

Our foreign policy now has no more urgent task than to reliably ensure security and peace for all peoples. This is why it is important to clarify above all the question of the nature and mechanism of the arms race and the starting of wars. "People," V. I. Lenin pointed out, "live within a state, and every state exists within a system of states that are in a condition of a certain political equilibrium relative to one another." Any desire on the part of a major state (or bloc of states) to sharply expand its sphere of influence would disrupt this equilibrium. To restore it, other states would unite in an "anticoalition" against the potentially or

---

[1] This treaty ended Russian participation in World War I.

actually strongest state (in a given region or in the world). Moreover, the counterweight that would be created might even be more powerful, because the "anticoalition" would be joined by more states and would mobilize to the maximum all of its material, spiritual, and human resources.

This "feedback" effect was often diminished by a series of factors. While the strength of a power that was expanding its sphere of influence rallied its enemies, its rejection of expansionist aspirations caused hesitation and disintegration within the "anticoalition" camp. Difficulties also emerged as a result of disagreements between its actual or potential members. Nonetheless, the "anticoalition" ultimately became so strong that the power challenging it could not withstand the military and economic confrontation. Consequently, any hegemony contains the seeds of its own downfall. Evidence of this is provided by the experience of two world wars.

Hegemonic behavior has always been founded on a desire for political and economic subjugation of peoples and states. But from the time of the French bourgeois revolution, or rather the Napoleonic wars, it began to acquire increasingly ideological overtones and to operate beneath the banner of messianism, in other words, the imposition of certain ideological values, a certain way of life, and a certain social structure on other peoples and states. This hegemony is typical mainly of countries in the grip of broad ideological movements. This ailment also afflicts the policy of the United States, which has for a long time striven to implant American values and the American way of life in the rest of the world. The famous U.S. diplomat R. Barkley wrote that "ever since the first settlers, Americans have acted as if they were carrying out a divine mission. The foreign policy complications stemming from this factor are obvious. Because to be guided in one's actions by the feeling of being chosen by destiny and the awareness of one's own messianic role means pitting oneself against the mighty forces of the international community."

States with different sociopolitical systems may unite to counteract hegemony. Let us recall that, soon after the October Revolution's victory in Russia, France, Britain, and the United States offered to give help to the Soviet government provided it agreed to continue the war against

Germany on the Entente's side. (The subsequent intervention by these powers between 1918 and 1921 partially stemmed from their desire to bring to power in Russia a government that would continue the war.) A similar "anticoalition" of countries belonging to different social systems emerged, albeit greatly delayed, against Germany and its allies during World War II.

The classic configuration of forces in Europe, which had developed by the end of the nineteenth century and prevailed until the middle of the twentieth century, consisted of the central European grouping of states headed by Germany and the opposing triangle of "Russia (USSR), France, Britain," which was joined by the United States and other states in wartime. Germany's two attempts to decisively alter the European balance in its favor by military means and to establish its domination in Europe ended in total collapse. The classic European balance of forces ensured the national security interests of Russia (USSR), France, and Britain in the face of German expansionism. V. I. Lenin realized the geostrategic importance of France and Britain for Soviet Russia. During the Brest-Litovsk peace talks, he categorically insisted that the armistice agreement with Germany include a provision prohibiting all transfers of German troops from the eastern front to the west. The Soviet government thus demonstrated its consideration of the interests of the Western powers, against which the German command was planning to deliver a decisive blow after Russia's withdrawal from the war.

The classic configuration of forces in Europe did more than provide the Soviet Union with a counterbalance to German aggression. One of its other advantages was the ruling out of a formation of a united front of Western powers against the Soviet Union. This was because France and Britain needed, as much as the Soviet Union did, an effective counterbalance to Germany in Eastern Europe. Ultimately, these national-state interests of France and Britain were more powerful than their class and ideological differences with the Soviet Union.

German fascism reared its head in the 1930s. All of the major powers realized that matters were leading to war. This was also realized in Moscow, and right until 1939 attempts were made to create a collective security system in Europe. At that time there was just one way possibly to curb a new German aggression: Revive the Entente. But the French and British ruling circles at the time did not make the proper efforts to create a coalition with the USSR in the face of the Nazi threat. As a matter of fact, they played up to Hitler, and Munich rests on their conscience.

This policy was dictated not only by anticommunism and anti-Sovietism. After Stalin had decapitated the Red Army by exterminating its best command cadres, Britain and France no longer considered the Soviet Union a serious and reliable military ally. Furthermore, they found it difficult to deal with a supreme leader who had trampled all human morality, committing unprecedented repressions by cruel and criminal methods merely for the sake of establishing his authoritarian power.

Finding himself in an extremely difficult situation, Stalin ultimately concluded the nonaggression pact with fascist Germany. He hoped to avert war at any cost, even if only temporarily.

When the Soviet Union left the traditional European configuration of forces, France and Britain were left to face fascist Germany alone. As a result, Hitler's command could concentrate 136 divisions along the western front by the start of the offensive against France, leaving only 10 ineffective divisions in the east against the USSR. This enabled fascist Germany to swiftly crush France and take over nearly all of Western Europe's resources. This would later have a grave effect on the security of the Soviet Union, when it found itself face to face with Hitler's *wehrmacht* on June 22, 1941. Under such circumstances, the Western powers could have remained on the sidelines, adopting the posture of pleased third parties. Nevertheless, overcoming prejudices, antipathies, rejection of Stalin's regime, and the ill feeling stemming from the Soviet-German pact, political circles in Britain and later those in the United States chose what was, from the viewpoint of their national interests, the only correct path—that of supporting the Soviet Union in its struggle against fascist Germany. The mechanism of balancing opposed forces on the European continent was in operation once again.

The military-political situation in Europe changed sharply following World War II. The world socialist system started to emerge. The Soviet Union gained friendly neighbors along its western border, while the Yalta and Potsdam decisions defined a postwar structure in Europe which took into account the legitimate interests of our security and our tremendous contribution to the rout of fascism.

The results seemed perfectly satisfactory to us. But the obvious consolidation of Soviet positions and the spread of Soviet influence in central and southeast Europe were perceived by our recent allies from the anti-Hitler coalition as an intolerable disruption of the European balance and a threat to their interests. Immediately after the end of the war, the Western powers began to hatch plans to counter the growing Soviet influence. In subsequent years, these plans materialized in the form of the "Cold War" launched against the Soviet Union. Backed by Britain and France, the United States filled the power vacuum created after Germany's defeat. The U.S. military and political presence on the European continent became a mighty (and enduring, even to the present day) factor in anti-Soviet policy. All of the Western powers united within the NATO military-political bloc against the Soviet Union. West Germany, with its powerful potential, was brought into this bloc. The Warsaw Pact organization which was created in response could rely, especially at the beginning, only and exclusively on the Soviet Union's potential.

A united front of the Western powers against the USSR thus emerged. An anti-Soviet coalition of unprecedented size and strength was formed, backed with both nuclear weapons and the means for their delivery.

Was such a demarcation inevitable? Probably. The imperialist centers of power saw the growth of world socialism as a direct threat to their interests and turned to the concepts of "containment," "rolling back," and "deterrence." Their priority in the arms race that was launched after World War II was obvious. But, while we have extensive knowledge of the West's unseemly behavior, we still are inclined to assess our own stance at various stages as unequivocally correct. As a matter of fact, trends that could have been and were perceived as hegemonistic also operated in Soviet foreign policy.

Let us recall Vladimir Lenin who, like Karl Marx and Friedrich Engels before him, was a decisive opponent of "bringing happiness" to "other peoples." He mercilessly criticized the leftist plans (put forward by Trotskyites after October) for the violent spread of revolution to Western Europe, Afghanistan, India, and other countries, bluntly pointing out that "so far, no decree has been promulgated to the effect that all countries must live according to the Bolshevik revolutionary calendar, and even if it were to be promulgated, it would not be implemented."

These principles did not differ from our country's deeds. The dangerous illusions about "world revolution" were overcome. Conditions were created for peaceful coexistence with the capitalist countries. Is it not striking today that, after the civil war and right until 1931, the Soviet republic allowed itself an army of only 560,000 men? This shows the great services of a brilliant constellation of diplomats (Georgy Chicherin, Maxim Litvinov, Leonid Krasin, Vaclav Vorovsky, and others) who managed to reduce the external threat to our country to a minimum. The size of our armed forces also indicated that the Soviet Union had no intention of threatening anyone. Only the growing military danger in the early 1930s, especially after fascism's coming to power in Germany, forced the Soviet Union to multiply its defense efforts.

Lenin's principles of domestic as well as foreign policy were seriously distorted during the time of Stalin's rule. In essence, the foreign policy practice of Stalin and his closest associates was based on the ultraleftist ideas of Blanquism[2] and Trotskyism, which are alien to the nature of socialism. What came to the fore, particularly after World War II, was the spread of Stalinist socialism wherever possible and its standardization in all countries regardless of their national features.

Overcentralization in domestic policy inevitably engendered hegemony and a great-power mentality in foreign policy. One indicative example was Yugoslavia's expulsion from the socialist system in 1948 and the attribution of all deadly sins to its leadership, simply because it had refused to submit to Stalin and obey his orders. This was followed by the breach with China and

---

[2] Louis Auguste Blanqui was a French left-wing revolutionary who advanced a theory of the dictatorship of the proletariat.

Albania, and here once again we made mistakes. Conflicts and frictions developed with other socialist countries.

Expectations that relations within the socialist framework could be built on the rigid principles of party "democratic centralism"[3] and that the unity of socialism could thus be ensured were not to materialize. Sad to say, matters went as far as sharp confrontation and armed clashes between socialist countries.[4]

The hegemonistic, great-power ambitions of Stalinism became rooted in foreign policy and repeatedly jeopardized political equilibrium between states, especially between those of East and West. In the process, the interest of expanding the social revolution pushed the task of preventing the threat of war into the background. Approximately the following propaganda argument was made for internal consumption: "Since Western imperialism is resisting the progressive social and territorial changes in the world emanating from the Soviet Union, it is the aggressor." On the one hand we heightened the level of military danger by advancing toward the West's positions, and on the other we mounted a broad campaign in defense of peace and spared no resources to organize a mass movement of champions of peace. (It is no accident that a joke current in the 1950s said: "There will be such a struggle for peace that everything will be razed to the ground.") Over the years all of this was embodied in stereotyped and cliché-ridden thinking in the mentality of leading cadres, who effectively were prisoners of their own propaganda.

How did the opposing side perceive the USSR's policy and goals, and, indeed, how does it continue out of inertia to perceive them even now? In the eyes of an overwhelming portion of the Western public, the Soviet Union is a dangerous power whose leadership wants to eliminate the bourgeois democracies by military means and to establish a Soviet-type Communist system throughout the world.

---

[3] The CPSU is theoretically governed according to the principle of democratic centralism; that is, the election of all governing bodies and the subordination of the minority to the majority after a resolution is approved.

[4] Armed clashes occurred between the Soviet Union and China and between China and Vietnam; also, Vietnam occupied Cambodia.

The thesis of Soviet expansion served as the main cement for rallying the states of the other social system against the USSR. The NATO countries' ruling circles viewed any progressive social processes almost exclusively through the prism of a further change in the global political balance in favor of the Soviet Union. This greatly impeded the activity of progressive forces in the capitalist and developing worlds, and massive repressions rained down upon them.

Washington actively exploited the "Soviet military threat" to secure a dominant influence in Western Europe, to advance its own hegemonic interests in various regions of the world, and to create an extensive network of strategic military bases. Ill-considered actions on our part provided U.S. expansionist circles with the desired pretext for acts of aggression against many peoples, for the deployment of powerful armed forces, and for the creation of more and more new types of lethal weapons. What about the dangerous extremism and adventurism of U.S. policy? These too leeched on the "Soviet threat."

By the early 1970s the Soviet Union had reached a level of nuclear preparation that made global nuclear conflict unacceptable to the United States. A period of East-West détente began. Western politicians' gazes turned toward peaceful means of achieving anti-Soviet political goals. Particular hopes were pinned on the economic decline of the Soviet Union and the inefficiency of its economy. To the West, these factors indicated the prospect of an erosion of the USSR's international position and a contraction of its sphere of influence. The implementation of this policy required a departure from the "Cold War," a lessening of tensions in relations with the USSR, and attainment of compromises on a wide range of issues.

Détente also gave the Soviet Union the opportunity to reduce confrontation with the West to a minimal level and thereby prevent a buildup in the forces of the "anti-coalition." Additional resources could be used for the resolution of internal tasks, political and social development, and the democratization of the country, and its economy could be switched to the path of intensive development.

It soon transpired that détente was acceptable to the United States and its allies only if the international political and strategic-military status quo was preserved. However, as the West saw it, the Soviet leadership was actively exploiting détente to build up its own military forces, seeking military parity with the United States and in general with all the opposing powers—a fact without historical parallel. The United States, paralyzed by the Vietnam catastrophe, reacted hypersensitively to the expansion of Soviet influence in Africa, the Near East, and other regions.

The West interpreted all of this as a further increase in the Soviet threat. The extreme right-wing political circles that came to power in the United States and the other NATO countries turned sharply away from détente toward confrontation.[5] The Soviet Union found itself faced with unprecedented new pressure from imperialism.

The expansion of the Soviet sphere of influence reached critical limits in the West's eyes with the introduction of Soviet troops into Afghanistan. In earlier times this could have been grounds for unleashing war. But the threat of nuclear annihilation did not permit the West to resort to a direct military clash with the USSR. The "anticoalition" turned to other means of pressure. The main one was such a massive race in the most modern arms that even the mighty Western economy finds it difficult to sustain. The spiritual and material resources of the capitalist world united against the Soviet Union. A "crusade" against the USSR was proclaimed.

The operation of the "feedback effect" placed the Soviet Union in an extremely difficult foreign policy and economic position. It was opposed by the major world powers: the United States, Britain, France, West Germany, Italy, Japan, Canada, and China. Opposition to their vastly superior potential was dangerously far beyond the USSR's capabilities.

Could such a severe exacerbation of tension in Soviet-Western relations in the late 1970s and early 1980s have been avoided?

Unquestionably so. It is our conviction that the crisis was caused chiefly by the miscalculations and incompetent

---

[5] Dashichev has in mind the election victories of Ronald Reagan, Margaret Thatcher, and Helmut Kohl.

approach of the Brezhnev leadership toward the resolution of foreign policy tasks.

The general goals were quite correctly formulated: peace, security, disarmament, cooperation, noninterference in internal affairs, and peaceful coexistence. But there was a manifest lack of purposeful, competent, scientifically substantiated, and tested actions. We were wrong in our assessment of the global situation and the correlation of forces, and no serious efforts were made to settle the fundamental political differences with the West. Although we were politically, militarily (with weapons supplies and advisers), and diplomatically involved in regional conflicts, we disregarded their influence on the relaxation of tension between the USSR and the West and on the entire system of relationships.

There were no clear ideas of the Soviet Union's true state interests. These interests by no means lay in pursuing petty and essentially formal gains resulting from leadership coups in certain developing countries. The genuine interest lay in ensuring an international situation favorable for profound transformations in the Soviet Union's economy and sociopolitical system. However, at that time it was believed that no transformations were needed.

The uncreative nature of the decisions resulted in an exceptionally costly foreign policy. The Reagan administration foisted a colossal increase in military spending on us. Defense expenditures in the United States grew from $122 billion in 1979 to $284 billion in 1985. To maintain military parity, we tried to keep up with the United States in this colossal unproductive spending, which totaled over $1 trillion during the five-year period.

The arms race, like war, may be regarded as the continuation of politics by other means.[6] To abate the arms race and make it pointless, you must remove political contradictions and balance both sides' interests.

Of course, it is wrong to separate the solution of political and military problems. It is certainly possible to solve them in parallel. But the primacy of political issues is self-evident. Evidence of that is provided by the sad failure of all

---

[6] Paraphrase of a well-known quote attributed to Karl von Clausewitz.

efforts to curtail or limit the arms race between the United States and the USSR in the 1970s. What defeated these efforts was precisely the fact that fundamental political problems were unsolved.

To radically and irrevocably curb the arms race, it is necessary to fundamentally reorganize Soviet-Western political relations. Mere talks on military issues are not enough here. Ultimately the point is not what quantity of nuclear and other weapons each side possesses or how far the level of armaments should be reduced. The main problem is whether a political modus vivendi is attainable between the USSR and the Western powers, whether they can secure a high level of mutual trust. It is here, in the political-ideological sphere, that the key to disarmament lies. It is in this that the further operation of the "feedback" effect and the strength or weakness of the "anticoalition" opposing the USSR will depend.

The USSR and the Western powers must renounce total confrontation, must not interfere in one another's internal affairs or in the affairs of third countries, must organize broad peaceful cooperation, must refrain from pressing each other's sore points, must not damage each other's interests, and must not seek unilateral benefits and advantages.

The removal of political and military tension between the USSR and the West requires mutual effort. For our part we must completely surmount Stalinism in domestic and foreign policy, theory and practice, organizational structures, and the public mind. We must also work to create favorable international conditions for socialist building. The narrowly elitist nature of foreign policy decision making, the distorted picture of the outside world, and the Soviet Union's isolation from the international community for a long time doomed it to sociopolitical, economic, scientific and technical, and cultural stagnation.

Throughout the twentieth century the nature and content of the struggle for social progress have changed substantially. After 1945 the Soviet Union played the role of military guarantor of the expansion of socialism in the world. As a result it was dragged into an extremely sharp confrontation with the main forces of imperialism.

Nuclear missile weapons lent an exceptionally dangerous and risky nature to this confrontation.

Now socialism has become an invincible force. So it is vitally important not only for the preservation of peace but also for the further development of world socialism to ensure that the center of gravity of the struggle for social progress moves again from the sphere of Soviet-Western interstate relations into the sphere of the internal sociopolitical development of the Soviet Union, the socialist countries, and the Western and Third World states. If in 1917 it was possible to break the chain of imperialism in a single country, Russia, without outside assistance, immeasurably better conditions now exist for the advance toward socialism on a national basis. The Soviet Union can and must influence world social progress exclusively through its economic, political, scientific, and cultural successes. That is the fundamental Leninist tenet regarding the Soviet state's role and tasks in the international community. The full restoration of the significance of this Leninist idea is one of the noble aims of *perestroika*.

Such a turnaround in our policy in no way presupposes some kind of "socialist isolationism." On the contrary, it will greatly expand the scope for international collaboration and the mutual influence and enrichment of socialist forces in the political, economic, theoretical, scientific, and cultural spheres. Socialist solidarity will become richer and acquire an organic nature.

The totally new tasks of the struggle for social progress in the nuclear age also require radically new ways and methods of realizing them. This is the conclusion of the 27th Party Congress (February 1986), which initiated a fundamental reassessment of values in foreign policy thinking. What has been established as the keystone of our foreign policy activity is a principle that develops Lenin's ideas: The interest of saving human civilization from nuclear annihilation takes precedence over any class, ideological, material, personal, and other interests.

23

Afghanistan: Preliminary Results

Kim Tsagolov and Artyom Borovik

Ogonyok, no. 30, July 1988

Major General Tsagolov, doctor of philosophical sciences, director of the Department of Marxism-Leninism at the Frunze Military Academy, and the first military man to speak frankly on this subject, has been criticized by conservatives in the press for his comments to *Ogonyok* correspondent Artyom Borovik. Tsagolov makes several frank admissions in this article. For example, he argues that the Soviets "convinced" themselves that the April 1978 military coup d'état (which brought the Afghan Communists to power) was a socialist revolution. "We were victims of our own illusions," he asserts.

General Tsagolov criticizes the Afghan regime for political and economic mismanagement and for precipitating the conflict with the rebels by antagonizing the traditionally Islamic populace. Similarly his interviewer, Artyom Borovik, asserts that Afghan government forces have often allowed Soviet troops to perform duties that the Afghan army should have done. The Soviet Union's criticism of the NDPA (the ruling Communist party in Afghanistan) corresponds to a general disillusionment with the USSR's Third World allies. Tsagolov sees a future Afghanistan engaged in battles between rival Afghan mujahideen groups with the potential for an Iranian-style fundamentalist government. In a call for *glasnost* in coverage of foreign affairs, Tsagolov faults the reporting on Afghanistan during much of the war for misleading the Soviet population.

Borovik: Kim Makedonovich [Tsagolov], if we were to judge by the larger part of the reporting from Afghanistan at the beginning (to the mid-1980s), everything was going well. The Afghans were said to be achieving military victories like lightning, and they happily walked with our soldiers and embarked with them down the path of friendship with roses and carnations. In a word, everything was going excellently, the process of strengthening the revolution was accelerating as the opposition suffered defeat after defeat. The "bands" raced to surrender into the hands of the state power, and with unprecedented enthusiasm the perceptive ones were building a "new life." National reconciliation was occurring widely. What a triumphant procession of the revolution! But really, you knew the truth. Really, wasn't it funny or, more accurately, painful for you and for the majority of veterans of Afghanistan to read all that?

Tsagolov: Of course, it was painful. I have a very different point of view on the "Afghan question." The war has been going on for nine years, and, although the withdrawal of our troops is continuing, the end is not yet in sight. [This interview was published in July 1988.] We only recently decided to report the real figures of losses to the people. More than 13,300 of our soldiers died on Afghan soil. For many, the war continues in the cruel scars of the wounded and crippled. They include more than 35,000 people. This is our common pain, our general tragedy. And 311 are missing in action—that is also our pain.

There has not yet been any discussion about the coalition government. Not one of the representatives of the Peshawar "Seven" and not one of the major leaders of the internal armed opposition has responded to the NDPA's call.[1]

The territory on which we have firmly and definitely established state power has barely increased over the past year. It is impossible to name a single province or a single district where the question of "who defeats whom" has been definitely settled in favor of state power. In the tribal zone, also, there have not yet been any real successes that have permitted us to conclude that any tribe has irrevocably crossed over to national reconciliation.

Borovik: Kim Makedonovich! And was there a revolution in Afghanistan? Maybe we mistook an ordinary coup d'état for a revolution? How do you evaluate the events of April 1978?

Tsagolov: Briefly, I am convinced that a military coup, which had the potential to develop into a national democratic revolution, occurred in Afghanistan on April 27, 1978. Unfortunately, that development did not happen.

Borovik: Before analyzing the situation in Afghanistan after April 1978, it is necessary to clearly state that the April coup d'état took place in a feudal-bourgeois society

---

[1] The Peshawar Seven are seven resistance organizations fighting against the Soviet invasion. NDPA stands for People's Democratic Party of Afghanistan.

still wrapped in the remnants of tribal and religious tradition. At the end of the 1970s we had convinced ourselves that Afghanistan "was certainly going the way of the construction of socialism." What kind of socialism? It didn't smell of that. We were victims of our own illusions.

Tsagolov: It's true. For Afghan society, traditional attitudes and influences are not relics. They are a powerful social stratum. Just like religious attitudes. The Afghan clergy held a truly solid position among the masses. Its influence is immense even now. It is no coincidence that the same powerful clergy became the kernel of the armed opposition.

Borovik: It seems to me that the question of the clergy merits particular attention. Toward the end of the 1970s that large social group numbered about 260,000: the leaders of great mosques, teachers in the theological departments of scholarly institutions, teachers in the *medres* [Islamic religious schools], ministers of the *sharia* [a code of Islamic law that defines daily social customs], tribunals, village mullahs, and mullahs of the army.

Tsagolov: Yet among the clergy the heads of the religious communities, the sects and the orders, carried a particular political weight. They possessed indisputable authority among the believers and had a large number of followers. The clergy in Afghanistan was not monolithic. It was divided into a traditional-conservative circle and numerous groups of Islamic modernists. The Islamic nationalists were really influential. Already in 1966 they were grouped around the newspaper *Afghan mellyat* ("Afghan nation"), propagating militant chauvinism on the basis of Islam. Among the conservative clergy, there was also the fringe rightist group which pursued the creation of an Islamic republic as its goal. They were opposed not only to the left-democratic forces, but also to the regime of Mohammed Daud.[2] The orthodox-clerical groups, which also did not accept the republic of M. Daud, emigrated to Pakistan and established a framework for future opposition.

---

[2] General Mohammed Daud overthrew the Afghan king in 1973 and established friendly relations with the Soviet Union. He ruled Afghanistan from 1973 to 1978.

Borovik: But surely the fact that a large part of the clergy did not accept the events of April 1978 was the fault of the new leadership of Afghanistan?

Tsagolov: Of course. Although Nur Mohammed Taraki declared at a May 1978 press conference that the new authority respected the principles of Islam and that no one was being prevented from fulfilling religious duties, in practice many mistakes were made in relation to both the high-ranking clergy and the ordinary attendants of the cult. For example, a demagogical "restoration of legality" by Khaphizullah Amin turned into unjustified terror.[3] Really, it must be admitted that a large part of the clergy did not, at that time, see anything contrary to Islam in the beginning of the social economic reformation. But when the restraint of the religious sentiments of the faithful began, grumbling, dissatisfaction, and even open protest began to become apparent among many orthodox.

Borovik: Simply put, at the beginning the NDPA seemed unprepared to establish normal relations with the clergy, and all of the subsequent attempts to improve the situation were met with open distrust by the believers. The masses saw the NDPA as a party of "nonbelievers."

Tsagolov: Yes. And second, the leaders of the NDPA failed to learn that the authority of the religious representatives is respected by the people. This authority was consecrated both by the clergy's active participation in the struggle for national independence and in its antimonarchist, anti-Daud activity. Definite preparatory work was necessary in order to "distinguish" the past merits of the clergy from the current clergy in the eyes of the people. Without that type of work, the September 22, 1978, declaration by the new authority that the "Muslim brothers" were the number-one enemy and the call for their destruction "wherever they were" could not, to put it mildly, contribute to the popularity of the state's power. Considering these missed opportunities, it is impossible not to see that the NDPA did not know how to make Islam its ally. The political opposition took advantage of this miscalculation.

---

[3] Khaphizullah Amin was an orthodox Communist leader who was overthrown by Soviet troops in December 1979.

Borovik: You often had contact with the chieftains of the armed bands. What did they say about the leaders of the opposition, particularly about the Peshawar "Seven?" And what is your opinion?

Tsagolov: I think that the Afghan opposition does not present itself as a unified, organizationally linked social force. Here, at least, it is necessary to distinguish between three layers. First, the Peshawar "Seven." They had turned into an isolated force even before April 1978, under M. Daud. Take Gulbuddin Hekmatyar, the son of a landowner, who studied at a military academy. He was the leader of the reactionary group "Muslim Youth" and the organizer of the rebellion in 1976. After its collapse, he fled to Pakistan. He is a dedicated militant partisan of the establishment of an Islamic state in Afghanistan and an advocate of Islamic chauvinism. Look at this: In the program of the "Islamic Party of Afghanistan," which he leads, the jihad, or holy war, is affirmed, and the goals of the "liberation" of the territories populated by Muslims and the creation of an Islamic state are proclaimed.

Borovik: How, then, are the repeated invitations for the "Seven" to join in the coalition government to be evaluated?

Tsagolov: Personally, I consider that idea to be shortsighted. On the one hand, the "Seven" will not agree to enter a coalition in which they will only share power. Every one of the "Peshawars" calculates on having not a small share of power in the long run, but 100 percent of it. On the other hand, the leaders of the internal armed opposition will not be reconciled if it is not they, the "spillers of blood" for these nine years, who enter into the coalition government, but instead those who sat in Peshawar. I think that a dialogue, not with the "Seven" but with the leaders of the internal armed opposition, would be more farsighted.

The fact that not one of the major leaders of the internal armed opposition has yet been attracted to the coalition government can also be considered a missed opportunity of the Kabul leadership. I do not believe that it is impossible to find, through political flexibility, a point of contact with that part of the opposition.

Borovik: Now I want to talk with you for a while about economic problems. Nine years of war have caused serious problems in the Afghan economy. Immediately after the cessation of military action, the restoration of the destroyed economy will undoubtedly become the main concern of the Afghan leadership.

Tsagolov: As a result of the war, a large number of enterprises, transport systems, electrical lines, communications systems, and roads were partially or completely taken out of operation. We cannot forget that the war seriously upset the internal economic connections among provinces, as well as among and within branches of the national economy. The supply of raw materials, fuel, and electrical energy to industrial enterprises is becoming a big problem. The war and emigration have dealt a blow to the ranks of engineering, the technical workers, and to the intelligentsia as a whole. Many private industrialists were killed or left the country. The economic blockade by the West and the reduction of income from exports, along with the growth of expenditures on imports, seriously affected the condition of the national economy. Unemployment and inflation are rising. The quality of life of the workers is declining.

Borovik: The land-water reform. Is that, in fact, the central question of the NDPA's economic policy? In Afghanistan, I came across truly skeptical attitudes toward it. What do you think?

Tsagolov: Yes, that is the central economic problem, it is clear, if only because three quarters of the entire able-bodied population works in agriculture. The government has done much to try to stimulate agricultural production, but there have not been any noticeable results. High hopes were placed on the cooperatives. I think that these hopes were unjustified. The state sector of the economy is just the same. The tempo of the implementation of land-water reforms is very slow. Only 30 to 35 percent of them have been implemented.

Borovik: The unfolding of the situation in Afghanistan after the withdrawal of Soviet troops will depend to a great extent on the unity and prestige of the NDPA. If the land-water reform is the central economic problem, then the central political problem is the position of the NDPA and the situation within the NDPA.

Tsagolov: I absolutely agree. But, unfortunately, after the split of the NDPA into two factions in November 1967 (the "khal'k" under the leadership of N. M. Taraki, and the

"Parcham" under the leadership of Babrak Karmal), the party could not become a single political organization. Even now, it does not act with a single purpose, a single will.

Borovik: You see, even following the takeover during the April days of 1978, rivalry among factions did not cease. In fact, it turned into a bitter struggle.

Tsagolov: Yes, that's right. All methods, including physical extermination, were implemented. The factional struggle did irreparable damage to the party. And the paradox is that everyone understood and understands the perniciousness of the factional struggle, but they simply cannot escape from it. Everyone is for unity in their words, but in practice there is no unity. This is the main reason why a substantial portion of the people who were once a social support for the party left the NDPA, having ceased to believe in it as a vanguard force capable of bringing the planned reforms to completion.

Borovik: During my trips to Afghanistan I was, like yourself, convinced that the NDPA is in a deep crisis. It suffers from serious political ailments. Is that understood in the party?

Tsagolov: I think so. Look at the words of General Secretary [Afghan leader] Najibullah at the 19th *plenum* of the Central Committee of the NDPA. He said:

> An unfortunate situation has developed, for which several members of the Central Committee, social organizations, ministries, and institutions have been carefully brought under criticism. The transfer of leaders who have obstructed our work from one armchair into another has become a system. The absence of activism, factionalism, the absence of strict controls, insufficiently high principles, and serious errors have cost us dearly. This has happened because, for several of them, the revolution ended the day that they gained everything from it; that is, a station, a position, an office, and personal dignity. The leaders and the responsible individuals were chosen for their posts, not on the basis of their loyalty to the party and to its goal, but in accordance with tribal, ethnic, and sectarian interests, and also on the basis of personal loyalty to individuals. They occupied themselves with intrigues and subversive activities, instead of work, in the internal party work,

and they looked for any occasion for conflict and disagreement.

Borovik: The withdrawal of our troops is going now at full speed. However, after their final departure at the beginning of next year, it seems to me that not only will the war not stop, but also we can expect still more military action.

Tsagolov: That is exactly why I believe that the dominant aspect of the discussions about the coalition government should shift to the side of the leaders of the internal armed opposition. The "Alliance of Seven" is not tired of the war; for it, the war is good business. The armed opposition, which carries out firsthand military action in Afghan territory, is tired of war. It is precisely its leaders who, to a greater degree than the Peshawar "Seven," are ready for a dialogue with the NDPA.

Borovik: Do you have any confidence that the Afghan armed forces will be able to defend their power from attacks by the opposition after the withdrawal of Soviet troops?

Tsagolov: It is hard to answer that question in a single way. The condition and capabilities of the Afghan armed forces are directly dependent on the condition of the NDPA and the state power. The Afghan leadership, in my opinion, is not sufficiently attentive to the dangers that threaten the party and the state power from within. Judging the Afghan army by its present condition, I do not have the confidence of which you speak. That is precisely why I think that the party-state apparatus is faced with an immense task: the mobilization of all resources, even the most insignificant ones, for the upgrading of the military capabilities of the army.

Borovik: Kim Makedonovich, in your opinion how will the situation in Afghanistan look in the spring of 1989?[4]

Tsagolov: I am not a prophet, I am an analyst. Many predict a bloodbath in Afghanistan. Others insist that, after the withdrawal, the opposition will not have an argument to continue the "blessed war" with the "nonbelievers." In that connection, I want to note that, even today, a

---

[4] The withdrawal of Soviet troops was scheduled for completion on February 15, 1989.

significant amount of the military activity on Afghan soil is among opposing detachments of the internal opposition. They are fighting for power, for territory, and for spheres of influence. I think that this internecine war will not subside immediately after our departure.

Borovik: In Afghanistan, I am repeatedly convinced that many party and state functionaries, both in Kabul and in other localities, would not have wanted the withdrawal of our troops. They have felt self-confident and secure leaning on our shoulder. They have often passed on to us things that they should have done themselves. Doesn't it seem to you that the prospect of the withdrawal of Soviet troops will cure them of this illness of dependency?

Tsagolov: That is why I consider the decision about the withdrawal of troops, agreed upon by the Soviet government and the Afghan leadership, to be exceptionally timely.

Borovik: Even now, many of our foreign friends who are overflowing with leftist psychology see a virtual departure from the principles of internationalism in this decision of the Soviet leadership. How would you evaluate this type of leftist criticism?

Tsagolov: I do not share this criticism. A consistent effort to resolve regional conflicts by political means is a courageous step. Our call to new political thinking is directed, not only toward the United States, to Pakistan, and to the leaders of the Afghan armed opposition, but also to our friends both in Afghanistan and in other countries of the world.

Borovik: And a final question. What would you wish for the representatives of our press?

Tsagolov: In the beginning of the 1980s, Afghanistan was moved into the category of so-called "closed subjects." Readers and television viewers were under the impression that Soviet troops were occupied more with their own interests than with war. That was only a small part of the truth. The Soviet people began to see in the sparkle of military medals and orders not the value of the difficult and mortally dangerous work of soldiers, but some kind of false showiness. This was nothing but insulting to those who served in wars. It is a graphic example of the absence of *glasnost*.

What would I wish for the press? To avoid both false "trench" truth and speculation about Afghan events. However, it is necessary to make up for the lack of truth that accumulated during the war.

24

Instead of Mountains of Weapons: On the Principle of Reasonable Sufficiency

Lev Semeyko

Izvestiya, August 13, 1987

In one of the first Soviet press articles to advocate the doctrine of "reasonable sufficiency," Colonel Semeyko cites the need to reduce military expenditures and the desire to alleviate tensions abroad as the cornerstones of this doctrine. Semeyko implicitly asserts that past Soviet efforts to merely declare publicly peaceful intent served no practical purposes for Soviet-Western relations. He argues that the number of soldiers and weapons on the potential battlefield and their structure and location should give an impression of a defensive posture regardless of the intentions or even the imagined fears of an adversary.

This doctrine represents a rebuke of the previous conduct of Soviet military policy, particularly as Semeyko criticizes the idea of "the more, the better," which has dominated Soviet military philosophy. Semeyko uses the analogies of the Roman Empire as well as the United States to argue that "the desire for a surplus of military might always has led inevitably" to economic and technological stagnation. Semeyko is a leading researcher at the USSR Academy of Sciences' United States and Canada Institute. Like Viacheslav Dashichev (author of Document #22), his status as either an active or a retired military officer is not cited in nonmilitary publications.

The question of what should be the size, nature, and function of a state's military power is one of the main questions separating the new and the old political thinking in the security sphere. The old thinking proceeds in principle from the idea of "the more, the better," the idea that gaining military supremacy over an opponent can almost automatically guarantee a victorious outcome in a potential war.

The new thinking denies this antagonistic approach. It favors a minimum and not a maximum of military might for both sides, and it also favors excluding the idea of seeking a military solution to disputed international problems. This quest is senseless, for with the continuation of the arms race, war will increasingly appear to mean universal destruction. It will become even more senseless if all states are oriented to exclusively defensive military doctrines, not only in declarations, but also in actions.

We can pride ourselves on the fact that it is our country that has proclaimed the new political thinking, transforming it from the good intentions of perspicacious scientists and public figures into the directives of a practical policy. The 27th Party Congress clearly formulated these directives. Subsequent actions by the USSR and its Warsaw Pact allies enacted them both conceptually and, if you like, materially. This is illustrated by our repeated unilateral measures to contain the arms race, our constructive proposals for the creation of an all-embracing system of international security, and the terms of the recently announced Warsaw Pact military doctrine.

Among the most important political directives of the new thinking, special significance is attached to the principle of reasonable sufficiency. It is this concept that is the basis for the structuring of the USSR and Warsaw Pact armed forces. It makes a large contribution to shaping the socialist countries' approach to reducing military potential and demonstrates the truly defensive thrust of the military doctrine of the Warsaw Pact and the national doctrines of its member states. What is the essence of this concept?

Its political aspect lies in its emphasis on the strictly defensive function of armed forces and their readiness for defense against outside attack and not for attack and aggression. Priority is given to the political solution of international disputes, to the continual reduction of the level of military confrontation, to the support and strengthening of strategic stability through strictly monitored arms limitation, and to the reduction of arms to reasonable limits ensuring the interests of reliable defense. The desire for purely peaceful solutions to international disputes must be confirmed by the defensive, nonthreatening nature of the entire array of indicators of the size of potential military might. The existing disproportion between political directives to strengthen peace and security (there are more than enough of the appropriate declarations today) and the menacing size and nature of military might must be eliminated, irrespective of whether the military threats are real or invented.

Indisputably, the creation and maintenance of a particular level of military might is determined, above all, by security interests, that is, by political aims. However, in any case the size and nature of military might must be reasonable. They must conform to the realities of the nuclear age and have an exclusively defensive thrust.

I am talking about the military-political philosophy of the countries of the socialist commonwealth, and it is not hard to imagine the significance that its adoption by the whole international community (above all, its adoption by the NATO states) would have. This would ensure most completely both mutual (USSR-U.S.) and universal security and would create an atmosphere of genuine trust.

The concept of reasonable sufficiency is oriented to the future, and it carries a charge of ideas for long-term action. It may be fully implemented in a nuclear-free world with the elimination of nuclear weapons and other types of mass destruction weapons. But, it is necessary to ensure right now the permanent, increasingly large-scale reduction of weapons arsenals to the minimum reasonable limits.

The concept's military aspect lies in the fact that specific indicators of military potential must actually confirm the defensive (nonoffensive, nonaggressive) nature of the military doctrines while at the same time ensuring reliable security.

What does this mean? Here I think one can discern at least two essential criteria.

The first is that the level of military might of a state or a coalition of states must ensure that no one has grounds for fears, even imaginary fears, for its security. This criterion demands reasonable sufficiency for exclusively defensive purposes and not an unreasonable surplus of military potential, from which a military threat can always be perceived. Here the mere proclamation of the defensive thrust of one's military doctrine, as is characteristic of NATO in particular, is not enough. Confirmations are needed on the size of the armed forces, their distribution and structure, the nature of their armaments, the military activity undertaken, and, of course, the constructive actions taken to reduce the level of military strategic equilibrium. Without this, declarations will remain declarations, and mutual suspicions not only will be a permanent feature but also will be capable of causing the swift emergence of crisis situations.

The sufficiency of military potential is expressed both in the precise quantity and quality of armaments and in the troops themselves intended for defense, and also in their structure and stationing. These and other factors must convincingly show the absence of aggressive intentions. In this context the Warsaw Pact countries' doctrinal purpose is of fundamental significance: to implement the reduction of armed forces and conventional armaments in Europe to a level at which neither of the sides, while ensuring its defense, has the means to suddenly attack the other side or to unleash offensive operations. This purpose is indeed revolutionary, because it proposes for the first time that both sides reject such a military action as an attack, which is traditionally considered to be fundamental. The proposals for the mutual withdrawal of the most dangerous offensive types of armaments from the zone in which the two sides are directly contiguous and for a reduction in the concentration of armed forces and armaments in this zone to an agreed minimum level are also innovative.[1] This approach is mutually beneficial and once again confirms the need for international recognition and adoption of the principle of reasonable sufficiency.

The second criterion is that military might and combat readiness must be sufficient to permit them not to be taken unawares (let us recall the sad experience of 1941) and, if a hostile attack occurs, to deal the aggressor a crushing rebuff. While the first criterion is aimed at ensuring that the other side has no unwarranted fears, the point of the second is that we and our allies equally want to be spared the sense of an imminent threat looming over us.

Sufficiency does not preclude but rather presupposes the presence of strategic parity, that decisive factor in preventing war. It is necessary to have within the framework of parity a reasonably sufficient military potential capable of reliably ensuring the security of the USSR and its allies. This means that, under contemporary conditions, we must have a guaranteed potential for

---

[1] Mikhail Gorbachev's unilateral cut announced at the United Nations in December 1988 incorporated these principles.

nuclear retaliation designed to prevent an unpunished nuclear attack under any, even the most unfavorable, nuclear attack scenarios. In any situation, an answering strike must unacceptably damage the aggressor. The inevitability of this must discourage him from attack. In turn, sufficiency with regard to conventional weapons means the capability to reliably ensure the collective defense of the socialist community countries.

To be spared the sense of an imminent threat, the Warsaw Pact's military potential must be a sufficiently reliable shield to defend us, and the NATO bloc must actually demonstrate renunciation of its aggression, of its gamble on military supremacy, and of its maintenance and especially its buildup of menacingly large armed forces.

But at the moment there is no proof that the North Atlantic (NATO) bloc has embarked on this, the only correct path. Since so much of our security depends on the resolutions and actions of the United States and its allies, the limits of sufficiency for our armed forces cannot be permanent. We cannot fail to take into consideration the fact that the U.S. armed forces' structure is now based not on the concept of reasonable sufficiency but on the concept of military supremacy. We cannot fail to be alarmed at the contradictions in the policy and statements (and this is also policy) of U.S. leaders. Here is an example from President Reagan's speeches: The first (and commendable) statement, "There can be no greater happiness than reaching an agreement that will rid the earth of nuclear weapons for all time." And the second statement, which really chills the soul, "May our adversary go to sleep each night in fear waiting for us to use nuclear weapons."[2] Under these conditions we need special precision in assessing our own capabilities, self-possession, and supreme responsibility in making decisions. But in any case the limits of our armed forces' sufficiency must be reasonable and not exceed actual defensive requirements. We do not support the idea of eternal nuclear deterrence, just as we resolutely oppose the hypocritical, totally

---

[2] President Reagan began to receive more positive Soviet press treatment after his and Mikhail Gorbachev's Washington summit meeting in December 1987.

unrealistic plans to ensure the creation of a nuclear-free world with the help of SDI. Lasting security can only be guaranteed by taking the path of consistent disarmament and by reducing military potential to a reasonable nuclear-free minimum for ensuring the interests of defense. That is precisely how the 27th Party Congress put the question.

The economic aspect of the concept under review is obvious. Its implementation means saving the huge means and resources that every state and all mankind need so badly to resolve constructive tasks. The experience of history convincingly confirms that the law of diminishing returns is valid when the level of military competition is raised, yielding increasingly reduced efficiency of additional quantities of arms and increasingly large expenditures on them. The situation is obviously absurd. Furthermore, the desire for a surplus of military might always has led inevitably to the slowing down of socioeconomic and technological processes. For four hundred years the Roman Empire directed its technological achievements above all to meeting military requirements. The result was stagnation in all spheres. The Pentagon is also a kind of huge black hole sucking up the achievements of the scientific and technical revolution and providing practically nothing in return. In the opinion of leading U.S. economists, over the past thirty years the military has been responsible for one half of the instances of U.S. economic backwardness with regard to particular targets. We do not want this practice either for the United States or for ourselves, or for anyone else.

The mutual orientation of the USSR and the United States, the Warsaw Pact and NATO, toward reasonable sufficiency of military might would ensure not only an accelerated transition from nuclear confrontation to a nuclear-free world (and, consequently, the consolidation of mutual and universal security), but also a broad scope for resolving the global tasks facing mankind. This is the tremendous importance for all mankind of the military-political concept proclaimed by the Soviet Union and now enshrined in the Warsaw Pact military doctrine.

25

Five Years of SDI: What Next?

D. Klimov

Krasnaya Zvezda, March 23, 1988

Klimov recites standard arguments made in both East and West against an ABM (antiballistic missile) system. The article utilizes many arguments commonly heard in the West to make its points including (1) SDI (Strategic Defense Initiative) is designed to ensure American military superiority, (2) the system will jeopardize arms control by violating the 1972 ABM treaty, and (3) SDI will increase the likelihood of nuclear war.

The tone of the article and the absence of nasty attacks in the Soviet press on the fifth anniversary of SDI suggest that SDI has subsided as an impediment to a START (Strategic Arms Reduction Talks) treaty, having been replaced to a degree by discussions about sea-launched cruise missiles and mobile ICBMs (intercontinental ballistic missiles). With START negotiations ongoing, it is possible that some important elements of the Soviet view of SDI are not being openly discussed in the press. It is interesting, however, that the idea to develop a limited ABM system against accidental launches, as proposed by Senate Armed Services Committee Chairman Senator Sam Nunn and others, is not completely discounted.

It is five years since the day U.S. President Ronald Reagan proclaimed the program for the establishment of a large-scale ABM system with space-based elements, which subsequently received the official title "Strategic Defense Initiative." In our view, however, those who described it as the "Star Wars" program were far more accurate.

The president did not provide a clear definition of what the system he proposed would be like. But he declared that it was designed to make nuclear arms "impotent and obsolete" and so would remove the threat of nuclear war. In fact, that is far from true. The purpose of SDI is to achieve military superiority over the Soviet Union. In a statement to the Senate Armed Services Committee, Caspar Weinberger, then U.S. defense secretary, cynically admitted that. Here are his exact words: "If we were able to acquire a system that was efficient, and if we knew that it could make their weapons (that is, the Soviet Union's weapons—KLIMOV) impotent, we would return to the situation where we were the only country to possess nuclear weapons."

The extremely dangerous nature of such a program was obvious right from the start. The very next day after Ronald Reagan's statement, Congressman Tom Downey declared that the president's proposal to build an ABM system in outer space "is a most horrific and absurd idea." "The president believes that lasers and beam weapons would be defensive by nature, but it is quite obvious that this is not so," another congressman, Jim Moody (D-WI), pointed out. "The introduction of more sophisticated weapons," he continued, "can lead only to the introduction of more powerful counterweapons." Another congressman, Les AuCoin (D-WI), said these words: "The president wants military superiority. But the Soviets will not stand still or allow us to achieve superiority. Instead, they will create new weapons which will in turn be capable of neutralizing space weapons."

As though summing up all of these statements, the *New York Times* wrote that "the president decided to develop research work on a new type of ABM system, despite the fact that many of his aides at the White House and the Defense Department believed that this idea had not been studied sufficiently." Valid concern was also aroused by the fact that the implementation of SDI runs counter to the 1972 Soviet-U.S. treaty on the limitation of ABM systems. It is no coincidence that even now, in the early stages of SDI implementation, the administration is trying to circumvent its provisions by resorting to the so-called "broad interpretation" and, essentially, rejecting a number of the treaty's provisions.[1]

The opposition to the "Star Wars" program even among U.S. legislators is evidenced by the fact that Congress is systematically reducing the administration's requests for funds to be allocated to SDI. Thus, the requests for fiscal 1988 were cut from $5.7 billion to $3.9 billion. Nor has the

---

[1] The Reagan administration asserted that tests of the most advanced elements of SDI are permitted under a "broad interpretation" of the 1972 ABM treaty.

idea of a "broad interpretation" of the ABM treaty met with the expected support in the Senate.

Nevertheless, the United States has been carrying out intensive development in the ABM sphere throughout these five years. Although Lieutenant General James Abrahamson, who heads the SDI organization, has acknowledged that budget cuts have somewhat slowed down the pace of research, he has, however, declared that the SDI organization has entirely abandoned the examination of only a small number of systems.

A considerable role is undoubtedly played here by pressure from the military-industrial corporations, which reckon on making superprofits out of implementing the program. But probably no less significant is the fact that the champions of "Star Wars" have managed to enlist considerable support by means of a forceful propaganda campaign. For the average American, who does not understand all the subtleties of foreign and military policy, the promises to safeguard the country against a possible nuclear strike with the help of a "space shield" appear very alluring. Many Americans have been enthralled by the usual illusions and stereotypes. So many people in the United States, even those who are skeptical about SDI, deem it necessary to continue research to find out whether it is possible, from a scientific and technical viewpoint, to create a strategic defense system.

What is the position today of this widely publicized program? The signing of the Soviet-U.S. treaty on intermediate- and shorter-range missiles (the INF treaty), which has opened up new prospects for the achievement of corresponding agreements, above all for a 50 percent reduction in strategic offensive arms, has still further increased skepticism about it. "SDI makes a nuclear war more likely," Eugene Carroll, deputy director of Washington's Center for Defense Information, emphasized, "because it pushes toward a buildup of offensive nuclear arms. And yet it is precisely this process that the United States and the Soviet Union are seeking to reverse during the Geneva talks on reducing strategic arms." This is why such fundamental significance is attached to a clause of the Soviet-U.S. joint statement signed in Washington on December 10, 1987, that the two countries' leaders have entrusted their delegations in

Geneva with "elaborating an accord obliging the sides to observe the ABM Treaty in the form in which it was signed in 1972 in the process of carrying out the research, development, and, where necessary, testing permitted under the ABM Treaty and not to abrogate the ABM Treaty during the agreed term."

The U.S. press reports that SDI has also encountered a number of purely technical problems. In the opinion of U.S. specialists, its command and management programs, without which the whole system cannot function, are "suffering total failure." *Newsweek* magazine, for example, believes that "unless there is some unforeseen technological leap, SDI is threatened with gradually fading away." However, champions of "Star Wars" are seeking to give it a new boost and to achieve its unconditional implementation. Attempts are being made to technically revamp the program. Tests within the SDI framework are designed, in the opinion of its adherents, to convince skeptics of the program's efficiency and technical feasibility.

Thus, in December 1987, the first ground tests of a laser code-named "Zenith Star" were conducted on a California range. And in February 1988 another SDI-related experiment was conducted, "Delta-181," during which a laser radar device was put into orbit and tested. Originally this experiment, which cost $250 million, was declared "very successful." However, it later became known that one of the sensors, the most important among the other analogous instruments launched into space, had gone out of commission.

Certain U.S. figures are already proposing the rejection of the ambitious plans to create a "space shield" and the reorientation of research within the SDI framework toward developing a considerably more modest system. But this is a complex issue. Thus, Senator Sam Nunn has proposed turning SDI into a "sensible defense initiative." "If we cautiously changed the thrust of our research, it could enable us to develop a limited system to counter the frightening possibility of an accidental or unsanctioned launch," Nunn declared. But champions of SDI are inclined to regard this proposal as a first step toward deploying a large-scale ABM system with space-based elements. This was said by Abrahamson, in particular, who called Nunn's proposal "very constructive."

It is still too early to draw a conclusion about how events will develop further around SDI. Its future appears rather uncertain. But there is no doubt that today it remains an adventurist undertaking with extremely dangerous consequences.

26

Pooling Resources to Get a Computer

The Naval Combat Training Department
of the Editor's Office

Krasnaya Zvezda, May 3, 1988

This article addresses the very serious problem of military personnel who lack both computers and computer literacy. Bureaucrats are blamed for the odd situation in which students at a submarine training facility have had to buy computers with their own money. A conclusion one can draw from this article is that the Soviet armed forces do indeed have significant budget constraints.

Any article carried by *Krasnaya Zvezda* that refers to the problems of using computers in combat training evokes numerous responses. This mail can be divided into two parts. The first contains proposals, while the second contains fully pertinent questions such as: How can we ever get our hands on them, these computers, if they reach the troops and the fleets in such limited quantities?

Letters from readers concerning the article "The Unattainable Computer" by Senior Lieutenant Ye. Tarasov, published January 21, 1988, are no exception. Let us recall one of the problems examined by the author. When it comes to submarines, many of the training sites are equipped with obsolete instruments. These are no longer used aboard ship, but for some reason the training has to be done with them. On the other hand, not too long ago a personal computer that could be used to solve navigation problems was offered for sale to the submariners. But it was never purchased; the financial experts objected. Strictly speaking they were in the right; there were certain documents that supported their objections, even though they were fifteen years old.

"May I hope that competent organizations will in the end resolve this issue?" the author of one letter asks. "If you think about it, nothing will come of all of this. It's not that easy to change even obsolete instructions. But I do support the newspaper's stand: Universal computer literacy can't be achieved without computers." In this Warrant Officer

N. Lankovets came close to predicting the subsequent course of events.

Here are excerpts from the reply by Colonel I. Radutny, chief of the Pacific Fleet's Financial Service:

> The article's author correctly asserts that the marketing network offers these goods for sale, but the following prohibitions on their purchase exist:
>
> 1. Military units, services, and military educational institutions are prohibited from using money to pay for computers supplied centrally on the basis of approved tables of equipment and supply norms.
>
> 2. The purchase of miniature calculators, computers, and felt-tip pens is not foreseen by the USSR Ministry of Defense's budget.
>
> But even if the money were allocated, it would be impossible to purchase computers because the marketing network can sell felt-tip pens, miniature calculators, and personal computers (the latter were available at a price of 650 rubles) only to the public at large, and it refuses to do so to military units, enterprises, and services in light of the "Rules of Sale of Marketable Goods to Institutions, Organizations, Enterprises, and Collective Farms on a Minor Wholesale Basis" approved by the USSR Ministry of Trade and the USSR State Bank on 1 August 1977 and supplemented by a letter from this ministry and the governing board of the USSR State Bank dated 10 June 1980.

As we can see, the editor's office was essentially unable to establish a dialogue with one of the naval departments. There was but one answer: It is not permitted, and that's final. But if the realities of life demand it, then the appropriate officials should sweep this "it is not permitted" from the path of progress. So far, the initiative is coming only from below. Cadet Ya. Ivanko from the Marshal of Aviation Alexander Pokryshkin's Higher Engineer Radiotechnical School of Air Defense Forces in Kiev, for example, is prepared to share his experience with submariners. "We have been using personal computers in our training for over a year now," he writes the editor's office. "They have extensive graphics capability, and this allows them to work not only with numerical data but also with graphic information. I think that they can be used to solve navigational problems as well. It is easy to create any combat and training program with computers." All that is left to be said is that, even in this school, the only kind of support that is available to the cadets was purchased with their own money. If they were to follow this route, the submariners would have to pool their own resources to get the computers. And what do competent organizations feel about all of this? The questions raised in "The Unattainable Computer" remain open.

27

No, I Do Not Want to Be a "Granddad"

Sh. Salimgareev

Krasnaya Zvezda, May 3, 1988

This letter is the Soviet Army's response to an especially sharp criticism of military life by the civilian press. Unlike the U.S. armed forces the Soviet military has been exempt from public critique. The phenomenon of *dedovshchina* ("granddads") reflects serious nationality and social problems rooted in the loss of ethnic homogeneity within the Soviet armed forces brought by the increased ratio of draftees from Central Asia.

Dear Editors:

I have not written before, but I feel that the time has come. Everyone is writing and causing a fuss, saying that there is real hell in the army and that young soldiers are humiliated and beaten. And all of this because of these notorious "granddads," "old men," etc.

I can be considered one of those who are "privileged"— this is my second year of military service—but I have no desire to become a "granddad."

To be honest, when all this information about "granddads" started to appear in the media, I began to ponder this issue. Shouldn't I, too, enjoy a piece of this "pie"? But I believe that to be able to ridicule, to humiliate a buddy who is younger by about a year and a half, well, I don't know, I guess one must be totally asinine. It's possible that tomorrow we could be fighting side by side for our homeland. How would we look to the eyes of our fathers and oldest brothers, who served with dignity, and to the teacher Albina Nikolaevna Guseva, who always told us that love for a country is not conceivable without love for fellow human beings?

I am a third-generation Muscovite. I was born in Moscow, went to college here, and then went to the army. I love my city and am proud of it. It was very painful in the beginning to hear all the uncomplimentary opinions of my fellow townsmen. Then, after a while, I understood that there is some truth to it, that some of the Muscovite soldiers are not prepared for a life in the army, but behave, at the same time, in a very provocative and arrogant manner. That's why they are caustically called "Children of the Arbat."[1] The conflicts began to arise. It's not surprising, for example, that the men from the village can quickly finish household tasks and are not afraid of hard work, but my townsmen enjoy discussing and debating before actually picking up a broom or a shovel. However, in the army, demagoguery is not encouraged, as we all know.

Now after serving for a year and a half, I can contemplate the idea of the "old man" from experience and not from hearsay. Yes, I had an encounter with this too. What are the advantages of being a "granddad"? What privileges does he have? First of all, to shift some of his work to the shoulders of young soldiers. After being freed from work there is even time to idle. The latter is especially disturbing. In the army, a person not involved in necessary, daily work can easily get on the path of disobedience. In their search for entertainment, "granddads" yearn for alcohol and try to amuse themselves by antagonizing the young. On this premise, barracks delinquency is born. My opinion of "granddads" is as follows: I am not pretending to make discoveries, I am simply speaking as a man who lives in the barracks.

This ugly and uncivilized behavior is receiving too much press coverage. I don't want to repeat the thoughts of others, especially because I disagree with many of the publications that are printing sensationalist speculation. But somehow, in all of my reading, I did not find the answer to the key question: What is the origin of "granddads"? From my experience as a sergeant, the situation seems like this. We received a higher rank and became distressed that more than half of our young soldiers cannot themselves pull up on the crossbar and almost all can't pull themselves up and over over a wall. Not the best picture, and it's greatly disturbing. The picture is a usual one, but from it the "granddad" begins. The strong automatically group together; it is unnecessary to be extremely perceptive to realize that the hardest jobs will be

---

[1] After *Children of the Arbat*, a book by Anatoly Rybakov, published in 1987.

performed by the weakest. Unless, of course, life in the unit will be strictly in accordance with the Statutes.

Another factor is that many of the young men join the service with a "home" assignment. For a year they follow the unwritten rules, and then they receive the benefits of being "granddads." From my point of view, some writers and journalists are at fault for literally attaching that name to these youths. How could we not remember the article by Yuri Polyakov, "A Hundred Days Till the Order," in the magazine *Yunost*? In that article the author publicly legitimized ranking frameworks and divided all soldiers into categories according to how much time they will serve. In the pads and notebooks of many of my coworkers, it is possible to find the chart that was published in the youth journal. Whether the author wanted to or not, he has created for us a huge hindrance.

This evil has such roots that it is not immediately discernible. For example, whose parents do not want for their son a good service? Everyone wants the best, but they understand it differently. For instance, the mother and father of my subordinate, Private I. Stepanov, came to visit him. They were shown the barracks and the cafeteria and told about the traditions of the unit and their son's studies. It seemed that the guests were satisfied, but then that evening I found out that Stepanov was caught trying to sneak in alcohol.

"Why do you need vodka, Igor?" I asked Stepanov. "Did you start drinking?"

"The folks gave it to me," he replied, almost crying, "so that I could offer it to the 'granddads,' so they wouldn't affront me."

Here, in our unit today, we do not have "granddads" or serious conflicts, yet the parents of this soldier thought otherwise. They did not provide their son with the best lesson. However, it's not only them, but also those who send in the mail illegal packages with liquor, as well as those who send lots of money to their sons. As if it will be easier for their son if he bribes someone. Such "compassion" of their seniors is convincing the young soldiers that it is possible to pay off responsibility and shift it onto the shoulders of someone else. And then, at the end of his service, a son like that becomes a master "granddad" and ends up in the rehabilitation center or somewhere else behind bars.

There are probably other grounds for becoming a "granddad." In army units today there are hard rockers, punks, heavy metal listeners, and others not used to discipline or spoiled by too much attention and laziness. To understand them, just study sociology. But I would like to discuss the ways of battling this unstable relationship (again, from my point of view as a sergeant). It seems counterproductive, for example, to make officers work twenty-four hours a day without a break and to sometimes make them sleep in the barracks with the soldiers. The commander of any rank must work no more than his subordinates, but work well. His success is measured by how good his subordinates think his work is. I have noticed that if a commander gets wrapped up in his daily routine and does not read the newspapers or magazines or watch television, he is unable to interest the soldiers. The soldiers and the sergeants like an erudite and, most important, just and fair officer.

I would like to conclude this letter with a question: Is there a connection between "granddads" and the conditions of life of the soldiers? The soldiers in my unit live in fair conditions, but others are located in barracks that were built, as they say, in the last century with a minimal level of comfort. The building of new barracks has been delayed, and I am not sure that by the end of my term of service their doors will be open. Since we live in the *glasnost* epoch everyone knows about this, but nothing has been done.

"Granddads" will keep spreading, if nothing blocks their path. As for myself, I can guarantee that I will never become a "granddad." But what about everyone else? No one is born a "granddad"; people become them. It is embarrassing to talk about it, but we have to.

Bibliography

Belan, Lieutenant Colonel N. *"Glasnost* against 'Granddads.' "
Krasnaya Zvezda, August 6, 1988.
   A story describing a military unit in which the social
   phenomenon of *dedovshchina* (granddads) is evident.
Belichenko, Colonel Yu., and Lukashevich, Captain V. "A Word
about the Military Formation." *Krasnaya Zvezda*, December 17,
1987.
   At a meeting in the Ministry of Defense, Defense Minister
   Dmitry Yazov and conservative Russian writers defend the
   army against liberal criticism on a wide range of topics.
Bocharov, Gennady. "Afghan." *Literaturnaya Gazeta*, February
15, 1989.
   This realistic portrayal of the nine-year war in Afghanistan
   includes a description of a civilian massacre perpetrated by
   Soviet soldiers.
Defense Ministers' Committee of the Warsaw Pact. "On the
Balance of Numerical Strength and Weapons between the
Warsaw Pact and NATO." *Krasnaya Zvezda*, January 31, 1989.
   This publication about military balance is an expression of
   glasnost and an unprecedented step toward establishing
   military trust between the Soviet Union and the West.
Prokhanov, Alexander. "Defense Thinking and New
Thinking." *Literaturnaya Rossiya*, May 6, 1988.
   This conservative defense of the Soviet armed forces argues
   that the army is the main reason why the Soviet regime
   survived and the "new thinking" and *perestroika* became
   possible.

Chapter Six

Party Struggle and Political Reform

For decades Western observers have studiously analyzed who stood next to whom at the May Day parade, which party official delivered the longest speech at a *plenum*, and whether a Soviet leader's illness was a serious ailment or simply a case of the sniffles. The secrecy surrounding internal party struggles frustrated Western attempts to determine the political meaning of Soviet domestic and foreign policies. Today, for the first time since the 1920s, serious debate in the party is made public for all to see. The most dramatic manifestations of this party struggle—Nina Andreyeva's letter to *Sovetskaya Rossiya* and *Pravda*'s response (Documents #28 and #29)—are included in this chapter. Articles by Alexander Gelman, Tatyana Zaslavskaya, and Andrei Sakharov (Documents #30, #31, and #32) discussing the future of *perestroika* and the prospects for reforming the Soviet political system are also included in this chapter.

Party officials share the goal of economic reform but differ on how to achieve it. Neither side of the debate denies the need for a *perestroika* of the Soviet system; the question is how high a price to pay for modernization. Mikhail Gorbachev has decided that the political price will be *glasnost*.

Gorbachev came to power in March 1985, succeeding three old and ill leaders who had come to symbolize the system they led. The long, drawn-out spectacle of dying rulers convinced the party leadership of the need to promote a younger man. Gorbachev defeated his Politburo rival Grigory Romanov by gaining the confidence of the party leaders. As a protégé of Yuri Andropov, Gorbachev proved his abilities executing policy decisions in the early 1980s. Yet, according to conservative Yegor Ligachev's statements at the 19th Party Conference, Gorbachev won the post of general secretary by a narrow margin.

Gorbachev inherited a stagnant economy, a war in Afghanistan, and an oligarchical leadership structure resistant to radical change. Seweryn Bialer writes that "an oligarchical leadership, which by its very nature has to act through bargaining, trade-offs, and compromise, is ill-suited to initiating and executing major reforms of structures, procedures, or even policies. In this sense the future of such reforms in the Soviet Union depends to a large degree on the inclinations of the top Soviet leader and on his ability to pursue and realize those inclinations."[1]

Gorbachev came to power with a narrow mandate for change. A consensus within the Politburo recognized the need for a moderate reform of the Soviet economy. Yuri Andropov's reforms sought to improve economic performance by waging war on corruption and improving discipline in the workplace. Gorbachev's mandate was to carry Andropov's reforms through to their logical conclusion, but with the fresh energy needed to invigorate the economy and inspire workers.

For his first year and a half, Gorbachev continued the official course of "acceleration of economic and social development." He concentrated on improving the policies of Andropov and Konstantin Chernenko as well as inaugurating a campaign against alcoholism. Gorbachev firmly believed that these policies would improve economic performance. It soon became apparent, however, that more sober workers in the factory and fewer corrupt officials in the bureaucracy would not by themselves solve the endemic political and economic problems of the Stalinist system.

The turning point for Gorbachev came in August 1986, during his trip to the Soviet Far East. Before this trip no one at home or abroad believed that he intended to radically reform the Soviet economic or political system. In 1986, Timothy Colton wrote that "the regime has little if any urge at this juncture to democratize the Soviet Union or embark on truly fundamental reforms. . . . Radical reform is not at all likely to be carried out in the Soviet Union in the near future."[2]

The three-day Far Eastern trip consumed seven hours of prime-time television in the Soviet Union and was meticulously stage-managed to project the image of a new type of leader. Surrounded by women, children, and elderly men, Gorbachev repeatedly stressed the need for better housing and consumer goods. It was a tailor-made forum for the Soviet leader to expound his key themes. For the first time Gorbachev declared his reforms to be "revolutionary" and used the slogan "*perestroika.*"

Gorbachev soon introduced more radical proposals. The Law on State Enterprises, designed to decentralize industry and to create incentives for profitable enterprises, and the introduction of cooperatives were the first major initiatives. At the same time the press, in the spirit of *glasnost*, began to attack the perks of party officials and to uncover corruption in the republics. Grumbling and

---

[1]Seweryn Bialer, *Stalin's Successors* (New York: Cambridge University Press, 1984), p. 75.

[2]Timothy J. Colton, *The Dilemma of Reform in the Soviet Union*, 2d ed. (New York: Council on Foreign Relations, 1986), p. 5.

resistance grew so loud that Gorbachev publicly threatened to punish recalcitrant bureaucrats.

The story of Boris Yeltsin, former party first secretary in Moscow, illustrates the power of the bureaucracy to block real change. Yeltsin represents a one-man radical wing in a party in which the majority are conservatives. He gained a populist image in Moscow by attacking the party *apparat* and calling for the elimination of party privileges. Conservatives sought to render Yeltsin and his populist initiatives ineffectual by having their powerful friends in the Politburo neutralize his actions.[3]

Yeltsin believed that reforms in Moscow and across the nation could not occur unless Gorbachev supporters seized control of the party. He called for a radical reorganization of the CPSU bureaucracy and a realignment of forces within the Politburo. Feeling threatened, conservative Politburo members portrayed Yeltsin as a troublemaker and forced Gorbachev to reject his most loyal ally. Yeltsin offered to resign two weeks before the November 7, 1987, 70th Anniversary of the Bolshevik Revolution, but party officials refused to allow such a display of disunity. Instead, they unceremoniously removed Yeltsin on November 11th.

Gorbachev's failure to support Boris Yeltsin, and Yeltsin's inappropriate timing for a political confrontation, resulted in a wasted important opportunity for the Soviet leader to strike decisively at the conservative opposition. With Yeltsin's ouster Gorbachev lost control of the Moscow party organization, and reformers in panic viewed the ouster as a grave threat to *glasnost* and *perestroika*. In the end, however, the Yeltsin affair proved to be simply a minor skirmish in the war between reformers and conservatives.[4]

The second battle in this war came in March 1988. Emboldened by Gorbachev's failure to boldly attack the Stalinist legacy in his 70th Anniversary speech, and by their successful attacks on Yeltsin,

---

[3]Since his removal, Boris Yeltsin has mentioned publicly that he and conservative Politburo member Yegor Ligachev clashed on several occasions.

[4]Yeltsin's overwhelming victory in the March 26, 1989, elections signaled danger for the conservatives as well as for Gorbachev in the continuing process of democratization. Nearly six million Muscovites, 89 percent of those who voted, expressed their deep dislike of the party *apparat* by voting for Yeltsin. Although Yeltsin has no positive program of his own, his insistence that *perestroika* needs to be more radical and more rapid makes Gorbachev seem moderate by comparison. But despite his political usefulness for Gorbachev, Yeltsin can also be used against Gorbachev by the conservatives, who can point to Yeltsin as an example of the forces unleashed by *perestroika* that are threatening to split the party into factions.

conservatives mounted a fresh offensive against the reform movement. They were worried that incessant press attacks against Stalinist institutions and the reformist platform for the 19th Party Conference would weaken the party's dominant role in society. Conservatives hoped to break the party stalemate in their favor.

On March 13, 1988, *Sovetskaya Rossiya* published a letter from Leningrad chemistry teacher Nina Andreyeva which became known as the "manifesto of conservative forces." The letter attacked *glasnost* but avoided the issue of the faltering economy. By taking an ideological position in favor of the "class struggle" it justified Stalin's repressive policies. The letter also portrayed the supporters of reform as brethren of the West, Jewish refuseniks, and the children of the White Guard.

Reformers saw the letter as a well-planned attack involving Politburo conservative Yegor Ligachev and Leningrad party First Secretary Yuri Solovyov. The day after the *Sovetskaya Rossiya* article was published, Leningrad television aired a special program to discuss the letter's main points, and local party officials convened a special study session. Several regional newspapers in provincial towns took the unusual step of reprinting the Andreyeva letter. With careful timing *Sovetskaya Rossiya* published the letter on March 13, the day before Gorbachev was to depart on a previously announced trip to Yugoslavia. This tactical maneuver presented the general secretary with a *fait accompli* upon his return.

Gorbachev supporters failed to act, and for three weeks the country plunged into doubt and panic. Almost no one publicly criticized the Andreyeva letter. Reformers believed that the end was near. Finally, on April 5, the Gorbachev forces rallied back. *Pravda* printed a stinging editorial (Document #29) excoriating conservatives for engineering the letter's publication and warning that the "revolutionary principles of *perestroika*" would carry on. The *Pravda* editorial, likely written by Gorbachev's Politburo ally Alexander Yakovlev, closely mirrors the arguments made in Alexander Gelman's March 23 speech to Soviet filmmakers (Document #30).

Following *Pravda*'s reply to *Sovetskaya Rossiya* some newspapers published letters from reform advocates who had viewed the Andreyeva letter as a signal for a crackdown. Reformers told of preparing to "pack their small suitcase," a euphemism for imprisonment in work camps. Boris Yeltsin's removal had aroused similar fears. The average Soviet citizens already feared questioning their superiors as advocates of *glasnost* had implored. The public reaction to the Yeltsin ouster and the Andreyeva letter proved that after decades of persecution the Soviet people are exceedingly sensitive to signs of political fluctuation. In both cases people feared that *glasnost* was over.

Although the Andreyeva letter displayed the conservatives' ability to strike, reformers naively believed that the 19th Party Conference scheduled for June 1988 would solve their political dilemma. Conservatives, however, controlled the selection of delegates and filled the hall with the usual assortment of party bureaucrats, factory workers, and milkmaids. The party *apparat* arrogantly excluded many prominent intellectual supporters of *perestroika*, although the bureaucrats later consented to including some of these individuals as delegates and observers. This thoroughly contradicted the edicts of Gorbachev and the Central Committee that only ardent supporters of *perestroika* should participate in the conference. Party bureaucrats had once again repudiated the spirit of Gorbachev's proposals.

Despite the delegate selection fiasco, the party conference demonstrated *glasnost* at its best. For the first time in Soviet history, the leadership permitted extensive television and newspaper coverage of such an event. Gorbachev proved to be skillful at the helm, engaging in spontaneous disputes and spirited conversation with delegates. The most startling moment during the three-day event came during the speech of Vladimir Melnikov, the first secretary of the party committee of the Komi autonomous republic, when he called for the removal of old-guard members of the Politburo. When Gorbachev prompted him to openly state to which Politburo members he was referring, Melnikov named Andrei Gromyko and Mikhail Solomentsev. The conservative admonition of Russian writer Yuri Bondarev, "Could our *perestroika* be compared to an airplane that has taken off without knowing if there is a landing strip at its destination?" remains the most frequently quoted statement from the conference.

At the September 1988 *plenum* Gorbachev made an important move in his fight against the conservatives. He removed from power such conservative remnants of the Brezhnev period as Gromyko, Solomentsev, and Vladimir Dolgikh. Although these individuals had been instrumental in Gorbachev's gaining power over Romanov in the fight to become general secretary, they had to be removed to speed up the implementation of reforms. New Politburo members such as Vadim Medvedev and Anatoly Lukyanov will be more inclined toward Gorbachev's viewpoint. However, Gorbachev still does not control the Politburo. A strong conservative element remains, represented by Yegor Ligachev, Lev Zaikov, Viktor Chebrikov, Yuri Solovyov, and Vladimir Shcherbitsky. Gorbachev's most valuable supporters are Alexander Yakovlev, Eduard Shevardnadze, Nikolai Slyunkov, and the newest appointment, Vadim Medvedev.

To understand the political dynamics of the Politburo it should be viewed as a council of party elders, in some respects similar to the board of a large corporation. As the Communist party's highest ruling body, the Politburo tries to reach consensus and avoids deciding major policy issues with simple majority votes. The long-term relationships among members resemble those of U.S. Supreme Court justices, as disagreement over particular issues does not preclude working side by side for decades. The group nature of the institution means that powerful personalities, such as those of Ligachev or Gorbachev, can be decisive in policy disputes.

In September 1988, Ligachev was nominally demoted by being placed in charge of agriculture; however, he still represents a potent force within the Politburo. Seweryn Bialer writes that "Ligachev seeks a vastly different *perestroika* than that to which Gorbachev and his associates are committed. Ligachev is a proponent of the types of reform that were attempted so many times in the past rather than of the radical, comprehensive, and speedy reforms envisioned by *perestroika*."[5] Duke University's Professor Jerry Hough presents a different view of the political situation, one that does not appear to be supported by recent events. Writing before the publication of the Andreyeva letter, Hough scoffed at the notion of "Politburo opposition" and argued that Ligachev was only "supposedly conservative."[6]

Gorbachev and his supporters realize that in order to make economic reforms succeed, a fundamental reform of the Soviet political system is essential. The key component of political reform is restricting the power of the Communist party and giving control of daily management to local soviets, enterprise managers, and state officials in general. Gorbachev believes that the party should offer general guidance but should be removed from the micromanagement of economic policy.

Despite the majority of conservative delegates Gorbachev, unlike Khrushchev, succeeded at the 19th Party Conference in restricting the tenure of party officials to ten years. Limiting tenure is aimed at curtailing the power and corruption of party bureaucrats. By not blocking this initiative, these individuals at the conference either lacked the political organization or did not comprehend that the essence of Gorbachev's proposals was to deprive the party bureaucracy of power. A testament to Gorbachev's skill at the conference came in the decision to build a monument to Stalin's victims, presumably against the beliefs of many delegates; this is a further proof of de-Stalinization under Gorbachev.

The most important conference decision, however, concerned the reform of the Soviet political system manifested in the creation of a two-tier parliament and an American-style presidency. Although the

---

[5]Seweryn Bialer, ed., *Inside Gorbachev's Russia* (London: Westview Press, 1989), p. 201.

[6]Jerry Hough, *Opening Up the Soviet Economy* (Washington, DC: Brookings Institution, 1988), pp. 45, 53.

proposed changes in the political system are very confusing and complex, they are first steps on the road to genuine democratization. Under the March 1989 election laws voters are allowed to cast at least two votes, one for local "territorial districts" of equal population and another for "national-territorial districts" comprising the country's fifteen republics. In addition, a block of 750 seats has been reserved for members of "social organizations" such as the Communist party or trade unions. Drawbacks in the election system emerged as conservatives succeeded at "pre-election" meetings in Moscow in blocking the candidacies of reformers such as *Ogonyok* editor Vitaly Korotych. "It was impossible for me to fight against the party *apparat*," said Korotych, contending that Communist officials had blocked his candidacy by skillfully exploiting extremely complicated electoral procedures.[7]

The March elections to the Congress of the People's Deputies was a unique and uncertain experience for the Soviet people who, despite an enormously complicated electoral system, got their first taste of Western-style election politics. For the first time in Soviet history, in over 70 percent of the districts, there was more than one candidate per seat. Conservatives were decisively defeated in Moscow and Leningrad in this first step toward democratization.

Reformers hope, however, that the parliament that emerges from the elections will benefit *perestroika* more than could the docile and ineffectual Supreme Soviet. As Tatyana Zaslavskaya argues, "As far as I know, in the past twenty-five years not a single deputy has displayed any genuinely radical social initiative. . . . But, as we know, until the last session, when the draft Law of Cooperatives underwent stormy discussion, the Supreme Soviet essentially rubber-stamped decisions prepared by the *apparat*."[8]

The fundamental objective of the new presidency is to redistribute power from the party to the state. A powerful president theoretically would be capable of ignoring the Politburo and regional party leaders. This could be crucial, because conservative forces control all party leadership positions in the republics and in the big cities. The leaders of the Leningrad, Moscow, and Ukrainian party organizations—the three most influential party organizations in the country—are rigid conservatives. The newly designed office of the presidency raises two central questions. First, how can the president overrule the Politburo, the leading party organ, if the Soviet constitution proclaims the leading role of the party? Second, how can the irreversibility of *perestroika* and the establishment of a legalistic

---

[7]"Ousted Moscow Party Boss Gets His Chance for Revenge," *Washington Post*, February 23, 1989. Nonetheless, Korotych managed to get elected on May 14 in Kharkov, in the Ukraine.

[8]Document #31.

state be guaranteed if the country retains its one-party system? These and many more questions will have to be resolved if the Soviet Union is to evolve into a more democratic state.

The most immediate political task for Gorbachev is overcoming the opposition his reforms are encountering from the bureaucracy. The Soviet bureaucracy consists of three groups: party, state, and industrial. Considerable mobility exists between these groups. They also interact and collaborate on issues of mutual interest. Party bureaucrats, who control the management of daily affairs in the Soviet Union, have thus far emasculated the essence of Gorbachev's reforms. Conservative holdovers from the Brezhnev era dominate the party *apparat* and remain unwilling to abdicate their power over state bureaucrats and enterprise managers. Gorbachev has, in fact, replaced the majority of party bureaucrats. Their continued defiance of reform directives from Moscow indicates that the new people are as conservative as their predecessors. After four years, Gorbachev controls no more than 5 to 10 percent of positions within the party bureaucracy.

Party bureaucrats have impeded Gorbachev's reforms in two ways. First, they have made numerous changes in the text of the new laws which weaken the intentions of reformers. In the Law on State Enterprises, for example, enterprises remain dependent on central ministries for the distribution of funds and materials. Second, party bureaucrats have sabotaged new laws by purposefully misinterpreting them.

Gorbachev proclaims that his reforms are "revolutionary," yet the slow pace of the Soviet leader's political moves endangers the reform process. By perpetuating the rule of the conservative bureaucracy, and by trying the patience of the population with continued shortages of high-quality food and consumer items, the fate of *perestroika* grows more perilous. In an article in the Leningrad journal *Neva*, radical reform advocate Sergei Andreyev argues that a "new class" of Communist party bureaucrats is "strangling" Gorbachev's reforms. He asserts that economic reforms have been a "complete failure," because party officials have opposed seeing their power and influence diminished. Andreyev was also the first Soviet journalist to dare to criticize Gorbachev for his indecisive, compromising stance toward the conservatives concerning radical economic and social reforms.[9]

Mikhail Gorbachev persists in occupying a middle ground both in policy implementation and in his speeches. In an important speech made to intellectuals on January 6, 1989, the Soviet leader criticized both radical reformers and conservatives as if both were his political

---

[9]Sergei Andreyev, *Neva*, no. 1, 1989.

opponents. Gorbachev's reform allies fear that a halfway reform—all ideas and no substance—will guarantee the Soviet leader's downfall. If Gorbachev truly wants to modernize the economy, democratize the political system, and expand *glasnost,* then he must decisively seize power in the party by removing conservative elements within the Politburo and the *apparat.* Only then will historians write about Gorbachev's "revolution from above."

28

Polemics: I Cannot Waive Principles

Nina Andreyeva

Sovetskaya Rossiya
March 13, 1988

Soviet citizens viewed this letter to the editor from a Leningrad college lecturer published in the influential newspaper *Sovetskaya Rossiya* as an attack against Gorbachev's reforms by conservative forces. The manner in which the Andreyeva letter was published clearly showed the active involvement of the newspaper's editorial staff: The letter covered the entire front page, with one-inch-high headlines. Moreover, a photograph of Nina Andreyeva speaking with her students accompanied the text. Letters to the editor never receive this type of attention in Soviet newspapers, and no one believed that such an influential newspaper as *Sovetskaya Rossiya* would publish such a letter without the permission of the party leadership.

The Andreyeva letter is written from a Stalinist perspective that combines Russian nationalism and Marxism. She advocates viewing events in their "class" context and calls Stalin's repressions justified because they advanced the cause of socialism. Gorbachev and his supporters rallied back three weeks later in the pages of *Pravda*. However, that a single article could paralyze political discourse in the country for three weeks illustrates how thin the layer of reform was and how little would have been needed to turn the country back to the days before Gorbachev.

I decided to write this letter after lengthy deliberation. I am a chemist, and I lecture at Leningrad's Lensovet Technology Institute. Like many others, I also look after a student group. Students nowadays, following the period of social apathy and intellectual dependence, are gradually becoming charged with the energy of revolutionary changes. Naturally, discussions develop about the ways of restructuring and its economic and ideological aspects. *Glasnost*, openness, the disappearance of zones where criticism is taboo, and the emotional heat of mass consciousness (especially among young people) often result in the raising of problems that are, to a greater or lesser extent, "prompted" either by Western radio voices or by those of our compatriots who are shaky in their conceptions of the essence of socialism. And what a variety of topics that are being discussed! A multiparty system, freedom of religious propaganda, emigration to live abroad, the right to broad discussion of sexual problems in the press, the need to decentralize the leadership of culture, abolition of compulsory military service. There are particularly numerous arguments among students about the country's past.

Of course, we lecturers must answer the most controversial questions, and this demands, in addition to honesty, knowledge, conviction, broad cultural horizons, serious reflection, and considered opinions. Moreover, these qualities are needed by all educators of young people and not only by members of social science department staffs.

Petergof Park is a favorite spot for the walks I take with my students. We stroll along the snow-covered paths, enjoy looking at the famous palaces and statues, and we argue. We do argue! The young souls are eager to investigate all complexities and to map out their path into the future. I look at my ardent young interlocutors, and I think to myself how important it is to help them to discover the truth and shape a correct perception of the problems of the society in which they live and which they will have to restructure, and how to give them a correct perception of our history, both distant and recent.

What are the misgivings? Here is a simple example: You would think that plenty has been written and said about the Great Patriotic War against the Nazi invasion and the heroism of those who fought in it. Recently, however, a student hostel in our Technology Institute organized a meeting with Hero of the Soviet Union and Colonel of the Reserve V. Molozeyev. Among other things, he was asked a question about political repressions in the army. The veteran replied that he had never come across any repressions and that many of those who fought in the war with him from its beginning to its end became high-ranking military leaders. Some were disappointed by this reply. Now that it has become topical, the subject of repressions has been blown out of all proportion in some young people's imaginations and overshadows any objective interpretation of the past. Examples like this are by no means isolated.

It is, of course, extremely gratifying that even "technicians" are keenly interested in theoretical problems of the social sciences. But I can neither accept nor agree with all too much of what has now appeared. Verbiage about "terrorism," "the people's political servility," "uninspired social vegetation," "our spiritual slavery," "universal fear," "dominance by boors in power"—these are often the only yarns used to weave the history of our country during the period of transition to socialism. It is, therefore, not surprising that nihilistic sentiments are intensifying among some students and that there are instances of ideological confusion, loss of political bearings, and even ideological omnivorousness. At times you even hear claims that the time has come to take Communists to task for having allegedly "dehumanized" the country's life since 1917.

The Central Committee's February *plenum* emphasized again the insistent need to ensure that "young people are taught a class-based vision of the world and an understanding of the links between universal and class interests, including an understanding of the class essence of the changes occurring in our country." Such a vision of history and of the present is incompatible with the political anecdotes, base gossip, and controversial fantasies that one often encounters today.

I have been reading and rereading sensational articles. For example, what can young people gain (apart from disorientation) from revelations about "the counterrevolution in the USSR in the late 1920s and early 1930s," or about Stalin's "guilt" for the rise to power of fascism and Hitler in Germany? Or the public "reckoning" of the number of "Stalinists" in various generations and social groups?

We are Leningraders, and therefore we were particularly interested in watching recently the good documentary movie about Sergei Kirov.[1] But at times the text that accompanied the film not only diverged from the movie's documentary evidence but even made it appear somewhat ambiguous. For example, the movie would show

---

[1] Sergei Kirov, a popular Bolshevik leader in Leningrad, was killed in 1934. This killing was allegedly organized by Stalin, who considered Kirov a dangerous rival and who used it as a pretext to start repressions.

the outburst of keenness, joie de vivre, and spiritual enthusiasm of people building socialism, while the announcer's text would be about repressions, about lack of information.

I am probably not the only one to have noticed that the calls by party leaders asking the "exposers" to pay attention also to the factual and real achievements at different stages of socialist construction seem, as if by command, to bring forth more and more outbursts of "exposures." Mikhail Shatrov's plays are a notable phenomenon in this—alas!—infertile field. On the day the 26th Party Congress opened, I went to see the play "Blue Horses on Red Grass." I recall the young people's excitement at the scene in which Lenin's secretary tries to empty a teapot over his head, confusing him with an unfinished clay sculpture. As a matter of fact, some young people had arrived with prepared banners whose essence was to sling mud at our past and present. In "The Brest Peace" the playwright and director make Lenin kneel before Leon Trotsky. So much for the symbolic embodiment of the author's concept. This is further developed in the play "Onward! Onward! Onward!" A play is, of course, not a historical document. But even in a work of art truth is guaranteed by nothing but the author's stance. Especially in the case of political theater.

Playwright Shatrov's stance has been analyzed in detail in a well-reasoned way in reviews by historians published in *Pravda* and *Sovetskaya Rossiya*. I would like to express my own opinion. In particular, it is impossible not to agree that Shatrov deviates substantially from the accepted principles of socialist realism. In covering a most crucial period in our country's history, he absolutizes the subjective factor in social development and clearly ignores the objective laws of history as displayed in the activity of the classes and the masses. The role played by the proletarian masses and the Bolshevik party is reduced to the "background" against which the actions of irresponsible politicians unfold.

The reviewers, on the basis of the Marxist-Leninist methodology of analyzing specific historical processes, have convincingly shown that Shatrov distorts the history of socialism in our country. He objects to the state of the dictatorship of the proletariat, without whose historical contribution we would have nothing to restructure today. The author goes on to accuse Stalin of the assassinations of Trotsky and [Sergei] Kirov and of "isolating" Lenin while he was ill. But how can anyone possibly make biased accusations against historical figures without bothering to adduce any proof?

Unfortunately, the reviewers have failed to show that, despite all his pretensions as an author, the playwright is far from original. I got the impression that, in the logic of his assessments and arguments, he rather closely follows the line of Boris Suvarine's book published in Paris in 1935. In his play, Shatrov makes his characters say things that were said by the adversaries of Leninism about the course of the revolution, about Lenin's role in it, about the relationships between Central Committee members at different stages of inner party struggle. This is the essence of Shatrov's "fresh reading" of Lenin. Let me add that Anatoly Rybakov, author of *Children of the Arbat*, has frankly admitted that he borrowed some incidents from émigré publications.

Without having read the play "Onward! Onward! Onward!" (it had not been published yet), I read rapturous reviews of it in some publications. What could have been the meaning of such haste? I learned later that the play was being hastily staged.

Soon after the February *plenum*, *Pravda* published a letter entitled "Coming Full Circle?" signed by eight of our leading theatrical figures. They warned against what they saw as possible delays in staging Shatrov's play. This conclusion was drawn on the basis of some critical reviews of the play in the press. For some unknown reason, the authors of the letter excluded the writers of the critical reviews from the category of those "who treasure the fatherland." How can this be reconciled with their desire for a "stormy and impassioned" discussion of our history, both distant and recent? It appears that they alone are entitled to their opinion.

In the numerous discussions now taking place on literally all questions of the social sciences, as a college lecturer I am primarily interested in the questions that have a direct effect on young people's ideological and political education, their moral health, and their social optimism. Conversing with students and deliberating with them on controversial problems, I cannot help concluding that our country has accumulated quite a few anomalies and one-sided interpretations that clearly need to be corrected. I would like to dwell on some of them in particular.

Take, for example the question of Joseph Stalin's place in our country's history. The whole obsession with critical attacks is linked with his name, and in my opinion this obsession centers not so much on the historical individual himself as on the entire highly complex epoch of transition, an epoch linked with unprecedented feats by a whole generation of Soviet people who are today gradually withdrawing from active participation in political and social work. The industrialization, collectivization, and cultural revolution which brought our country to the ranks of the great world powers are being forcibly squeezed into the "personality cult" formula. All of this is being questioned. Matters have gone so far that persistent demands for "repentance" are being made of "Stalinists" (and this category can be taken to include anyone you like). There is rapturous praise for novels and movies that lynch the epoch of "storms and onslaught," which is presented as a "tragedy of the peoples." It is true that such attempts to place historical nihilism on a pedestal do not always work. For example, a movie showered with praise by critics can be extremely coolly received by the majority of viewers despite the unprecedented publicity hype.[2]

Let me say right away that neither I nor any members of my family were in any way involved with Stalin, his retinue, his associates, or his extollers. My father was a worker at Leningrad's port, my mother was a fitter at the Kirov plant. My elder brother also worked there. My brother, my father, and my sister died in battles against Hitler's forces. One of my relatives was repressed and then rehabilitated after the 20th Party Congress. I share all of the Soviet people's anger and indignation about the mass repressions that occurred in the 1930s and 1940s and with the party-state leadership of the time, which is to blame. But common sense resolutely protests against the

---

[2] Andreyeva has in mind Tenghiz Abuladze's movie *Repentance*, which condemns Stalinism.

monochrome depiction of contradictory events that now dominates in some press organs.

I support the party's call to uphold the honor and dignity of the trailblazers of socialism. I think that these are the party-class positions from which we must assess the historical role of all leaders of the party and the country, including Stalin. In this case, matters cannot be reduced to their "court" aspect or to abstract moralizing by persons far removed both from those stormy times and from the people who had to live and work in those times, and to work in such a fashion as to still be an inspiring example for us today.

For me, as for many people, a decisive role in my assessment of Stalin is played by the candid testimony of contemporaries who clashed directly with him on our side of the barricades as well as on the other side. It is the latter who are quite interesting. For instance, take British Prime Minister Winston Churchill, who, back in 1919, was proud of his personal contribution to organizing the military intervention by fourteen foreign states against the young Soviet republic and who, exactly forty years later, used the following words to describe Stalin, one of his most formidable political opponents:

> He was an outstanding personality who left his mark on our cruel time during his lifetime. Stalin was a man of exceptional energy, erudition, and unbending willpower, harsh, tough, and ruthless in both action and conversation, and even I, brought up in the English Parliament, could not oppose him in any way. . . . A gigantic force resounded in his words. This force was so great in Stalin that he seemed unique among the leaders of all times and all peoples. His effect on people was irresistible. Whenever he entered the Yalta conference hall, we all rose as if by command. And strangely, we all stood to attention. Stalin possessed a profound, totally unflappable, logical, and sensible wisdom. He was a past master at finding a way out of the most hopeless situation at a difficult time. . . . He was a man who used his enemies to destroy his enemy, forcing us—whom he openly called imperialists—to fight the imperialists. . . . He took over a Russia still using the wooden plow, and left it equipped with atomic weapons.

This assessment and admission by the loyal custodian of the British Empire cannot be attributed to either pretense or political timeserving.

Long and frank conversations with young interlocutors lead us to the conclusion that the attacks on the state of the dictatorship of the proletariat and our country's leaders at this time have not only political, ideological, and moral causes, but also a social substratum. There are quite a few people interested in expanding the bridgehead for these attacks, and they are to be found not just on the other side of our borders. Along with professional anti-Communists in the West who picked the supposedly democratic slogan of "anti-Stalinism" a long time ago, the offspring of the classes overthrown by the October Revolution (by no means all of whom have managed to forget the material and social losses incurred by their forebears) are still alive and prospering. One must add to them the spiritual heirs of Dan and Martov and other adherents of Russian social democracy, the spiritual followers of Trotsky or Yagoda, and the offspring of NEP-men, *basmachy*, and *kulaks* with grudges against socialism.[3]

I think that, no matter how controversial and complex a figure in Soviet history Stalin may be, his genuine role in the building and defense of socialism will sooner or later be given an objective and unambiguous assessment. Of course, unambiguous does not mean an assessment that is one-sided, that whitewashes, or that eclectically sums up contradictory phenomena making it possible subjectively (albeit with slight reservations) "to forgive or not forgive," "to reject or retain." Unambiguous means primarily a specific historical assessment detached from short-term considerations which would demonstrate—according to historical results!—the dialectics of the correlation between the individual's actions and the basic laws governing society's development. In our country these laws were also linked with the answer to the question "Who will defeat

---

[3] Fyodor Dan and Yuli Martov were leaders of the Menshevik wing of the Russian Social-Democratic party who opposed Lenin's policies. Genrikh Yagoda was Stalin's head of the security forces during the 1930s. NEP-men were entrepreneurs who flourished during the period of the New Economic Policy. *Basmachy* were members of the local resistance to Soviet control of Central Asia in the 1930s.

whom?" in its domestic as well as international aspects. If we are to adhere to the Marxist-Leninist methodology of historical analysis then, in Mikhail Gorbachev's words, we must primarily and vividly show how the millions of people lived, how they worked, and what they believed in, as well as the coupling of victories and failures, discoveries and errors, the bright and the tragic, the revolutionary enthusiasm of the masses and the violations of socialist legality and even crimes at times.

I was puzzled recently by the revelation of one of my students that the class struggle is supposedly an obsolete term, just like the leading role of the proletariat. It would be alright if she were the only one to claim this. A furious argument was generated, for example, by a respected academician's recent assertion that present-day relations between states from the two different socioeconomic systems apparently lack any class content. I assume that the academician did not deem it necessary to explain why it was that, for several decades, he wrote exactly the opposite, namely, that peaceful coexistence is nothing but a form of class struggle in the international arena. It seems that the philosopher has now rejected this view. Never mind, people can change their minds. It does seem to me, however, that duty would nevertheless command a leading philosopher to explain—at least to those who have studied and are studying his books—what is happening today; does the international working class no longer oppose world capital as embodied in its state and political organs?

It seems to me that many of the present debates center on the same question: Which class or stratum of society is the leading and mobilizing force of *perestroika*? This in particular was discussed in an interview with writer Alexander Prokhanov published by our city newspaper *Leningradskii Rabochii*.[4] Prokhanov proceeds from the premise that the specific nature of the present state of social consciousness is typified by the presence of two ideological currents or, as he puts it, "alternative towers" which are trying, from different directions, to overcome the "socialism that has been built in battles" in our country. Although he exaggerates the significance and acuteness of

---

[4] Alexander Prokhanov is a conservative writer who actively defends the military establishment.

the duel between these two "towers," the writer is nevertheless correct in emphasizing that "they agree only on the slaughter of socialist values." But both of them, so their ideologists claim, are "for *perestroika*."

It is the champions of "left-wing liberal socialism"[5] who shape the tendency toward falsifying the history of socialism. They try to make us believe that the country's past was nothing but mistakes and crimes, keeping silent about the greatest achievements of the past and the present. Claiming full possession of historical truth, they replace the sociopolitical criterion of society's development with scholastic ethical categories. I would very much like to know who needed to ensure, and why, that every prominent leader of the party Central Committee and the Soviet government—once they were out of office—was compromised and discredited because of actual and alleged mistakes and errors committed when solving the most complex of problems in the course of historical trailblazing? Where are the origins of this passion of ours to undermine the prestige and dignity of the leaders of the world's first socialist country?

Another peculiarity of the views held by the "left-wing liberals" is an overt or covert cosmopolitan tendency, some kind of non-national "internationalism." I read somewhere about an incident after the revolution when a delegation of merchants and factory owners called on Trotsky "as a Jew" at the Petrograd soviet to complain about the oppression by the Red Guards, and he declared that he was "not a Jew but an internationalist," which really puzzled the petitioners.

In Trotsky's view, the idea of "nation" connoted a certain inferiority and limitation compared with the "international." This is why he, emphasizing October's "national tradition," wrote about "the national element in Lenin," claimed that the Russian people "had inherited no cultural heritage at all," and so on. We are somehow embarrassed to say that it was indeed the Russian proletariat, whom the Trotskyites treated as "backward and uncultured," who accomplished—in Lenin's words—

---

[5] According to Nina Andreyeva these liberals are writers, artists, and historians who strongly denounce Stalin's crimes and advocate radical reforms.

"three Russian revolutions" and that the Slavic peoples stood in the vanguard of mankind's battle against fascism.

This, of course, is not to denigrate the historical contribution of other nations and ethnic groups. This, as it is said nowadays, is only to ensure that the full historical truth is told. When students ask me why thousands of small villages in the nonblack-soil lands and Siberia are deserted, I reply that this is part of the high price we had to pay for victory and for the postwar restoration of the national economy, just like the irretrievable loss of large numbers of monuments of Russian national culture. I am also convinced that any denigration of the importance of consciousness produces a pacifist erosion of defense and patriotic consciousness as well as a desire to categorize the slightest expressions of Great Russian national pride as manifestations of the chauvinism of a great power.

Here is something else that worries me: The practice of "refusenikism" of socialism is nowadays linked with militant cosmopolitanism.[6] Unfortunately, we remember this suddenly only when its adherents plague us with their outrages in front of the Smolny or at the Kremlin walls. Moreover, we are gradually being trained to perceive the aforementioned phenomenon as some sort of almost innocent change of "place of residence" rather than as class or national betrayal by persons who (most of them) graduated from colleges and completed their postgraduate studies thanks to our own country's funds. Generally speaking, some people are inclined to look upon "refusenikism" as some sort of manifestation of "democracy" and the "rights of man," whose talents were prevented from flourishing by "stagnant socialism." And if it so happens that people over there, in the "free world," fail to appreciate bubbling entrepreneurship and "genius" and the special services are not interested in the trading of conscience, one can always return.

While "neoliberals" look toward the West, the proponents of the other "alternative tower," to use Prokhanov's expression, the "protectionists and

---

[6] "Cosmopolites and refuseniks" are code words for Jews, who are often perceived as overtly liberal troublemakers who do not possess Russian national pride. The term "cosmopolites" was coined during the Stalin period.

traditionalists," are striving "to overcome socialism by regression," in other words, by reverting to the social forms of presocialist Russia. The spokesmen for this variety of "peasant socialism" are fascinated by this image.[7] In their opinion, the moral values accumulated by peasant communes in the misty fog of the centuries were lost a hundred years ago. The "traditionalists" certainly deserve credit for what they have done for the exposure of corruption, the fair solution of ecological problems, the struggle against alcoholism, the protection of historical monuments, and the opposition to dominance by mass culture, which they correctly evaluate as consumerist media.

At the same time, the views of the ideologists of "peasant socialism" show a lack of understanding of October's historical importance for the fate of the fatherland, a one-sided assessment of collectivization as a "terrible atrocity against the peasantry," an uncritical perception of mystical religious Russian philosophy and the old czarist concepts in our historical science, and an unwillingness to perceive the postrevolutionary stratification of the peasantry and the revolutionary role of the working class.

When it comes to the class struggle in the countryside, for example, excessive emphasis is often placed on the "rural" *commissars* who "shot middle income peasants in the back." There were, of course, all sorts of *commissars* at the height of the revolutionary conflagration in our vast country. But in the mainstream of our life are *commissars* who were shot at, *commissars* who had stars carved on their backs or who were burned alive. The price the "attacking class" had to pay consisted not only of the lives of *commissars, chekists*, rural Bolsheviks, members of the committees of poor peasantry, or the "Twenty Thousand," but also those of the first tractor drivers, rural correspondents, girl teachers, rural Komsomol members, and the lives of tens of thousands of other unknown fighters for socialism.[8]

---

[7] "Traditionalists" and "peasant socialists" refer to Russian nationalists who identify with the Russian peasantry.

[8] Andreyeva emphasizes the losses of the *commissars* (political workers of the party) and the *chekists* (members of the security forces),

The education of young people is made even more complex by the fact that informal organizations and associations are being formed around the ideas of "neoliberals" and "neo-Slavophiles." Sometimes the upper hand in their leadership is gained by extremist elements capable of provocations. A politicization of these informal organizations on the basis of a by-no-means socialist pluralism has recently emerged. Leaders of these organizations often speak of "power sharing" on the basis of a "parliamentary system," "free trade unions," "autonomous publishing houses," and so on. In my view, all this leads to the conclusion that the main and cardinal issue of the debates now taking place in the country is this: whether or not to recognize the leading role of the party and the working class in socialist building and therefore in *perestroika* with all the ensuing theoretical and practical conclusions for politics, economics, and ideology.

It seems to me that the question of the role and position of socialist ideology is extremely acute today. The authors of timeserving articles[9] circulating under the guise of moral and spiritual "cleansing" erode the dividing lines and criteria of scientific ideology, manipulate *glasnost*, and foster nonsocialist pluralism, which applies the brakes on *perestroika* in the public conscience. This has a particularly painful effect on young people which, I repeat, is clearly sensed by us, the college lecturers, schoolteachers, and all who have to deal with young people's problems. As Mikhail Gorbachev said at the CPSU Central Committee February *plenum*, "our actions in the spiritual sphere—and maybe primarily and precisely there—must be guided by our Marxist-Leninist principles. Principles, comrades, must not be compromised on any pretext whatever."

This is what we stand for now, and this is what we will continue to stand for. Principles were not given to us as a

---

who supported Stalin's policies, rather than their far more numerous victims.

[9]Conservatives often accuse proreform writers of duplicity for condemning Brezhnev-era policies that they previously supported wholeheartedly.

gift, we have fought for them at crucial turning points in the fatherland's history.

29

Principles of *Perestroika*: The Revolutionary Nature of Thinking and Acting

Pravda editorial
April 5, 1988

This *Pravda* editorial signaled a resolute and authoritative rebuke to Nina Andreyeva's letter to *Sovetskaya Rossiya* (Document #28). It reassured supporters of reform and encouraged them to continue to fight for *perestroika* and *glasnost*. *Pravda* chastises conservatives for engineering the placement of the letter and questioned the role of *Sovetskaya Rossiya*'s editorial staff in the affair. No mention is made of Andreyeva as the author of the letter, further evidence that Gorbachev supporters view the article as the product of a plot.

The editorial marks the first time that a Soviet newspaper specifically identifies a conservative opposition movement. One of the chief complaints expressed in the *Pravda* editorial is that Andreyeva's letter offers no specific suggestions for improving *perestroika* and resorts to labeling people with derogatory terms. *Pravda* defends the reinterpretation of Soviet history and maintains that a great deal has been accomplished in three years, but notably does not hail economic achievements since *perestroika* has thus far yielded few. The editorial asserts that the country's lack of a public political culture and an "ability to listen to one another" has exacerbated the tensions in society during the reform process. Most important, the editorial is an affirmation that conservative opponents did not succeed in stopping *glasnost*.

The CPSU Central Committee February *plenum* solidified the party's new tasks in restructuring all spheres of life at the present stage. The *plenum* speech of Mikhail Gorbachev, general secretary of the CPSU Central Committee ("Revolutionary *Perestroika* Requires Ideology of Renewal") made a clear analysis of today's problems and set forth a program of ideological support for *perestroika*. People want to be better aware of the nature of the changes that have begun in society, to see the essence and significance of the proposed solutions, and to know what is meant by the new quality of society we want to achieve. The struggle for *perestroika* is being waged both in production and in the spiritual sphere. And even though this struggle does not take the form of class antagonisms, it is proceeding sharply. The emergence of something new always excites attitudes toward and judgments about the new thing.

The debate itself and its nature and thrust attest to the democratization of our society. The diversity of judgments, assessments, and positions is one of the most important signs of the times and attests to the socialist pluralism of opinions which really exists now.

But it is impossible not to notice one very specific dimension of this debate. It occasionally declares itself not in a desire to interpret what is happening and to investigate it nor in a wish to advance the cause but, on the contrary, in attempts to slow it down by shouting the usual incantations: "They are betraying ideals!" "Abandoning principles!" "Undermining foundations!"

Probably we are not just dealing here with sociopsychological phenomena. Such a stance has its roots in command and edict-based bureaucratic management methods. It is also bound up with the moral legacy of the time as well as naked pragmatic interests and considerations and the desire to defend one's own privileges (material, social, or spiritual) at any price.

It is an axiom of Marxism that ideas and interests are linked. Any interest is expressed in certain ideas. Behind all ideas there is invariably a particular interest. Conservative opposition to restructuring carries the weight of custom and habitual thinking and action derived from the past and the belligerent, selfish interests of those accustomed to living at others' expense and reluctant to kick the habit. It is against those interests that restructuring is objectively aimed, because restructuring, like every revolution, is not just for something, it is also against something. It is against everything that impedes our living a better, cleaner, and fuller life, making more rapid progress, and paying the least price for the inevitable mistakes and miscalculations that are made along the new path.

Some people maintain that "we are heading for petty bourgeois socialism based on commodity-money relationships. And who is dragging it into our society?

Idealists with a Menshevik mentality.[1] This is the main danger for us and for world peace in general. This is the twentieth-century plague that Vladimir Lenin put so much effort into combating."

"Don't rock the boat!" others say, intimidatingly. "You'll overturn and destroy socialism."

There are also those who bluntly propose stopping or else turning back altogether.

The long article "I Cannot Waive Principles" [Document #28] that appeared in the newspaper *Sovetskaya Rossiya* on March 13 was a reflection of such feelings.

The article, written in the form of a "letter to the editorial office," attracted readers' attention. It contains observations with which one is bound to agree. There is energetically expressed concern about certain negative phenomena. There is a heatedness of expression which also communicates itself to the reader.

But there is something else that is nevertheless more important: the reason it was written, the kind of solutions it proposes, and the overall spirit and style of those solutions. It is by those criteria that the utter incompatibility and antithesis between the stances adopted in the article and the basic thrusts of *perestroika* are revealed.

Whether the author wanted it or not, primarily the article artificially sets off certain categories of Soviet people against one another. And this at precisely the moment when the unity of creative forces, despite all the shades of opinion, is more necessary than ever and when such unity is the prime requirement of *perestroika* and an absolute necessity simply for normal life, work, and the constructive renewal of society. Herein resides the fundamental feature of *perestroika*, which is designed to unite the maximum number of like-minded people in the struggle against phenomena impeding our life. Precisely and principally against all of these phenomena, not only or simply against certain incorrigible proponents of bureaucracy, corruption, abuse, and so forth.

---

[1] When party bureaucrats are short of reasonable arguments they often resort to accusations of "menshevism" and "idealism," which signify bourgeois mentality.

In addition, the article is unconstructive. In an extensive, pretentiously titled article essentially no space was found to work out a single problem of *perestroika*. Whatever it discussed—*glasnost*, openness, the disappearance of areas free from criticism, youth—these processes and *perestroika* itself were linked only with difficulties and adverse consequences.

Perhaps readers were able to observe for the first time in such a concentrated form in this "letter to the editorial office" not inquiry, not reflection, not even simply an expression of perplexity or confusion in the face of the complex and acute problems that life poses, but rather nonacceptance of the very idea of renewal in a rigorous exposition of a highly defined stance, an essentially conservative and dogmatic stance.

There are, in point of fact, two basic theses running throughout the article: Why all of this *perestroika*, and haven't we gone too far with democratization and *glasnost*? The article urges us to amend and adjust *perestroika*; otherwise, it is alleged, "people in authority" will have to rescue socialism.

It is evident that not everyone has realized clearly yet the dramatic nature of the situation the country found itself in by April 1985, a situation which today we rightfully describe as precrisis. It is evident that not everyone is fully aware yet that administrative edict methods are totally obsolete. It is time that anyone who still places hopes in these methods or in their modification understands that all of this has already been tried, tried repeatedly, and it has failed to produce the desired results. Any ideas about the simplicity and effectiveness of these methods are nothing but illusions without any historical justification.

So, how is socialism to be "saved" today?

Should authoritarian methods, the practice of blind obedience, and the stifling of initiative be retained? Should we retain the system in which bureaucratism, lack of control, corruption, bribery, and petty bourgeois degeneration flourished lavishly?

Or should we revert to Leninist principles, whose essence is democratism, social justice, economic accountability, and respect for the individual's honor, life, and dignity? Do we have the right, in the face of the real difficulties and unsatisfied needs of the people, to adhere to the same old approaches that prevailed in the 1930s and 1940s? Has not the time come to clearly differentiate between the essence of socialism and the historically restricted forms of its implementation? Has not the time come for a scientifically critical investigation of our history, primarily in order to change the world in which we live and to learn harsh lessons for the future?

Almost half of the article is devoted to an assessment of our distant and recent history. The last few years have provided graphic proof of the growing interest in the past shown by the broadest strata of the population. The principles of scientific historicism and truth are increasingly the basis on which the people's historical awareness is taking shape. At the same time, there are instances of people playing on the idea of patriotism. Those who loudly scream about alleged "internal threats" to socialism, those who join certain political extremists and look everywhere for internal enemies, "counterrevolutionary nations," and so on, those are not patriots. The patriots are those who act in the country's interests and for the people's benefit, without fearing any difficulties. We do not need contemplative or verbal patriotism, we need creative patriotism. Not nostalgic and backward-looking patriotism, but the patriotism of socialist transformations. Patriotism based not only on love for the area of your birth, but also imbued with pride in the accomplishments of the great motherland of socialism.

Past experience is vitally necessary for the present, for solving the tasks of *perestroika*. Life's demand—"More socialism!"—makes it incumbent upon us to investigate what we did yesterday and how we did it, what has to be rejected and what has to be retained. Which principles and values ought to be considered really socialist? And if today we are taking a critical look at our history, we are doing so only because we want a better and more complete idea of our path into the future.

We are reinstating the truth, cleansing it of the false and sly half-truths that led to the blind alley of public apathy; we are learning the lesson about truth taught by the 27th Party Congress. But the truth has proved bitter in many respects. An attempt is already being made to whitewash the past, to justify political deformities and crimes against socialism with references to emergency conditions.

Today we know that many thousands of Communists and nonparty people, economic and military cadres, scientists and cultural figures, were subjected to mass repressions. This is the truth, it is unavoidable. The party has spoken bluntly about this. Many accusations have already been dropped, and thousands and thousands of innocent people who suffered have been fully rehabilitated. The restoration of justice is continuing. It is well known that a Central Committee Politburo commission is at work, studying all aspects of the facts and documents referring to these issues.

To keep silent about painful issues in our history means to disregard the truth and show disrespect for the memory of the innocent victims of illegality and arbitrariness. There is only one truth. We need clarity, accuracy, and consistency as a moral guideline for the future.

Numerous discussions taking place today sharply raise the question of Joseph Stalin's role in our country's history. The article in *Sovetskaya Rossiya* does not overlook him, either. While declaring its support for the 1956 CPSU Central Committee resolution on overcoming the personality cult and its consequences and its approval for the assessment of Stalin's activity contained in the party's latest documents, in practice the article makes a virtual attempt to refute these assessments and to separate socialism from morality.

To suit her purpose the author turns to Churchill for support. Let us note that the eulogy of Stalin she quotes did not originate with Churchill. Something along these lines was said by the famous British Trotskyite Isaac Deutscher.[2] Be that as it may, though, it would be legitimate to ask: Is it tactful to turn indiscriminately to bourgeois sources when assessing leaders and eminent figures of our party and state? Especially if we already have a clearly stated assessment by the party itself or, as in this specific case, an assessment by Vladimir Lenin.

Stalin's personality was extremely contradictory. Hence the furious arguments. But principled assessments were

---

[2] Isaac Deutscher, *Stalin: A Political Biography*, New York, 1949.

made at the 20th and 22nd Party Congresses and in the report "October and *Perestroika*: The Revolution Continues" by M. Gorbachev, general secretary of the CPSU Central Committee. Holding to our position of historical truth, we must see both Stalin's indisputable contribution to the struggle for socialism and the defense of socialist gains on the one hand, and, on the other hand, his flagrant political errors and the arbitrary rule exercised by him and his entourage, for which our people paid a great price and which had serious consequences for our society. People can sometimes be heard to claim that Stalin did not know about acts of lawlessness. Not only did he know about them, he organized and directed them. That is now a proven fact. And Stalin's guilt—along with that of his closest entourage—toward the party and the people for the mass repressions and lawlessness he permitted is enormous and unforgivable.

Yes, all historians are molded by specific socioeconomic, ideological, and political conditions. But the cult was not inevitable. It is alien to the nature of socialism and only became possible because of deviations from fundamental socialist principles.

But why, now that the party has provided a clear and direct answer to this question, should we return to it again and again? Probably for two reasons. Primarily because in defending Stalin people thereby defend the retention in our life and practice of the methods engendered by him for "resolving" disputed questions and the social and state structures and norms of party and social life he created. The main point here is that they are defending the right to arbitrary rule. Arbitrary rule, upon closer inspection, invariably turns out to be just an egotistic interest, although in some people this interest can be aimed at taking more and giving less, while in others it is wrapped in the outwardly respectable garb of claims to a monopoly in science, or to one's own infallibility, or to something else.

Another reason to keep coming back to the question of Stalin's personality is that around this assessment there is speculation on what people hold most dear, the essence of the lives they have led. Concepts get confused: If Stalin was guilty of crimes, people say, how are we to assess our past achievements? How are we to assess the labor and heroism of people who caused the land of socialism to achieve historic gains? Are we not denying them, too, in condemning Stalin and rejecting his methods?

No, we are not, we are actually extolling them even further. Honest workers, soldiers in the battlefield, and all Soviet people who proved their patriotism and their devotion to the motherland and socialism through their work did their duty. It was their work, selflessness, and heroism that brought our country to unprecedented heights. Only an immoral person would cast aspersions on the people's work and achievements. And today we are better aware than ever of how difficult it was to do real work at that time, a time that was difficult in every respect.

It would be wrong to label these people as advocates of Stalin's lawlessness. It would also be wrong because we realize and are obliged to realize just how much greater the results of their efforts would have been for the whole country and for each of us if their creative input and material effectiveness had not been impaired by objectively anti-Leninist and antisocialist practices.

No, the lives of party, war, and labor veterans were not in vain! All subsequent generations owe them a debt that can never be repaid.

But some people just cannot rid themselves of nostalgia for the past, when certain people would speak and others would listen and submissively do their bidding. Certain people's nostalgia can be understood, but it is not a press organ's job to propagandize such sentiments, not only by not making a proper assessment of them, but also by creating the impression that they are offering some kind of "new" political platform.

The author's argument on the use of the class approach to the assessment of the arguments and opinions expressed in the discussions is also worthy of attention. The author's view is that certain controversial positions that people may adopt are engendered not by problems but by people's social or national origins. This focuses the question not on what is being said and disputed, but rather on who precisely is doing the saying and disputing.

A class approach is undoubtedly needed. But even in those cases in which we must deal with people who have ideas alien to socialism, the class approach is not a "hallmark" that makes "selection" easier, but a tool of scientific analysis. The article states that the "descendants of the classes overthrown by October are alive and well" along with the "spiritual heirs of Dan and Martov and other Russian Social Democrats, the spiritual followers of Trotsky or Yagoda, and the descendants of NEP-men, *basmachy*, and *kulaks*." The article is prepared to seek a virtually genetic reason for antisocialist sentiments. Is this position not consonant with Stalin's well-known directive on the exacerbation of the class struggle in the process of socialist building, a directive which had tragic consequences?

The article also expresses concern about the well-known spread of nihilism among a section of our young people. Should this be a cause for concern? Yes. But it should be noted that today's "distortions" in young people's consciousness are symptoms of what is by no means a modern disease. This disease is rooted in the past. It is the consequence of the spiritual diet that we fed to young people for decades and of the discrepancies between what was said on rostrums and what actually happened in real life.

The best teacher of *perestroika*—the one to whom we should constantly listen—is life, and life is dialectical. We should constantly remember the words of [Friedrich] Engels to the effect that nothing has been unconditionally established once and for all as sacrosanct. It is this continual motion and the constant renewal of nature, society, and our thinking that is the point of departure for and the initial, most cardinal principle in our thinking.

Let us return to the question: What has been done already? How are the party's course and the decisions of the 27th Party Congress and Central Committee *plenums* being implemented? What positive changes are taking place in people's lives?

We have really got down to tackling the most pressing, highest priority problems: housing, food, and the supply of goods and services to the population. A turn toward accelerated development of the social sphere has begun. Concrete decisions about restructuring education and health care have been adopted. Radical economic reform, our main lever for implementing large-scale transformations, is being put into practice. "That is the main political result of the last three years," M. Gorbachev said at the 4th All-Union Congress of *kolkhoz* members.

The voice of the intelligentsia and of all the working people has begun to make itself heard powerfully and strongly in society's spiritual life. This is one of the first gains accomplished by *perestroika*. Democratism is impossible without freedom of thought and speech, without the open, broad clash of opinions, without keeping a critical eye on our life.

Our intelligentsia has done much to prepare the public to understand the need for profound, cardinal changes. It has itself become actively involved in *perestroika*. It takes up the best traditions created by its predecessors, calls for conscience, morality, and decency, and it upholds humanist principles and socialist norms of life.

Many words have been spoken and written about unifying the intelligentsia with the working class and the *kolkhoz* peasantry. And with what new light these truths now shine, at a time of nationwide support for *perestroika* from the broad masses of working people! It is a time in which genuinely patriotic, moral assessments of thoughts, deeds, and the whole of our life unify all strata of society. How many patriotic initiatives in *perestroika* are associated with the names of our writers and poets, dramatists, and critics? Here we should recall the brilliant, attacking journalism, imbued with the ideology of renewal, of Ivan Vasiliev, which has found such a worthy place, in the pages of that same *Sovetskaya Rossiya*, in the ranks of the best materials on *perestroika*.

But we see something else, too. In certain works there is a lack of shared experience with the people, their history, their joys and griefs. Some authors, as if they were apostles of truth, pontificate and instruct everyone on what must be done and how. There are many attempts to make one's mark, to cause a sensation, and to amuse oneself with "facts" and "snippets," not for the sake of the truth, but to suit one's own insatiable pride. This leads to juggling the facts and misrepresenting them, and—most important—it substitutes the history of the leadership's errors for the history of the people. Naturally, this approach offends the sensibilities of millions of honest people, and it does not help us to draw objective, useful lessons from history.

The roots of such phenomena lie in that same legacy of stagnation. People's thoughts and feelings were seething even then, as they reflected on what was happening and its consequences for the future. But people were forced to keep to themselves the results of their analysis, the outcome of their quest, and their own proposals. Now all of this bursts out into the open with an energy multiplied by years without *glasnost*, and this does not always happen in a thoughtful and responsible way.

Culture also is subject to renewal and cleansing. The more profoundly and actively the intelligentsia is involved in the life of the people and the party, the quicker this process will become. Tact, goodwill, respect, and recognition of the right to one's own opinion, but also the honest, competent, open identification of errors—that is what many party committees lack today in their work with the intelligentsia. "On questions of culture," V. Lenin stressed, "haste and recklessness are more harmful than anything else" (vol. 45, p. 389).

A different phenomenon is observed in the practice of party work. This can be seen particularly clearly in examples of attitudes toward the critical voice of the press. Some people are prepared to see all the troubles, all the unpleasantness of daily life in the fact that the newspapers "have gotten out of hand, express opinions about everything, stir up public opinion," and so forth. It must be recognized that a newspaper column is a secondary phenomenon. The primary phenomenon is in life itself! If we are not to read about shortcomings in newspaper columns, they must not exist in life.

Once again we see the value, the responsibility, of the printed word. Sometimes unverified facts or claims to a monopoly on the truth, and sometimes simply attempts to adapt the facts to fit a concept formulated beforehand by the author, tend to backfire against the very best intentions. Conservatives represent such errors as absolute, and they reduce the fruits of democratism and *glasnost* to them alone. And what is the result? Forces that at first glance are diametrically opposed in their convictions are united in practice into one bloc that retards *perestroika*.

There are no prohibited topics today. Journals, publishing houses, and studios decide for themselves what to publish. But the appearance of the article "I Cannot Waive Principles" is part of an attempt little by little to revise party decisions. It has been said repeatedly at meetings in the party Central Committee that the Soviet press is not a private concern, that Communists writing for the press and editors should have a sense of responsibility for articles and publications. In this case the newspaper *Sovetskaya Rossiya*, which, let us be frank, has done much for *perestroika*, departed from this principle.

Debates, discussions, and polemics are, of course, necessary. They lie in store for us in our future, too. There are also many pitfalls in store for us, traps laid by the past. We must all work together to clear these traps from our path. We need disputes that help to advance *perestroika* and lead to the consolidation of forces, to cohesion around *perestroika*, and not to disunity.

It is less than three months until the 19th All-Union Party Conference. That is a great event in the life of the party and of all the people. Preparations are under way. The main thing is to bring to the conference the experience of *perestroika* and an analysis of how the concept of *perestroika* is being implemented in practice and what result it is yielding. In order to really see what is happening, to see the new phenomena in life, Communists must be in control of events and not tag along in their wake. V. Lenin said repeatedly: "A firm line by the party, its unswerving determination is also a factor in determining the mood, especially at the most critical revolutionary moments. . . ." (vol. 34, pp. 411–12). *Perestroika* is the cause of every Communist, the patriotic duty of every citizen.

More light. More initiative. More responsibility. A more rapid mastery of the full profundity of the Marxist-Leninist concept of *perestroika*, of the new political thinking. We can and must revive the Leninist practice of the socialist society—the most humane, the most just. We will firmly and steadily follow the revolutionary principles of *perestroika*: more *glasnost*, more democracy, more socialism.

30

Time to Assemble Forces

Alexander Gelman

Sovetskaya Kultura, April 9, 1988

Alexander Gelman's speech to Soviet filmmakers, delivered at the March 23 open meeting of the USSR Cinematographers Union, is the only well-known public criticism of Nina Andreyeva's letter (Document #28) to appear prior to *Pravda*'s editorial rebuke (Document #29). Gelman delivered this important address nearly two weeks before the *Pravda* editorial, yet *Sovetskaya Kultura* did not publish Gelman's speech until four days after *Pravda*'s reply—further evidence of the paralysis that followed in the wake of Andreyeva's letter.

Film director Alexander Gelman is one of the leading proponents of *perestroika*, a group which includes Yuri Afanasiev, Tatyana Zaslavskaya, and Abel Aganbegyan. He was among the first intellectuals to vigorously support Gorbachev's reforms. Many of the points made in this speech also appeared in *Pravda*'s editorial reply to the Andreyeva letter.

No one set me any tasks as the keynote speaker, so I have set myself the task of making a statement of a personal nature and imparting my own ideas and concerns in the light of the forthcoming 19th All-Union Party Conference.

Some three years have elapsed since the start of *perestroika*. What is the main positive result? In my opinion it is that, despite the fact that three years have elapsed, *perestroika* has not yet become irreversible.

For all those who link the destiny of our future with *perestroika*, the fact that we have not yet created adequate democratic structures that would make the democratic way of life reliable and self-generating is a tremendous anxiety, a tremendous concern which does not relax its grip on us for a single day or hour. And in my opinion this will be the main question of the 19th Party Conference: elaborating and adopting decisions whose implementation will guarantee the complete irreversibility of the democratic process in society.

As I feel it now, in the course of preparation for the conference, all forms of the struggle for and against the revolutionary nature of *perestroika* are being sharpened. It is not out of the question that this struggle will also make itself felt in the work of the conference itself.

The open and backstage opponents of *perestroika* are realizing increasingly clearly that the ideals of *perestroika* are winning over new hearts and minds with every passing day. They understand that the interval of time within which *perestroika* can be halted or at least palpably driven from its resolute revolutionary path is a small one. Sensing this lack of time, they have come to attention. They realize that they must make haste while the decision-making mechanisms are still operating, with whose aid public opinion can be bypassed and a blow dealt to *perestroika*. These mechanisms are in many cases in their hands. I admit that preparation for the party conference or even the party conference itself could be the bridgehead from which they will try to engage in a resolute battle with *perestroika*.

Perhaps my fears are exaggerated. God grant that they are, but it is a case of such serious matters, a case of such potential tragic consequences, that I consider I have the right not to be inhibited in expressing my fears.

In this sense I do not regard as accidental *Sovetskaya Rossiya*'s publication of an article by Nina Andreyeva [Document #28], who has expressed some of the program aims of the conservative forces in the party. This article's main thrust is to cast doubt on the correctness of the moral criteria for assessing the past and present of Soviet society. It preaches as a Marxist idea the incompatibility of politics and morality and contrasts the class and ethical approaches. Speaking of a Leningrad film devoted to [Sergei] Kirov, she says she is angered by the commentator's text, which reminds viewers of the repressions of the 1930s while the film shows scenes of enthusiasm from those years. She sees in this an act of violence against the truth. She is generally angered by the fact that very little is now being written about the labor enthusiasm of that time, while everything is about tragedies and more tragedies. It does not seem to occur to her that the laws of normal human responsiveness state that people are more concerned with the fate of those who died innocently and prematurely in Stalin's camps than with the fate of those who undoubtedly deserve respect for the labor heroism they displayed but who nonetheless lived and worked normally and who are still alive or died a natural death. At all times tragedies have met with a greater response in people's hearts than the normal course of life, especially when it is tragedy on a scale like Stalin's actions. Nina Andreyeva also demands some kind of state-historical criterion of assessment rather than a moral criterion with regard to Stalin himself. She believes that we have simply not grown to the point where we can define Stalin's place in history; anything big, she says, can only be seen from a distance.

In general a certain skittishness can be traced in some comrades' assessments of the figure of Stalin. In an interview with *Ogonyok* Sergei Mikhalkov says that yes, of course, on the one hand Stalin was a butcher, but on the other hand just think, he would not allow himself to remove a comma from the text of the USSR's anthem without the author's permission, and he sought out the author at the front to ask his permission.[1] You see, he says, what a contradictory, complex personality he really had. And someone else has written that yes, Stalin was a butcher, but he was an ascetic, he needed absolutely nothing, he was as poor as a church mouse. Just like a second Mahatma Gandhi.

Yes, Stalin was indifferent to objects and money, it was something else that brought him pleasure. He liked to enjoy full power over people, over entire peoples, and in that respect he was no ascetic. He took inordinate pleasure in it.

Who gains from Andreyeva's position? The people? The party? In no way. This position, whether she wants it to or not, serves the vital interests of the bureaucracy, including the party bureaucracy. It is to their advantage to separate policy and morality. They need this to avoid denunciation for their old sins and to ensure that nothing prevents them from committing new ones.

The most intelligent and farsighted opponents of *perestroika* use a different strategy: they try to replace democratization with liberalization. What is the difference? Democratization provides for the redistribution of power, rights, and freedoms and the creation of a number of

---

[1] See Vladimir Aleksandrov, "How the Anthem of the Soviet Union Was Written," *Moskva*, no. 3, 1988, pp. 190–94.

independent structures of management and information. Liberalization conserves all of the foundations of the administrative system but in a milder form. Liberalization is an unclenched fist, but the hand is the same, and at any moment it could be clenched again into a fist. Only outwardly is liberalization sometimes reminiscent of democratization, but in actual fact it is a fundamental and intolerable usurpation.

One more method is used to discredit *perestroika*. It is claimed that an exhaustive critical analysis of the past and of Stalin's actions strikes against the authority of the party as the leading force of society. Yes, in a certain sense it does. But in opening up to society the opportunity to criticize it and to deprive it of a few pages of specious glory, the party at the same time opens up the opportunity, thanks to its policy's resolute turn, to acquire new, untarnished glory. We must think not only of the party's past but also of its future. You cannot bring back the past, but the party's future is being laid today on a purged foundation of truth. If we are speaking of the past, we can say today that the moral nucleus within the party never died. It was dying of fear and defenselessness in the Stalin era, but even after contracting and shrinking it retained its inner worth. Otherwise neither the 20th Party Congress nor today's *perestroika* would have taken place. The party bore its loyalty to moral principles through its entire, very complex history as a living, unfading value.

The party has done very major services to the people, but it is also in their debt. The main debt is democracy, full socialist democracy, which the party did not implant promptly in our social existence. I will put it even more sharply: throughout entire, quite protracted periods the party, especially its leading organs, acted in the role of a force opposing democracy. Sufficiently strong antidemocratic traditions were created in the party. This should be admitted without reservation, otherwise it is hard to explain the need for a drastic change of course or to implement *perestroika* in practice and in the spirit of the new course. Yes, the party has accumulated a debt to society, and it is now beginning to pay this debt. When this imposing work on the democratic restructuring of society has been completed, the gratitude of the people and of the whole world will cover many times over the damage to the party's authority connected with an exhaustive critical analysis of its history.

Without democratic management of public property, it is in fact not public property, not the property of all the people. Being the owner of property means being the master of management, otherwise property belongs to the bureaucratic stratum of society and not to the people. Removing the land and the plants from the exploiters still does not mean transferring them to the people. Only with the implementation of democratic structures of management is the act of handing the people their property accomplished. This seems to be acknowledged today, but frequently only verbally, while in practice, I repeat, we can observe a persistent attempt to supplant democratization with liberalization, the obsolete, discredited liberalization of the bureaucratic system of management.

The opponents of *perestroika* have no conclusive logical or persuasive program, but they do still have power. They have strength. That is why I believe that we rank-and-file Communists should not sit idly by and await the decisions of the party conference on the basis of the "whatever God sends" principle. Our concern for the fate of *perestroika* must be transformed into real action. Not only into books, screenplays, plays, and films, but also into real, direct, political action. The progress of preparation for the conference today cannot be wholly assigned to the party apparatus. It is very important that the conference delegates should sense the mood of the party masses and the position of the party organizations.

I want to propose for your attention the draft mandate to the 19th Party Conference from our party organization:

First. It would be desirable for the 19th Party Conference to be held openly, with the publication of the delegates' speeches without cuts, with the televised broadcast of substantial parts of the conference's work, for the Communists and society as a whole to sense the atmosphere, and for people to be able to respond not formally but effectively to what is happening at the conference even while it is working. For a lively hourly feedback, so to speak, to exist between the party and the conference.

Second. In the spirit of this openness the conference should make the decision that CPSU Central Committee *plenums* also be held openly. A Central Committee *plenum* is in fact the main party parliament, and, considering that the party rules in our country, it is in general the country's main, deciding parliament. If Central Committee *plenums* are held openly this will intensify the Central Committee's beneficial influence on society and at the same time increase Central Committee members' responsibility for their words and for their mission as a whole.

Third. We associate ourselves with those Communists who propose that the term of continuous office in elected posts should be limited to eight to ten years.

Fourth. There is an urgent need for the activity of party leaders of any rank, including Central Committee secretaries and Central Committee department chiefs, to be constantly on view so that people know who is who, have a more detailed and real knowledge of their personal qualities, and have an idea of any nuances of their world outlook, the features of their character, the features of the position they hold on particular issues, their style of work, style of communication, and cultural purview. We can no longer allow, as has frequently been the case in the past, that society and the party itself should suddenly learn of the shortcomings and errors of a particular party figure. There have already been enough of those information shocks, those blows to the head, when at first a person is for a long time considered to be a really good man and then suddenly—bang!—it turns out that he is an adventurist or an extremist or is in favor of "*glasnost* without limits." One reader of mine wrote to say, just you wait, "your Gorbachev will be thrown out yet for *glasnost* without limits." You see, he has the formula all ready. I am sure that the adoption of a decision on access to observe the activity of the leaders will meet with approval among the leaders themselves and the Communists. People's fates cannot be decided abruptly and without open debate. Who knows, perhaps even Stalin, had he worked under conditions of *glasnost*, would have found the strength to curb his evil proclivities and would have gone down in our party's history not as a butcher but as an entirely respected figure.

The question of *glasnost*, of greater autonomy and independence for the media, is in need of additional and in-depth discussion at the conference. The activation of the ideological backup for democratic transformations is connected with this. A program to eliminate illiteracy in democracy is needed, perhaps on television. People have a poor knowledge of the historical path of democratic values. These values were not revealed today for the first time in the course of historical creation, as it seems to some people. Democracy has performed outstanding services in the history of mankind. The fact that today we are having endless debates and heartrending polemics about the harm or benefit of *glasnost* is evidence, not least, of our insufficiently high standard of culture. Essentially these are routine debates, the question of the benefit of *glasnost* is a historically decided question, and marking time for years on this tiny piece of political culture is simply intolerable. Incidentally, when it was necessary to ensure and to provide ideological justification for the lack of *glasnost* in recent years, the Central Committee culture and propaganda departments were far more skillful than they are today, when the authority of *glasnost* has to be strengthened.

We must treasure *glasnost* as the apple of our eye. And I want to mention one important thing here. A mass of negligence, a mass of stupidity has accumulated over the years when a veritable dictatorship of mediocrity existed in many regions. Many of these questions were not discussed, were not touched on in polemics, and were not explained for decades. And suddenly there is *glasnost* and freedom. And in many heads everything has become confused; hence, alongside the fair, justified, necessary demonstrations and protests, we can observe (and there may be more of them in the future) protests connected with thoughtlessness, false certainties, and extremist feelings. That is why, in addition to the danger that *perestroika* may be halted by its direct opponents, there is also a danger from the extremist forces who support *perestroika*. These extremes can join without ceremony, particularly now, in the period of transition, when democratic foundations are still only beginning to take root, when they have not yet been reinforced with the cement of perfected procedural instructions. In brief, our feet may be ahead of our heads, the entire frame of *perestroika* may tilt and even topple, and here the ironclad boot of excessive administration will try not to let slip the chance to attack *perestroika* and put an end to it.

I think the party conference should draw society's attention to the need, especially in the period of transition, to distinguish between freedom for the head and freedom for the feet. Our heads need complete freedom, so that people can read and think about everything and work out what is what and why, clarify the obscure, and check their feelings against reason. But our feet need restraint. I realize that it is hard to separate feet from heads, and my wish will look speculative. Nonetheless, if you have a good think about it, methods will be found that are entirely acceptable under the conditions of democracy for the self-limitation of freedom for the feet with complete freedom for the head.

Like everyone, I am very concerned by the events in Nagorno-Karabakh, Azerbaijan, and Armenia. Blood has been shed there. The culprits must be sought out to the last man and punished, punished. Unfortunately, the press has uttered no words of grief for the innocent lives that have been taken. Our media have proved unready to cover dramatic events in a human and honest way. Some turns of phrase in the items published have angered Muscovites, never mind readers in Yerevan or Sumgait! Our union and the cinematographers' union secretariat must contribute their share of considered, sympathetic efforts to promote the consolidation of the spirit of reason in the actions of these republics' creative intelligentsia.

Democracy is not above reason; there is nothing in people's lives that is above reason, and democracy itself is the child of reason, the child of human wisdom. It does happen that, for the sake of self-preservation, democracy is obliged, is compelled to display for a while a firmness and even a toughness that is not inherent in it. But even in that case it should do everything openly, persuasively explaining to society the moral justification for the measures that are being taken. Reason responds to reason, and human hearts are reassured when they are addressed sincerely, caringly, without ulterior motive.

Today it would be sensible to create a ministry or committee for the affairs of nations. This organ could investigate in detail all problems among these nations, take preemptive measures, and not allow the solution of these problems to degenerate into mass protest demonstrations. There is a lot to do here, especially in the autonomous republics and *oblasts*. The purely administrative classification of a particular people as autonomous should not lead to any violations of their opportunities for developing their own culture. In attitudes toward nations there should not be a trace of division into ranks. In that sense our union must think about Tatars, Bashkirs, and other peoples as having conditions for developing their national cinema. We must not wait for a resolution to do this to appear. The creation of conditions for developing national cinemas where they do not exist should be part of the program to restructure the cinema, should be its most important component.

The forthcoming party conference should define the new, nonauthoritarian nature of the party's leadership activity, its ideological, spiritual activity. And that is more complex than appointing and removing the next leaders. The party must learn to operate by using only its ideological and spiritual power. And this is a kind of power to which people can subordinate themselves only voluntarily.

When you can order people, no one will try to persuade them. When you can order people, any complexities of life and activity are oversimplified, reduced to their outline, to dogma. The authoritarian principle of activity became the reason for massive oversimplification. The sin of oversimplification is an old sin of ours, and it is very difficult to break the habit of this sin. It is one of the reasons for opposition to democratization; many party workers are simply unable to cope with complex tasks and do not have the qualities required for it. And each person wants what he is capable of. If he is not capable of something, he says it is not needed, that it is harmful and dangerous to the foundations of socialism.

The party's well-organized *perestroika* to a nonauthoritarian style needs several, admittedly not big but sensible and high-quality, films and effective cinematic assistance. The creation of such films today will obviously require special organizational efforts. In my opinion cinematographers today have investigated exclusively general human themes and problems, and that is fine and I welcome it, but we must also remember that our *perestroika*, the *perestroika* in our party today has a real, practical, general human importance.

I think that as a whole, since its renowned fifth congress, our union has somewhat lost its importance as one of the ideological and intellectual bastions of *perestroika* and democratization. That is normal, that can be understood, and efforts have been dispersed for specific jobs, but I think that we should have sufficient dynamism and ability, when necessary, to focus our efforts on concerns of general importance. Now, in the period of preparation for the 19th Party Conference, is just such a time for mustering and concentrating our forces.

The following question seems legitimate to me: If restructuring is halted, who primarily will be responsible, its supporters or its opponents? I personally have just one answer: Its supporters will be to blame.

Somehow we have rapidly become lazy, and we let slip unheeded things that should not be let slip. Some people have been seized by euphoria caused by the opportunities opened up, and some people are rushing to pluck their little piece of the freedom that has only just begun to emerge from the iron shell of tyranny. I address these rebukes not only to you but also to myself, above all to myself.

We must take in air for a second wind; now is the right time to do so. The struggle has not ended. Its decisive, hardest stage is only beginning.

31

19th Party Conference: Considering the CPSU Central Committee Theses and Fundamental Questions of *Perestroika*

Tatyana Zaslavskaya and Yelena Manucharova

Izvestiya, June 4, 1988

Sociologist Tatyana Zaslavskaya is a leading and long-standing proponent of reforms. She views *glasnost* and *perestroika* as a "social revolution," with all the corresponding ramifications. In this interview on the eve of the 19th Party Conference, she criticizes the entrenched command and administrative system and emphasizes that there are social groups who oppose the reforms. She supports the further development of the unofficial movement. Conservatives deeply dislike Zaslavskaya and prevented her election as a delegate to the 19th Party Conference.

Manucharova: Tatyana Ivanovna! The CPSU Central Committee theses offer absolutely new conditions of life.[1] They commit every person to a great deal. But the people who grew up in the era when social activeness was not encouraged and initiative was punished remain fettered. It is as though a "circle of prohibition," invisible to others but highly imperative, has been drawn around each of us, separating the "accepted" from the "unaccepted."

Zaslavskaya: This circle is a dangerous thing. It is widespread. And traditional. Much comes within it. For instance, the passiveness of the majority of Supreme Soviet deputies. As far as I know, in the past twenty-five years not a single deputy has displayed any genuinely radical social initiative, although he ran no risk and no actions would have been taken against a single deputy, whatever he demanded. But, as we know, until the last session, when the draft Law of Cooperatives underwent stormy

---

[1] The theses published by the Central Committee of the CPSU on the eve of the 19th Party Conference were limited in scope compared to Gorbachev's proposals.

discussion, the Supreme Soviet essentially rubber-stamped decisions prepared by the *apparat*.

You are right. After a long period of stagnation it is hard to immediately acquire different habits and to behave in a truly free manner, as you consider necessary. Our consciousness is overgrown with many erroneous ideas, illusions of prohibition, and skepticism. And that is characteristic of all strata of society. But a very great deal in the fate of *perestroika* now depends on the level of public awareness.

Manucharova: Forgive me for interrupting you, but different people have different understandings of what *perestroika* is. Some people think it pertains only to the quality of work, others to the number of goods, and this correspondingly determines their position. Skepticism is manifested when goods disappear from the shelves. But few people think about the underlying meaning of the breakthrough period.

Zaslavskaya: I believe that the key to an understanding of *perestroika* is given in Mikhail Gorbachev's words to the effect that *perestroika* is a social revolution. That is how I see it (or at any rate want to see it) in the CPSU Central Committee theses.

Manucharova: It is the theses that our talk is about today. But it would be a good thing to determine also what should be understood in this case by the word revolution. Precise terms are particularly important here.

Zaslavskaya: There are no variant readings here. Revolution is a radical means of changing the socioeconomic formation. Marx called revolutions the "locomotives of history."

Manucharova: What is the main question that any revolution must resolve to ensure its victory?

Zaslavskaya: Power. Without resolving the question of power there are no revolutions. Our present-day revolution is no exception. The transfer of a large part of incomes, rights, and social privileges from the top stories of the social pyramid to the lower is connected with the redistribution of power. This is a profoundly democratic action, but it is understandable that it can only be carried out by encroaching on the interests of those groups who occupy a privileged position today, primarily the *apparat* of party, soviet, and economic management. The principle of the radical redistribution of power is "built into" the very concept of *perestroika*, and that is what makes it a social revolution. Fundamental transformations are required to lead our society onto a Leninist path of socialist development.

But it would be premature to conclude from the fact that these changes are essential that they are already taking place, in other words, that the measures that are being implemented in society are of a revolutionary nature. To assert this would mean deceiving ourselves and others. From my viewpoint, the system of measures that are being implemented so far can be assessed only as a rather uncomprehensive, contradictory reform based on many compromises, a reform whose pace and only slight efficiency are so far curbing society's development.

We have yet to attain genuinely revolutionary transformations. Or, to be more precise, they must be won in a hard sociopolitical struggle that will markedly change today's balance of social forces.

Manucharova: Let's dwell on today's obstacles to reform. The situation is complex, after all.

Zaslavskaya: Naturally. The *perestroika* of social relations is not being implemented in an empty space, but rather where the vitally important interests of different classes, strata, and groups of our society intersect. Each of them is seeking to protect its own interests, to achieve their implementation, and to prevent a threat to them. The professional demands made on leaders under the new conditions are naturally growing. Labor is becoming more complex, and the intellectual level it requires is increasing. This alone is enough for a proportion of leaders to take a conservative stance, to be in no hurry to make practical changes in production management methods.

To these factors we must add insufficient thought and the inconsistencies and confusion that inevitably arise in connection with the first attempts to switch enterprises to new conditions of economic management. This is expanding still further the circle of leaders who are displeased by the course of *perestroika*. While supporting the fundamental concept of *perestroika* they believe that it is not being implemented, that many of the innovations that are actually being introduced are in fact only consolidating a leadership based on administration through command.

Hence the skepticism and the reservation of their own established positions.

A very high concentration of power has always been characteristic of our society. The majority of representatives of the top group hold responsible jobs in several ruling organs simultaneously. CPSU Central Committee members have become Supreme Soviet deputies, republican leaders have become CPSU Central Committee members, and ministers have joined the Supreme Soviet and the Central Committee. In brief, a powerful ruling nucleus subordinate to no one has always taken shape. The centralist principle always drastically dominated the democratic principle.

During the time of stagnation the management apparatus wielded enormous power. A command-based style of managing the lower echelons, the unconditional execution of orders from higher-ranking echelons, formalism and bureaucracy in resolving questions affecting people's interests, and the minimizing of direct contacts with working people became characteristic features of behavior here.

That is why it is precisely in this group that we can now find the staunchest champions of the ideological views of the period of stagnation. Many of them are reluctant to concede their positions, to surrender even a small amount of power, and they allow themselves to ignore even keen criticism in the press.

The pseudosupporters of *perestroika* working in the management apparatus also present a great danger. While creating a semblance of great activeness and effective participation in the elaboration of directive documents and instructions, they are in fact bit by bit reducing transformation efforts to nothing.

I think that this group will wield a large number of rights for a long time. That is why many "prohibited zones" are still preserved which seem not to be affected by the transformations taking place in other regions. The changing of leading cadres at least improves the situation, but it is taking place relatively slowly and not always successfully.

Many unseen but tangible barriers are obviously dividing society into groups that are constantly seeking to consolidate their positions and which are aware of the opposing nature of their interests. On the one hand there are the initiators, champions, and allies of *perestroika*, on the other hand the opponents of *perestroika*. In this connection there arises the question of the "social price" that our society can, should, and is prepared to pay for overcoming its backwardness, for purging itself of the accumulated dirt, and for moral renewal.

Manucharova: Please name the points in the CPSU Central Committee theses that you consider to be truly momentous.

Zaslavskaya: First of all, of course, the transformation of the soviets of people's deputies into fully empowered organs of power and the party organs' renunciation of interference in the solution of economic questions. In other words, spheres of power are being precisely differentiated. The management of the country and of socioeconomic processes will be undertaken by the soviets, while the party organs will fulfill actual political and ideological functions. This allocation will make it possible to overcome the political organs' unnecessary and harmful tutelage over economic activity.

The slogan "All power to the soviets" put forward by October has acquired particular popularity among the masses in recent years. It seems to me that the theses express precisely this truly Leninist revolutionary idea. The theses suggest a system of specific measures for the life support and implementation of this idea. One of these measures is aimed against the "private unions" of which I was speaking, against the merging of executive and legislative power. For instance, it will no longer be possible to elect *ispolkom* [municipality] members to the soviets, the soviet is to be the supreme legislative organ, while the *ispolkom* will be under the control of and subordinated to the soviet.

So far deputies have divided their time between their workplace and representation at sessions, and their main profession naturally dominated. That is why they readily agreed to vote for any decision prepared by the *apparat*. And they did not even think particularly about its content; frequently they did not even have time to understand it properly. To strengthen the soviets, for the period of their election a proportion of deputies will be relieved of their professional work.

The restriction of the terms in office of leading elected posts also seems to me to be important. This ensures the rotation of cadres.

One more fundamental position, the rejection of the *nomenklatura* system for forming cadres, is being submitted for discussion. This is very important, but I should like to see this thesis formulated even more precisely.

The idea of the self-purging of the Communists' ranks is very important; this will help the party to protect itself against those people who, without sharing its basic ideas, have joined the CPSU for selfish reasons. There are undoubtedly such people in the party. We must free ourselves of them, but how? After all it is not clear who will undergo recertification and who will be able, with a full knowledge of all the circumstances, to offer an objective decision on the alienation of a particular party member. For instance the example of Uzbekistan, with which everyone is familiar, shows that under certain conditions it is precisely the people for whom there ought to be no place in the party who can seize the upper hand in the party *apparat*.

Manucharova: Perhaps you have already switched to a criticism of the theses.

Zaslavskaya: The theses are the fruit of collective thinking. They reflect a compromise between people's different positions, hence the large number of streamlined formulations. In fact they have been put forward as a platform for subsequent discussion and undoubtedly need to be given practical concrete form.

Their text is concentrated more on what has to be done rather than on how to achieve it. In them you will find no answer to how the most important demands can and will be implemented: intensifying the role of the USSR Supreme Soviet, altering the election system, and subordinating the *apparat* to the elected organs. Only general words are uttered about a drastic reduction of the party *apparat*.

The discussion of the theses has already developed, and people are demanding more radical changes. In my view this is extraordinarily important. The raising of the level of public awareness is having an effect here. Some three years ago the very publication of such theses would probably simply have caused a mass shock.

Manucharova: The value of feedback. . . .

Zaslavskaya: It is important for society that feedback should travel upward through many channels, and not just one. It is a good thing that we have a large and powerful press and television and that social initiatives are growing.

Manucharova: What do you think of informal associations? A march and meeting by the Civic Dignity group was held in front of our newspaper building recently. Their slogans are "All power to the soviets" and "Long live *perestroika*." Are they of any use?

Zaslavskaya: For the time being they are still perhaps not mature enough on the social plane. But they should be supported. In my view organizational forms are needed into which the desire of many people to take an active part in transforming social relations could merge. People are now talking increasingly frequently about creating a "people's alliance for assisting *perestroika*" that would operate on a public basis. This has already been done in Estonia. Why should the experience not be extended to all of the Soviet Union? If this initiative is supported, the organization could exist on the people's money, not state money.

There are funds protecting children, culture, and peace. There should be a fund for assisting *perestroika*. Informal organizations could be of considerable benefit to society, becoming one more channel of feedback for the government.

Manucharova: Many people do not accept the very idea of informal associations and have probably lived their whole lives without seeing such enterprising and uninvited organizations. That is why they consider the informal associations to be simply savages that some "evil forces" will be able to launch into any conflict between nations or between groups.

Zaslavskaya: Distrust scarcely extends only to young social initiatives. The development of society is never without conflicts. Denying the inevitability of the struggle of group interests in connection with *perestroika* means closing your eyes to reality. But our path will not be so hard if we consciously and promptly enlist science for our assistance. It is necessary for the elaboration of a strategy for the social management of *perestroika*. And it will make it possible to minimize and to "domesticate" intergroup conflicts, to reduce social tension in society so that it is possible to achieve the projected goals at the least social cost.

The least cost—I want to stress that. Here an understanding of the measure of things is extraordinarily important. Under the conditions of antagonism of the interests of different social groups, an attempt to ease conflicts can in reality result in the emasculation of the main ideas of *perestroika*. And a one-sided orientation toward compromises, an excessive fear of offending the interests of a particular group will delay progress. Then the slow progress of *perestroika* will lead to acute dissatisfaction among working people, although it is being implemented precisely in their interests. The implementation of a thoughtful strategy for managing *perestroika* will make it possible to accelerate the progress of the revolution.

After all, it is only the convinced, self-sacrificing participation of the broadest masses which can ensure its victory. Social revolution implemented through the efforts of the *apparatchiks*, revolution "from above" cannot work. It should be the business of those who are vitally interested in it: the progressive section of workers, *kolkhoz* members, and the intelligentsia. It is essential to sharply intensify their influence on the progress of *perestroika*. The theses show how much can be done if you alter the political power structure.

Manucharova: You will repeat all of your bold ideas at the party conference?

Zaslavskaya: I will not be there. I was not elected. But you can consider that I have already delivered my speech here.

32

The Inevitability of *Perestroika*

Andrei Sakharov

Knizhnoe Obozrenie
no. 25, June 17, 1988

Andrei Sakharov, a Nobel Peace Prize winner and father of the Soviet hydrogen bomb, became the country's leading dissident during Brezhnev's rule. Sakharov's exile in Gorky ended in December 1986, when he received a personal phone call from Mikhail Gorbachev. In his well-known March 1970 *samizdat* letter to Leonid Brezhnev entitled "Appeal for a Gradual Democratization" (which he coauthored with Valery Turchin and Roy Medvedev), Sakharov warned that without fundamental political reforms, the Soviet Union faced ever-increasing economic difficulties and the prospect of turning into a "second-rate provincial power." Sakharov's ideas are today congruent with much of the current reform program. Going beyond support for individual human rights cases, Sakharov has long fought for the development of a legalistic state, a much-discussed topic today in the Soviet press. One can also see striking parallels between Sakharov's and Gorbachev's views on East-West relations and on the need to abolish nuclear weapons.

In this article published in a small proreform weekly, Sakharov argues that for economic reform to succeed, *glasnost* must be expanded to ensure the "moral and economic health of the country." He also calls for a free flow of information, genuine pluralism, and an end to bureaucratic rule. Sakharov is convinced of the absolute "historical necessity" of *perestroika*, but he sees difficult times ahead.

Our society has become deeply sick—not suddenly, of course, but as a result of a complex historical process. We know the symptoms of this illness, whose most recent stage is being called "the epoch of stagnation," and to some extent we understand its causes and inner mechanism, although we are still far from understanding it in its entirety.

In the first place, we understand that there is an absence of pluralism in the power structure, in the economy (with the exception of the NEP period), and in ideology. Connected with this is the bureaucratization of the daily life of our country. All the reins of control are concentrated in the hands of those people who possess power by dint of their position in the state-economic or party apparatus. It is they who constitute the "bureaucratic class."

Bureaucracy is a necessary part of contemporary society and of organized society in general. Everywhere, the bureaucracy's functioning, although often very useful, is in some manner associated with negative phenomena such as elitism, inflexibility, and the command structure of management which mechanically subordinates middle levels to higher levels, exhibits a disregard for democratic controls from below, and sometimes turns against the interests of business. But in our country's "antipluralistic" tradition, these phenomena have acquired a qualitatively different, self-contained character.

A new social force arose [in the years after Lenin's death], the personification of which was, for a long time, Stalin. This does not mean, however, that the bureaucracy under Stalin had an easy life. In fact, a one-man dictatorship, characterized by an increase of harshness and other generally known qualities of Stalin, was instituted during that period. In truth, however, it was from the bureaucracy that he received a mandate to rule, but not only from the bureaucracy.

Having liquidated NEP [New Economic Policy], the new force showed its "teeth." One can assume that the basis of our society's pluralistic development could have been that very NEP, in conjunction with the voluntary, that is, partial, creation of labor cooperatives in the countryside and the rational construction of state industry on a healthy economic foundation. But this is exactly what would have been unacceptable for the "new bureaucracy." What happened afterward is known: forced collectivization, dispossession of the *kulaks*, destruction of the peasantry for the sake of rapid industrialization, forced starvation, and monstrous isolation of those areas doomed to death. There was practically no aid for those dying of starvation. It was at that time that the export of grain and timber to the West reached its maximum level. Then there was the "great terror," which had its tragic culmination in 1937 and consumed not only the old revolutionary guard and military leaders, but all living forces of society. Then there was much more.

The attempts at reform undertaken by Khrushchev and his assistants and those initiated in the 1960s were resisted by the *nomenklatura* and turned out to be largely ineffectual (especially the later reform attempts). To a significant degree, these failures predetermined the psychological climate of the next decades. Yet another attempt at *"perestroika"* within the socialist camp was crushed by tanks in 1968.[1]

Nevertheless, after the 20th Party Congress, the system shed the extremes and excesses of the Stalinist period and became more "civilized" with a face which, although not completely human, was in any case not that of a tiger. In a certain sense, this epoch was psychologically comforting for some parts of the population. At the same time, it was actually a period of stagnation as the country slowly became more deadlocked.

During this period, the possibilities for extensive economic development exhausted themselves, while the system turned out to be incapable of intensive development. Technical progress was not advantageous to the industrial executives who acted within the bounds of the administrative-bureaucratic structure; new ideas did not take root, nor were they cultivated as bureaucratization enveloped even the scientific sphere. A large portion of scientific-technical ideas came from the West, although often years or decades later.

Another facet of this era of bureaucratic dominance, one closely related to the economic abnormalities and no less tragic, was the moral degradation of society. Hypocrisy and lies flourished in the press, on the radio and television, in school, in the Komsomol, at the university, and in the family. The people, who had been repeatedly deceived with pretty words, didn't believe them anymore. Indifference crept over society.

This suffocating psychological situation had a particularly severe effect on youth, demoralizing and corrupting them. No social portrait of this era of stagnation would be complete if it did not take into account the colossal development of various forms of corruption. Mafia-like groups arose that were connected to the local party and government apparatus from which, as a rule, the threads

---

[1] Sakharov considers the Prague Spring of 1968 to be a forerunner of *perestroika.*

extended upward. A classic example is the Uzbekistan mafia with its many embezzlements of billions of rubles for cotton that was never produced, its systematic bribery, and its exploitation of cotton harvesters. Thus did thousands of people, especially children, become victims of the uncontrolled mass use of defoliants and other chemicals and the cruelest violence over malcontents in private underground prisons and "psychiatric wards."

Such a general picture of a dead-end street, of stagnation, became visible in the mid-1980s. Fortunately, strong forces have turned up in the USSR that have realized that we cannot continue in this manner. We are all familiar with the slogans and ideology of *perestroika*. They are economic reform, *glasnost*, democratization (particularly new principles concerning the promotion of leaders), social justice, and new political thinking that declares the common human goals of survival and world development as priorities over all state, class, national, bureaucratic, and private interests.

Is the program of *perestroika* really feasible? This is the question on everyone's mind.

First of all, I want to emphasize that I am convinced of the absolute historical necessity of *perestroika*. It is like war: Victory is necessary, but great hardships and obstacles of an economic, psychological, and organizational nature are inevitable. For decades, the people studied in a corrupting "antischool" that trained many not to work and created a vision of work that was accustomed to hypocrisy, lies, egoism, and time serving (when I say "the people" I mean also the intelligentsia). Do the people still possess sufficient moral strength? If not, our path will be slow and contradictory, with deviations and pitfalls.

But I believe that in the people, and particularly in youth, an animated fire is always burning beneath the surface. It makes itself known. This depends on all of us. There must be both moral and material motivation for *perestroika* if everyone is to take an interest in its success. But still, a grand sense of a common goal cannot be achieved through orders and persuasion. Without this, however, all remains undecided. The people must believe that they are being told the truth. But for this, one thing is necessary: to speak only the truth and nothing but the truth, and to confirm words with deeds.

Yet even in the most favorable of cases, there will be great difficulties. Already for many people the transition to self-accounting and self-financing, to a new system of supply and cooperativization, has led to a loss of part of their revenues and even their jobs. Indeed, this is only the beginning of a difficult path on which way we will see a little less stupidity, a little more common sense, and a little more feeling of responsibility.

The chief obstacles facing *perestroika* are the general stagnation resulting from decades of the administrative-bureaucratic system and the practical interests of millions of that system's members at all levels. They simply don't need a self-regulating, effective system. Indeed, they would find themselves excluded from it. Hence the danger is that someone either actively or passively, through incompetence, may impede, distort, or caricaturize *perestroika* and portray its temporary setbacks as definitive failures. Through all of this *perestroika* must pass.

What do I think about and what do I expect from *perestroika*? First and foremost, I think about *glasnost*. Specifically, *glasnost* must create a new moral climate in this country! It is generally known that we have made the greatest progress of all in this sphere. As fewer subjects are forbidden, we begin to see our society as it really was in the past and is in the present. People must know the truth and must have the opportunity to express their thoughts freely. The corrupting lie, silence, and hypocrisy must be forever and irrevocably removed from our lives. Only an internally free man can take initiative. This is also true of a society.

Another, no less important, basis of a morally healthy society is social justice. This is a broad and many-sided concept, and I have written about such aspects of it as the privileges of the elite, the level of wages and pensions, and social equality.

Not being a specialist, I shall refrain from discussing critically important economic questions, and shall limit myself to a few "outsider's" remarks. We must create economic and legal conditions that foster profitable initiative, flexible responses to the economic situation, favorable technical progress, and valuable, good, individual work, without any obstacles or limitations of a dogmatic nature. Now we have the Law on State Enterprises, a draft of a Law on Cooperatives (most likely preliminary), and the Law on Individual Labor Activity.[2] These documents are all very important, and in principle they open qualitatively new political-economic possibilities.

At the same time, the disagreements and contradictions in the spirit of the documents are striking. For example, what does "party organization control" mean under the conditions of a cooperative? The preamble of the draft Law on Cooperatives stipulates the right of free exit from the cooperative. But, for some reason, the exit matter is not mentioned in the discussion of the functions of the general assembly of the collective farm. In other words the general assembly, in contradiction to the preamble, is endowed with the right to refuse to allow exit from the *kolkhoz*. In the Law on Cooperatives and the regulations of the *kolkhoz* it is necessary to stipulate the right of free exit for each member, with appropriate compensation for labor expended, preservation of the length of service [for pension purposes], and, at the desire of the person exiting, the apportionment of a plot of land. The collective farm worker is not a serf. The collective farm should be an absolutely voluntary association. Any violation of this principle is fraught with a very deep social, psychological, and economic danger for society, as we are now observing.

The subsequent development of a system of familial and collective contracts with legal, economic, and social-moral support is very important. Long-term apportionment of good land (with the right of inheritance) to those who desire it is necessary. This is the only way to guarantee careful preservation of one of the main riches of our society: fruitful land. An especially large role should be played by the "small cooperatives," together with a series of transitional forms of collective contracts.

We must give individual labor activity maximum support, create the most favorable economic and legal conditions for this activity, and foster a psychological atmosphere for a longer range outlook. Of course, all resolutions which, like the Decree on Unearned Income,

---

[2] The Law on Individual Labor Activity took effect on July 1, 1987, the Law on State Enterprises on January 1, 1988, and the Law on Cooperatives on July 1, 1988.

contradict the goals of individual labor activity development must be changed. One shouldn't be afraid of large profits for individual citizens if the source of the profits is personal labor, initiative, invention, utilization of the situation, or use of personal property. The principle that "everything that is not prohibited by law is permitted" should be taken literally. Certain socially useful aspects of individual labor activity should be exempt from taxation (beekeeping, for example).

Perestroika must promote "openness of society" as a basic condition for the moral and economic health of the country, and for international trust and security. The concept of openness includes public control over key decisions (repetition of the mistakes made in the invasion of Afghanistan should be made impossible),[3] freedom of conviction, freedom to receive and disseminate information, and freedom to choose one's country of residence and one's place of residence within the country. Many acute problems which had been latent surfaced at the beginning of *perestroika*: social, economic, moral, cultural, and, unfortunately, national problems. The touchstone of *perestroika* has become its capability to overcome resistance and the obstacles of the past. The people's belief in *perestroika* depends to a significant extent on whether the deeds correspond to the words.

---

[3] Sakharov was exiled to Gorky for his condemnation of the Soviet invasion of Afghanistan.

Bibliography

Elkin, Valery. "I Want to Help My Party." *Izvestiya*, May 11, 1988.
> A letter from a rank-and-file party member which argues that the hypocrisy of the party leaders and bureaucracy has resulted in the passivity of party members.

Ilyin, Alexander. "To Restore the Leninist Concept of the Party." *Pravda*, January 2, 1989.
> An analysis of the party's role in the reform process and the need to restructure the party through *glasnost* and democratization.

Kurashvili, Boris. "What the Power Structure Should Be." *Izvestiya*, July 28, 1988.
> A criticism of the electoral reform system establishing a bicameral legislature and what the author views as excessive concentration of power in the presidency.

Kuznetsov, Pobisk. "Questions to a Historian." *Pravda*, June 25, 1988.
> A conservative criticism of the reformer Yuri Afanasiev and his views on party history, including the idea of a "Bukharin alternative."

Selivanov, V. "About the Power and Authority of the Party." *Pravda*, May 2, 1988.
> A sharp criticism of the concentration of power in the hands of the party *apparat* during the Brezhnev years.

Yakovlev, Alexander. "In Favor of Realistic Thinking and the Responsibility of Action." *Izvestiya*, August 12, 1988.
> Politburo member Alexander Yakovlev's philosophical interpretation of economic reform and democratization.

33

Mikhail Gorbachev Addresses the United Nations

Soviet Life, special supplement
no. 2, February 1989

We are now entering into a period in the superpower relationship which appears destined to transcend both the hostility of the Cold War and the euphoria of détente. Mikhail Gorbachev's "new thinking" in foreign policy and the doctrine of "reasonable sufficiency" in military defense offer Americans both opportunity and challenge as we look to the next decade.

In his speech to the United Nations on December 7, 1988, Mikhail Gorbachev announced a dramatic unilateral cut of 500,000 Soviet troops and 10,000 tanks. Lost, however, in the minutiae of military analysis that followed the speech was Gorbachev's continuing "de-ideologization" of foreign policy. While past Soviet leaders and conservative Politburo rival Yegor Ligachev have emphasized the "class struggle" against the West, Gorbachev advocates instead the non-Marxist ideals of universal human values and cooperation among nations.

The specific cuts and their locations as declared in the UN speech clearly indicate Gorbachev's intent to back up "reasonable sufficiency" with actions. Gorbachev's cutbacks are an attempt to alleviate Western anxiety about Soviet doctrine (whether forces are trained for defense or for attack), location (the proximity of troops to the European border, which affects the warning time for an attack), and the composition of its armed forces (which in the case of Europe refers to offensive-oriented items such as tanks and mechanized troops). Gorbachev specified that 10,000 tanks and 800 aircraft, as well as assault-crossing support units and their combat equipment, are to be withdrawn from Eastern Europe and the western part of the USSR. This action addresses a number of NATO concerns and should accelerate efforts for conventional arms reduction.

Standing before the United Nations, Gorbachev symbolized the Soviet Union of this period of *perestroika* and *glasnost*: more peaceful, less ideological, and more willing to be a participant in international cultural and trade exchanges. This energetic and eloquent Soviet leader has captured the attention and imagination of the West.

Esteemed Mr. President,
Esteemed Mr. Secretary-General,
Distinguished delegates,

We have come here to show our respect for the United
Nations, which increasingly has manifested its ability to
act as a unique international center in the service of peace
and security.

We have come here to show our respect for the dignity of
this organization, which is capable of accumulating the
collective wisdom and will of humankind. Recent events
have made it increasingly clear that the world needs such
an organization and that the organization itself needs the
active involvement of all of its members, their support for
its initiatives and actions, and their potential and original
contributions, which enrich its activity.

A little more than a year ago, in an article entitled "The
Reality and Guarantees of a Secure World," I set out some
ideas on problems of concern to the United Nations.

The time since then has given fresh food for thought.
World developments have indeed come to a crucial point.

The role played by the Soviet Union in world affairs is
well known and, in view of the revolutionary *perestroika*
under way in our country, which has a tremendous
potential for peace and international cooperation, we are
now particularly interested in being properly understood.

That is why we have come here to address this most
authoritative world body and to share our thoughts with its
members. We want it to be the first to learn of our
important new decisions.

I

What will humankind be like as it enters the twenty-
first century? People are already fascinated by this not too
distant future. We are looking forward to it with hopes for
the best and yet with feelings of concern.

The world in which we live today is radically different
from what it was at the beginning or even in the middle of
this century. And it continues to change, as do all its
components.

The advent of nuclear weapons was a tragic reminder of the fundamental nature of all these changes. A material symbol and expression of absolute military power, nuclear weapons at the same time revealed the absolute limits of that power. The problem of humankind's survival and self-preservation has come to the fore.

Profound social changes are taking place.

Whether in the East or the South, the West or the North, hundreds of millions of people, new nations and states, new public movements and ideologies have moved to the forefront of history.

Broad-based and frequently turbulent popular movements have given expression, in a multidimensional and contradictory way, to a longing for independence, democracy and social justice. The idea of democratizing the entire world order has become a powerful sociopolitical force.

At the same time, the scientific and technological revolution has turned many economic, food, energy, environmental, information and demographic problems, which only recently we treated as national or regional problems, into global concerns.

Thanks to the advances in mass media and means of transportation, the world seems to have become more visible and tangible. International communication has become easier than ever before. Today it is virtually impossible for any society to remain "closed." We need a radical review of approaches to the totality of the problems of international cooperation, which is a major element of universal security.

The world economy is becoming a single organism, and no state, whatever its social system or economic status, can normally develop outside it.

This places on the agenda the need to devise a fundamentally new machinery for the functioning of the world economy, a new structure of the international division of labor.

At the same time, the growth of the world economy reveals the contradictions and limits inherent in the traditional type of industrialization. Its further extension and intensification spell environmental catastrophe.

But there are still many countries without sufficiently developed industries, and some have not yet industrialized.

One of the major problems is whether the process of their economic growth will follow the old technological patterns or whether they can join in the search for environmentally clean production.

Another problem is the widening gap between the developed and most of the developing countries, which is increasingly becoming a serious global threat.

Hence the need to begin a search for a fundamentally new type of industrial progress that would meet the interests of all peoples and states.

In a word, the new realities are changing the entire international situation. The differences and contradictions inherited from the past are diminishing or being displaced. But new ones are emerging.

Some former differences and disputes are losing their importance. But conflicts of a different kind are taking their place.

Life is making us abandon traditional stereotypes and outdated views; it is making us discard illusions.

The very concepts of the nature of and criteria for progress are changing.

It would be naive to think that the problems plaguing humankind today can be solved with the means and methods that were applied or seemed to work in the past.

This is one of the signs of the crucial nature of the current phase in history.

The greatest philosophers sought to grasp the laws of social development and to find an answer to the main question: how to make human life happier, fairer and more secure. Two great revolutions, the French Revolution of 1789 and the Russian Revolution of 1917, had a powerful impact on the very nature of history and radically changed the course of world developments.

These two revolutions, each in its own way, gave a tremendous impetus to humankind's progress. To a large extent, the two revolutions shaped the way of thinking that is still prevalent in social consciousness. It is a precious intellectual heritage.

But today we face a different world, and we must seek a different road to the future. In seeking it, we must, of course, draw on the accumulated experience and yet be aware of the fundamental differences between the situation yesterday and what we are facing today.

But the novelty of the tasks before us, as well as their difficulty, goes beyond that. Today we have entered an era when progress will be shaped by universal human interests.

The awareness of this dictates that world politics, too, should be guided by the primacy of universal human values.

The history of past centuries and millennia was a history of wars that raged almost everywhere, or of frequent desperate battles to the point of mutual annihilation. They grew out of clashes of social and political interests, national enmity, and ideological or religious incompatibility. All this did happen.

And even today many people would like these vestiges of the past to be accepted as inexorable law.

But concurrently with wars, animosities and divisions among peoples and countries, another objective trend has been gaining momentum—the emergence of a mutually interdependent and integral world.

Today, further world progress is only possible through a search for universal human consensus as we move forward to a new world order.

We have reached a point at which disorder and spontaneity lead to an impasse. The international community must learn how it can shape and guide developments in such a way as to preserve our civilization, to make the world safe for all and more conducive to normal life.

I am referring to the kind of cooperation that could be more accurately termed cocreation and codevelopment.

The concept of development at the expense of others is on the way out. In the light of existing realities, no genuine progress is possible at the expense of the rights and freedoms of individuals and nations or at the expense of nature. Efforts to solve global problems require a new scope and quality of interaction of states and sociopolitical currents, regardless of ideological or other differences.

Of course, radical changes and revolutionary transformations will continue to occur within individual countries and social structures. This is how it always was and how it always will be.

But here too, our time marks a change. Domestic transformations no longer can achieve their national goals if they develop just along "parallel courses" with others, without main use of the achievements of the outside world and of the potential inherent in equitable cooperation.

In these circumstances, any interference in those domestic developments, designed to redirect them to alien ways, would have destructive consequences for the emergence of a peaceful order.

In the past differences were often obstacles to cooperation. Now they have a chance of becoming a factor for mutual enrichment and mutual attraction.

Specific interests underlie all differences in social systems, in the way of life and in preferences for certain values. There is no escaping that fact.

But equally, there is no escaping the need to find a balance of interests within an international framework. Such a balance is a condition for survival and progress.

Pondering all this, one comes to the conclusion that if we are to take into account the lessons of the past and the realities of the present, if we are to reckon with the objective logic of world development, we must look for ways to improve the international situation and build a new world—and we must do it together.

And, if so, we ought to agree on the basic, truly universal prerequisites and principles of such policy.

It is obvious, in particular, that force or the threat of force can no longer be an instrument of foreign policy. This applies above all to nuclear arms, but not only to nuclear arms. All of us, and primarily the stronger of us, must exercise self-restraint and totally rule out any use of force in international affairs.

That is the cornerstone of the ideal of a nonviolent world, which we proclaimed together with India in the Delhi Declaration and which we invite you to follow.

After all, it is now quite clear that building up military power makes no country omnipotent. What is more, one-sided reliance on military power ultimately weakens other components of national security.

It is also quite clear to us that the principle of freedom of choice is essential. Refusal to recognize this principle is fraught with extremely grave consequences for world peace.

Denying that right to the peoples under whatever pretext or rhetorical guise means jeopardizing the fragile balance that has been attained. Freedom of choice is a universal principle that should allow for no exceptions.

It was not simply out of good intentions that we came to the conclusion that this principle is absolute. We were driven to it by an unbiased analysis of the objective trends of today.

More and more characteristic is the increasingly multi-optional nature of social development in different countries. This applies to both the capitalist and the socialist systems. The diversity of the sociopolitical structures that have grown over the past decades out of national liberation movements also attests to this.

This objective fact demands respect for the views and positions of others, tolerance, a willingness to perceive something different as not necessarily bad or hostile, and an ability to learn to coexist with others while retaining our differences and the ability to disagree with each other.

As the world asserts its diversity, attempts to look down on others and to teach them one's own brand of democracy become totally improper, to say nothing of the fact that democratic values intended for export often very quickly lose their worth.

What we are talking about, therefore, is unity in diversity. If we recognize this politically, if we reaffirm our adherence to the principle of freedom of choice, then there is no room for the view that some live on earth by virtue of divine will while others are here quite by chance.

The time has come to discard such thinking and to shape our policies accordingly. That would open up prospects for strengthening the unity of the world.

The new phase also requires freeing international relations from ideology. We are not abandoning our convictions, our philosophy or traditions, nor do we urge anyone to abandon theirs.

But neither do we intend to be hemmed in by our values. That would result in intellectual impoverishment, for it would mean rejecting a powerful source of development— the exchange of everything original that each nation has independently created.

In the course of such exchange, let everyone show the advantages of their social system, way of life or values— and not just by words or propaganda, but by real deeds.

That would be a fair rivalry of ideologies. But it should not be extended to relations among states. Otherwise, we would simply be unable to solve any of the world's problems, such as:

—developing wide-ranging, mutually beneficial and equitable cooperation among nations;

—making efficient use of the achievements of the scientific and technological revolution;

—restructuring international economic ties and protecting the environment;

—overcoming backwardness and eliminating hunger, disease, illiteracy and other global scourges;

—and last, but not least, eliminating the nuclear threat and militarism.

Those are our reflections on the patterns of world development at the threshold of the twenty-first century.

We are, of course, far from claiming to be in possession of the ultimate truth. But, on the basis of a thorough analysis of the past and newly emerging realities, we have concluded that it is along those lines that we should jointly seek the way to the supremacy of the universal humane idea over the endless multitude of centrifugal forces, the way to preserve the vitality of this civilization, possibly the only one in the entire universe.

Could this view be a little too romantic? Are we not overestimating the potential and the maturity of the world's social consciousness? We have heard such doubts and such questions both in our country and from some of our Western partners.

I am convinced that we are not completely unrealistic.

Forces have already emerged in the world that in one way or another encourage us to enter a period of peace. The peoples and large sectors of the public do, indeed, ardently wish for an improvement in the situation; they want to learn to cooperate. This trend is sometimes amazingly powerful. Even more important, such trends are beginning to shape policies.

Changes in philosophical approaches and in political relations form a solid prerequisite for imparting, in line with worldwide objective processes, a powerful impetus to the efforts to establish new relations among states.

Even those politicians whose activities used to be associated with the cold war, and sometimes even with its most critical phases, are now drawing similar conclusions. They of all people find it particularly hard to abandon the old stereotypes and practices of the past.

And if even they are changing course, it is clear that when new generations take over, such opportunities will increase in number.

In short, the realization that there is a need for peace is gaining ground and beginning to prevail. This has made it possible to take the first real steps toward improving the international situation and toward disarmament.

What are the practical implications? It would be natural and sensible not to abandon everything positive that has already been accomplished and to build on all the gains of the past few years, on all that we have created working together. I am referring to the process of negotiations on nuclear disarmament, conventional weapons and chemical weapons, and to the search for political approaches to the solution of regional conflicts.

Of course, I am referring above all to political dialogue—a more intensive and open dialogue pointed at the very heart of the problems instead of confrontation, at an exchange of constructive ideas instead of recriminations. Without political dialogue the process of negotiations cannot advance.

We regard prospects for the near and more distant future quite optimistically.

Just look at the changes in our relations with the United States. Little by little, mutual understanding has started to develop and elements of trust, without which it is very hard to make headway in politics, to emerge.

These elements are even more pronounced in Europe. The Helsinki process is a great process. I believe that it remains completely valid. Its philosophical, political, practical and other dimensions must all be preserved and enhanced, while at the same time taking into account new circumstances.

Current realities make it imperative that the dialogue that ensures the normal and constructive evolution of international affairs involves, on a continuous and active basis, all countries and regions of the world, including such major powers as India, China, Japan and Brazil and other countries—large, medium and small.

I am in favor of a more dynamic and substantive political dialogue, of consolidating the political prerequisites for improving the international climate. That would make it easier to find practical solutions to many problems. Tough as it may be, this is the road that we must travel.

Everyone should join in the movement toward greater unity of the world.

Today, this is particularly important, for we are approaching a very important point when we shall have to face the question of how to ensure the world's solidarity and the stability and dynamism of international relations.

And yet, in my talks with foreign government and political leaders, with whom I have had more than 200 meetings, I could sometimes sense their dissatisfaction over the fact that at this crucial time, for one reason or another, they sometimes find themselves, as it were, on the sidelines of the main issues of world politics.

It is natural and appropriate that no one is willing to resign himself to that.

If, although different, we are indeed part of the same civilization, if we are aware of the interdependence of the contemporary world, then this understanding must be increasingly present in politics and in the practical efforts to harmonize international relations. Perhaps the term *perestroika* is not quite appropriate in this context, but I do call for building new international relations.

I am convinced that our time and the realities of today's world call for internationalizing dialogue and the negotiating process.

This is the main general conclusion that we have come to in studying global trends that have been gaining momentum in recent years, and in participating in world politics.

II

In this specific historical situation, we face the question of a new role for the United Nations.

We feel that states must to some extent review their attitude toward the United Nations, this unique instrument without which world politics would be inconceivable today.

The recent reinvigoration of its peace-making role has again demonstrated the United Nations' ability to assist its members in coping with the daunting challenges of our time and in working to humanize their relations.

Regrettably, shortly after it was established, the organization went through the onslaught of the cold war. For many years, it was the scene of propaganda battles and continuous political confrontation. Let historians argue who is more and who is less to blame for it. What political leaders today need to do is to draw lessons from that chapter in the history of the United Nations, a chapter that turned out to be at odds with the very meaning and objectives of the organization.

One of the most bitter and important lessons lies in the long list of missed opportunities. As a result, at a certain point the authority of the United Nations diminished, and many of its attempts to act failed.

It is highly significant that the reinvigoration of the role of the United Nations is linked to an improvement in the international climate.

In a way the United Nations embodies the interests of different states. It is the only organization capable of channeling their bilateral, regional and global efforts. New prospects are opening up for it in all areas that fall naturally under its responsibility—in the political-military, economic, scientific, technological, environmental and humanitarian areas.

Take, for example, the problem of development, which is a truly universal human problem. Conditions in which tens of millions of people live in a number of Third World regions are becoming a real threat to all humankind.

No closed entities or even regional communities of states, important as they are, are capable of untangling the main knots that tie up the principal avenues of world economic relations—North-South, East-West, South-South, South-East and East-East.

We need to combine these efforts and take into account the interests of all the different groups of countries, something that only this organization, the United Nations, can accomplish.

Foreign debt is one of the gravest problems.

Let us not forget that in the age of colonialism the developing world, at the cost of countless losses and sacrifices, financed the prosperity of a large portion of the world community. The time has come to compensate the developing countries for the privations that accompanied their historic and tragic contribution to global material progress. We are convinced that here, too, internationalizing our approach is the solution.

Looking at things realistically, one has to admit that the accumulated debt cannot be repaid or recovered on the original terms.

The Soviet Union is prepared to institute a lengthy moratorium—up to 100 years—on debt payments by the least developed countries, and in quite a few cases to write off the debts altogether.

As regards other developing countries, we invite you to consider the following propositions:

—limiting their official debt payments depending on the economic performance of each of them or granting a long deferral in the repayment of a major portion of their debt;

—supporting the appeal of the United Nations Conference on Trade and Development to reduce debts owed to commercial banks;

—guaranteeing governmental support for market arrangements to assist in Third World debt settlement, including the formation of a specialized agency that would repurchase loans at a discount.

The Soviet Union favors a substantive discussion of ways to settle the debt crisis at multilateral forums, including consultations under the auspices of the United Nations among heads of government of debtor and creditor countries.

International economic security is inconceivable unless it is related not only to disarmament but also to the elimination of the threat to the world's environment. In a number of regions, the state of the environment is simply appalling.

A conference on the environment under UN auspices is scheduled for 1992. We welcome this decision and are working to have this forum produce results commensurate with the scope of the problem.

But time is running out. Much is being done in various countries. Here again I would just like to underscore most emphatically the prospects opening up in the process of disarmament—for environmental revival.

Let us also think about establishing within the framework of the United Nations a center for emergency environmental assistance. Its function would be to promptly send international groups of experts to areas with a badly deteriorating environment.

The Soviet Union is also prepared to cooperate in establishing an international space laboratory or manned orbital station designed exclusively for monitoring the state of the environment.

In the general area of space exploration, the outlines of a future space industry are becoming increasingly clear.

The position of the Soviet Union is well known: Activities in outer space must exclude the deployment of weapons there. Here again, there must be a legal base. The groundwork for it—the provisions of the 1967 treaty and other agreements—is already in place.

However, there is already a compelling need to develop an all-embracing regime for peaceful activity in outer space. The verification of compliance with that regime would be entrusted to a world space organization.

We have proposed the establishment of such an organization on more than one occasion. We are prepared to incorporate within its system our Krasnoyarsk radar station. A decision has already been made to place that radar under the authority of the USSR Academy of Sciences.

Soviet scientists are prepared to receive their foreign colleagues and discuss with them ways of converting the station into an international center for peaceful cooperation by dismantling and refitting certain units and structures, and to provide additional equipment.

The entire system could function under the auspices of the United Nations.

The whole world welcomes the efforts of the United Nations organization and Secretary-General Perez de Cuellar, and his representatives in untying knots of regional problems.

Allow me to elaborate on this.

Paraphrasing the words of the English poet that Hemingway took as an epigraph to his famous novel, I will say: The bell of every regional conflict tolls for all of us.

This is particularly true since those conflicts are taking place in the Third World, which already faces many ills and problems of such magnitude that it must be a matter of concern to us all.

The year 1988 has brought a glimmer of hope in this area of our common concerns as well. This has been felt in almost all regional conflicts. In some of them, there has been movement. We welcome it, and we did what we could to contribute to it.

I will single out only Afghanistan.

The Geneva accords, whose fundamental and practical significance has been praised throughout the world, provided a possibility for completing the process of settlement even before the end of this year. That did not happen. This unfortunate fact reminds us again of the political, legal and moral significance of the Roman maxim: *Pacta sunt servanda!* Treaties must be honored.

I don't want to use this rostrum for recriminations against anyone.

But it is our view that, within the competence of the United Nations, the General Assembly resolution adopted last November could be supplemented by some specific measures. In the words of that resolution, "for the earliest comprehensive settlement by the Afghans themselves of the question of a government on a broad basis," the following measures should be undertaken:

—A complete cease-fire should take effect everywhere as of January 1, 1989, and all offensive operations or shelling should cease, with the opposing Afghan groups retaining, for the duration of negotiations, all territories under their control.

—Accordingly, all supplies of arms to all belligerents should be stopped as of the same date.

—While a broad-based government, as provided in the General Assembly resolution, is being established, a contingent of UN peace-keeping forces should be sent to Kabul and to other strategic centers throughout Afghanistan.

—We also request the Secretary-General to facilitate early implementation of the idea of holding an international conference on the neutrality and demilitarization of Afghanistan.

We shall most actively continue to assist in healing the wounds of the war and are prepared to cooperate in this endeavor with the United Nations and on a bilateral basis.

We support the proposal to create under the auspices of the United Nations a voluntary international peace corps to assist in the revitalization of Afghanistan.

In the context of the problem of settling regional conflicts, I have to express my opinion on the serious incident that has recently affected the work of this session. The chairman of an organization that has observer status at the United Nations was not allowed by U.S. authorities to come to New York to address the General Assembly. I am referring to Yasser Arafat.

Moreover, this happened at a time when the Palestine Liberation Organization has taken a constructive step, which facilitates the search for a solution to the Middle East problem with the involvement of the United Nations Security Council.

This happened at a time when a positive trend has become apparent toward a political settlement of other regional conflicts, in many cases with the assistance of the USSR and the United States. We express our deep regret over the incident and our solidarity with the Palestine Liberation Organization.

Ladies and Gentlemen,

The concept of comprehensive international security is based on the principles of the United Nations Charter and is predicated on the binding nature of international law for all states.

While we champion demilitarizing international relations, we want political and legal methods to prevail in solving whatever problems may arise.

Our ideal is a world community of states that are based on the rule of law and subordinate their foreign policy activities to law.

The achievement of this goal would be facilitated by an agreement within the United Nations on a uniform understanding of the principles and norms of international law, their codification with due regard to new conditions, and the development of legal norms for new areas of cooperation.

In a nuclear age the effectiveness of international law should be based not on enforcing compliance but on norms reflecting a balance of state interests.

As we become ever more aware of our common fate, every state becomes more genuinely interested in exercising self-restraint within the bounds of international law.

Democratizing international relations means not only a maximum degree of internationalization in the efforts of all members of the world community to solve major problems. It also means humanizing those relations.

International ties will fully reflect the genuine interests of the peoples and effectively serve the cause of their common security only when man and his concerns, rights and freedoms become the center of all things.

In this context, let my country join the chorus of voices expressing their great esteem for the significance of the Universal Declaration of Human Rights adopted 40 years ago on December 19, 1948. This document retains its significance today. It reflects the universal nature of the goals and objectives of the United Nations.

The most fitting way for a state to observe this anniversary of the declaration is to improve its domestic conditions for respecting and protecting the rights of its own citizens.

Before I inform you about what specifically we have undertaken recently in this respect, I would like to say the following. Our country is experiencing a period of truly revolutionary enthusiasm.

The process of *perestroika* is gaining momentum. We began with the formulation of the philosophy of *perestroika*. We had to evaluate the nature and the magnitude of problems, to understand the lessons of the past and express that in the form of political conclusions and programs. This has been done.

Theoretical work, a reassessment of what is happening, the finalization, enrichment and readjustment of political positions have not been completed. They are continuing.

But it was essential to begin with a general philosophy, which, as now confirmed by the experience of these past years, has generally proved to be correct and which has no alternative.

For our society to participate in efforts to implement the plans of *perestroika* has now spread to politics, the economy, intellectual life and ideology. We have initiated a radical economic reform. We have gained experience. At the start of next year the entire national economy will be redirected to new forms and methods of operation. This also means profoundly reorganizing relations of production and releasing the great potential inherent in socialist property.

Undertaking such bold revolutionary transformations, we realized that there would be mistakes and also opposition, that new approaches would generate new problems. We also foresaw the possibility of slowdowns in some areas.

But the guarantee that the over-all process of *perestroika* will steadily move forward and gain strength lies in a profound democratic reform of the entire system of power and administration.

With the recent decisions by the USSR Supreme Soviet on amendments to the Constitution and the adoption of a new electoral law, we have completed the first stage of the process of political reform.

Without pausing, we have begun the second stage of this process with the main task of improving the relationship between the center and the republics, harmonizing inter-ethnic relations on the principles of Leninist internationalism that we inherited from the Great Revolution, and at the same time reforming the local Soviets.

A great deal of work lies ahead. Major tasks will have to be dealt with concurrently. We look to the future with confidence. We have a theory and a policy, and also the driving force of *perestroika*—the party—which also is restructuring itself in accordance with new tasks and fundamental changes in society as a whole.

What is most important is that all our peoples and all generations of citizens of our great country support *perestroika*.

We have become deeply involved in building a socialist state based on the rule of law. Work on a whole series of new laws has been completed or is nearing completion.

Many of them will enter into force as early as 1989, and we expect them to meet the highest standards with regard to ensuring the rights of the individual.

Soviet democracy will then be placed on a solid legal base. I am referring, in particular, to laws on the freedom of conscience, on *glasnost*, public associations and organizations, and many others. People are no longer kept in prison for their political or religious beliefs.

Additional guarantees are to be included in the new draft laws that rule out any form of persecution on those grounds.

Naturally, this does not apply to those who committed actual criminal offenses or state crimes such as espionage, sabotage, terrorism, and so forth, whatever their political or ideological beliefs.

Draft amendments to the criminal code have been prepared and are awaiting their turn. Among the articles being revised are those concerning capital punishment.

The problem of emigration from and immigration to our country, including the question of leaving it for family reunification, is being resolved in a humane spirit.

Permission to leave, as you know, is denied to persons with knowledge of state secrets. Strictly warranted time limitations are being introduced in relation to the knowledge of classified information. Every person seeking employment at certain agencies or enterprises will be informed of this rule. In case of disputes the law provides a right of appeal.

This removes from the agenda the problem of the so-called "refuseniks."

We intend to expand the Soviet Union's participation in the human rights monitoring arrangements under the aegis of the United Nations and within the European process. We believe that the jurisdiction of the International Court of Justice at the Hague as regards the interpretation and implementation of agreements on human rights should be binding on all states.

We also see an end to the jamming of all foreign radio broadcasts beamed at the Soviet Union within the context of the Helsinki process.

Overall, this is our credo: Political problems must be solved only by political means; human problems, only in a humane way.

III

Now let me turn to the main issue—disarmament, without which none of the problems of the coming century can be solved.

International development and communication have been distorted by the arms race and militarization of thinking.

As you know, on January 15, 1986, the Soviet Union proposed a program to build a world free from nuclear weapons. Translated into actual negotiating positions, it has already produced material results.

Tomorrow marks the first anniversary of the signing of the Treaty on the Elimination of Intermediate-Range and Shorter-Range Missiles. I am therefore particularly pleased to note that the implementation of the treaty—the destruction of missiles—is proceeding normally, in an atmosphere of trust and constructive work.

A large breach has thus been made in a seemingly impenetrable wall of suspicion and animosity. We are witnessing the emergence of a new historic reality—the principle of excessive arms stockpiling is giving way to the principle of reasonable defense sufficiency.

We are witnessing the first efforts to build a new model of security—not through the buildup of arms, as was almost always the case in the past, but on the contrary, through their reduction on the basis of compromise.

The Soviet leadership has decided to demonstrate once again its readiness to reinforce this healthy process not only by words but also by deeds.

Today, I can report to you that the Soviet Union has decided to reduce its armed forces.

Over the next two years their numerical strength will be reduced by 500,000 men. The numbers of conventional armaments will also be substantially reduced. These cuts will be made unilaterally, without relation to the talks on the mandate of the Vienna meeting.

By agreement with our Warsaw Treaty allies, we have decided to withdraw by 1991 six tank divisions from the German Democratic Republic, Czechoslovakia and Hungary, and to disband them.

Assault-landing troops and several other formations and units, including assault-crossing support units with their weapons and combat equipment, will also be withdrawn from the groups of Soviet forces stationed in those countries.

Soviet forces stationed in those countries will be reduced by 50,000 men and 5,000 tanks.

All Soviet divisions remaining, for the time being, on the territory of our allies are being reorganized. Their structure will be changed. A large number of tanks will be withdrawn, and the divisions will become strictly defensive.

At the same time, we shall reduce the numerical strength of the armed forces and the numbers of armaments stationed in the European part of the USSR.

In total, Soviet armed forces in this part of our country and in the territories of our European allies will be reduced by 10,000 tanks, 8,500 artillery systems and 800 combat aircraft.

During these two years we intend to reduce significantly our armed forces in the Asian part of our country, too. By agreement with the government of the Mongolian People's Republic a major portion of Soviet troops temporarily stationed there will return home.

In making this fundamental decision, the Soviet leadership expresses the will of the people, who have undertaken a profound reconstruction of their entire socialist society.

We shall maintain our country's defense capability at a level of reasonable and reliable sufficiency so that no one is tempted to encroach on the security of the USSR or its allies.

By this action, and by all our efforts to demilitarize international relations, we wish to draw the attention of the international community to yet another urgent matter— the problem of converting from an economy of armaments to an economy of disarmament.

Is conversion of military production a realistic idea? I have already had occasion to speak about this. We think that, indeed, it is realistic.

The Soviet Union is prepared:

** To formulate and make public its own internal plan of conversion as part of its economic reform efforts;

** To draw up as an experiment, in the course of 1989, conversion plans for two or three defense plants;

** To make public its experience in reemploying military specialists and in using defense equipment and facilities in civilian production.

We consider it desirable for all states, in the first place major military powers, to submit their national conversion plans to the United Nations.

It would also be useful to set up a group of scientists to undertake a thorough analysis of the problem of conversion as a whole and as applied to individual countries and regions and report its findings to the Secretary-General of the United Nations. Later this matter should be considered at a session of the General Assembly.

IV

And finally, since I am here on American soil, and for other obvious reasons, I want to turn to the subject of our relations with this great country. I had a chance to appreciate the full measure of American hospitality during my memorable visit to Washington exactly a year ago.

The relations between the Soviet Union and the United States have a history of five and a half decades. As the world has changed, so have the nature, role and place of those relations in world politics.

For too long these relations were characterized by confrontation and sometimes animosity—either overt or covert.

But in the past few years people all over the world have breathed a sigh of relief as the substance and the atmosphere of the relationship between Moscow and Washington took a turn for the better.

I do not intend to underestimate the seriousness of our differences and the complexity of our outstanding problems. We have, however, already graduated from the primary school of learning to understand each other, and we seek solutions in both our own and common interests.

The USSR and the United States have built up immense nuclear-missile arsenals. But these very countries have acknowledged their responsibility, becoming the first to conclude a treaty on the reduction and physical elimination of a portion of these armaments, which posed a threat to both them and to all nations of the world.

Both countries possess the greatest and the most sophisticated military secrets. Those two countries have laid a basis for and are further developing a system of mutual verification of both the destruction of armaments and the reduction and prohibition of their production.

Those two countries are accumulating the experience for future bilateral and multilateral agreements.

We value this experience. We acknowledge and appreciate the contribution made by President Ronald Reagan and by the members of his administration, particularly Mr. George Shultz.

All this is our capital in a joint venture of historic importance. We must not lose this investment or leave it idle.

The next U.S. Administration, headed by President-elect George Bush, will find in us a partner that is ready—without procrastinating or backtracking—to continue the dialogue in a spirit of realism, openness and good will, and determined to achieve concrete results working on an agenda that covers the main issues of Soviet-American relations and world politics.

I have in mind, above all, consistent movement toward a treaty on 50 percent reductions in strategic offensive arms while preserving the ABM Treaty; working out a convention on the elimination of chemical weapons—here, as we see it, prerequisites exist to make 1989 a decisive year; and negotiations on the reduction of conventional arms and armed forces in Europe.

We also have in mind economic, environmental and humanitarian problems in their broadest sense.

It would be quite wrong to ascribe the positive changes in the international situation exclusively to the USSR and the United States.

The Soviet Union highly values the great and original contribution of the socialist countries toward the creation of a healthier international environment.

During the course of negotiations we are constantly aware of the presence of other great nations, both nuclear and nonnuclear.

Many countries, including medium and small ones, and, of course, the Nonaligned Movement and intercontinental Group of Six play a uniquely important constructive role.

We in Moscow are happy that an ever increasing number of statesmen, political, party and public figures and—I want to emphasize this—scientists, cultural figures, representatives of mass movements and various churches and activists of what is called people's diplomacy are ready to shoulder the burden of universal responsibility.

In this context I believe that the idea of convening an assembly of public organizations on a regular basis under the auspices of the United Nations deserves consideration.

We have no intention of oversimplifying the situation in the world.

True, the trend toward disarmament has been given powerful impetus, and the process is gaining a momentum of its own. But it is not yet irreversible.

True, there is a strong desire to give up confrontation in favor of dialogue and cooperation. But this trend has not yet become a permanent feature in the practice of international relations.

True, movement toward a nonviolent world free from nuclear weapons can radically transform the political and intellectual identity of our planet. But only the first steps have been made, and even they have been met with mistrust and resistance in certain influential quarters.

The legacy and inertia of the past continue to be felt. Profound contradictions and the roots of many conflicts have not disappeared. And there remains another fundamental fact, which is that a peaceful period will be taking shape in the context of the existence and rivalry of different socioeconomic and political systems.

However, the aim of our international efforts and one of the key elements of the new thinking is that we must transform this rivalry into reasonable competition on the basis of freedom of choice and a balance of interests.

Then it will even become useful and productive from the standpoint of global development.

Otherwise—if the arms race, as before, remains its basic component—this rivalry will be suicidal.

More and more people throughout the world—leaders as well as ordinary people—are beginning to understand this.

Esteemed Mr. President,

Distinguished delegates,

I am concluding my first address to the United Nations with the same feeling I had when I began it—a feeling of responsibility to my own people and to the world community.

We are meeting at the end of a year that has meant so much for the United Nations and on the eve of a year from which we all expect so much.

I would like to believe that our hopes would be matched by a joint effort to put an end to an era of wars, confrontation, and regional conflicts, to aggressions against nature, to the terror of hunger and poverty and to political terrorism.

This is our common goal, and we will be able to reach it only by working together.

Thank you.

Glossary

aktiv	a group comprised of party members in leadership positions and other party activists
apparat	party/government functionaries who make up the machinery of government
apparatchik	a functionary, a member of the *apparat*
Comintern	the central organ that was in charge of the Communist International movement
CPSU	acronym for the Communist Party of the Soviet Union
glasnost	openness, publicity
Gosplan	the powerful agency in charge of determining the yearly quotas for various industries and enterprises
kolkhoz	a collective farm
Komsomol	the Soviet organization for Communist youth ages fourteen to twenty-eight
kulaks	well-to-do peasants who were considered to be enemies of the Soviet regime

NEP New Economic Policy, a relatively liberal Soviet economic program followed from 1921 to 1928

NKVD acronym for the People's Commissariat of Internal Affairs, the Soviet secret police from 1934 to 1946, predecessor to the KGB

nomenklatura a select group of party members occupying key positions

obkom provincial party committee

oblast province

Pamyat "Memory," the name of an extreme Russian nationalist organization

Party Conference an irregularly scheduled meeting at which party delegates from all over the USSR discuss an agenda of issues listed by the party leadership

Party Congress a regularly scheduled meeting of party delegates from all over the USSR at which party leadership is selected

perestroika "restructuring," a slogan signifying Gorbachev's agenda for changing the structure of the Soviet economic, social, and political system

plenum a plenary meeting of the Central Committee CPSU

raikom a district-level party committee

samizdat illegal "underground" publications, either printed or handwritten

samogon illegally produced alcoholic beverages; homebrew, moonshine

vozhd the top party or national leader

Index